Register Now for O[...]
to Your Bo[...]

x

MW00851190

SPRINGER PUBLISHING COMPANY

CONNECT™

Your print purchase of *EMDR Toolbox, Second Edition*, **includes online access to the contents of your book**—increasing accessibility, portability, and searchability!

Access today at:
http://connect.springerpub.com/ content/book/978-0-8261-7256-3 or scan the QR code at the right with your smartphone and enter the access code below.

9D4YKKDN

Scan here for quick access.

The online access with your print purchase is available at the publisher's discretion and may be removed at any time without notice.

CS

SPRINGER PUBLISHING COMPANY

View all our products at springerpub.com

Jim Knipe, PhD, has been a licensed psychologist in private practice in Colorado since 1976 and has been using eye movement desensitization and reprocessing (EMDR) since 1992. He is a Trainer with Trauma Recovery/EMDR Humanitarian Assistance Program, an Eye Movement Desensitization and Reprocessing International Association (EMDRIA)-approved consultant and instructor, and was designated a "Master Clinician" by EMDRIA in 2007. He was a keynote speaker at the 2010 EMDRIA conference; 2015 EMDR Canada conference; and was an invited guest speaker at the 2006, 2007, 2010, 2014, and 2015 EMDRIA Annual Conferences; the 2006, 2008, and 2012 EMDR Europe Annual Conferences; the 2010 EMDR Asia Conference; and national EMDR conferences in Australia, Denmark, Germany, Scotland, Italy, Belgium, Sweden, Spain, the Netherlands, Turkey, Brazil, and Japan. He has been involved with Trauma Recovery/EMDR Humanitarian Assistance Programs (HAPs), serving as coordinator for training programs in Turkey and Palestine, and serving on the board of directors and as research and training director. He has also been involved in HAP in Oklahoma City, New York (following 9/11), Sri Lanka, and Indonesia. In addition, he is a coauthor of published outcome research documenting the effects of EMDR with survivors of 9/11 and with those traumatized by the 1999 Marmara earthquake in Turkey. Dr. Knipe has contributed chapters to *EMDR Casebook* (Manfield, 2002), *EMDR Solutions*, Volumes I and II (R. Shapiro, 2005, 2009), *Healing the Heart of Trauma and Dissociation* (2007), *EMDR Scripted Protocols: Special Populations* (Luber, 2009), and *EMDR and Dissociation: The Progressive Approach* (Gonzalez & Mosquera, 2012). He is a coauthor (with Dolores Mosquera) of articles describing EMDR-related methods of narcissistic self-idealization, and idealization of a partner in an abusive relationship.

EMDR Toolbox: Theory and Treatment of Complex PTSD and Dissociation

Second Edition

Jim Knipe, PhD

SPRINGER PUBLISHING COMPANY

Springer Publishing Company, LLC
11 West 42nd Street
New York, NY 10036
www.springerpub.com

Acquisitions Editor: Sheri W. Sussman
Compositor: S4Carlisle

ISBN: 978-0-8261-7255-6
ebook ISBN: 978-0-8261-7256-3

18 19 20 21 22 / 5 4 3 2 1

The author and the publisher of this Work have made every effort to use sources believed to be reliable to provide information that is accurate and compatible with the standards generally accepted at the time of publication. The author and publisher shall not be liable for any special, consequential, or exemplary damages resulting, in whole or in part, from the readers' use of, or reliance on, the information contained in this book. The publisher has no responsibility for the persistence or accuracy of URLs for external or third-party Internet websites referred to in this publication and does not guarantee that any content on such websites is, or will remain, accurate or appropriate.

Library of Congress Cataloging-in-Publication Data
Names: Knipe, Jim, 1944– author.
Title: EMDR toolbox : theory and treatment of complex PTSD and dissociation / Jim Knipe.
Other titles: Eye movement desensitization reprocessing toolbox
Description: Second edition. | New York, NY : Springer Publishing Company, [2018] | Includes bibliographical references and index.
Identifiers: LCCN 2018028120| ISBN 9780826172556 | ISBN 9780826172563 (e-book)
Subjects: | MESH: Stress Disorders, Post-Traumatic—therapy | Dissociative Disorders—therapy | Eye Movement Desensitization Reprocessing—methods | Models, Psychological
Classification: LCC RC489.E98 | NLM WM 172.5 | DDC 616.85/210651—dc23 LC record available at https://lccn.loc.gov/2018028120

Contact us to receive discount rates on bulk purchases.
We can also customize our books to meet your needs.
For more information please contact: sales@springerpub.com

Printed in the United States of America.

*To Nancy, who has given me the gift of love,
friendship, and life partnership, and whose unequivocal
support, encouragement, and unfailing patience were essential
in the writing of this book.*

Contents

Preface   ix
Acknowledgments   xiii

PART I: AN ADAPTIVE INFORMATION PROCESSING FRAMEWORK FOR TREATING COMPLEX PTSD

1. The Need for a Theoretical Framework and Additional "Tools" for Using EMDR With Complex PTSD   *3*
2. Traumatic Memory and EMDR, When Dual Attention Is Possible   *27*

PART II: ADAPTIVE INFORMATION PROCESSING METHODS FOR RESOLVING PSYCHOLOGICAL DEFENSES

3. An Adaptive Information Processing Model for Treating Psychological Defenses   *51*
4. EMDR With Avoidance   *75*
5. Targeting Idealization Defenses   *97*
6. Treating Addictive Disorders With Adaptive Information Processing Methods   *125*

PART III: AN ADAPTIVE INFORMATION PROCESSING MODEL FOR TREATING DISSOCIATIVE PERSONALITY STRUCTURE

7. Treating Dissociation Within an Adaptive Information Processing Model   *159*
8. The Basic Framework for the Preparation Phase   *175*
9. Preparation: The Language of Ovals   *185*
10. Preparation: Drawings   *197*
11. Loving Eyes: "Looking" From One Part to Another   *211*
12. Treating Defensive Shame   *223*
13. The CIPOS Procedure   *235*
14. The Persistence of Dissociative Personality Structure and the Internal Healing Dialogue (IHD) Procedure   *247*

PART IV: CASE EXAMPLES

15. Veronica *259*
16. Doug *279*
17. Rhonda *291*
18. Some Closing Thoughts *303*

Index *305*

Preface

In 1974, Hiroo Onoda, a Japanese soldier, came out of the jungle in the Philippines and was surprised to learn that World War II, which actually ended in 1945, was now over. This man had been caught in a time warp, stuck in a "reality" that no longer existed, with intense but unfortunate loyalties to people and institutions long gone. His situation resembled that of many adult psychotherapy clients suffering from complex posttraumatic stress disorder (Complex PTSD) and dissociative personality structure. For many of these individuals, who come to us with hope and even some degree of trust that we will help them, the war is not yet over. They are attempting to live life in a way that other people deem to be "appropriate" and "normal," while also frequently experiencing "relivings" of a past trauma world—a world that, in many cases, no longer exists.

Many clients come to therapy with "issues" and emotional problems that do not fall clearly into the category of single-incident PTSD. Oftentimes, a client's clinical picture might include significant psychological defenses, problems in forming and maintaining relationships with others, addictive disorders, and dissociative separation between personality parts. This is a book for therapists who are trained and experienced in using standard eye movement desensitization and reprocessing (EMDR; as taught in the basic Eye Movement Desensitization and Reprocessing International Association [EMDRIA]-approved trainings), but who are stymied sometimes about how to structure therapy sessions to help clients with more complex emotional problems. The methods described in the chapters that follow are meant to supplement, not replace, standard EMDR procedures (Shapiro, 1995, 2018). The standard procedures are extremely useful and effective (Maxfield & Hyer, 2002) with a wide variety of clinical presentations that originate in or include disturbing traumatic memories. However, for some clients, those who have suffered early, complex, and prolonged abuse or neglect, additional therapy "tools"—conceptual models and specific therapy interventions—can significantly extend the therapeutic power of EMDR-related methods.

I began using EMDR in 1992. At that time, I had a practice as a therapist for several decades, with the particular focus of treating complex emotional problems—personality disorders, addictive disorders, clients with "thought disorders" and poor reality contact, and clients with histories of childhood abuse. EMDR met a need that had repeatedly come up in my work with clients. Many people who had been in therapy over the years had developed cognitive understanding of *why* they were unhappy, and this had helped, but part of the affective element of their initial problem had remained. One person said, "I know why I am nervous around my father, after everything that happened when I was a kid. I know all that, but when he calls on the phone, I still feel anxious, like I am 10 years old, all over again!" For many clients who endured sexual abuse or sexual assaults, the therapy process was very arduous, and for those who had gained insight into their history, but still had intense feeling of shame or fear, all I could suggest was continuing exposure to these irrational affects, either in my office or when these feelings arose between sessions.

EMDR was a solution to this problem. It was a way to break through, relatively quickly, and help these individuals tame the flashbacks and the disturbing emotions that had resulted from their prior life experience. My enthusiasm for EMDR was channeled into several research projects, work with the Trauma Recovery/EMDR Humanitarian Assistance Program, and, in my practice and in writing, exploration of ways that EMDR-related procedures could be used in the treatment of the more complex psychological disorders.

Therapists who are trained and experienced in the use of EMDR often report a particular phenomenon during the first year after their training. The composition of the therapist's clinical practice is likely to significantly change. Those clients with simple, single-incident posttraumatic disturbance—a traumatic event that the person was depressed or anxious about, and was reliving mentally—were able to finish therapy fairly quickly, say "Thank you very much!" and be on their way. Consequently, within the practice of a newly trained EMDR therapist, there tends to be a shift to an increasing proportion of clients with more complexity in their clinical picture. The great majority of clients come to therapy with "issues," not just of troubling memories but also of interpersonal problems and significantly problematic personality structure. Oftentimes, that is when additional conceptual models and additional procedures—additional therapy tools—are needed.

This book has two main goals: to provide descriptions of specific EMDR therapeutic "tools" and, by incorporating these tools, to develop an overview of an Adaptive Information Processing (AIP) model of the treatment of Complex PTSD. The development of EMDR-related tools has been ongoing since the introduction of EMDR three decades ago (Shapiro, 1989). Since that time, many advanced applications and extentions of the EMDR Therapy approach have been developed. What will EMDR be in 2030? Unfortunately, our field—the field of psychotherapy for trauma-related disorders—has at times had a kind of dissociative disorder. Some therapists identify with one theoretical approach, and others are strong adherents of another identity. Often, these two "identities" do not communicate sufficiently, and sometimes they mistakenly think they have to fight with each other. Clearly, my primary identification as a therapist is with EMDR-related methods based on an AIP approach, but in each of the following chapters, I am also attempting to integrate the concepts and methods of cognitive approaches—approaches that are not only useful, but at times essential in the treatment of dissociative clients.

The use of the word "tools" is intended here to be metaphorical: a person who builds houses for a living needs to use power tools, but that person also needs to know, in general, how to build houses! A contractor or carpenter needs to know how to put up drywall, read blueprints, put in the electricity and plumbing, and so on. The tools I will be describing in this book are meant to be blended, for the reader, with other skills previously acquired as a psychotherapist.

Many EMDR therapists are quite aware of the need in their work for additional concepts and interventions, particularly when working with clients who have extensive trauma histories going back to childhood abuse and neglect. Some new EMDR therapists take the approach of alternating between "doing psychotherapy" and then putting their psychotherapy skills on the shelf so that they can "do EMDR." Often, therapists will attempt to create a "hybrid" therapy, combining elements of EMDR with whatever therapy model the therapist was using before. This mixing of models can be useful if the therapist remains alert to the ways that the best elements of each model can be successfully integrated. But it can be problematic if the "hybrid" leaves out crucial elements of EMDR such as the targeting of specific key memories; the focused use of sets of bilateral stimulation; the identification of negative beliefs about self that are related to traumatic events; the identification of a positive, more realistic cognition about self that might replace the negative belief; and/or the emphasis on including physical sensations in the processing. Fidelity to the basic EMDR eight-phase model has been shown to be very important for the effectiveness of the method (Maxfield & Hyer, 2002), and so alterations and extensions of EMDR for therapy for more complex clients require the careful judgment of the therapist (as well as the informed consent of the client). As a general rule, we can say that, for experienced therapists, everything previously learned about how to do effective therapy prior to EMDR training—all understandings about people, all the ideas and interventions learned through reading and workshops and from previous clients—is still important, is necessary, and provides a context for doing effective EMDR therapy. The tools described in the chapters to come are meant to supplement, not replace, the skills and understandings of experienced psychotherapists.

The chapters of this book are divided into four parts. The first, comprising Chapters 1 and 2, is an overview of the application of the AIP model to Complex PTSD and other dissociative conditions. The second part, Chapters 3 to 6, presents ways of treating (i.e., resolving) psychological defenses that are often linked intrinsically to disturbing memories but can be conceptually defined as separate entities because defenses typically contain dysfunctional *positive* affect, as opposed to the disturbing affect within memories of traumatic events. The third part, Chapters 7 to 14, focuses on several issues important in the EMDR treatment of dissociative conditions. And Chapters 15 to 17 are detailed case reports illustrating how these AIP "tools" can be employed in actual treatment sessions.

REFERENCES

Maxfield, L., & Hyer, L. A. (2002). The relationship between efficacy and methodology in studies investigating EMDR treatment of PTSD. *Journal of Clinical Psychology, 58,* 23–41. doi:10.1002/jclp.1127

Shapiro, F. (1989). Efficacy of the eye movement desensitization procedure in the treatment of traumatic memories. *Journal of Traumatic Stress Studies, 2,* 199–223. doi:10.1002/jts.2490020207

Shapiro, F. (1995). *Eye movement desensitization and reprocessing: Basic principles, protocols and procedures.* New York, NY: Guilford Press.

Shapiro, F. (2018). *Eye movement desensitization and reprocessing: Basic principles, protocols, and procedures* (3rd ed.). New York, NY: Guilford Press.

Acknowledgments

First of all, I am indebted to each client who has given me permission to write about the moments of his or her hard work in therapy. In each case, this permission was given with the hope of helping others.

I am also indebted to several colleagues who generously gave their time to review drafts of chapters in this book. Their thoughtful suggestions and encouragement were essential at several points in the process. Thank you to Susan Brown, Esta Porter, Christine Wilson, Vivian Dent, David House, Karen Wray, and Ellen Rossier. Their comments comprise a large contribution to whatever may be useful in this book. Of course, I am responsible for any errors in what was written.

Thank you to Dr. Francine Shapiro for the gift of eye movement desensitization and reprocessing (EMDR). Her steadfast commitment has significantly helped hundreds of thousands of people throughout the world. And, on a more personal level, her insights and her example have transformed the way I work as a psychotherapist. The clarity of her vision has often been a guiding light. Also, thank you to Robbie Dunton for her support, many times, in our work together through the EMDR Institute and with the Trauma Recovery/EMDR Humanitarian Assistance Program. I would like to thank Phil Manfield for inviting me in 1998 to write a chapter in *Extending EMDR*, and for the many engaging conversations about EMDR during all these years. I have a warm and grateful feeling when I think of Liz Snyker, who left us too early. She and Phil were my Eye Movement Desensitization and Reprocessing International Association (EMDRIA) copresenters in 1998, and colleagues in the initial EMDR HAP Turkey project. I want to send a very special thank you to Carol Forgash, for her wisdom in the many projects we have shared, in our work with HAP, in our joint presentations at EMDRIA and in Japan, and in our collaboration for chapters in her fine 2007 book, *Healing the Heart of Trauma With EMDR and Ego State Therapy*. Carol's positive energy has been contagious, and I have benefitted in many ways from the privilege of being her friend. Bob Gelbach has my great appreciation for his patient, intelligent management and development of EMDR

HAP, and his frequent good advice during the earlier days of that organization. Thanks to Lene Jacobsen and to Emre Konuk for their encouragement to take the ideas in this book to an international audience. Thanks to Arne Hofmann for his very persuasive list of reasons why I should write this book. Robin Shapiro has been, many times, an inspiring presence for me, and I very much appreciate her asking me to contribute to her two groundbreaking volumes of *EMDR Solutions*. I also appreciate very much the insights I was able to glean from conversations with Benek Altayli, Katie O'Shea, Paul Miller, Roger Solomon, Onno van der Hart, Anabel Gonzales, Dolores Mosquera, Andrew Leeds, A. J. Popky, Gus Murray, Sally Standart, Mary Rixford, Susan Brown, Sonya Farrell, Eric Legoe, Manuela Spadoni, and Katie Murray. And thank you to Sheri W. Sussman, my editor at Springer Publishing Company, for her strong support in every stage in the writing of both the first and second editions of this book.

Jim Knipe
Longmont, Colorado

An Adaptive Information Processing Framework for Treating Complex PTSD

1

The Need for a Theoretical Framework and Additional "Tools" for Using EMDR With Complex PTSD

Many experienced therapists who take the standard eye movement desensitization and reprocessing (EMDR) initial training are impressed, and even surprised, by how quickly this therapy approach can transform the disturbing feelings that are held within dysfunctionally stored traumatic memories. But, even with this realization, it is often challenging to bring the full power of EMDR into therapy and work with clients who have a variety of presentations that do not line up exactly with the definitions of acute stress disorder (ASD) or posttraumatic stress disorder (PTSD). Often, in order to meet this challenge, the therapeutic procedures and understandings described in the basic EMDR standard training program need to be supplemented in order to successfully treat individuals with significant attachment disorder, dissociative personality structure, and rigid psychological defenses (Forgash & Knipe, 2007, 2012)—a condition that has been called Complex PTSD. This condition has also been called *disorders of extreme stress* (van der Kolk, Roth, Pelcovitz, Sunday, & Spinazzola, 2005). In children and adolescents, the pattern has been referred to as *developmental trauma disorder* (van der Kolk, 2005). Herman (1992), in her landmark book *Trauma and Recovery*, first used the term *Complex PTSD* to describe a complex of symptoms seen in many clients with a background of extensive abuse and/ or neglect. These descriptions resemble a symptom picture described over 100 years ago by Pierre Janet in Paris. The characteristics often seen in clients with this problem are shown in Figure 1.1.

- Dysfunctionally stored traumatic memories
  - Implicit (not overtly conscious) memories of repeated difficult experiences with caretakers, resulting, in the adult, in insecure, disorganized patterns of attachment to other people. These implicit memories may not be connected to visual images, and may not be recognized as memories, but still are influential as basic assumptions about self in relationship to other people.
  - Explicit memories that are so highly disturbing, or threatening, that these memories cannot be incorporated into the individual's larger life narrative.
- Psychological defenses—that is, mental actions that function to prevent the intrusion into awareness of unresolved posttraumatic images and feelings.
  - Avoidance defenses, including addictive behaviors. Avoidance defenses are probably the most frequently occurring obstacle to the use of standard EMDR procedures.
  - Idealization defenses, positive mental images that are unrealistically and dysfunctionally overvalued. These positive images may be of others (parents, children, a spouse, or an ex-lover) or of self (as in the case of an individual with a narcissistic personality disorder, or simply a situation-specific narcissistic style). Idealizing overvaluation can also occur with regard to other entities—a behavior (e.g., an addiction), a religion, a political party, a geographic location, or an employer. Any of these may serve as a defense, to the extent that it blocks awareness of unresolved posttraumatic material.
  - Shame defenses, that is, the inappropriate blaming of the self for negative events that were not in fact controllable.
- Dissociative personality structure
  - Division of the personality into separate parts or identities
  - Parts may be coconscious, or have limited mutual awareness, or have no conscious awareness of each other
- Problems in regulating disturbing affect, frequently due to insecure disorganized patterns of attachment to other people

Figure 1.1 Primary characteristics of clients with Complex PTSD.
EMDR, eye movement desensitization and reprocessing; PTSD, posttraumatic stress disorder.

There is not a specific diagnosis for Complex PTSD within the *Diagnostic and Statistical Manual,* either the fourth edition (*DSM-IV;* American Psychiatric Association [APA], 1994) or the fifth edition (*DSM-5;* APA, 2013). When the *DSM-IV* was being developed in the early 1990s, it was the unanimous recommendation of both the APA committee defining PTSD and the committee defining categories of dissociative disorder that both these conditions be encompassed within a new single diagnostic category. These recommendations were not accepted at that time, and the categories of PTSD and dissociative disorders remain separate in *DSM-5*. Within *DSM-5*, PTSD is no longer listed as an anxiety disorder, but now is included within the coding for Trauma- and Stressor-Related Disorders. This appears to be a positive development, in that traumatic experiences not only leave their mark in terms of anxiety, but also can create a residue of despair, anger, helplessness, and withdrawal. The current criteria for PTSD still include the symptoms listed in the *DSM-IV* definition: (a) exposure to actual or threatened death, serious injury, or sexual violence; (b) intrusive symptoms such as flashbacks, nightmares, and emotional triggering by reminders of trauma; (c) avoidance thoughts and behaviors; and (d) symptoms of hyperarousal and emotional reactivity associated with the traumatic event. In *DSM-5*, other criteria are also listed: negative alterations in cognitions and mood; memory difficulties; negative, irrational, self-blaming thoughts about self; persistent negative emotions; social withdrawal; and inability to experience positive emotion. The PTSD definition also now includes reference to dissociative subtypes, individuals who meet criteria for diagnosis with PTSD and who also show symptoms of depersonalization (perceiving one's self as not real, or whole or connected) and/or derealization (perceiving the world or the immediate environment as unreal). However, the category of Dissociative Disorders, in *DSM-5*, remains separate and does not specifically reference the origins of dissociative personality structure. It is widely assumed by therapists that dissociative disorders do, in fact, originate in traumatic events during childhood, although, as will be discussed later in Chapter 7, parental nonengagement during very early childhood may also be a very significant contributing factor.

The phenomenon of traumatization extends beyond the criteria listed for PTSD in *DSM-IV* and *DSM-5*. Events that are highly impactful, but not necessarily life threatening—which we can refer to as "small-t" traumas (Shapiro, 1995, 2018)—are often the origin of severe emotional problems in both children and adults. Small-t does not mean that the occurrence was minor or small in its impact. Teicher, Samson, Polcari, and McGreenery (2006) found that parental verbal aggression during childhood contributed more to adult psychiatric symptoms (depression, dissociative symptoms, "limbic irritability," anxiety, and anger-hostility) than physical abuse occurring within the family. Teicher (2000) also found that the combined effect of parental verbal aggression and domestic violence contributed to measures of adult psychiatric symptoms as much or more than familial sexual abuse. Mol et al. (2005) found that many childhood events that were disturbing but not diagnosable as PTSD tended nevertheless to be more troubling than identified PTSD. As shown in Figure 1.2, the damaging effects of adverse childhood experiences (ACEs; Felitti, 2013; Felitti et al., 1998) appear to be cumulative—that is, the greater the exposure to domestic violence, parental divorce, harsh punishment, or witnessing caretaker addictive disorder, depression, suicidal potential, or incarceration, the greater the likelihood that

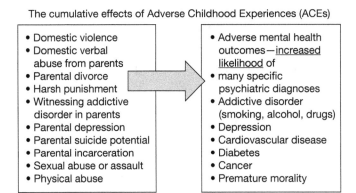

Figure 1.2 Adverse Childhood Experiences have a cumulative damaging effect on mental health, physical health and mortality (Felitti, 2013; Felitti et al., 1998).

a child from that family will have adverse physical or mental health outcomes, such as substance abuse, depression, cardiovascular disease, diabetes, cancer, and/or premature mortality. Other studies found similar correlations between rough physical maltreatment during childhood and a variety of mental health problems (Afifi, Mota, Dasiewicz, MacMillan, & Sareen, 2012) and even risk for psychosis (Varese et al., 2012) in adults.

In other words, emotional disturbance and behavior problems in the present often have their origins in prior events that were not life threatening, but were very damaging. This is true not only for children who have had active exposure to adverse events ("traumas of commission") but also for children who had "traumas of omission"—failure to receive adequate nurturing, mirroring, engagement, or guidance during childhood (Lyons-Ruth, Dutra, Schuder, & Bianchi, 2006). There is much evidence that both PTSD and small-t traumas are similar in that they have very similar symptom pictures—and follow the same course of resolution through EMDR treatment (Wilson, Becker, & Tinker, 1995, 1997).

The therapist who is treating childhood-onset Complex PTSD needs to have additional understandings and procedures beyond those needed for treating single-incident, adult-onset PTSD. This conclusion is illustrated in the results of a study done by van der Kolk et al. (2007). Subjects in this study were randomly assigned to eight 90-minute sessions of EMDR, 8 weeks of appropriately prescribed fluoxetine (Prozac), or a placebo control group. Within the latter two groups, the prescribing psychiatrist was blind to whether the pill was an antidepressant or an inert substance. The EMDR therapy was given in a strict manualized manner, with ongoing monitoring of the session to ensure that EMDR treatment was being carried out in a way that was faithful to the standard protocol. Subjects in all conditions were further divided into those who had adult-onset PTSD and those for whom PTSD originated prior to the age of 18. All the subjects in this childhood-onset EMDR condition had reported ongoing, repeated physical and/or sexual abuse in their families of origin. On several measures of treatment outcome, there were differences between the adult-onset and childhood-onset groups—differences that were both statistically and clinically significant. For example, one measure was the percentage of each group that was "symptom free" (asymptomatic score on the Clinician-Administered PTSD Scale; CAPS) immediately following treatment, as well as at a 6-month follow-up. Immediately following the 8 weeks of treatment, 46.2% of the adult-onset PTSD subjects were now symptom free, and 100% of these were no longer diagnosable with PTSD. However, in contrast, the group with childhood-onset PTSD was only 9.1% symptom free, and 72.7% were no longer diagnosable with PTSD. At the 6-month follow-up for these groups, the adult-onset group was symptom free at 75%, but the childhood-onset group was symptom free at 33.3%. "Symptom free" is pretty good, and a large proportion of each group attained this high standard, but we can look at these data and ask the question: "Why was there a difference, in response to EMDR, between the childhood-onset and the adult-onset PTSD subjects?"

van der Kolk's results, along with clinical experience, suggest that appropriate and comprehensive therapy for the childhood-onset people would have required more than eight therapy sessions. Why is that? It is likely that the childhood-onset clients had a larger number of traumatic events, and also it is likely that those clients had developmental disruptions due to adverse experiences within dysfunctional family environments—the pattern of Complex PTSD: attachment disorders, difficulty in achieving specific developmental tasks and interpersonal learning, psychological defenses embedded within developing personality structure, and, to some degree, dissociative separation of self into personality parts.

The subjects with childhood-onset PTSD almost certainly required a more individualized approach to their treatment, that is, individualized treatment plans based, for each client, on an overview of that client's unique personality structure. This type of overview would have allowed the clinician to broaden the focus of bilateral stimulation (BLS) to include, for each client, not only dysfunctional memories but also pathological adaptations to that client's difficult childhood environment—defensive processes and dissociative separation of self-states. Often, these particular adaptations do not easily fall into the category of "dysfunctionally stored specific memory." Instead, we can think of these as "dysfunctionally stored elements" (DSEs; Gonzales & Mosquera, 2012; Gonzales et al., 2012) which, though originating in particular life experiences, require a different type of treatment than one focused on discrete remembered events. These DSEs include pathological defenses, the dissociative separation of parts of self, blocking beliefs about self and others, and disrupted attachment patterns. Consistent with this reasoning, the study done by van der Kolk and colleagues gives support to the idea that, in order to treat childhood-onset Complex PTSD within an Adaptive Information Processing (AIP) model, we need additional EMDR-related therapy "tools" to address specific posttraumatic elements, in addition to dysfunctionally stored memories.

The groups of ovals in Figure 1.3 represent a visual language to describe different personality configurations. Often visual representations like this are very useful for clients, as a way to understand their own personality structure. Each oval is meant to symbolize a specific state of mind, and this state of mind—a phenomenological conscious experience—is assumed to originate in a physically based memory network within an individual's neurology. Throughout this book, ovals like these will be used to illustrate various personality configurations, both before treatment and after.

The groupings of ovals (Groupings 1, 2, and 3) in Figure 1.3 represent three main ways that difficult life experience can negatively influence personality development. A basic tenet of the AIP model is that emotional problems originate in dysfunctionally stored memories. The word *memory* can be defined in a narrow way to mean simple recollection of a specific event, or we could think of memory in a larger context as any and all the ways an individual's prior life experience affects present functioning—not only recall but also perception, prediction, ways of protecting the self from intense feelings, and even ways of defining self. Within this formulation, single-incident traumatic memories are a subcategory of DSEs.

Grouping 1 represents a situation that is familiar to experienced EMDR therapists. The solid large oval represents an individual with a *well-integrated, pretraumatic* personality structure. The smaller oval, with wavy lines, represents a dysfunctionally stored memory of a particular traumatic event. The trauma memory continues to be triggered by reminders, in a very unwelcome way, with some or all of the sensory elements of the original event. What happened was so disturbing, or threatening, that it could not be integrated into the person's larger life narrative.

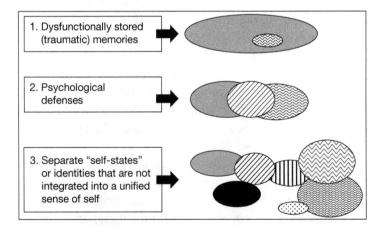

Figure 1.3 We can think of three different ways that difficult early life experience can negatively influence the development of personality structure.

When, in early sessions, I am explaining EMDR to a client, and we are identifying therapy goals and a likely treatment plan, it is often useful to introduce a shift in language. It can be clarifying to note that what are commonly called traumatic memories are not memories in the usual sense, but are *relivings*. The purpose of therapy is to *turn these relivings into normal memories*—"Oh yes, I remember that," or "I know that." This is the language that most clients will understand. We all have normal memories that are available when we need them throughout each day—as we draw on what we know from the past. For example, it is usually not hard to remember how to access favorite websites on the computer. It is not hard to remember how to add 12 plus 3, or start up the car, or remember the names of friends, or recall the location of a good grocery store or favorite restaurants. This is not memory information that comes flashing in the mind in an unwelcome way. Normal memories arise when needed, and are in the background at other times. What we call traumatic memories is different. An unfinished piece of the past is being triggered and experienced all over again, often with a strong sense of "right now" realness. Some type of reliving of the past—emotions, cognitions, sensations, and/or visual images—is usually a core element of the present problem of any psychotherapy client. This shift in language—that traumatic memories are relivings—is a shift that most clients understand and find helpful.

With this approach, a client may better understand why any reminder of an abusive parent may bring up anxiety (i.e., a reliving of previous feelings of fear), or why just thinking about horrible combat experiences may feel like stepping back into combat. Many clients come to therapy with a certain kind of self-blame—"Why can't I just get over this?! I know I'm safe now! But it's like, my mind won't let me rest. Something reminds me and I'm back there all over again! It is reassuring for clients to hear, and then realize that their therapist can explain the origin of these "relivings," as a normal human reaction to a difficult history. One client, at the end of therapy, said, "I thought I was abnormal! I was a normal person in an abnormal world!"

The "reliving" experience may be minor—a reminder may lead to a brief increase in apprehension or tension. Or it may be a full dissociative switch—the client may suddenly feel mentally transported into "trauma time," with the identity, feelings, limited problem-solving skills, and worldview of a much younger person. The felt "realness" of the actual present situation may be much diminished or even absent. A person might say, "Half of me is here, and half of me is there!" The trauma half, when triggered, is likely to keep replaying in a stereotyped way.

This "reliving" aspect is a hallmark of a trauma memory. That is, a reminder triggers a sudden intrusion into consciousness of flashback visual images, negative thoughts about self, emotions, body sensations, and/or behaviors that reproduce all or part of the experience an individual had at the time the trauma was actually occurring. It may feel like the event is happening all over again, or just happened, even though it may actually have occurred 50 years before! There was not adequate "processing" and/or resolution of the event, at the time, because it was too intense, too awful, too threatening, and too much outside of the person's experience to be integrated into that individual's sense of himself or herself in the world.

When an experienced EMDR-trained therapist is treating a clearly remembered, adult-onset, single-incident trauma, that therapist knows what to do. Treatment follows the eight phases of EMDR, with attention to the three prongs of events in the past, dysfunctional triggers in the present, and anticipatory disturbance, as well as positive planning regarding the future. EMDR, when administered with fidelity to the standard procedures, is highly effective in resolving single-incident posttraumatic disturbance (Maxfield & Hyer, 2002; Wilson et al., 1995, 1997).

The "issues" that most clients bring to therapy are often more complex than single-incident trauma—for example, anxiety, depression, low self-esteem and shame about self, addictive disorders, difficulty in relationships, and, very often, low expectations regarding the possible benefits of therapy. Typically, many unhappy memories are connected to these "issues."

Underlying these difficulties, there is usually an internally contradictory personality structure, with distinct states of mind that are activated at different times and which are functioning at cross-purposes with regard to each other; sometimes they even lack conscious awareness of each other. For example, one part of the personality may long for a satisfying life, connection with others, positive experiences, and healthy adaptation, while other parts are stuck in continually reliving the emotions and self-doubts of the worst moments of the person's past. Difficult life experience, especially during childhood, can prevent healthy personality integration; instead, children living in adverse circumstances may develop different and separate parts of the personality—different self-states—which may or may not be fully aware of each other, and which may have different purposes, functions, values, agendas, histories, perceptions, and predictions about the anticipated future—resulting in much confusion and a helpless unhappiness in the client. This type of confusion and unhappiness is typically the reason a person is motivated to pick up their phone and call a therapist for an appointment. The ways that these separate self-states develop, as adaptations to a difficult childhood environment, and the reasons that these self-states often continue into adult life, are discussed in Chapters 7 to 9. Chapters 10 to 14 address therapy considerations in assisting clients in integrating discrepant or conflicting self-states.

Separate states of mind may be triggered (i.e., emerge and function) differently during different life conditions or circumstances. Most clients with serious emotional problems have a personality part that is focused on *appearing* normal, *feeling* normal, and even wishing to *be* normal. This part is described in different ways by different theories of dissociation. For example, it has been called the apparently normal part of the personality within the Theory of the Structural Dissociation of the Personality (TSDP; van der Hart, Nijenhuis, &

Steele, 2006), and designated a Manager Part, or a collection of Manager Parts, within the Internal Family Systems (IFS) model (Schwartz, 1995). These terms from different theoretical models have somewhat different definitions, but they seem to overlap to a high degree in designating the part of the personality that faces the world; is oriented to present, external, consensual reality; and manages, in a relatively "normal" way, relationships and tasks of daily living.

In Figure 1.4, the solid oval represents this present-oriented part—the way a person keeps connections with others, and with the world, by looking "normal" (i.e., evidencing behavior that is regarded by others as being within the normal range of acceptability). If a person does not look normal, that person is jeopardizing connections with other people, and therefore a part of the personality is usually tasked with monitoring adherence to external expectations of "normality." Clients can be very aware of the danger of rejection if they step outside of their "normal" self-presentation, as when very personal information is revealed to the therapist, and then the client asks the therapist, with apprehension, "Do you think I'm weird?" People who are regarded by others as "weird" are vulnerable to rejection by those others. The need to be loved, accepted, and connected to other people is a very basic human motivation, grounded in the obvious importance for survival. In an evolutionary sense, there is strength and safety in being connected with others, and there is danger in being disconnected and alone. This need for connection and acceptance may be intensified for those individuals who unfortunately suffered frustration in their early attachment experiences with caretakers. Whether healthy or problematic, an adult's attachment style nearly always has its origins in early interactions; for most people, this style, learned early, tends to continue all through life, especially in the absence of therapy.

In Figure 1.4, the oval with the wavy pattern is meant to represent, for an individual, the *many* sources of unresolved emotional disturbance—overwhelming or threatening events in the past—that are still stuck dysfunctionally in traumatic "relivings." The wavy oval contains trauma memory images, thoughts, feelings, and physical sensations—the residue of many unhappy events. This unresolved material may intrude and interfere with the functioning of the part of self that wants to look normal and be normal. For example, consider the example of a man who had repeated experiences with his father of frequent physical abuse, unfair criticism, and emotional abandonment during his growing up years. He left this dysfunctional family environment when he was 18, and went on to make a stable and coherent life for himself, with a good job, friends, and a loving spouse. But in his present life, when he receives criticism, even constructive criticism, from a male boss, or coworkers, or his partner, memories of his father's rage and feelings of helplessness and terror flood over him, even though today he has options and choices, and there is not a present danger.

This type of situation can create an additional type of self-state or part: psychological defense. In the previous example, this man might become inappropriately angry—expressing the anger that could never be shown to his father.

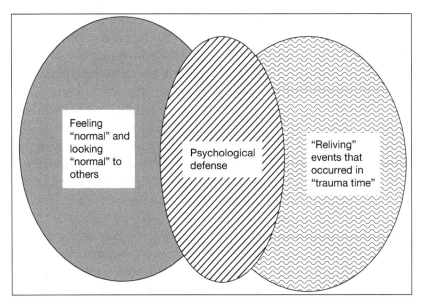

Figure 1.4 Psychological defense: Any mental action or behavior that has the purpose and function of preventing intrusion of posttraumatic disturbing memory material into the functioning of the part that is trying to look "normal" and be "normal."

Or he may become inappropriately submissive, or go into denial, or develop an addictive disorder, or simply try to avoid thinking about his ongoing feeling of inadequacy. When a defense like this is activated, this man might appear to others to be "not acceptable, not normal," but the defense may continue nevertheless because it is serving the important purpose of preventing disturbance from coming into awareness.

When emotional intrusions from the past happen over and over again—and these intrusions can happen in hundreds of different ways—defense will become more solidified and stronger within the individual's personality structure (represented by the striped oval in Figure 1.4). In this book, defense will be defined in a way that may be useful for therapists who are working within an AIP model of psychotherapy. Defense, of course, is a term that is borrowed from psychodynamic writers (e.g., Freud, 1937; Kernberg, 1967; Plutchik, Kellerman, & Conte, 1979; Vaillant, 1992). Within an AIP therapy model, it is useful to define defense as follows: any mental action or behavioral action that has the *function of blocking the emergence of posttraumatic disturbance*, that is, preventing intrusion *from* traumatized parts of self into the "normal" part or parts of self. For example, addictive disorders often serve a defensive purpose. Many addictive disorders begin, and then continue, because the addictive behavior contains or prevents the emergence of disturbing feelings and/or memories. Treatment of addictions, within this model, will be the focus of Chapter 6.

Because defenses protect the "normal-appearing" self in this way, by putting in place a mental wall to prevent intrusions of posttraumatic disturbance, defenses may also *prevent full access* to unresolved memories, and thereby prevent the use of standard EMDR, for many people. A client will often present initially in therapy as the apparently normal part (van der Hart et al., 2006). In order to heal and have comprehensively therapeutic results, that person may need to fully access the most damaging pieces of his or her own traumatic past, and resolve those memories. But defenses (e.g., avoidance defenses) stand in the way. To illustrate, a person in therapy might say, "I don't want to think about what happened with my stepfather!" or "Yes, the death of my mother hit me pretty hard, but I don't want to talk about it." A person may be using a defense, and not even be aware of it—"I don't think I was really affected very much by the death of my mother. Life had to go on, and we didn't have time to think much about it" (said with a tremor in the voice). If there is a strong defense in place, preventing direct conscious access to something disturbing in the past, the therapist cannot just jump to using standard EMDR. If the client expresses an unequivocal wish to avoid thinking of something, the therapist cannot say, "Well, in spite of that, can you get a picture of the worst part?"

Avoidance behaviors are part of the very definition of PTSD (APA, 2013) and avoidance defenses arise very often in therapy. There are many different examples. For example, a woman came into therapy after a car accident. She had heard that EMDR could help with her current anxiety about driving. Toward the end of the first session, she said, "One thing . . . can we agree from the outset, here, that we are not going to talk about my mother? I spent 3 years in therapy talking about my mother, and it didn't really go anywhere." Based on my assessment, I did not believe that her issues with her mother would affect her ability to resolve the anxiety about driving, and so I agreed to not bring up the subject of her mother, and she was able to successfully work on her anxiety regarding driving. Later in therapy, we explored other issues, and, with a greater sense of self-efficacy, she was able to recognize that she was able to productively explore how her parents were involved with those other issues.

Some degree of avoidance urge appears to be intrinsic to any dysfunctionally stored traumatic memory. For some clients with only a moderate level of avoidance defense, the motivation to resolve the traumatic material will override the avoidance urge; when the client proceeds with standard EMDR processing, and that processing is seen to be effective in reducing the intensity of the traumatic disturbance, the avoidance urge is likely to evaporate. But for other clients, for whom avoidance has been a powerful protection over the years, it may be better to shift the focus of treatment to the avoidance itself. In the end, most clients have, along with their avoidance urges, a strong wish to benefit from therapy, and a willingness to confront unhappy memories if sufficient safeguards are in place and the client does not feel that he or she is being asked to do something that feels impossible.

The following transcript, taken verbatim from a video recording and used with the client's generous permission, illustrates the interaction between fear, avoidance urges, and a client's need to look "normal." This client was a man in his early 40s who was coming to therapy because he had had an intense feeling of terror while trying to teach his young children to swim. He knew what the terror was about. Thirteen years prior to our first session, he had nearly drowned while swimming near the outlet for a large powerful river that was flowing into the ocean. He got caught up in the current from the river, was tumbled around, did not know up from down, and for a brief period of time he was certain that he was about to die. He was able to get to the surface, and then to shore, but in the years since this incident he had never attempted to go swimming again. Prior to this event, he had been a strong swimmer. He had heard about EMDR as a treatment for fears and disturbing memories and he was coming to therapy to see if he could relax enough to be able to teach his children to swim.

During the initial sessions, we got to know each other. We talked about his background and established his goals for therapy. He was able to easily identify a "safe place" image, which gave him a feeling of comfort. He was able to describe the drowning incident clearly and with some, but not an unusual amount of, emotional disturbance. We then used the EMDR Phase 3 procedural steps to target this incident. His image of the "worst part" was when he was tumbling in the sandy water, not knowing up from down. His negative cognition with this image was "I am in danger." He had two corresponding positive cognitions, neither of which, at the outset, had a strong feeling of truth: "I survived," and "I can easily and comfortably go swimming and teach my children how to swim." The following transcript begins when we are starting EMDR Phase 4, with the first set of eye movements to process the memory.

> Therapist: Notice the feelings in your chest, and in your abdomen and the top of your head. And hold in mind, being disoriented under the water. Just think of that and watch my fingers. Just stay with that. Just think of that. **[EM]** That's good. That's right. Okay. Let it go now.

During this first set of eye movements, fear was evident in his face. A trace of a tear was at the side of each eye. When I stopped moving my fingers, he arched his body back, with his eyes closed, and he was clearly experiencing a high level of distress. Because of this distress, I said some things to him to help him become oriented once again to the safety of my office.

> Therapist: Come back here. That's good. That's good. Just look around the room here. See where you are. You are really here.

In spite of these attempts on my part, he still appeared to be very disoriented. He looked like he was having trouble even listening to what I was saying. And so I suggested that he think of his "safe place," his home.

> Therapist: So, just let yourself go to your home right now. Put all this aside for the moment. We will get back to it. But just let it go for now.

This helped a little, but not enough. He still had a "faraway" look in his eyes, indicating he was not fully oriented to the safety of my office.

> Therapist: I am going to ask you another question. Can you hear the cars outside right now? **(Client: Yes.)**
>
> Can you look around my office here, and see the things I have on my wall? I am asking you to do things right now to deliberately bring your attention back here, because this is a place that is safe. Look around. That's right.

With these interventions, he appeared to be calming down quite a bit, and so I suggested that we continue.

> Therapist: Okay, when you are ready, let yourself go back into it. Okay? And when you go back into it now, tell me what comes into your mind. **(Client: I don't feel like I want to. I don't want to go back there again. I just don't feel like it.)** It is too much? **(Client: It is just an unpleasant feeling.)**

He was telling me that he did not want to go back and think once again of the drowning incident. This was understandable, since he had just had a very fearful "reliving" of it. He was attempting to manage, contain, and control his fear by avoiding thinking of the incident. If he had told me, unambiguously, that he *did not want to think of this incident* again, I certainly would have respected that. However, I also knew that he was highly motivated to resolve this drowning incident, for the sake of both himself and his children. And so I suggested something else, to explore our options.

> Therapist: Okay. Toss me the pillow next to you there on the couch (client hands therapist the pillow). This may seem silly, but let's do it anyway. Here. (Therapist tosses the pillow. There is a short game of catch, back and forth, for about 5 seconds. Client begins to smile.) **(Client: Take my mind away?)** Yes, exactly. Good.

We stopped the pillow tossing.

> Therapist: What is happening now? Check in again. **(Client: Yes. It feels much better than it was.)**

This short game of "catch" apparently had the effect of reorienting him to the safety of the present. Using other language, we could say that tossing the pillow helped him shift from the self-state that was reliving the drowning incident (not just remembering) to another self-state that knew where he was, and knew he was safe. It is difficult to stay in the trance of a trauma memory while following the trajectory of a tossed object. In spite of this apparent shift, though, I still had to have his permission before proceeding with targeting the drowning incident.

> Therapist: Isn't it nice to know that you can come back? **(Client: Yes.)** Now, knowing you can come back actually can be a great help. How about if we do this? If it is too frightening to go all the way back into it . . . check and see, right now. Do you still prefer to not go back into it? Because that's okay. We can work with that if you prefer not to. **(Client: I still can go. I can.)** You can? **(Client: Yes.)** Good. Go back into it now, and what comes into your mind, when you go back into it now? **(Client: Actually, the other picture just interferes a little bit. I could float. I still have some sort of a mix between the most horrible feeling and the joy. I could see both mixed together. The joy I could breathe again. They come as flashes together.)**

> Therapist: Just think of that, and follow my fingers. **[EM]**

When he allowed himself to go back again and think of the incident, he discovered that it already had begun to shift—the memory was already beginning to therapeutically process. He would not have realized this if he had not gone back to think of it again. What he experienced is consistent with how disturbing memories generally are processed during EMDR Phase 4. This is Francine Shapiro's well-known train metaphor for how EMDR processing occurs. It is like a train going down a track and then getting to a stop, where passengers get on and passengers get off (Shapiro, 1995, 2018). With each set of eye movements, or other BLS, negative information about the trauma event leaves the person's awareness (i.e., "reliving" feelings diminish), and positive, adaptive, and realistic information enters awareness. This is what this man experienced, but only when he let himself return to thinking of the drowning incident.

> Therapist: And now, when you are ready, go back into it again. And what do you get now? **(Client: I still have the feeling, but it is not as intense as the very first time we talked about it.)** Okay. Notice that difference. Just watch my fingers, and think of that. **[EM]**

We continued with this session, and after 40 minutes of standard EMDR Phase 4 processing, he reported that his intensity of disturbance regarding this incident was at a total zero (no disturbance) on the Subjective Units of Disturbance Scale (SUDS; 0–10). With a few additional sets of eye movements, he was able to verify the complete truth of the statement, "I survived that, and I'm just fine. I can easily enjoy swimming now, and teach my kids to be good swimmers." He laughed, and said,

> **Client: What the hell was I so upset about!? I am in the water, but there is the shore. I can get there. It is a sunny day! Everything is just fine! This is the feeling that came. I'm just laughing at it.**

Immediately after this late-afternoon session, he went home, put on a swim-ming suit, and went swimming. In the weeks following, he enjoyed teaching swimming to his children.

This was an example of a strong emotional abreaction, one that was not predicted by anything in his initial presentation. He was temporarily so over-whelmed by memory that an avoidance defense was activated. Through the pillow-tossing procedure, he was able to shift his mental state from traumatic reliving back to being aware of the safety of the present.

In a subsequent session, we looked for explanation for what had unexpect-edly occurred. He realized that when he began the first set of BLS, thinking about the near-drowning, he began to have tears in his eyes, and his awareness of tears triggered a whole separate series of unresolved traumatic memories. He told me that when he was 4 years old and crying one day, his father had told him, "If I ever see you crying again, I will kill you!" From that time on, throughout his child-hood, he had tried very hard never to cry. His father's words had stayed with him. So, although we started by working on the drowning incident, we actually tran-sitioned, in a way that was unexpected by either the client or myself, to a whole separate piece of unresolved life experience. We subsequently worked on these incidents with his father, and he was able to put this childhood incident in per-spective, realizing that his emotions, then and now, were normal and acceptable.

This excerpt illustrates several issues that can arise in the treatment of avoidance defenses.

- *The sudden emergence of an unresolved traumatic memory can be very unpleasant and disorienting to a client.* This is a dissociative abreaction— an experience of reliving the trauma all over again, and losing orientation to the safety of the therapist's office. This type of switch can happen very quickly, leaving the client frightened and disoriented. The client was able in this instance to return to being oriented, but this return to safety does not always happen so readily. Regardless of whether orientation is regained, this is generally not something that the client will regard as good therapy. In Chapters 7 to 16, several EMDR-related "Tools" will be described. Each of these Tools is a method of minimizing the chances of dissociative abreaction, and managing the clinical situation on those rare occasions when it nevertheless happens unexpectedly.
- *Avoidance defense can effectively contain phobic anxiety.* This client's avoidance response gave him a way to escape from feelings that were intolerable. When he was able to help himself in this way, the associated feeling was a positive feeling of containment. During our first session, I said to him, "It sounds like, during all these years, you have had fear about swimming. Is that true?" And he said, laughing, "No! I haven't had any fear at all! I just never went swimming!" This is exactly how avoidance can successfully prevent fear. For many people

with strong avoidance defenses, the discovery of their own ability to avoid something disturbing—a memory, an emotion, or a realization—is felt as a clear positive, because avoidance carries a feeling of relief. As described in Chapters 3 to 6, this has implications when we are targeting defenses using an AIP model.

- An avoidance defense often is an immediate and reactive response to overwhelming affect and has the purpose of shutting down that affect quickly. In other words, *defensive avoidance is often a "knee-jerk" impulse, uninfluenced by cognition.* Avoidance defenses, in general, are examples of what has been called *fast thinking* (Kahneman, 2011)—an immediate, reflexive type of response. Repeated sets of BLS tend to have the effect of shifting this type of fast thinking into what Kahneman describes as *slow thinking*, which is more deliberate, mindful, cognitive, and productive.
- The avoidance defense can quickly diminish in intensity if the person can return in some way to being oriented to the safety of the therapist's office. This *reorientation can often happen rapidly* through tossing a pillow, or drinking some water, or walking back and forth in the room, or counting the clocks or tissue boxes in the room, books with red covers on a bookshelf, and so on.
- This example also illustrates how *an avoidance defense is a separate mental action from the disturbance held within the traumatic memory.* In this example, it was still necessary, after resolution of the avoidance defense, to return to the client's original traumatic memory, using EMDR Phase 4. An avoidance response is an implicit memory experienced as a compelling impulse. This avoidance urge was developed and was maintained by a feeling of containment—containment of feelings of extreme threat. When this client was able to be aware of the safety of the therapist's office, that awareness disconfirmed an element of his implicit avoidance memory, and then allowed reconsolidation of that memory, and a resulting drop in his avoidance urge.
- This therapy excerpt also illustrates how, in spite of the therapist's best efforts and intentions, dissociative abreaction cannot always be prevented. *We want to prepare our clients adequately so that they will not be vulnerable to being overwhelmed, and that is why all of the preparation procedures prior to trauma processing are so important.* We also want our clients to have the confident sense that they are bigger than their own memories, bigger than the emotions that have frightened them in the past. At the start of therapy, this man appeared to have this type of empowered attitude with regard to the identified trauma—the near-drowning incident—but his chain of associations, initially hidden, led into something much more disturbing, in a way that was a surprise to both of us. Fortunately, when this rare event occurs, EMDR therapists can have some "tools" in their toolbox to help clients return to being oriented to the safety of the present. Pillow tossing is one effective method, and there are many others.

Along with avoidance, *idealization* defenses of various kinds also can be a major impediment to psychotherapy in general, and to EMDR psychotherapy in particular. For example, one woman in her 30s came to therapy, and as we were just beginning to get to know each other, I was asking questions about her background. I asked about her family, and she said, "My dad was just perfect! He was the best father anyone could ever have!" Later, it emerged that this father had done some very inappropriate things. But these very negative experiences with her father were much harder for her to realize and discuss because she also had a highly cherished image of how, at times, he was good and admirable. She had learned to protect a positive image—an image containing her positive memories of the good times—by pushing from awareness memories of the bad times. This is an example of how an idealization defense can interfere with a client's ability to fully utilize the healing power of EMDR. If the client cannot get to the traumas—cannot have a full realization of the shock, terror, anger, and helplessness associated with unresolved horrible events—then the client probably will not be able to fully resolve those memories, develop a realistic understanding of his or her own life history, and have clear perceptions of other people who have been part of that story. A good feeling, connected with an image that is highly valued but not consistent with past or present realities—that good feeling may be an obstacle to the standard use of EMDR. More examples of how to identify defensive self-states with dysfunctional positive affect, and ways of targeting these with sets of BLS, will be presented in Chapters 3 to 6.

Irrational shame about self often functions as a defense. At first, that might appear to be a strange idea. But shame is an emotion that does not always follow the rules of logic. The effect of shame is an intrinsic neurological activation pattern that has the function of shutting down other affects—particularly interest and/or excitement—that are untenable (Nathanson, 1992). Of course, shame can result when people realize that they have done something bad, something that violates their own moral rules so much that they feel they *are* bad. A husband caught having an affair might have shame (and perhaps also guilt and/or fear); in this instance, the shame may function to partially or completely flatten sexual interest. But shame affect can occur under other circumstances too—it is not always, or even most often, the result of moral transgression. Children and adults who are sexually assaulted often feel intense irrational shame afterward, including a search in the mind—"What did I do wrong?" or, "There must be something wrong with me." The perpetrator should feel ashamed; ironically, however, the perpetrator may have little or no shame. We could say that shame affect in an abuse victim is functioning as a defense. An illusion of personal responsibility for what happened can enable that person to deny the reality of his or her own powerlessness during the trauma. In this way, shame defense is maintained because it is relatively less disturbing than a full awareness of the horror of the traumatic experience. This is a double unfairness for the victim of abuse, one that is often stoked by perpetrators. Fortunately, within our culture, there appears to be a growing awareness of the appalling unfairness of this type of shaming.

Shame, as a defense, often occurs in connection with an idealization defense. Within the logic of a child, it is better to be a bad kid with good parents than a good kid with bad parents. For a child who is being abused or neglected by a caretaker, it is compelling to try to think, "I am—I *must* be—a bad child, and my parents *must* be good parents, or at least good enough parents. I will try very, very hard to be perfect, perhaps then they will love me, the way I need." It may be far too frightening for the child to be fully aware of the reality of the situation—that is, "I am a good, innocent child with abusive, neglectful, disengaged, or disinterested parents." That realization would lead to a sense of helplessness or hopelessness. It is a rare child who is able to accurately perceive the reality of his or her own innocence during abuse or neglect. A child in this situation realistically has no options. He cannot just move down the street into another family. However, if a child in this situation becomes intensely self-critical, searching his own behavior to find fault, that child will probably be able to find something negative, which will then result in an illusion of control: "If I caused it, I'm not powerless!" Ross (2012) describes this as the locus of control shift: an illusion of control, in a situation that in fact is without control, is purchased at the high price of a pervasive negative definition of self, and an inability to see the awful reality of the childhood environment. The child then is likely to take on beliefs—a self-definition—of badness or shame. And shame, in these unfortunate instances, is not just cognitive—it involves visceral responses—a feeling of giving up, or loss of energy in the body. This is the response of dorsal vagal parasympathetic activation (Porges, 2007), which is an unconditioned response to situations of impossible helplessness, or anticipation of impending death. Issues of conceptualizing and treating this type of shame affect, localized in body sensations, will be discussed in Chapter 12.

Figure 1.5 is meant to illustrate the sad situation of dissociated self-states or parts, with partial or complete amnesic separation between the parts. This type of personality structure is often the result of early, frequent, and severe parental disengagement, trauma, and neglect (Lyons-Ruth et al., 2006). Richard Schwartz, in his writings describing the IFS (1995) model of psychotherapy, has made the point that all human beings have "parts" to their personalities—separate states of mind that function to respond to different life circumstances. One main difference for people who are dissociative is that access between parts is significantly impaired. We all have ways of going about normal life tasks, such as meeting a new person, handling a frustrating situation, dealing with interpersonal conflict, expressing the need for affection in connection with another person, coping with unpleasant memories, and 1,000 other examples. For many of these, there is a certain state of mind that becomes routinized. For a child growing up in a coherent and supportive environment, these parts

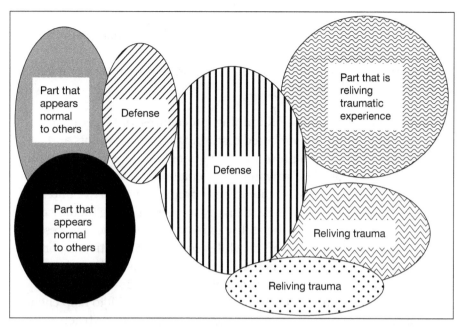

Figure 1.5 Separate personality parts ("self-states," identities) that are not integrated into a unified sense of self and that are not fully coconscious—that is, there is partial or complete dissociative, amnesic separation between the parts.

generally have access to one another and will be under the executive control of the person's unitary sense of self.

In contrast, tragically, there often is a different situation for the individual who has grown up under conditions of extreme, early, and frequent parental disengagement, abuse, and neglect. For these people, parts of the personality often do not have free and unfettered access to one another. A unified sense of self is impaired, and instead a "feeling of self" shifts and switches from one part to another, depending on circumstances, in a way that is very disorganizing and confusing to the individual (and to others who are attempting to relate to that individual). These switches may happen suddenly with only limited cognitive awareness of what has occurred. The divisions in the personality tend to be structured along certain "fault lines" (van der Hart et al., 2006). Specifically, for such a child, some parts may be focused on appearing normal and maintaining connection with caretakers (whatever the cost), and other parts—more hidden parts—may contain "reliving" experiences, feelings, and realizations that the caretakers did not give any attention to, or could not tolerate. Additional parts may have been developed that function to prevent intrusions of disturbing feelings and memories into consciousness.

The clinical picture of Complex PTSD, then, includes, to varying degrees, not only attachment difficulties but also dissociative personality structure, dysfunctionally stored traumatic memories, and psychological defenses—particularly avoidance, idealization, addictive behavior patterns, and shame defenses.

What are the AIP-related tools that are useful in treating Complex PTSD? They are listed as follows:

- From the standard EMDR training: procedures for targeting and resolving clearly remembered disturbing traumatic events and resource installation procedures for strengthening and bringing to the foreground the client's awareness of emotional safety, effectiveness, lovability, worthiness, ability to be appropriately assertive and say "no," and—a skill that is particularly important in the therapy of clients with Complex PTSD—the ability to remain oriented to the present safety of the therapist's office while accessing traumatic memory.
- Conceptual/cognitive/phenomenological models of dissociative personality structure and dissociative symptoms.
- Specific procedures (described in Chapters 9 and 10) to help clients form a visual representation of their own personality structure, in order to prepare for trauma processing, and also to facilitate the clients' ability to contain and have emotional distance from their own painful memory material. These procedures include a method of "Ovals," the many variations of the dissociative table method (Fraser, 1991, 2003), and the use of drawings by clients to create "maps" representative of internal experience.
- Targeting and resolving psychological defenses, primarily defenses of avoidance, addictive behaviors, idealization (dysfunctional positive affect), and shame. These are described in Chapters 3, 4, 5, 6 and 12.
- The Loving Eyes method (Chapters 11 and 14, with additional examples in other chapters): that can be used if a client has either *too much* psychological defense to be able to consciously access a traumatic memory, or *too little* psychological defense, leaving that client open to a nontherapeutic dissociative flooding of disturbing affect if the traumatic memory is accessed.
- The Back-of-the-Head Scale (BHS; Chapter 13) which is a procedure for assessing, moment to moment, the degree to which a client is dissociating and no longer oriented to the safety of the therapist's office.
- The method of Constant Installation of Present Orientation and Safety (CIPOS; Chapter 13), a procedure that can extend the healing power of EMDR to many clients who are extremely frightened of their own traumatic memories and/or very vulnerable to dissociative abreaction.
- The internal healing dialogue (IHD; Chapter 14) procedure, the use of focused sets of BLS to safely bridge and then reduce the phobic barrier and dissociative distance between separate self-states that are initially separated and/or are incongruent with regard to each other.

As I hope will be evident from the examples that follow, these EMDR-related tools are not discrete and separate procedures, but are most usefully implemented in conjunction with each other, in response to specific client needs.

REFERENCES

Afifi, T. O., Mota, N. P., Dasiewicz, P., MacMillan, H. L., & Sareen, J. (2012). Physical punishment and mental disorders: Results from a nationally representative US sample. *Pediatrics, 130,* 1–9. doi:10.1542/peds.2011-2947

American Psychiatric Association. (1994). *Diagnostic and statistical manual of mental disorders* (4th ed.). Washington, DC: Author.

American Psychiatric Association. (2013). *Diagnostic and statistical manual of mental disorders* (5th ed.). Arlington, VA: American Psychiatric Publishing.

Felitti, V. (2013). *The adverse childhood experiences (ACE) study.* Presentation at the EMDR International Association Annual Conference, Austin, TX.

Felitti, V. J., Anda, R. F., Nordenberg, D., Williamson, D. F., Spitz, A. M., Edwards, V., . . . Marks, J. S. (1998). Relationship of childhood abuse and household dysfunction to many of the leading causes of death in adults: The adverse childhood experiences (ACE) study. *American Journal of Preventive Medicine, 14,* 245–258. doi:10.1016/s0749-3797(98)00017-8

Forgash, C., & Knipe, J. (2007). Integrating EMDR and ego state treatment for clients with trauma disorders. In C. Forgash & M. Copeley (Eds.), *Healing the heart of trauma and dissociation with EMDR and ego state therapy* (pp. 1–55). New York, NY: Springer Publishing.

Forgash, C., & Knipe, J. (2012). Integrating EMDR and ego state treatment for clients with trauma disorders. *Journal of EMDR Practice and Research, 6*(3), 120–128. doi:10.1891/1933-3196.6.3.120

Fraser, G. A. (1991). The dissociative table technique: A strategy for working with ego states in dissociative disorders and ego state therapy. *Dissociation, 4*(4), 205–213.

Fraser, G. A. (2003). Fraser's dissociative table technique revisited, revised: A strategy for working with ego states in dissociative disorders and ego state therapy. *Journal of Trauma & Dissociation, 4*(4), 5–28. doi:10.1300/J229v04n04_02

Freud, A. (1937). *The ego and the mechanisms of defence* (Rev. Ed. 1966 [US], 1968 [UK]). London, UK: Hogarth Press and Institute of Psycho-Analysis.

Gonzales, A., & Mosquera, D. (Eds.). (2012). *EMDR and dissociation: The progressive approach.* Charleston, SC: Editors.

Gonzales, A., Mosquera, D., Knipe, J., & Leeds, A. (2012). Introducing healthy patterns of self-care. In A. Gonzales & D. Mosquera (Eds.), *EMDR and dissociation: The progressive approach.* (1st ed. rev., pp. 87-138). Charleston, SC: Editors.

Herman, J. L. (1992). *Trauma and recovery: The aftermath of violence from domestic abuse to political terror.* New York, NY: Basic Books.

Kahneman, D. (2011). *Thinking, fast and slow.* New York, NY: Farrar, Straus and Giroux.

Kernberg, O. (1967, July). Borderline personality organization. *Journal of the American Psychoanalytic Association, 15*(3), 641–685. doi:10.1177/000306516701500309

Lyons-Ruth, K., Dutra, L., Schuder, M. R., & Bianchi, I. (2006, March). From infant attachment disorganization to adult dissociation: Relational adaptations or traumatic experiences? *Psychiatric Clinics of North America, 29*(1), 63–86, viii. doi:10.1016/j.psc.2005.10.011

Maxfield, L., & Hyer, L. A. (2002). The relationship between efficacy and methodology in studies investigating EMDR treatment of PTSD. *Journal of Clinical Psychology, 58,* 23–41. doi:10.1002/jclp.1127

Mol, S. S. L., Arntz, A., Metsemakers, J. F. M., Dinant, G., Vilters-Van Montfort, P. A. P., & Knottnerus, J. A. (2005). Symptoms of post-traumatic stress disorder after non-traumatic events: Evidence from an open population study. *British Journal of Psychiatry, 186,* 494–499. doi:10.1192/bjp.186.6.494

Nathanson, D. L. (1992). *Shame and pride: Affect, sex, and the birth of the self.* New York, NY: W. W. Norton.

Plutchik, R., Kellerman, H., & Conte, H. R. (1979). A structural theory of ego defences and emotions. In C. E. Izard (Ed.), *Emotions in personality and psychopathology* (pp. 229–257). New York, NY: Plenum Press.

Porges, S. W. (2007). The polyvagal perspective. *Biological Psychology, 74,* 116–143. doi:10.1016/j.biopsycho.2006.06.009

Ross, C. (2012). *Trauma attachment, dissociation and EMDR.* EMDRIA annual conference, Austin, TX.

Schwartz, R. (1995). *Internal family systems therapy.* New York, NY: Guilford Press.

Shapiro, F. (1995). *Eye movement desensitization and reprocessing: Basic principles, protocols and procedures.* New York, NY: Guilford Press.

Shapiro, F. (2018). *Eye movement desensitization and reprocessing: Basic principles, protocols, and procedures* (3rd ed.). New York, NY: Guilford Press.

Teicher, M. (2000, Fall). Wounds that time won't heal. Cerebrum: The Dana Forum on Brain Science. Presentation at the Dana Forum, October 1, 2000, 505 Fifth Ave. New York, NY.

Teicher, M. H., Samson, J. A., Polcari, A., & McGreenery, C. E. (2006). Sticks stones and hurtful words: Relative effects of various forms of childhood maltreatment. *American Journal of Psychiatry, 163,* 993–1000. doi:10.1176/ajp.2006.163.6.993

Vaillant, G. E. (1992). *Ego mechanisms of defense: A guide for clinicians and researchers.* Washington, DC: American Psychiatric Press.

van der Hart, O., Nijenhuis, E., & Steele, K. (2006). *The haunted self: Structural dissociation and the treatment of chronic traumatization.* New York, NY: W. W. Norton.

van der Kolk, B. A. (2005, May). Developmental trauma disorder: Towards a rational diagnosis for chronically traumatized children. *Psychiatric Annals, 35,* 401–408. doi:10.3928/00485713-20050501-06

van der Kolk, B. A., Roth. S., Pelcovitz, D., Sunday, S., & Spinazzola, J. (2005, October). Disorders of extreme stress: The empirical foundation of a complex adaptation to trauma. *Journal of Traumatic Stress, 18*(5), 389–399. doi:10.1002/jts.20047

van der Kolk, B. A., Spinazzola, J., Blaustein, M. E., Hopper, J. W., Hopper, E. K., Korn, D. L., & Simpson, W. B. (2007). A randomized clinical trial of eye movement desensitization and reprocessing (EMDR), fluoxetine, and pill placebo in the treatment of posttraumatic stress disorder: Treatment effects and long-term maintenance. *The Journal of Clinical Psychiatry, 68,* 37–46. doi:10.4088/jcp.v68n0105

Varese, F., Smeets, F., Drukker, M., Lieverse, R. Lataster, T., Viechtbauer, W., . . . Bentall, R. P. (2012). Childhood adversities increase the risk of psychosis: A meta-analysis of patient-control, prospective- and cross-sectional cohort studies. *Schizophrenia Bulletin, 38,* 661–671. doi:10.1093/schbul/sbs050

Wilson, S. A., Becker, L. A., & Tinker, R. H. (1995). Eye movement desensitization and reprocessing (EMDR) for psychologically traumatized individuals. *Journal of Consulting and Clinical Psychology, 63,* 928–937. http://dx.doi.org/10.1037/0022-006X.63.6.928

Wilson, S. A., Becker, L. A., & Tinker, R. H. (1997). Fifteen-month follow-up of eye movement desensitization and reprocessing (EMDR) treatment for PTSD and psychological trauma. *Journal of Consulting and Clinical Psychology, 65,* 1047–1056. doi:10.1037//0022-006x.65.6.1047

2

Traumatic Memory and EMDR, When Dual Attention Is Possible

The eye movement desensitization and reprocessing (EMDR) psychotherapy approach is founded on the Adaptive Information Processing (AIP) Model (Shapiro, 1995, 2018). We can think of standard EMDR procedures for processing specific disturbing memories as one of several applications of the AIP—one that can be highly effective when the client is able to maintain dual attention (simultaneous awareness of present safety and past trauma) with regard to a troubling memory. As will be described in the chapters to follow, the AIP can also guide the treatment of defenses and dissociation between personality parts, when access to dual attention tends to be more difficult (Knipe, 2005, 2007, 2009).

The core assumption of the AIP model—the theoretical basis of EMDR—is that there is a natural, physically based mechanism in all human beings for processing and resolving disturbing or incongruent life experiences. Within this model, memories that are disturbing, but not traumatically overwhelming, are processed in the same way that all life experience is processed into memory (Figure 2.1). Following an event, the person thinks about it, talks about it, and perhaps dreams about it. As this occurs, the recollection of the event connects with memories of other life events, and it then takes its place in whatever context is appropriate within the individual's overall life narrative (Shapiro, 1995, 2018). These AIP assumptions are very similar to what has been expressed by other theorists and therapists—for example, Carl Rogers, Abraham Maslow, and Richard Schwartz. All of these have asserted that there is a tendency that we all have, mentally, to move remembered experience from reactive disturbance to realistic, objective perception—with the result of knowing "That was then; and this is now. The past is over, and I am living in the present. I can learn from what has happened without being trapped in what happened or terrorized by

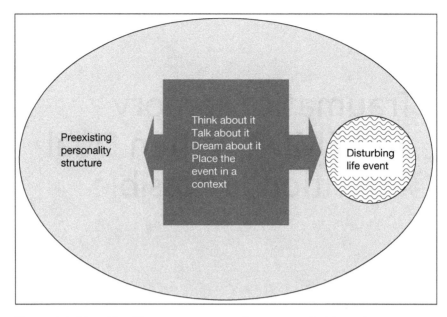

Figure 2.1 Disturbing life events are normally processed without therapy.

what happened." Within the EMDR community, this type of objectivity regarding past and present realities is referred to as "adaptive resolution" (Shapiro, 1995, 2018).

For example, imagine you are driving home one night after work, and you pass a terrible accident on the highway. The police are there, as well as an ambulance. You are waved on through, but as you go by you see some gruesome things. It would not be surprising if 10 minutes later you still might have flashing pictures in your mind of what you saw. That makes sense. And when you get home, you might talk to someone about it. You might have a dream about it that night. You might think about it again the next morning. Little by little (unless the accident somehow activates your unresolved memory networks), what is likely to happen, over the course of several days, is that the disturbance will become less and less and the memory picture will fade, so that a week later you might pass that same place on the highway and remember it differently. There might be some learning that accompanies the processing—"I need to drive through this part of the highway more carefully"—but you would not feel the same emotional impact as when it first happened (Figure 2.2).

This is how the mind usually processes disturbing events without benefit of therapy. Metaphorically, it is similar to what happens if you cut your finger. Once you stop the bleeding and clean and seal up the wound, the healing process in your finger takes over. It is not necessary to wake up the next morning and say to yourself, "I have to remember my healing thoughts! I have to remember today to heal my finger!" Your finger "knows what to do." Similarly, the mind has the capacity to automatically process disturbing experiences. This is the mechanism we all have—that all clients have—that the EMDR

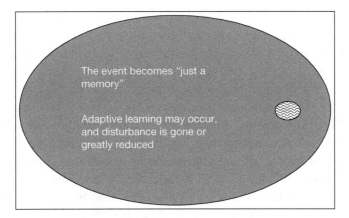

The event becomes "just a memory"

Adaptive learning may occur, and disturbance is gone or greatly reduced

Figure 2.2 After a time has passed ....

therapy approach taps into and utilizes for therapeutic healing of disturbing pieces of the past. This process is not primarily cognitive but occurs naturally, "off the radar."

However, as we know, there is such a thing as psychological trauma, and trauma can be defined in many ways. One simple, clear, and easily understandable way is this: Trauma is when the natural information processing system fails, and the memory of the disturbing event becomes dysfunctionally stored as a "right now," immediate reliving experience within the individual's memory networks. The information processing system might fail because the event is so terrible and totally outside the person's previous life experience that it cannot be taken in and understood. Or, sometimes, the AIP fails because there is a defense in place that prevents the person from fully perceiving and processing the disturbing memory information.

This is an example of the latter: A man in his 50s came to therapy following his arrest for severely assaulting another person. We discussed this incident, as well as other similar incidents that had occurred during his adult life, and also explored his family background. He told me of his deep, reverential respect for his father. As therapy proceeded, he also described many times when his father would beat him with a belt, and even hit him painfully and unexpectedly for no reason whatsoever. At the time, his father's explanation for this was, "You have to always be on guard!" My client initially did not regard these incidents as disturbing; he said, "It was really good that he taught me that lesson." Later, in therapy, this man came to realize that his illegal and inappropriate physical aggressiveness toward others was a behavioral piece of unresolved posttraumatic stress, putting others in the role of the helpless recipient of violence. His idealized image of his father had served as a psychological defense, which had prevented him from being fully aware of the pain created by his father's assaults. With this realization in mind, he was able to process these childhood incidents with compassion for his younger self. This man's case is an example of how a trauma memory sometimes is expressed, not so much as a visual flashback, or an irrational negative cognition (NC), or a feeling or body sensation, but as a behavioral reenactment. If a trauma is unresolved, but not remembered, a person may reproduce that trauma "not as a memory but as an action; he repeats it, without knowing, of course, that he is repeating, and in the end, we understand that this is his way of remembering" (Freud, 1914/1962). This phenomenon may be especially likely to occur with dissociative individuals who are not consciously aware of the traumas of their lives.

Within this model, all posttraumatic dysfunctional memory storage is basically a problem of incomplete integration of the memories of life events. The verbal description of this might be a little confusing because the word *experience* is both a noun and a verb. We could describe traumatic memory storage as experience that is not fully experienced. The inexperienced portion of the traumatic event can be thought of as an impulse pushing the unresolved memory material toward expression through conscious awareness. This impulse toward completion and resolution of memory probably has a neurological basis, at this time not yet well understood, but described in detail by the original Gestalt learning theorists 80 years ago (Koffka, 1935). The purpose of this impulse is to bring about completion and closure with regard to the memory of the disturbing event. This push for conscious experiencing of the unfinished disturbance clashes directly with another strong need of the individual—the need for comfort, emotional safety, and clear orientation to present reality, each of which is disrupted by the memory intrusion. This is the core of the dilemma faced by the person with posttraumatic stress.

Figure 2.3 illustrates this dilemma. Something happens that is overwhelming and stressful, and the information processing system fails. The result is that the individual's conscious experience is divided into two distinct and easily recognizable states of mind—you could say, two distinct experiences of self. For example, imagine the situation of the person who barely escapes from a burning building. Before the escape, that person is feeling intense terror, and the thought, "I'm about to die." And then the person is able to get out of the building safely. The next day, much of this individual's life is still the same. He might go to the same job, have the same car, and have the same people in his life—assuming they all escaped too. The person looks out his eyes and sees the same things in his world, albeit with a diminished sense of the reality of what he sees. However, when there is any reminder of the fire, flashbacks—"relivings"—may intrude into his awareness. The flashbacks may be visual or cognitive—that is, the thought, "I'm in danger!" Or the emotions and physical sensations that occurred at the time of the event may "flash" in that person's body. This response can occur, undiminished, even a year to 5 or 10 years later if the person happens to smell smoke in the air. When a reminder occurs, there is an activation of some or all of the moments of being helplessly trapped in the fire. The "reliving" images and feelings may flood into the mind in a way that is

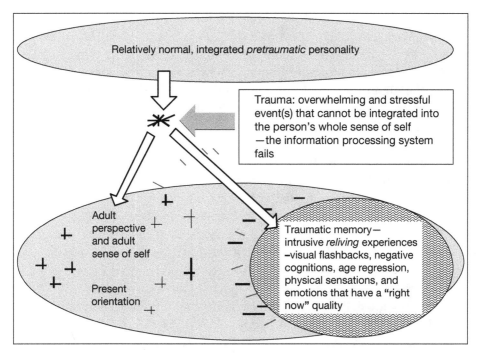

Figure 2.3 *Traumatic* memories result from a failure of the brain's natural information processing system.

terribly upsetting, and may give the person a thought: "I must be crazy! I know I survived! Why can't I just get over this?"

Faulkner (1950) wrote, "The past is never dead. In fact, it's not even past." Traumatic memories highlight the truth of his statement. Academicians have ways of categorizing different types of memory: implicit versus explicit, narrative versus procedural, long term versus short term. With clients, it is often useful to bypass this terminology, and simply point out that posttraumatic disturbance is best described as like time travel—an odd *reliving* of some or all of an event in the past. The purpose of therapy, actually, is to transform traumatic memories into being "just normal memories." Posttraumatic stress disorder (PTSD) is a nonrational, strange mental phenomenon in which the past seems to be the present. It can be helpful to clients, at the beginning of therapy, to introduce some psychoeducation by describing examples of PTSD that are far removed from the client's situation. For example, the survivor of childhood abuse may have read about how sometimes combat veterans, now safely back home, may have a flashback when they hear the sound of a car backfiring or a helicopter overhead. The traumatic memory typically has a quality of happening "right now" or "just moments ago," even if half a century has passed since the event.

In 2003, I provided therapy to a man in his 80s. He had been suffering all his adult life with a recurring nightmare of witnessing the death of three close friends while landing on a beach in the South Pacific in 1943 during

World War II. His case illustrates both the timelessness of traumatic memory and the remarkable effectiveness of EMDR. He went through the EMDR standard phases in basically the same way that most clients do. In two sessions, he was able to resolve his disturbing memory images, with no subsequent recurrence of the nightmares, and he was astonished with that result. Most EMDR therapists can report similar situations with their clients. Time, by itself, does not always heal these very old "relivings," and that is why it is so valuable that therapists have a way to help clients jump-start their AIP systems.

Figure 2.4 shows another example of a client with PTSD. A woman was sexually assaulted 18 years ago when she was in college; in the time since the incident, she has had the support of friends, family, and a loving partner. The client understands she is safe in the therapist's office. She knows she survived after the sexual assault. She realizes she is a good and worthy person. She knows all these things. However, when a very warm, supportive, and safe lover touches her in a certain way, the unresolved traumatic memory is reactivated, and this person is once again reliving—partially or fully—the assault.

Even though all these thoughts are going on in the same brain, the trauma material cannot connect with the person's sense of safety. There is a barrier in the person's awareness—a barrier between the self-state of safety and worthiness, and the state of "reliving" the assault. The thing that EMDR therapy does so beautifully is to remove the barrier so that the client can begin connecting the positives and safety of the present with the pain of the past. This—the

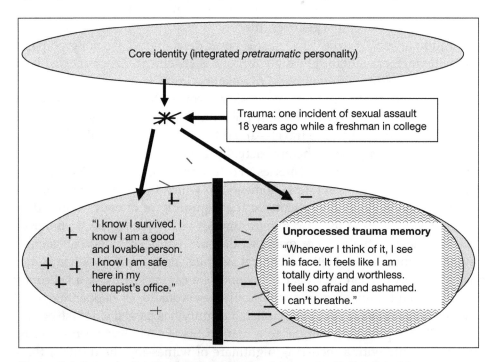

Figure 2.4 Example: Positive information cannot connect with the disturbing memory.

facilitation of access and integration of memory information—is a good thing about standard EMDR procedures.

However, there is an issue with standard EMDR; if the client has a *huge amount* of unresolved traumatic material—from repeated, severe, and early horrible events—there is a danger that the different phases of EMDR, the Phase 3 steps, the bilateral stimulation (BLS), can invite this material to come more and more into awareness in a way that overwhelms the person. Unresolved, unintegrated disturbing memory information may flood the individual, creating an unwelcome, disorienting experience of being much more in the trauma than in the safety of the therapist's office. This is why EMDR cannot be properly regarded simply as an isolated technique—an add-on to another therapy approach. The skill of being a good EMDR therapist involves knowing how to focus the power of BLS directly on the points of dysfunction within the client's personality structure, in a way that is carefully titrated and measured, *and maintains emotional safety*. EMDR work with Complex PTSD requires a high level of awareness of the typical characteristics of dissociative disorders, and the importance of establishing sufficient feelings of safety with dissociative clients, at all phases of therapy. With clients who have a large amount of unresolved trauma, extensive psychological defenses, and/or dissociative personality structure, we have to take extra measures to maintain an appropriate level of emotional containment throughout the therapy. Particular interventions to assist dissociative clients in maintaining a sense of safety during processing of trauma-related information will be described in Chapters 7 to 14.

A traumatic memory, when activated, may contain visual images, cognitions about the self or about others, emotions, and kinesthetic experience connected with reliving the traumatic event. These are all experiential elements that are measured within EMDR Phase 3, prior to initiating the sets of eye movements, or other BLS, in Phase 4.

The target of EMDR therapy is not just an isolated memory, in the narrow sense of that word. When the memory of a traumatic event is dysfunctionally stored, there will not only be a distortion in *recall* of the past, but also distortion in *perception of the present and prediction of the future*. Distortion in perception of the present is actually the most common reason why people pick up the phone to make an appointment with a therapist. This is one reason why it is inaccurate to regard EMDR as simply a treatment for disturbing memories.

For example, a person may have intense anxiety, and feel a sense of danger, in a situation that is actually, objectively, quite safe but nonetheless evokes past trauma. An example would be a person who has had unhappiness and betrayal in past relationships, perhaps in his or her family or in previous love relationships, and now that person is in a new relationship with someone who (objectively speaking) is very emotionally safe. There may be an inappropriate sense of threat with that person in the present, and a concern that what happened before will happen again, even though that may be unlikely or not based on any evidence. The popularity of many popular songs carrying this theme (e.g., Hank Williams' "Cold, Cold Heart") attests to the fact that this is a significant and widespread issue, frequently leading to unhappiness in relationships.

Here is another example of how a traumatic memory can distort present perception and prediction of the future. A person who is rear-ended in a traffic accident, and subsequently has driving-related PTSD, may, after the accident, look in the rearview mirror way too much, because that is where the danger is perceived. One such person I saw in treatment actually drove onto the island of the drive-up window at her bank and had a second accident, because she was giving too much attention to what might be behind her. Another example: A person with an "existential" depression may have feelings inconsistent with current, relatively positive life circumstances. That person's feelings of emptiness and lack of meaning in relationships, in the present, may persist because of distorted perception—the hidden influence of unresolved memories of early helplessness, loss, or abandonment.

There are also parallels to this with sexual assault survivors who, in current relationships, may be highly attentive and vigilant to protect themselves from an exact recurrence of the sexual assault, but who are inattentive, and therefore vulnerable, to new traumas that might occur differently from the first. It is as though unresolved trauma throws a person's danger-warning system off-kilter. Attention is focused on preventing the terrible thing *that has already happened* and this focus overrides the flexible attention that is necessary to protect against unexpected threats in the present. Trauma survivors often experience constant feelings of being "on alert" and are uncomfortably vigilant regarding the possibility of threat. This hypervigilance can spoil good times, as well as cause tension, interrupt sleep, and undermine the person's sense of self-efficacy, since these emotions feel so uncontrollable.

In addition, an unresolved traumatic memory may distort prediction of the future; there may be an absence of hope, or a fear that the future will be a repetition of past suffering, even though there is little or no evidence for that.

EMDR is effective in correcting and resolving these distortions, integrating memory material that is initially separately stored, and bringing the client to adaptive resolution with regard to an initially disturbing memory. A key element in the effectiveness of EMDR therapy is *dual attention*: the client's ability to simultaneously be aware of present safety, positive personal qualities, and strengths, while accessing disturbing traumatic memory material.

EMDR WHEN THE CLIENT IS ABLE TO MAINTAIN DUAL ATTENTION

Skill in using EMDR requires not just training (i.e., a training program recognized by the EMDR International Association), but also extensive consultation both during and following this training. Since this book is primarily aimed at the reader who has received training in EMDR therapy, the specifics of targeting and resolving disturbing memories will only be described generally here, not in detail. EMDR therapy has been widely used in the treatment of a variety of diagnoses other than PTSD, since many other conditions also have disturbing memory as an intrinsic contribution to the clinical picture (Mol et al., 2005). EMDR has been used successfully to treat disturbing memories that are part of panic disorder (de Jongh, Ten Broeke, & Renssen, 1999; de Jongh, van den Oord, & Ten Broeke, 2002; Feske & Goldstein, 1997; Goldstein & Feske, 1994; Goldstein, de Beurs, Chambless, & Wilson, 2000; Maxfield & Melnyk, 2000; Muris, Merkelbach, Holdrinet, & Sijenaar, 1998; Shapiro, 1999), body dysmorphic disorder (Brown, McGoldrick, & Buchanan, 1997), depression (Hofmann, 2011; Knipe, 2009; Lobenstine & Courtney, 2013; Manfield, 1998; Thomas & Gafner, 1993), phantom limb pain (Amano, Seiyama, & Toichi, 2013), posttraumatic symptoms in psychotic clients (de Bont, van Minnen, & de Jongh, 2013; van den Berg, van der Vleugel, Staring, de Bont, & de Jongh, 2013), and as an adjunct to successful treatment of addictive disorders (Bae & Kim, 2012; Cox & Howard, 2007; Hase, Schallmayer, & Sack, 2008; Knipe, 2005; Marich, 2009; Miller, 2010; Popky, 1994, 2005; Zweben & Yeary, 2006). With any of these applications, EMDR is an eight-phase approach. A general description of the standard EMDR phases follows. A detailed description of the complexities within each phase can be found in Shapiro's (1995, 2018) basic text as well as that of Leeds (2009).

> *Phase 1: Exploration of the client's history, particularly with regard to the history of the presenting problem or problems—the development of a contract for therapy—evaluation of the client's mental status—evaluation of elements within the client's clinical picture that will complicate the use of EMDR, such as dissociative personality structure, significant psychological defenses, addictive behaviors, and suicidal ideation. In Phase 1, the specific memories leading to current dysfunction are identified along with the context of those memories in the individual's life experience.*
>
> *Phase 2: Preparation/stabilization—the development of trust and rapport within the therapy relationship—the containment of therapy-interfering behaviors— installation and enhancement of positive resources that will fortify the individual prior to accessing traumatic memory material—resources include a feeling of emotional safety, empowerment, worthiness, lovableness, the ability to self-soothe in the face of stress. The primary purpose of Phase 2 is to help the client develop a sense of empowerment and even mastery over his or her own disturbing memories.*
>
> *Phase 3: In this phase, the specific experiential elements of the dysfunctionally stored traumatic memory are identified. The client is asked to describe a visual image that either represents or shows the "worst part" of the traumatic event. Next, with this image in mind, the client is asked to identify a self-referencing, negative thought (NC) that arises in connection with that memory image. A positive and more realistic cognition (positive cognition; PC) that is an answer to the NC is then identified, and the client is asked to rate the validity of cognition (VOC)—that is, on a 1 to 7 scale, how true that PC feels—while thinking of the*

traumatic event. The negative emotion or emotions connected with the event are named, and then the intensity of disturbance is measured on the 0 to 10 Subjective Units of Disturbance Scale (SUDS). This emotional disturbance is located in the person's physical sensations.

Phase 4: The client holds in mind the disturbing image, negative thoughts about self, and physical sensations while engaging in repeated sets of either eye movements or other forms of BLS, such as hand taps, alternating tones, or alternating buzzers in the hands. Between each set of BLS, the client is asked for a report of the client's immediate experience, which is followed by the therapist saying, "Notice that," "Stay with that," or "Continue with that." In some cases, additional procedures are necessary in order to remove obstacles to processing. Phase 4 is completed when the client reports a SUDS of one or zero, usually zero, unless there is some ecological reason (such as the loss of a loved one) for some disturbance to remain.

Phase 5: In this phase, the "felt truth" of the PC, in connection with the original traumatic event, is reevaluated. Oftentimes, there is a new and better PC that has emerged from the processing during Phase 4. The PC is then combined with an awareness of the original event, and additional sets of BLS are employed until the VOC reaches 7 (unless a lower number is reasonable for ecological reasons).

Phase 6: This is a phase to identify and resolve any remaining residual kinesthetic experience connected with the traumatic memory. The client is asked to hold the event in mind, along with the PC; if any odd or disturbing physical sensations are experienced, these become the focus of additional sets of BLS, with the usual result that the sensations fade. In some cases, these sensations reveal additional channels of disturbing information, which then are available for processing if time and safety considerations allow.

Phase 7: This is the closure phase, during which a client is asked to keep track, during the week to come, of any additional elements to the trauma being treated. If the session is incomplete, and some disturbance still remains, the client is helped to return to a comfortable and safe level of emotional functioning, through various procedures, prior to ending the session.

Phase 8: During this reevaluation phase, the EMDR processing that occurred in the previous session or sessions is brought up again to make sure that the initial processing was complete. Reevaluation typically occurs in the session immediately following the targeting of a traumatic memory, and then occurs again at the end of therapy, prior to termination.

Comprehensive EMDR therapy is not just about treating disturbing old memories. EMDR therapy for a particular issue addresses not only the events from the past that set the problem in motion but also the situational triggers that have perpetuated the problem in the present, as well as anticipated instances of the issue occurring again in the future.

Figure 2.5 illustrates the process and outcome of standard EMDR. Standard EMDR is robust, reliable, and effective in resolving posttraumatic

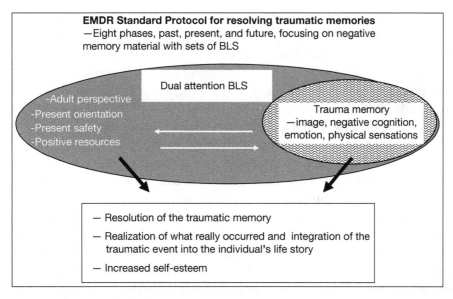

Figure 2.5 Sets of BLS combined with dual attention reliably result in resolution of a traumatic memory.
BLS, bilateral stimulation; EMDR, eye movement desensitization and reprocessing.

disturbance, especially for the client without significant psychological defenses or dissociative personality structure (Maxfield & Hyer, 2002). If the client is able to maintain simultaneous awareness of both present safety and past trauma, and utilize the eight phases of EMDR therapy—targeting the past, present, and future manifestations of a trauma memory (Shapiro, 1995, 2018)—the very reliable results are the following:

1. Resolution of the traumatic memory
2. Incorporation of the event into the person's life narrative and core sense of self, so there is a realization of "Yes, it happened. And, yes, it happened to me. And, yes, it's over"
3. An increase in self-esteem, as measured by the VOC scale

THE CRUCIAL IMPORTANCE OF DUAL ATTENTION

To achieve these results, EMDR requires dual attention, or coconsciousness, between the personality part that is well oriented to the safe present and the parts that hold the memory containing the posttraumatic disturbance. (Actually, this need for dual attention is necessary not only for therapy within the EMDR model but also within other models of treatment for trauma and dissociation.) Dual attention means that the person sitting in the therapist's office is able to maintain a sense of orientation to the present, orientation to needed positive qualities of self, and awareness of the therapist's liking, respect, and competence. And then, from this place of present orientation and safety, the client is able to access traumatic memory material, particularly the "live" disturbing emotions, without losing this orientation. If this ability is present, we can then proceed to use EMDR procedures—the eight phases, particularly Phases 3 to 7, targeting images from past, present, and the anticipated future—to bring this material to resolution. Figure 2.5 illustrates the important situation of dual attention stimulation—the initiation of sets of BLS with a client who is experiencing this state of dual attention. This is the situation we always want to get to as EMDR therapists, because the reliable result will be therapeutic processing of the trauma.

Dual attention is very difficult for many dissociative clients. It is true that *some* dissociative clients, with *some* disturbing situations, will be able to have simultaneous awareness of present safety and past trauma, and be able to use standard EMDR procedures effectively for those particular situations. But many clients with dissociative structure will not be able to do this, at least not initially in therapy. Instead, in the beginning, many clients will have a strong investment in remaining in the part of self that appears normal to others and is oriented to the present. There is likely to be reluctance to allow the emergence of the full traumatic memory. When a client is in the part that appears normal, it may be hard for the client to safely access trauma; when a client is in a personality part that is "reliving" the trauma, it may be hard to access safety. In the beginning, many dissociative clients just will not have the dual attention skill.

THE THERAPEUTIC SHIFTS OF EMDR ARE NOT PRIMARILY COGNITIVE

The therapeutic effects of standard EMDR are not cognitively driven, but occur through the operation of the intrinsic information processing system that all people have. Most EMDR therapists have had many clients who went through the following sequence. A client might come in with a disturbing traumatic memory, 8–9–10 on the SUDS, and when EMDR Phases 1 to 3 have been completed and Phase 4 processing of the memory has been underway for 15 to 20 minutes, the client may suddenly realize, with surprise, "The feeling doesn't seem as strong." Or, "That image in my mind—it seems hazy now." Or, "That negative thought about myself—it just doesn't seem to be as true now." The processing of the disturbance has occurred "off the radar." The conscious mind notices, but does not cause this shift. There are conscious cognitive results of this processing, as well as positive shifts in affect and other aspects of memory, but the cognitive shifts are secondary to the information processing. This accessing and utilization of the mind's automatic information processing capacity is a significant contribution of EMDR.

SPECIFIC EFFECTS OF BLS

So, we have this powerful therapeutic approach of EMDR, with eight phases, targeting identified situations in the past, present, and future, based on the AIP model, and utilizing sets of BLS. BLS is one of the defining characteristics of the EMDR approach.

Figure 2.6 shows a summary of theory and research (Christman, Garvey, Propper, & Phaneuf, 2003; Elofsson, von Scheele, Theorell, & Sondergaard, 2008; Hornsveld et al., 2010; Lee, 2008; Lee & Cuijpers, 2014; MacCulloch & Feldman, 1996; Propper, Pierce, Geisler, Christman, & Bellorado, 2007; Sack, Hofmann, Wizelman, & Lempa, 2008; Wilson, Silver, Covi, & Foster, 1996) showing the different theoretical explanations for how BLS influences and moves conscious experience, particularly with regard to retrieval of memory information. What does BLS do? These studies seem to indicate several specific effects. One is that BLS reduces sympathetic arousal (Amano & Toichi, 2016; Elofsson et al., 2008; Sack et al., 2007; Wilson et al., 1996).

Another is an increased conscious accessing of previously nonassociated (but related) memory elements (Christman et al., 2003; Christman, Propper, & Brown, 2006). A third factor may be that the procedures of EMDR Phase 4 (and other procedures described later in this book) facilitate reconsolidation of the trauma memory into a form that is less disturbing and more consistent with past and present realities (Ecker, Ticic, & Hulley, 2012). In standard EMDR, the memory is activated during Phase 3. Then in Phase 4, the dual attention situation—awareness of memory material combined with present safety—destabilizes the memory. With continuing focused sets of BLS, the mismatch between the disturbance held in the memory and the safety of the office creates a reconsolidation of the memory material. The reconsolidated memory no longer holds distorted, disturbing affect.

The Nobel Prize–winning psychologist, Daniel Kahneman, has focused his research program on a type of mental activity that is quite separate from emotional disturbance—the thinking process that occurs when consumers make choices. In his 2011 book, *Thinking, Fast and Slow*, Kahneman describes two modes of thinking (or information processing): System 1, which occurs quickly, is more intuitive, and operates automatically outside voluntary control, and System 2, which occurs more slowly and deliberately, takes more conscious effort, takes into account a wider network of associated considerations, and results in more accurate assessment of the object of the thinking. It seems reasonable to speculate that during sets of BLS, as the client lingers for a period of 5 to 20 seconds on each separate piece of dysfunctionally stored information associated with an initially troubling memory, the slowing down of the associational process allows the more thoughtful and accurate *slow thinking* to kick in, and replace the more automatic, but erroneous *fast thinking* associations. During focused sets of BLS, a chain of associations about a traumatic event is considered, piece by piece, slowly; as this occurs, each piece of information can more easily shift toward resolution—objectively accurate perception.

Many associational chains may be feeding feelings of disturbance into a traumatic memory image. As each of the many separate chains or channels of information is considered and processed with sets of BLS, "realization" of

Focused sets of BLS

- *Expand associational networks.* That is, repeated sets of BLS, with a person who is holding in mind an emotionally charged memory, will have the effect of inviting additional information regarding that memory into the person's awareness (Christman et al., 2003). Eye movements enhance retrieval of early childhood episodic memories (Christman et al., 2006).

- *Reduce sympathetic arousal* (i.e., fear, rage, or shock) (Amano & Toichi, 2016; Elofsson et al., 2008; Sack et al., 2007; Wilson et al., 1996).

- *Reduce disturbance by allowing reconsolidation of distorted memory elements* (Ecker et al., 2012). Repeated sets of BLS provide an element of present orientation and safety that disconfirms the distorted elements of a trauma memory (the emotional disturbance, the need to avoid accessing the memory), which are the affects held in implicit memory.

- Reduce mental avoidance of disturbance by taxing "working memory" (Andrade, Kavanagh and Baddeley, 1997) while decreasing "emotionality" of memory (de Jongh, Ernst, Marques, & Hornsveld, 2013; Hornsveld et al., 2010).

- *Activate parasympathetic elements of the orienting response* (MacCulloch & Feldman, 1996; Sack et al., 2007). The orienting response has a sympathetic element (when attention is directed to a novel stimulus) and a parasympathetic element (decrease in autonomic activation when the novel stimulus is recognized as nonthreatening).

- *Decrease interhemispheric coherence in frontal areas,* possibly inhibiting posttraumatic memory intrusions (Propper et al., 2007)

- *Increase capacity for distancing/noticing versus "reliving"* a remembered event (Lee, 2008; Lee & Cujpers, 2013, 2014).

- *Reduce the "vividness" of a traumatic memory* (Kavanagh, Freese, Andrade, & May, 2001; van den Hout, Eidhof, Verboom, Little, & Engelhard, 2014; van den Hout, Muris, Salemink, & Kindt, 2001).

- *Facilitate changes in neurological activation consistent with client reports of reduced disturbance*—specifically, reduced limbic activation in response to disturbing memories (Amano & Toichi, 2016); reduced overactivity of the lateral prefrontal cortex (Ohtani, Matsuo, Kasai, Kato, & Kato, 2009); and activation shift from frontal and limbic regions to temporo–parietal–occipital regions (Pagani et al., 2012).

- *May facilitate "slow thinking,"* which relies less on intuition and implicit memory, is less reactive, and results in more objective assessment (Kahneman, 2011). This feature of BLS is relevant because many emotional problems have an element of immediate reactivity—termed by Kahneman as "fast thinking." The structure of repeated sets of BLS, each set followed by a cognitive report of ongoing shifts in experience, has the effect of slowing mental reactivity, leading to an easier, more mindful, and more productive mental examination of a troubling memory.

All of the previously mentioned enhance accurate information processing and facilitate adaptive resolution.

Figure 2.6 Dual attention stimulation activates the AIP system.
AIP, adaptive information processing; BLS, bilateral stimulation.

the event is increased; in other words, there is accurate understanding of what occurred, including the important realization that it is now in the past. There is an increased "presentification" (van der Hart, Nijenhuis, & Steele, 2006) with regard to the memory—an increased ability to differentiate between remembered information and perception of what is occurring "right now." There is an expansion of associational networks related to the target memory, so that the individual who is thinking of an event in the past, while experiencing BLS, may initially have some increased disturbance ("I now can clearly see the look on his face. I'm feeling that fear more intensely now."), but may also have increased recognition of positive elements ("I really did survive that!" or, "I see now that I really did the best I could. What happened wasn't my fault.") and that increased recognition ultimately lowers the disturbance. It seems that BLS, combined with any remembered experience, brings that memory front and center in the person's awareness. As a disturbing memory is activated, yet coupled with disconfirming information (e.g., present safety, adult perspective), that memory can then be reconsolidated with accurate realization of past and present. Once that occurs, previously unseen linkages can be more apparent, and any incongruities within that experience can be identified and reconciled, resulting in clarity and a sense of closure. The incongruity between the fear and danger of the past and the safety of the present can be reconciled. The incongruity between the urge to use an addictive substance and the self-destructive consequences of the addiction can be reconciled. And, over the course of an extended therapy process, the incongruity between an experience of separate, disconnected self-states inside can be reconciled with the realization of having one heart, one brain, and one core self. In other words, appropriately focused sets of BLS seem to move conscious experience toward increasing accuracy of perception of "consensual reality"—the perception of present and past that most people would agree is normal and accurate. And this phenomenon, then, is instrumental in facilitating many positive results in therapy.

The reader who has been trained and has experience in effectively using EMDR can see how the earlier description matches what you have observed with your clients—sympathetic arousal goes down, associational networks expand, and the previously traumatic event is now remembered objectively, as it simply takes its place within the client's life story—no longer a "punch in the gut" or "knife in the heart." The client no longer has a sense of fear in the safe present, and no longer has a strong investment in defense (i.e., the urge to escape or find relief from posttraumatic fear). This is the therapeutic effect of BLS, stimulation of the natural, physically based information processing system of the mind: to move an individual's awareness and perception toward accurate perception of past and present realities and "adaptive resolution." Fifteen years ago, many of the critics of EMDR (e.g., Herbert et al., 2000) were saying something catchy: "What is effective about EMDR is not new, and what is new is not effective." This neat short statement was a stark contrast with the observations of many EMDR clinicians at that time. Now we know quite a bit more about how the specific effects of BLS are very useful at particular points in the therapy process.

These distortions of past, present, and future, which occur with simple PTSD, are present to an even greater degree with dissociated personality parts that have originated many traumatic experiences. For example, an unresolved traumatic memory, when triggered, may also induce age regression; this can occur even in a client who is not particularly dissociative. Consider a person who was traumatized at age 4, has never talked about it with anyone, has tried hard to never think of it, and now is in a therapist's office at age 44, talking about it for the first time. That person might, at that moment, go into a "reliving" of the childhood event and have only the problem-solving skills of a 4-year-old. He might also have the needs of a 4-year-old—for example, a need for the therapist to understand even things that are not being verbalized. There may be an activation of a deep need for nurturing by the therapist, or, conversely, an inaccurate perception of the therapist as critical. He might even be able to say, "Right now, I feel like I'm just 4 years old!" This type of age regression has many implications for therapy. Most of the transference events in therapy can be reconceptualized as posttraumatic intrusions from a previous trauma world into the relationship with a therapist.

Usually, a client requests psychotherapy following repeated unsuccessful attempts to solve a particular, present-day emotional problem on his or her own. Initially, there may be incomplete recognition of how the current issue is influenced by events in the past. Either during the history taking, or during the exploration of the identified problem, roots of the present difficulties in prior unresolved unhappy events are likely to become more evident. This is illustrated in Figure 2.7 (which is a close-up look at the traumatic memory oval in Figure 2.3). The dotted line in this figure illustrates how aspects of traumas and other dysfunctionally stored elements (DSEs) may initially be outside the client's awareness. EMDR "uncovers" these DSEs, so that they then can be brought to adaptive resolution. This is how EMDR works, very reliably, for those clients who do not have significant psychological defenses and/or dissociative personality structure. If the client is able to maintain sufficient orientation to the safety of the present while accessing emotional disturbance of the past, EMDR can be very effective in healing the distortions caused by traumatic memory.

Subsequent chapters (7 to 14) will focus on the more complex dissociative conditions, which typically include elements of self-defeating psychological defense and dissociative separation between personality parts that have "first person" identities. Often these parts have very different roles within the personality, and, to the extent they are mutually aware, they may have intensely conflictual agendas. Focused sets of BLS can also be very useful in the treatment of these additional elements. The intensity of psychological defense can

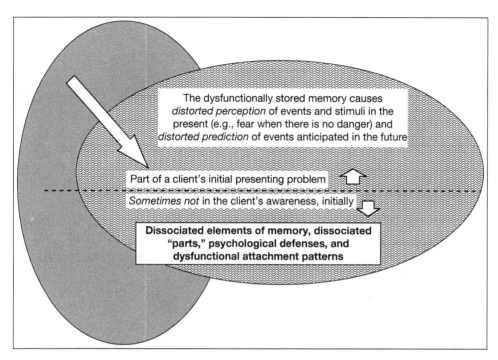

Figure 2.7 A traumatic memory causes not only distortion in recall but also distortion in perception and prediction, and may in turn result in the development of psychological defense, dissociative personality structure, and dysfunctional interpersonal relationship patterns.

be reduced. The internal phobic fear connected with contact between separate dissociative parts can be reduced, and healing dialogue between those parts can be initiated.

REFERENCES

Amano, T., Seiyama, A., & Toichi, M. (2013). Brain activity measured with near-infrared spectroscopy during EMDR treatment of phantom limb pain. *Journal of EMDR Practice and Research, 7*(3), 144–153. doi:10.1891/1933-3196.7.3.144

Amano, T., & Toichi, M. (2016). Possible neural mechanisms of psychotherapy for trauma-related symptoms: Cerebral responses to the neuropsychological treatment of post-traumatic stress disorder model individuals. *Scientific Reports, 6*, Article 34610. doi:10.1038/srep34610

Andrade, J., Kavanagh, D., & Baddeley, A. (1997). Eye movements and visual imagery: A working memory approach to the treatment of posttraumatic stress disorder. *British Journal of Clinical Psychology, 36*(2), 209–223. doi:10.1111/j.2044-8260.1997.tb01408.x

Bae, H., & Kim, D. (2012). Desensitization of triggers and urge reprocessing for an adolescent with Internet addiction disorder. *Journal of EMDR Research and Practice, 6*(2), 73–81. doi:10.1891/1933-3196.6.2.73

Brown, K. W., McGoldrick,. T., & Buchanan, R. (1997). Body dysmorphic disorder: Seven cases treated with eye movement desensitization and reprocessing. *Behavioural and Cognitive Psychotherapy, 25*(02), 203–207. doi:10.1017/s1352465800018403

Christman, S. D., Garvey, K. J., Propper, R. E., & Phaneuf, K. A. (2003). Bilateral eye movements enhance the retrieval of episodic memories. *Neuropsychology, 17*(2), 221–229. doi:10.1037/0894-4105.17.2.221

Christman, S. D., Propper, R. E., & Brown, T. J. (2006). Increased inter-hemispheric interaction is associated with earlier offset of childhood amnesia. *Neuropsychology, 20*(3), 336–345. doi:10.1037/0894-4105.20.3.336

Cox, R. P., & Howard, M. D. (2007). Utilization of EMDR in the treatment of sexual addiction: A case study. *Sexual Addiction & Compulsivity. The Journal of Treatment & Prevention, 14*(1), 1–20. doi:10.1080/10720160601011299

de Bont, P. A., van Minnen, A., & de Jongh, A. (2013). Treating PTSD in patients with psychosis: A within-group controlled feasibility study examining the efficacy and safety of evidence-based PE and EMDR protocols. *Behavior Therapy, 44*(4), 717–730. doi:10.1016/j.beth.2013.07.002

de Jongh, A., Ernst, R., Marques, L., & Hornsveld, H. (2013). The impact of eye movements and tones on disturbing memories involving PTSD and other mental disorders. *Journal of Behavior Therapy and Experimental Psychiatry, 44*(4), 477–483. doi:10.1016/j.jbtep.2013.07.002

de Jongh, A., Ten Broeke, E., & Renssen, M. R. (1999). Treatment of specific phobias with eye movement desensitization and reprocessing (EMDR): Protocol, empirical status, and conceptual issues. *Journal of Anxiety Disorders, 13,* 69–85. doi:10.1016/S0887-6185(98)00040-1

de Jongh, A., van den Oord, H. J. M., & Ten Broeke, E. (2002). Efficacy of eye movement desensitization and reprocessing (EMDR) in the treatment of specific phobias: Four single-case studies on dental phobia. *Journal of Clinical Psychology, 58,* 1489–1503. doi:10.1002/jclp.10100

Ecker, B., Ticic, R., & Hulley, L. (2012). *Unlocking the emotional brain: Eliminating symptoms at their roots using memory reconsolidation.* New York, NY: Routledge.

Elofsson, U. O. E., von Scheele, B., Theorell, T., & Sondergaard, H. P. (2008). Physiological correlates of eye movement desensitization and reprocessing. *Journal of Anxiety Disorders, 22,* 622–634. doi:10.1016/j.janxdis.2007.05.012

Faulkner, W. (1950). *Requiem for a nun.* New York, NY: Vintage.

Feske, U., & Goldstein, A. (1997). Eye movement desensitization and reprocessing treatment for panic disorder: A controlled outcome and partial dismantling study. *Journal of Consulting and Clinical Psychology, 65,* 1026–1035.

Freud, S. (1962). The aetiology of hysteria. In J. Strachey (Ed. & Trans.), *The standard edition of the complete works of Sigmund Freud* (Vol. 3, pp. 189–221). London, UK: Hogarth. (Originally published 1914)

Goldstein, A., & Feske, U. (1994). Eye movement desensitization and reprocessing for panic disorder: A case series. *Journal of Anxiety Disorders, 8*, 351–362. doi:10.1016/0887-6185(94)00023-9

Goldstein, A. J., de Beurs, E., Chambless, D. L., & Wilson, K. A. (2000). EMDR for panic disorder with agoraphobia: Comparison with waiting list and credible attention-placebo control condition. *Journal of Consulting and Clinical Psychology, 68*, 947–956. doi:10.1037/0022-006X.68.6.947

Hase, M., Schallmayer, S., & Sack, M. (2008). EMDR reprocessing of the addiction memory: Pretreatment, posttreatment, and 1-month follow-up. *Journal of EMDR Practice and Research, 2*(3), 170–179. doi:10.1891/1933-3196.2.3.170

Herbert, J. D., Lilienfeld, S. O., Lohr, J. M., Montgomery, R. W., O'Donohue, W. T., Rosen, G. M., & Tolin, D. F. (2000). Science and pseudoscience in the development of eye movement desensitization and reprocessing: Implications for clinical psychology. *Clinical Psychology Review, 20*(8), 945–971. doi:10.1016/S0272-7358(99)00017-3

Hofmann, A. (2011). *EMDR in the treatment of depression.* Paper presented at the EMDR Europe Association annual conference, Vienna, Austria.

Hornsveld, H. K., Landwehr, F., Stein, W., Stomp, M., Smeets, M., & van den Hout, M. (2010). Emotionality of loss-related memories is reduced after recall plus eye movements but not after recall plus music or recall only. *Journal of EMDR Practice and Research, 4*(3), 106–112. doi:10.1891/1933-3196.4.3.106

Kahneman, D. (2011). *Thinking, fast and slow.* New York, NY: Farrar, Straus and Giroux.

Kavanagh, D. J., Freese, S., Andrade, J., & May, J. (2001). Effects of visuospatial tasks on desensitization to emotive memories. *British Journal of Clinical Psychology, 40*(Pt. 3), 267–280. doi:10.1348/014466501163689

Knipe, J. (2005). Targeting positive affect to clear the pain of unrequited love: Codependence, avoidance and procrastination. In R. Shapiro (Ed.), *EMDR solutions* (pp. 189–211). New York, NY: W. W. Norton.

Knipe, J. (2007). Loving eyes: Procedures to therapeutically reverse dissociative processes while preserving emotional safety. In C. Forgash & M. Copeley (Eds.), *Healing the heart of trauma and dissociation* (pp. 181–226). New York, NY: Springer Publishing.

Knipe, J. (2009). "Shame is my safe place": Adaptive information processing methods of resolving chronic shame-based depression. In R. Shapiro (Ed.), *EMDR solutions II* (pp. 49–89). New York, NY: W. W. Norton.

Koffka, K. (1935). *Principles of Gestalt psychology.* New York, NY: Ronald Press.

Lee, C. (2008). Cultural process in EMDR—More than imaginal exposure. *Journal of EMDR Practice and Research, 2*(4), 262–268. doi:10.1891/1933-3196.2.4.262

Lee, C. W., & Cuijpers, P. (2013). A meta-analysis of the contribution of eye movements in processing emotional memories. *Journal of Behavior Therapy & Experimental Psychiatry, 44*, 231–239. doi:10.1016/j.jbtep.2012.11.001

Lee, C. W., & Cuijpers, P. (2014). What does the data say about the importance of eye movement in EMDR? *Journal of Behavior Therapy and Experimental Psychiatry, 45*(1), 226–228. doi:10.1016/j.jbtep.2013.10.002

Leeds, A. (2009). *A guide to the standard EMDR protocols for clinicians, supervisors, and consultants.* New York, NY: Springer Publishing.

Lobenstine, F., & Courtney, D. (2013). A case study: The integration of intensive EMDR and ego state therapy to treat comorbid posttraumatic stress disorder, depression, and anxiety. *Journal of EMDR Practice and Research, 7*(2), 65–80. doi:10.1891/1933-3196.7.2.65

MacCulloch, M. J., & Feldman, P. (1996). Eye movement desensitization treatment utilizes the positive visceral element of the investigatory reflex to inhibit the memories of post-traumatic stress disorder: A theoretical analysis. *British Journal of Psychiatry, 169,* 571–579. doi:10.1192/bjp.169.5.571

Manfield, P. (1998). Resolution of uncomplicated depression. In P. Manfield (Ed.), *Extending EMDR* (pp. 15–36). New York, NY: W.W. Norton.

Marich, J. (2009). EMDR in the addiction continuing care process case study of a cross-addicted female's treatment and recovery. *Journal of EMDR Practice and Research, 3*(2), 98–106. doi:10.1891/1933-3196.3.2.98

Maxfield, L., & Hyer, L. A. (2002). The relationship between efficacy and methodology in studies investigating EMDR treatment of PTSD. *Journal of Clinical Psychology, 58,* 23–41. doi:10.1002/jclp.1127

Maxfield, L., & Melnyk, W. T. (2000). Single session treatment of test anxiety with eye movement desensitization and reprocessing (EMDR). *International Journal of Stress Management, 7,* 87–101. http://dx.doi.org/10.1023/A:1009580101287

Miller, R. (2010). The feeling-state theory of impulse-control disorders and the impulse-control disorder protocol. *Traumatology, 16*(3), 2–10. https://doi.org/10.1177/1534765610365912

Mol, S. S. L., Arntz, A., Metsemakers, J. F. M., Dinant, G., Vilters-Van Montfort, P. A. P., & Knottnerus, J. A. (2005). Symptoms of post-traumatic stress disorder after non-traumatic events: Evidence from an open population study. *British Journal of Psychiatry, 186,* 494–499. doi:10.1192/bjp.186.6.494

Muris, P., Merkelbach, H., Holdrinet, I., & Sijenaar, M. (1998). Treating phobic children: Effects of EMDR versus exposure. *Journal of Consulting and Clinical Psychology, 66*(1), 193–198.

Ohtani, T., Matsuo, K., Kasai, K., Kato, T., & Kato, N. (2009). Hemodynamic responses of eye movement desensitization and reprocessing in post-traumatic stress disorder. *Neuroscience Research, 65,* 375–383. doi:10.1016/j.neures.2009.08.014

Pagani, M., Di Lorenzo, G., Verado, A. R., Nicolais, G., Monaco, L., & Lauretti, G. (2012). Neurobiological correlates of EMDR monitoring—An EEG study. *PLOS ONE, 7*(9), e 45753. doi:10.1371/journal.pone.0045753

Popky, A. J. (1994). *EMDR protocol for smoking and other addictions.* Presentation at the annual meeting of the EMDR network, Sunnyvale, CA.

Popky, A. J. (2005). DeTUR, an urge reduction protocol for addictions and dysfunctional behaviors. In R. Shapiro (Ed.), *EMDR solutions* (pp. 167–188). New York, NY: W.W. Norton.

Propper, R., Pierce, J. P., Geisler, M. W., Christman, S. D., & Bellorado, N. (2007). Effect of bilateral eye movements on frontal interhemispheric gamma EEG coherence: Implications for EMDR therapy. *Journal of Nervous and Mental Disease, 195,* 785–788. doi:10.1097/NMD.0b013e318142cf73

Sack, M., Lempa, W., & Lamprecht, F. (2007). Stress reactions during a traumatic reminder in patients treated with EMDR. *Journal of EMDR Practice and Research, 1*(1), 15–23.

Sack, M., Hofmann, A., Wizelman, L., & Lempa, W. (2008). Psychophysiological changes during EMDR and treatment outcome. *Journal of EMDR Practice and Research, 2*(4), 239–246. doi:10.1891/1933-3196.2.4.239

Shapiro, F. (1995). *Eye movement desensitization and reprocessing: Basic principles, protocols, and procedures.* New York, NY: Guilford Press.

Shapiro, F. (1999). Eye movement desensitization and reprocessing (EMDR) and the anxiety disorders: Clinical and research implications of an integrated psychotherapy treatment. *Journal of Anxiety Disorders, 13,* 35–67. doi:10.1016/S0887-6185(98)00038-3

Thomas, R., & Gafner, G. (1993). PTSD in an elderly male: Treatment with eye movement desensitization and reprocessing (EMDR). *Clinical Gerontologist, 14*(2), 57–59.

van den Berg, D. P. G., van der Vleugel, B. M., Staring, A. B. P., de Bont, P. A. J., & de Jongh, A. (2013). EMDR in psychosis: Guidelines for conceptualization and treatment. *Journal of EMDR Practice and Research, 7*(4), 208–224. doi:10.1891/1933-3196.7.4.208

van den Hout, M. A., Eidhof, M. B., Verboom, J., Little, M., & Engelhard, I. M. (2014). Blurring of emotional and non-emotional memories by taxing working memory during recall. *Cognition and Emotion, 28*(45), 717–727. doi:10.1080/02699931.2013.848785

van den Hout, M. A., Muris, P., Salemink, E., & Kindt, M. (2001). Autobiographical memories become less vivid and emotional after eye movements. *British Journal of Clinical Psychology, 40*(Pt. 2), 121–130. doi:10.1348/014466501163571

van der Hart, O., Nijenhuis, E., & Steele, K. (2006). *The haunted self: Structural dissociation and the treatment of chronic traumatization.* New York, NY: W. W. Norton.

Wilson, D., Silver, S. M., Covi, W., & Foster, S. (1996). Eye movement desensitization and reprocessing: Effectiveness and autonomic correlates. *Journal of Behavior Therapy and Experimental Psychiatry, 27,* 219–229. doi:10.1016/S0005-7916(96)00026-2

Zweben, J., & Yeary, J. (2006). EMDR in the treatment of addiction. *Journal of Chemical Dependency Treatment, 8*(2), 115–127. doi/abs/10.1300/J034v08n02_06

Adaptive Information Processing Methods for Resolving Psychological Defenses

3

An Adaptive Information Processing Model for Treating Psychological Defenses

The methods described in this chapter and previously (Knipe, 1998, 2005, 2007, 2010, 2014) are designed to expand the use of the eye movement desensitization and reprocessing (EMDR) Adaptive Information Processing (AIP) model to clients with strong psychological defenses. As described in Chapter 1, the term *psychological defense* is being used here to describe any mental action, or behavior, that has the function and purpose of blocking the full emergence into consciousness of posttraumatic disturbance. Defenses protect the self from being overwhelmed by the past; however, the same defenses also prevent access to unresolved traumatic memory information, and thereby prevent the full use of EMDR procedures for processing disturbing memories. The methods that will be described here, for targeting and resolving psychological defense, facilitate therapy moving more easily, more quickly, and more effectively for many people with Complex posttraumatic stress disorder (Complex PTSD). These methods are consistent with Milton Erickson's principle of utilization (Erickson & Rossi, 1979): any behavior or attitude of the client can be *utilized*. In therapy, a defense can be a starting point for therapeutic progress. Client "resistances" or "acting out behaviors" are seen not as obstacles to therapy but as aspects of the client's presentation that must be included in the therapy. Of course, there are many instances when "therapy-interfering behaviors" (Linehan, 1993), such as intoxication, threatening behavior, or other illegal behavior, have the potential to bring therapeutic progress to a standstill; in these instances, compassionate confrontation from the therapist is needed. But in general, all client behaviors presented in and out of therapy sessions directly express different aspects of a client's personality structure, and often there will be an intrinsic functionality in the way these aspects arise. For example, a client might present an avoidance defense within a therapy session, and this defense might appear to be a detour on the path the therapist had planned—to discuss and resolve some issue. But, in a sense, the client's avoidance is saying to the therapist, "I can't work on this issue yet. First we have to deal with my reasons for not wanting to work on it." Obstacles to therapy, within the client's presentation, usually express incongruities in the client's personality structure, and there are likely to be many ways to address these types of incongruity through specific targeting with bilateral stimulation (BLS).

Writers in the field of dissociation (Kluft & Fine, 1993; Putnam, 1989; Schwartz, 1995; van der Hart, Nijenhuis, & Steele, 2006), each with a strong rationale, have proposed different ways of categorizing personality parts. The categorization system proposed here is designed specifically for use by therapists working within the EMDR model. *Separate types of personality parts respond differently to focused sets of BLS*; therefore, it is useful to think of three categories of dissociated parts (Figure 3.1):

1. Oriented, adaptive, and effective "normal-appearing" parts
2. "Trauma-reliving" parts
3. Parts that prevent "trauma-reliving" parts from intruding into and disrupting the oriented, "normal" parts—parts that function as psychological defenses

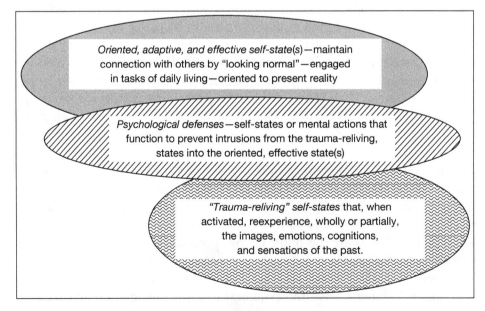

Figure 3.1 An AIP model of personality parts—under conditions of neglect and abuse, *certain types* of separate self-states or parts tend to develop.
AIP, adaptive information processing.

THE EFFECTS OF BLS ON DIFFERENT TYPES OF PERSONALITY PARTS

Within each of the three different categories of parts—oriented and effective parts, "trauma-reliving" parts, and psychological defense—BLS has different effects. If the therapist asks the client to hold in mind memory images that have to do with present safety, or worthiness, or lovableness, or personal strength, or any of a number of other positive qualities, and get in touch with the good feelings of those memories, and then combine memory images and feelings with sets of BLS, that is what is referred to in the EMDR community as resource installation. The client's awareness of that particular personal strength comes to the foreground, and is available to fortify the person in preparation for trauma work. For example, a client might say, "Aunt Betty loved me so much! I would go over there, and she would bake cookies. That is such a nice thing to remember!" The therapist can ask, "When you think of being with Aunt Betty, what is the emotion you feel? Where is that good feeling in your body? Can you just follow my fingers while you think of that?" The resource of lovableness is then strengthened through combining BLS with a representative image and associated feelings. Resource installation is often necessary for people with Complex PTSD, who need to have these positive elements enhanced in awareness prior to doing the difficult and potentially destabilizing trauma work.

And, of course, experienced EMDR therapists have witnessed many examples of how combining BLS with a troubling memory, or memory elements from a "trauma-reliving" part of the personality, can result reliably in trauma resolution. If the client is able to maintain sufficient present orientation (particularly present safety) and awareness of positives while accessing a representative disturbing memory, the distortions and disturbing affect of that memory are likely to be resolved through standard EMDR procedures.

There is an additional EMDR "tool" that is quite useful. If sets of BLS are combined with the *positive* affect of defense, the result will tend to be a lessening of the strength of that defense—the defense will become less powerful—revealing the traumatic material that has been held by the defense, which is then available for standard EMDR processing (Figure 3.2).

The therapist should be cautioned to not begin this procedure with only 20 minutes left in the session! Sufficient time should be available to target and begin to resolve any disturbing material that has been hidden behind the defense. However, bearing in mind this caveat, this method of targeting defense can be quite useful for clients who have defensive processes in place that prevent full access to traumatic material. If carried out with sufficient emotional safety, this procedure is doubly useful—less defense, yet more healing access to disturbing memories. An experienced therapist might ask, "Is that a good idea?" If clients are without their usual defenses, would not they feel horribly overwhelmed and vulnerable? This is a reasonable concern; however, in practice, this does not tend to occur in this way. Rather, as the defense is processed, there tends to also be a parallel reduction in the emotional intensity of the underlying traumatic material.

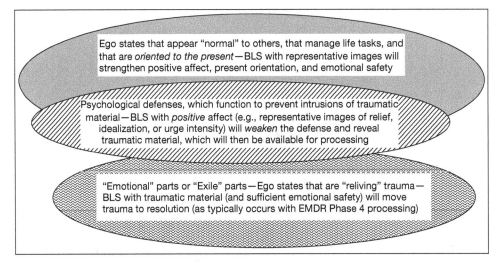

Figure 3.2 The effects of sets of BLS with different types of ego states or dissociated parts.
BLS, bilateral stimulation; EMDR, eye movement desensitization and reprocessing.

The dysfunctional affect of defense is positive affect; this positive affect is processed, resolved, and relinquished when these procedures are used. The defense functions to contain negative posttraumatic affect; therefore, successful containment is experienced as positive. If a person has a disturbing thought or memory, but is able to shift away from that disturbing material by denying it exists, or by blaming someone, or by learning to not think about it, that will be accompanied by a positive feeling of relief. If a person has a narcissistic defense, there will be—by definition—unrealistic positive thoughts and affect about self. Or a client from a dysfunctional home environment may have an unrealistic positive image of parents and enjoy the positive feelings of this image. The image may be based in part on actual positive experiences, but may also function to cover over, and prevent conscious access to, childhood abuse or neglect. This approach to targeting defense—by focusing on the positive affect of defense— really reverses the whole way of thinking about how to use EMDR when targeting negative trauma memories. When a defense is the focus of therapy, we target positive images, positive statements about self, positive feelings—these positively valenced mental actions serve a defensive purpose by standing in the way of accessing the disturbing memories that must be accessed in order for the person to comprehensively achieve his or her larger therapy goals.

Here is an example. The first time I ever used this method was in 1994. A woman in her 30s had recently had a serious car accident and had heard about EMDR. We used the standard procedures, successfully targeting the moment of impact, other images from the hospital, and then moving to more present-day targets, such as driving past the intersection where the accident occurred and highway driving in general. We then worked on a "future template" of driving comfortably in many situations. As this whole process of therapy was winding down, with good results, she came in one day and said, "This has really been helpful. But I want to ask you about something. When I was 8 years old, something happened I've never told anyone about. I'm wondering if EMDR could help me with it. . . . A neighbor did some bad things to me, and I never told anybody." She began to cry when she told me of this molestation. I told her that I thought EMDR might be helpful to her, in the same way that the work with the accident had been helpful. She said that she was pretty sure that it had only happened once, but it was very difficult for her to talk about the one occurrence. Over the course of several weeks, she told me all the information she was able to remember about it. We did not yet do any EMDR processing—she just told me what had happened, so that I would have a full picture. It was obvious that even telling me the basic details was very frightening for her. In spite of this, though, she was determined to proceed, now that she had bravely opened the door to working with this unfinished memory.

We set up a 90-minute session, with the plan that on this day we would begin EMDR Phase 3, assessment of the specific memory, and Phase 4, desensitization/reprocessing of the memory. She arrived at my office, out of breath, and said, "I know what we are going to do today, but before we do that, something just happened at work, something that was kind of upsetting, and could we talk about it for just 5 minutes?" Forty minutes later, we were still talking about work, and at that point it felt unwise to begin opening up the whole issue of what happened to her when she was 8 years old. So we set up another 90-minute session for the next week, and she was 25 minutes late! We set up another extended session for the following week, and something else came up—something less troubling, but a distraction that used up most of our time. It was becoming very clear, to both the client and myself, that she had a huge avoidance defense in place that was preventing healing access to this memory.

So, for the next week, we set up another 90-minute session. She was on time. She sat down. I said to her, "At this moment, we have 90 minutes that we could use to work on what happened when you were 8 years old. Here's a question. Right now, 0 to 10, with 10 the most, how much do you *not want to think about* what happened? How much would you rather talk about anything else?" She said, "10!" I asked, "Where's that 10 in your body?" She said, "In my stomach . . . and really all over!" For this type of intervention, in my notes, I record this number, not as a Subjective Units of Disturbance (SUDS) score but as a Level of Urge to Avoid (LOUA) score. This procedure is derived from A. J. Popky's Level of Urge measure, which is part of his protocol (Popky, 1994, 2005) for reducing dysfunctional urges that are part of an addictive disorder. It can also be used for avoidance that is internally generated, not substance induced.

This client had already had good results with EMDR, working with the car accident, and so, on that basis, I thought it would be emotionally safe for us to proceed. In order to check this out and ask her permission, I described the procedure I was proposing, and added the thought that this might be a softer and easier way to work with this memory.

I said, "Right now, can you hold in mind how much you *don't want* to talk about this, and be aware of that feeling in your body—the feeling of not wanting to talk about it? And just follow my fingers." She said, "I can do that." We did one set of eye movements. She then said, "I never told my mother." I said, "Stay with that." After another set, she said, "If I had told my mother, she would not have been able to stand it." Another set, and then the client said, "If *I* let myself think about it, *I* don't *I* think could stand it." I said, "Stay with that." As we continued in this way, information continued to come into her mind, both about the urge to avoid the memory and about the memory itself, in a way that was similar to what normally occurs in EMDR Phase 4. After about 10 minutes, I asked again the exact same question we started with, with the emphasis on the words *right now* (in order to help her observe any change in her urge to avoid). I said, "*Right now*, 0–10, how much do you not want to think about what happened?" She said, "It's a 7 now. I still don't want to think about it, but it's not so intense." As we continued on in this way, her LOUA score dropped to 5, and then 4, at which point she said, "I can think of it now." And so, I said, "Okay, and when you think of it, what do you get?" I did not ask her at that moment what her *Subjective Units of Disturbance Scale* (SUDS) score was, but I would guess that it went up to 9 or 10, because she became visibly distressed. But she now also had a sense of emotional control, and was able to continue from this point using the standard EMDR Phase 4 processing. In this one session, her distress level regarding this memory dropped significantly, and she felt very good about having been able to effectively face what had happened and bring about a partial resolution. The events of this session make sense if we conceptualize an avoidance defense as a mental action that is separate from the activation of the actual posttraumatic "reliving." The avoidance impulse is an implicit memory, colored with positive affect of relief, based on repeated instances of affect containment in the person's past. If that implicit memory can be approached gently in a way that maintains awareness of present safety, and thereby enables both activation of the avoidance urge and disconfirming information (safety of the present), the result is reconsolidation of the avoidance urge memory (i.e., less avoidance urge). When this occurs, direct processing of the trauma "relivings" can then proceed, with EMDR Phase 4.

Figures 3.3 to 3.5 are meant to illustrate the changes this client experienced during this session.

During the next 4 weeks, we continued to work directly on her memory of the molestation, and she was able to significantly reduce the amount of disturbance she felt while deliberately thinking of what had occurred (SUDS between 1 and 2). In subsequent weeks, we focused not just on the anxiety connected with this memory but also on the feeling of shame about herself that she had frequently experienced since the time of molestation (as will be discussed in Chapter 12, feelings of shame, without basis, often occur with childhood abuse). She continued in therapy for several months after this, because there were many ancillary problems that had occurred in her family relationships and in

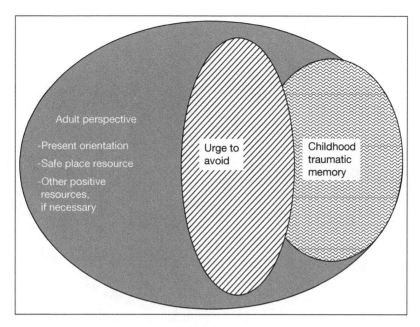

Figure 3.3 Example: Ego-state disorder with traumatized "inner child" and strong avoidance defense coconscious with the "adult" ego state. The AIP treatment strategy is to target, within a safe, supportive therapy relationship, the urge to avoid, and then, when the avoidance urge diminishes, directly target the disturbing memory.
AIP, adaptive information processing.

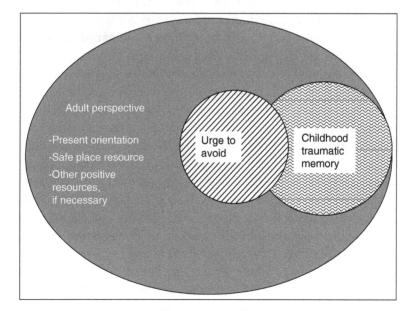

Figure 3.4 When the urge to avoid is targeted with sets of BLS, that urge lessens in intensity, and the intensity of the memory disturbance also tends to diminish.
BLS, bilateral stimulation.

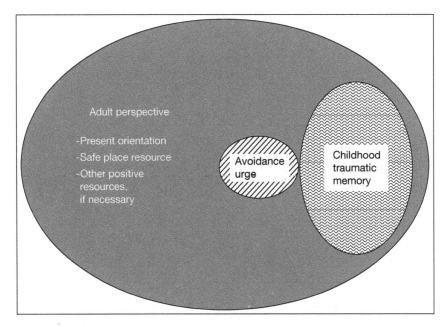

Figure 3.5 Continued targeting of the avoidance urge results in that urge becoming much less; the remaining posttraumatic disturbance can then be targeted using standard EMDR Phases 3 to 7.

her adult peer relationships, as part of the aftermath of what happened and her long-standing attempt to not think about it. But when she ended therapy 5 months later, this memory and many associated issues were resolved.

This example shows one way of targeting an avoidance defense. Over the years, this client's avoidance—avoidance of thinking or talking about the abuse—had served as a protection. The avoidance had continued because it had provided some degree of marginal relief and containment. This protection had partially worked to push away some of the disturbance; however, the client still continued to feel anxiety, shame about self, and very mixed feelings about sexual interest and sexual activities. During her therapy for the car accident, she had come to realize that the meager relief provided by the avoidance defense regarding the childhood incident was not sufficient. Also, her previous EMDR successes had given her some degree of confidence that she could resolve the old issues.

These cognitive realizations, though, were not enough for her to be able to overcome her intense response to not think of it. *That urge was primarily a feeling, rooted in implicit memory, and mainly outside the influence of cognitive insight or conscious decision.* That urge, however, was susceptible to change with repeated focused sets of BLS. When we targeted the urge to avoid—the positive feeling connected with the urge to obtain relief by pushing it out of awareness—that urge dissipated, making the underlying trauma much more accessible. In addition, as the urge to avoid went down, the actual disturbance from the traumatic event was also indirectly being targeted and lessened in intensity. For example, when the client said, "If I let myself think about it, I won't be able to stand it," she was actually already beginning to think about thinking about it! The focus on avoidance gave her a buffer and a protection—you could even say a positive resource—which made the EMDR targeting of this trauma significantly easier. By the time she got to an LOUA score of 4, she was able to maintain the "dual attention" condition—simultaneous awareness of both present safety and past trauma—and we were able to proceed successfully from this point with standard EMDR Phase 4. This was the first time I used this method to assist a client with an avoidance defense—one that was blocking the standard use of EMDR (Knipe, 1995). In the intervening years, I have continued to use variations on this procedure, often several times in a week with many different clients. Colleagues have also reported that the LOUA is one of their most-used EMDR "tools."

Sometimes a client's defensive structure will be more complicated, with avoidance arising in many different ways. The person might describe avoidance as part of an internal debate: "I know what happened. I know that it *did happen*. But I just don't want to think that it could have happened!" Or the internal debate might take a different form. One client, who had experienced successful EMDR working with present-day situations and issues, was nevertheless reluctant to let herself think of memories of childhood sexual abuse. She said, "Part of me wants to bring this up in here, and just deal with it, and part of me, when I think of that, screams, 'No! No! No!'" This illustrates how defenses of all kinds will often exist on two separate levels within the client's mind. There is the level of urge ("No! No! No!") and also the level of the client's larger sense of self ("I just want to deal with it.") and his or her desired outcomes for therapy. The two levels might also be evident with addictive disorders. Six months into sobriety, a previously alcohol-dependent man might say, "Right now, I really want a drink. I don't want to want a drink, but I still do want a drink." And it can go the other way—18 months in the sobriety, he might say, *"Right now, I really don't want a drink, but, you know, I kind of want to want a drink!"* This illustrates how some triggers for relapse with an addiction will only arise after a period of sobriety, and these must be taken into account, in many cases, in order for therapy to be successful.

Avoidance can take many forms. A client might say, "I just want to get this therapy over with!" which can be a way of avoiding the full processing and realization of all the disturbing elements of a traumatic memory. A person may have a strong avoidance defense, but not consciously know what is being avoided. For example, a therapist might say to a client, "Tell me about your family." The client might reply, "Oh, I really don't want to talk about my family." The client may not know why. There may not be a clear memory of a particular disturbing event. Or there may be a dissociative separation between the part of self that is talking to the therapist in the present and the part of self that holds memories of difficult times within the family, and these internal parts may be frightened of each other and avoidant of each other. Things are never so complicated that they cannot become more complicated!

PSYCHOLOGICAL DEFENSE AND VULNERABILITY TO DISSOCIATIVE ABREACTION

When EMDR-related procedures are used in the treatment of a client with dissociative personality structure, it is important for the therapist to be alert to client vulnerability to dissociative abreaction—an eruption of posttraumatic "relivings" accompanied by a loss of orientation to present safety. All the procedures of the preparation phase, described later in Chapters 8 to 10, are designed to minimize this nontherapeutic possibility. Dissociative abreaction can occur when an enormous amount of posttraumatic disturbance has been bottled up and unavailable to the client's apparently normal part (ANP), and then in the session, this material breaks through in consciousness, and the client feels overwhelmed. And there is also another possible cause when dissociative abreaction occurs. For many clients, a rigid defense has been in place, and somehow in the session that defense is loosened or becomes less effective in containing the posttraumatic material, and *that* is the cause of the sudden eruption of disturbance. For clients that fit this latter clinical picture, the targeting of apparent defenses prior to targeting of underlying disturbance is likely to significantly minimize the possibility of dissociative abreaction. Defense is a mental action, often not fully conscious and held in implicit memory, but that action can be brought into consciousness and reconsolidated using the procedures described in this chapter. When that defense is reduced in intensity, what is left is the underlying traumatic material. In many cases, that material has been indirectly processed during the targeting of the defense, and also, there is less danger of dissociative abreaction because of the reduced likelihood of the client being shocked—feeling "ambushed"—by the simultaneous breakdown of defense and the emergence of the posttraumatic disturbance. It has been my impression that, with complex clients, there is much less vulnerability to dissociative abreaction when these procedures of defense targeting are used.

A client may have many separate avoidance defenses, and also many idealization defenses, all of which prevent access to the memories of difficult times. Einstein (1933) once said, "In science, always keep your explanations as simple as possible . . . but no simpler!" This is something worth remembering as we attempt to provide therapy to clients with complex personality structures. In later chapters (particularly Chapters 12–14), EMDR-related methods of untangling and treating this type of complexity will be described.

OTHER EXAMPLES OF DEFENSE

Within the definition of defense stated here, any mental action or behavior that functions to prevent the conscious emergence of posttraumatic disturbance can be regarded as defensive. A person may have unresolved traumatic experience that is entirely dissociated (Figure 3.6), and then some type of reminder of that trauma may occur, resulting in a flood of unexpected feeling (Figure 3.7).

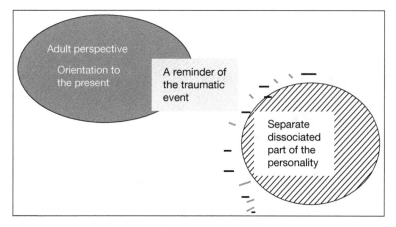

Figure 3.6 A dissociated memory or part of the personality intrudes into the awareness when an event occurs that is a reminder of the dissociated event(s).

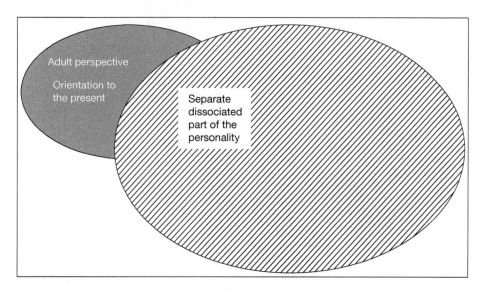

Figure 3.7 The dissociated memory material can flood into awareness in a very unpleasant and disorienting way.

The flood of "reliving" may be a complete switch—experientially becoming a younger traumatized self. Or it may be a reliving without certain elements—for example, an unexpected surge of anxiety, helplessness, or shame, without memory pictures, knowledge, or context. The memory surge is likely to be disturbing, perhaps very disturbing. The person might have an immediate impulse to push the traumatic material back out of consciousness, by any means possible, and the understandable result is a defensive mental action that functions to contain the unwelcome disturbance and soothe the adult part. If this sequence repeats again and again, a specific defensive part of the personality, a reactive implicit memory is likely to be created (Figures 3.8 and 3.9).

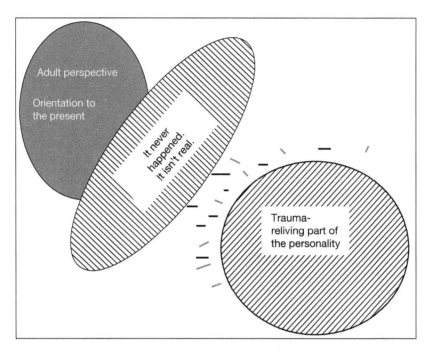

Figure 3.8 The defense of denial.

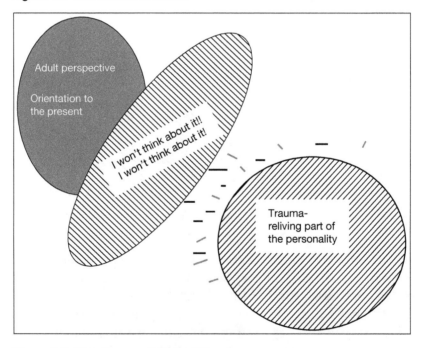

Figure 3.9 Conscious avoidance defense.

A common defense is denial—"It never happened." The client might report in great detail a situation of abuse. There might be descriptions of the perpetrator's face, the wallpaper of the room, the way the floor looked—a lot of detail. In spite of this detail, however, the client might turn to the therapist and ask, "Do you think it really happened?" Twenty years ago, a naïve therapist might have answered this question by telling the client that the abuse did in fact occur. We now know that it is a therapeutic mistake to tell clients that we as therapists know more about their lives than they do. Actually, oftentimes the perpetrator might have told the abused child, "It didn't happen." Essentially, this is an abusive message of "Don't trust your memory. Only trust what I tell you." We want our clients to trust their memories. A reasonable approach is to believe what clients say they remember, and trust what they are telling, unless there is a reason to doubt it. But therapists should be very cautious about attempting to fill in the gaps in clients' memories, or even the clients' uncertainty about those memories, because such guesses—even educated guesses—might not be accurate. It does happen, quite often, that a client, who has reported considerable detail about trauma, has not yet fully *realized* the truth of what occurred. In these instances, when a client is accessing a large amount of remembered sensory information, but has not yet fully realized the full extent of the trauma, there may be an idealization defense, perhaps of the perpetrator, that is standing in the way. The term *realize*, in this context, can have a very specific meaning—to be fully aware of the truth of what happened then and what is true now (van der Hart et al., 2006).

If the trauma involves feelings of being totally without control—no control whatsoever—the individual in his or her present life might be defending against reliving this out-of-control feeling by compulsively attempting to control everything and everyone, and then feeling embarrassed and ashamed for being a "control freak" (Figure 3.10).

If an overwhelming traumatic experience included unexpressed rage, which at the time had to be dissociated and disowned, the person coming into the therapy office years later might say, "I just never get angry. I know that in therapy you are supposed to get in touch with your anger, and my previous therapist told me I should be angry about what my stepfather did, but I don't want to just pretend. I just never feel angry." One client told me she was a member of a church that regarded any anger as a sin. She belonged to several political pacifist organizations (which I can be sympathetic with), but in her case, her pacifism expressed an adaptation to her history. This was an expression of an "I'm not angry" defense. Later in her therapy, when she was fully realizing what had happened to her during childhood sexual abuse, she connected with her childhood rage regarding her father's abuse, in a way that felt real, positive, and empowering (Figure 3.11).

If a client has grown up with inadequate nurturing, without sufficient attunement or mirroring by caretakers, then insecure, disorganized behaviors and attitudes toward other people can be the result, causing many types of relationship dysfunction. One type of dysfunction is when a young child— lacking sufficient attunement from caretakers—develops an impaired and disparaging sense of the value of other people, along with a negative self-definition of "I don't matter. I'm nothing." Primitive efforts to compensate by self-soothing—attending exclusively to one's own needs—may over time create

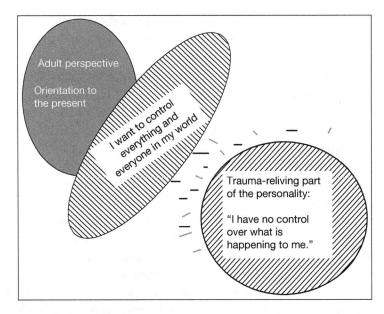

Figure 3.10 Excessively controlling defense.

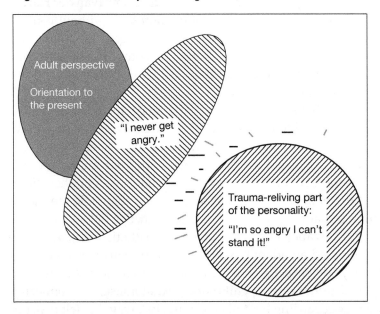

Figure 3.11 Denial of anger defense (reaction-formation defense).

a defensive self-state with a self-centered narcissistic style (Figure 3.12). Within the child-grown-up, this self-state may be dominant within the personality, or may emerge selectively, only in certain situations, but this state may be characterized by a lessened awareness of the needs and value of other people, as well as an attitude of perceiving other people primarily in terms of how they might be instrumental in meeting one's own needs. This way of relating, interpersonally, is likely to invite the ill will of others, and yet in many individuals

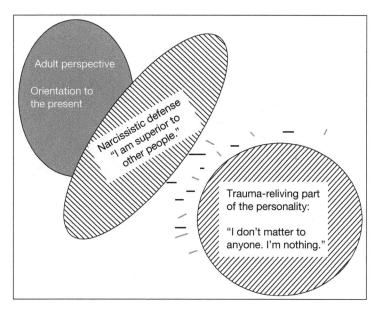

Figure 3.12 Narcissistic defense.

this grandiose interpersonal style tends to persist, because it is a defense. In other words, it is resistant to alteration through facts, logic, or disconfirming experiences, because it functions within the personality to wall off and prevent the emergence of disturbance—typically memories of perceived personal inadequacy, early attachment failures, and lonely abandonment. Narcissism is often connected with specific defenses of automatic blaming of others for one's own shortcomings (Figure 3.13), as well as the defense of remaining emotionally distant and unempathetic with regard to other people, which, in turn, is often a defense against the full realization of painful experiences that occurred early with emotionally distant caretakers. Narcissism, as a human condition, is very complex and differs between individuals; the description here is not comprehensive and complete. However, a hidden, very depressed part of the personality is often lurking beneath a surface grandiose persona. Chapter 5 includes a more detailed discussion of how idealization defenses such as narcissism develop, as well as how EMDR-related procedures can be an important element of treatment.

Addictive behaviors often function within the personality structure as a means to contain or reduce the intensity of unpleasant—feelings that, for the individual, are connected with a history of traumatization. Addictions have features of both avoidance defense and idealization defense, as will be discussed further in Chapter 6 (Figure 3.13).

Separate personality parts originate in, and consist of, complex memory networks, each with its own history, typically of many events that have a common theme. It is natural that, for any person, a repeated specific stress will tend to create a personality part to cope with that stress. If I have a neighbor with a terrible temper, I will have to develop a protective part of my own personality that is activated when I go outside my house and happen to see my neighbor.

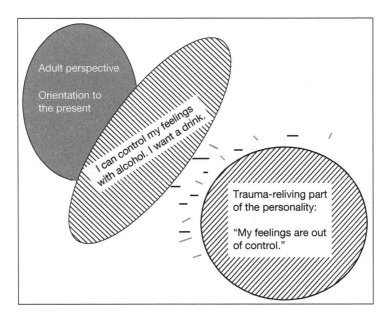

Figure 3.13 Addictive defense.

That part of me will have to either avoid that neighbor, or make great effort to never provoke the neighbor's anger. Similarly, and sadly, if a child has to cope repeatedly with an alcoholic parent's rage, or ongoing ridicule by older siblings, or with sexual abuse that occurs in the middle of the night, a personality part for each of these repeated events is likely to be created. This adaptive part, then, may be coconscious with another part that goes to school and looks normal. Or, by necessity, the adaptive part may be amnesiacally dissociated from the normal-appearing part.

In our culture, the concept of dissociative parts, within a single personality, may seem to many people to be very peculiar, even somewhat "crazy." There have been many movies and TV shows that depict dissociative disorders as bizzare and "weird." Many dissociative individuals are able to appear quite "normal" in most current life situations, while experiencing secret inner turmoil and fears of inadequacy and "weirdness." In this context, it is useful—for both client and therapist—to realize that separate dissociated parts were often developed in order to maintain some semblance of "normal" appearance and accurate contact with reality. In the words of one client, "I made these different parts to keep from going crazy!" It was easier to maintain an appearance of normal when the parts that coped with trauma were kept in a separate, dissociated place.

Dissociative individuals show different and distinct patterns of cortical activation while thinking of a traumatic event while in a present-oriented state of mind, as compared with having a flashback reliving of that event (Reinders et al., 2006) indicating separate physically based neurological networks corresponding to the experience of different personality parts. Parts are built from memories,

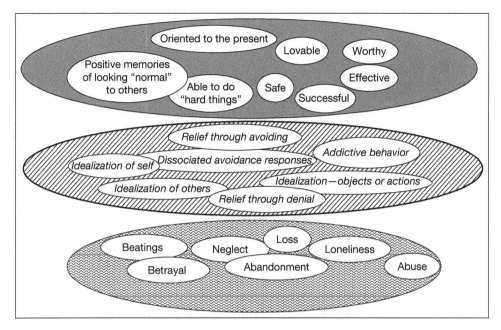

Figure 3.14 Parts are created from the memories of specific events, with repeated themes.

and can have parts of their own (Figure 3.14). Each part, or each part within each part, has a function, developed adaptively during the client's life experience. In addition, the parts within a dissociative person's personality tend to have consistent patterns of relationship with each other; these patterns may have a certain rigidity that is consistent over time. Parts may fear, avoid, dislike, invalidate, or ignore each other. Some parts may function to protect other parts. Some parts may have a narcissistic investment in separateness. ("I am a competent adult. I see that child part, but she is not important to me. She is pathetic and weak.")

The three different categories of parts—normal, oriented parts; trauma-reliving parts; and psychological defense parts—might be relatively coconscious, or be partially or wholly dissociated from each other (Figure 3.15). A person might come into therapy only aware of the part of self that appears normal to others, and not aware at all, initially, of the traumas of his or her life. In addition, that individual may not be particularly aware of the defenses that are used to prevent the emergence of disturbance—to prevent intrusions from the trauma-reliving part into his or her "normal" functioning. Or, at other times, the person may be strongly in a terrified "reliving" state of mind and be unable to get back to being in his or her "normal" part—in other words, back to feeling and functioning normally. It is important to be sure the client never leaves the therapy office while still in a dissociative abreaction—that is, stuck in a trauma-reliving part, vividly reexperiencing "trauma time," unable to access present orientation and safety. A person may also be stuck in a defense, without much awareness at that moment of the "normal" part of his or her personality,

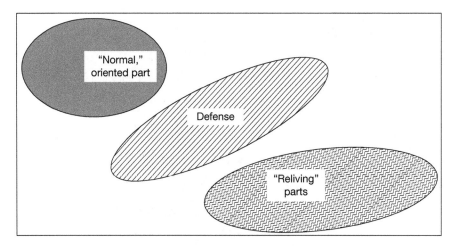

Figure 3.15 Personality parts may be entirely dissociated and unaware of each other.

or of his or her own underlying traumatic memories. For example, an addictive part may serve as a psychological defense, and an active alcoholic might say to himself, "I just want to get drunk tonight! I don't care! That's all I want!" At that moment, the individual is in his addictive defense. If such a person is asked, "Aren't you concerned about how you will feel tomorrow when you're trying to be a normal person in your family, or at work?" the answer might be, "No, I'm not thinking about that right now!" The person is not concerned that he is using alcohol to avoid feeling so bad about his divorce, or what his mother said last week, or what his father did to him when he was a child. If asked about it, he might say, with defensive vehemence, "Don't give me that therapy s____!" These are examples of how these separate parts of the personality—even parts characterized by psychological defense—might function very autonomously and even be quite separate and dissociated from each other. In each of these instances, a person's sense of self-identification—the feeling of "This is the real me. This is who I really am."—shifts from one part to another. If there is coconsciousness between parts, one part may be experienced as "self," while other parts are experienced as "not self."

This EMDR-related AIP model of psychological defense covers much of the same ground as other theoretical models, particularly the Theory of Structural Dissociation of the Personality (TSDP; van der Hart et al., 2006) and Internal Family Systems (IFS) theory (Schwartz, 1995). Exploration of the similarities and differences between these models can be useful in expanding the therapist's understanding of how to treat defensive elements to a client's problems. TSDP describes two major categories of personality parts, not three. ANPs are oriented to the present; they are focused on appearing "normal" to other people and maintaining the tasks of daily living. Emotional parts (EPs) are states of mind that reexperience elements of an unresolved traumatic event, with a sense of timelessness, as if the event is happening right now. The experiences of the EPs are not necessarily an exact recreation of the original event—an EP might have an ongoing experience of drowning or being severely injured when actually, during the original trauma, those were only the person's experiences of feared outcomes. In addition, within TSDP, there is a concept of "substitute action," which refers to any mental action or behavior that, while focused on a certain goal, is ineffective, or less than optimally effective, with regard to that goal (Figure 3.16). Substitute actions can occur in many forms. For example, if I do not have time for a good, nutritious lunch, and instead I grab a candy bar—that would be a substitute action. I would be doing something that is somewhat non-functional and ineffective, with regard to the goal of eating in the best way. If an 8-year-old boy is beaten by his father and does not fight back because his father is so much bigger, and then that boy goes to his room and hits the wall as hard as he can—that would be a substitute action. He cannot hit his father, so he hits something else (and maybe damages his hand in the process). If a person grows up in a family where relationships are difficult and distant, that person may have developed caution and apprehension with regard to close relationships in general. When a child coming from these circumstances gets to be 13 or 14 years old, and begins, with puberty, to have strong sexual needs, that person might be vulnerable to developing a sex addiction. Sexually addictive behavior, by definition, involves finding sexual outlets that do not require a deep relationship or commitment: one-night stands, the pattern of sexual conquest quickly followed by disconnection from the relationship, Internet pornography, and so on.

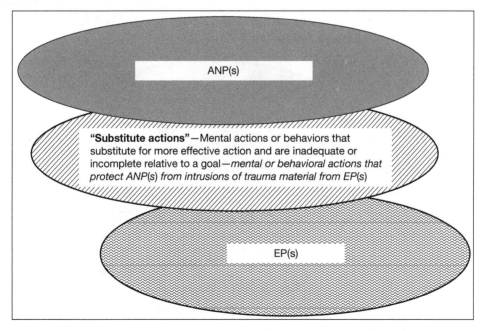

Figure 3.16 The TSDP (van der Hart et al., 2006) describes "parts" in a way that is comparable.
ANPs, apparently normal parts; EPs, emotional parts; TSDP, Theory of Structural Dissociation of the Personality.

These behaviors could be considered substitute actions, in that there are ways of achieving some degree of sexual gratification without having to confront a phobia of having a close and intimate relationship. Blaming others for one's own faults is a substitute action—it creates an explanation for who is to blame, but it is inaccurate, and often destructive to relationships. Using alcohol excessively to avoid bad feelings, or as the primary way to get good feelings, is an example of a substitute action. Procrastination is often a substitute action, in that it is a way to gain short-term relief from the nagging awareness of some difficult task, but does not result in that task being accomplished. Substitute actions can often serve a defensive function to the extent that they are created and maintained in order to prevent posttraumatic intrusions from an EP into an ANP, or from an EP into another EP (O. van der Hart, private conversation, April 2010).

There are also parallel concepts between the AIP model of dissociation presented here and Schwartz's IFS model (Schwartz, 1995; Twombly, 2005): "Managers," "Exiles," and "Firefighters" (Figure 3.17). Within IFS, "Manager" parts of the personality are in charge of proactively running the day-to-day life of the person, staying alert and oriented to ongoing realities, and anticipating future problems that might threaten the person's sense of control. The term *Firefighter* is used to designate a personality part that is reactive to an emotional crisis in the present, and functions to contain (and *extinguish*) impending disruptive intrusion of emotion or information from an "Exile part"—a part that is continuing to relive highly disturbing memories from the past, and has been banished because of its disruptive influence on the Manager parts. The concept of a "Firefighter" part seems to overlap quite a bit with what is referred to, here within this AIP model, as a psychological defense.

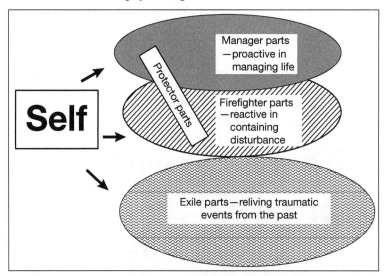

Figure 3.17 Schwartz's IFS (1995) model of "parts" also has a similar method of categorization, and emphasizes the valuable unifying concept of *Self*.
IFS, internal family systems.

This discussion, comparing AIP and IFS models of defense, would not be complete without a discussion of Schwartz's important and useful conceptualization of the term *Self* (indicated here with a capital "S"). Within IFS, the "Managers" and the "Firefighters" together are defined as "Protector parts." These parts protect the Self against intrusions from "exile" parts. Schwartz's conceptualization of Self is, for many clients, a crucial concept in facilitating both the processing of trauma and the integration of the personality after traumas have been resolved. Within this model, dissociated personality parts experience themselves, erroneously, as separate from each other, and each is "burdened" by the distortions and emotional residue of difficult life experiences. Therapeutic interventions are designed to facilitate the client looking compassionately at each of these parts from a place of overview, from Self, so as to lift away these burdens. Self is viewed as a healing capacity of the mind—always present as a force for personality integration, but often, initially in therapy, dormant (and "blended" with posttraumatic "burdens") in a dissociative individual. Schwartz's use of the term *Self* is consistent with Schore's (2001) description of steps in the normal development of self during infancy, and also the ways that self can become distorted and divided during this early time, due to inadequate parental engagement and/or abuse.

For *single-incident, adult-onset* PTSD, there is often less need to conceptualize the client's problem as a disorder of Self. An adult with a relatively well-integrated pretraumatic personality structure who is suffering from an isolated traumatic memory will generally have a sense of self—a feeling of "This is the real me"—within the state of mind that is oriented to the present. The flashing memory of the trauma is likely to be experienced as "not self," as something the person regards as alien and just wants to get rid of. If the clinical picture does not include strong and pathological defenses or significant dissociative personality structure, usual procedures of EMDR will nearly always resolve memories of this kind. Perhaps for this reason, "Self" is not a term that is discussed extensively during EMDR training, except when the focus is on the interface between EMDR and dissociative disorders.

However, for clients who have clearly differentiated separate parts, many of which are in polarized, extreme conflict with each other, the IFS concept of Self is very useful therapeutically in assisting case conceptualization, treatment planning, and the increasingly active involvement by the client in directing his or her own therapy. Within IFS, Self is almost synonymous with "true self," or even "soul" (though without necessarily including specific religious connotations). As therapy proceeds successfully, and personality parts become less polarized and are able (through specific IFS interventions) to release their posttraumatic "burdens," a larger awareness of Self emerges, which is "above" and can compassionately witness how each of the separate self-states or parts became so extreme in a misguided effort to do something positive for the Self. Within Schwartz's model, Self is a person's intrinsic capacity to acknowledge the real events that have occurred in that person's life, as well as the ways in which internal personality parts were formed to adapt to those events. This definition of Self is very similar to Demassio's (2010) conceptualization of self as the internal mental process that "knows" and "observes" other mental processes, with a "first person" sense of agency and perspective.

Self, within this context, is not a personality part, but is an experiential place from which to witness how the separate personality parts came into being. This compassionate witnessing is seen as the crucial element in healing both "trauma-reliving" experiences (Exile parts) and mental actions that serve a defensive purpose (Manager parts and Firefighter parts). Little by little, as resolution of trauma-based memory material occurs, the client is likely to develop, more and more, a unified sense of knowing, "I am the person who can see how rough I had it as a child, and see how I spent so many years trying to protect myself by not thinking about it, or by going to my addiction, or by maintaining an illusion of how I wanted things to be. I can see now, from a unitary vantage point, that sometimes I may be in one state of mind, and at other times I am in another state of mind, but I remain myself all through these changes. I can see it all now with some distance and perspective, and compassion for myself. *Who I really am*, is the person who is able to see all of this." For many clients in my practice who were initially highly dissociative, this concept of Self has been very useful in bringing about full personality integration following resolution of memories of abuse and neglect. As therapy proceeds with people with Complex PTSD, Self can increasingly become a resource in the subsequent targeting of additional traumatic material. With continuing successful therapy, the person develops increasing compassion for the child he or she once was, and this compassion, in turn, facilitates continuing integration of previously separate personality parts. The Self takes on a "leadership role" within the therapy process. This idea of Self overlaps to some degree with Shapiro's (1995, 2018) assumption of an intrinsic, physically based information processing system that moves dysfunctionally stored memory information to adaptive resolution and health; it also overlaps with the writings of others who have described a potential within human beings toward personal growth and healing (e.g., Carl Rogers and Abraham Maslow).

In Chapters 7 to 14, there will be an attempt to integrate features of the TSDP model and the IFS model with EMDR-related therapy "tools," in a way that is faithful to the unique contributions of each model.

REFERENCES

Demassio, A. (2010). *Self comes to mind*. New York, NY: Pantheon.

Einstein, A. (1933). *On the method of theoretical physics. Herbert Spencer lecture*. Oxford, UK: Oxford University Press.

Erickson, M., & Rossi, E. (1979). *Hypnotherapy: An exploratory casebook*. New York, NY: Irvington.

Kluft, R. P., & Fine, C. G. (1993). *Clinical perspectives on multiple personality disorder*. Washington, DC: American Psychiatric Press.

Knipe, J. (1995, August). Targeting avoidance and dissociative numbing. *EMDR Network Newsletter, 5*(2), 6–7.

Knipe, J. (1998). It was a golden time: Healing narcissistic vulnerability. In P. Manfield (Ed.), *Extending EMDR* (pp. 232–255). New York, NY: W. W. Norton.

Knipe, J. (2005). Targeting positive affect to clear the pain of unrequited love: Codependence, avoidance and procrastination. In R. Shapiro (Ed.), *EMDR solutions* (pp. 189–211). New York, NY: W. W. Norton.

Knipe, J. (2007). Loving eyes: Procedures to therapeutically reverse dissociative processes while preserving emotional safety. In C. Forgash & M. Copeley (Eds.), *Healing the heart of trauma and dissociation* (pp. 181–226). New York, NY: Springer Publishing.

Knipe, J. (2010, October 3). *Invited keynote address, the use of AIP therapy methods with dissociative symptoms and Complex PTSD.* EMDR International Association annual conference, Minneapolis, MN.

Knipe, J. (2014). *EMDR toolbox: Theory and treatment of Complex PTSD and dissociation.* New York, NY: Springer Publishing.

Linehan, M. M. (1993). *Cognitive-behavioral treatment of borderline personality disorder.* New York, NY: Guilford Press.

Popky, A. J. (1994). *EMDR protocol for smoking and other addictions.* Presentation at the annual meeting of the EMDR network, Sunnyvale, CA.

Popky, A. J. (2005). DeTUR, an urge reduction protocol for addictions and dysfunctional behaviors. In R. Shapiro (Ed.), *EMDR solutions* (pp. 167–188). New York, NY: W. W. Norton.

Putnam, F. (1989). *The diagnosis and treatment of multiple personality disorder.* New York, NY: Guilford Press.

Reinders, A. A., Nijenhuis, E. R., Quak, J., Korf, J., Haaksma, J., Paans, A. M., . . . den Boer, J. A. (2006). Psychobiological characteristics of dissociative identity disorder: A symptom provocation study. *Biological Psychiatry, 60,* 730–740. doi:10.1016/j.biopsych.2005.12.019

Schore, A. N. (2001). Effects of a secure attachment relationship on right brain development, affect regulation, and infant mental health. *Infant Mental Health Journal, 22*(1–2), 7–66.doi:10.1002/1097-0355(200101/04)22:1<7::aid-imhj2>3.0.co;2-n

Schwartz, R. (1995). *Internal family systems therapy.* New York, NY: Guilford Press.

Shapiro, F. (1995). *Eye movement desensitization and reprocessing: Basic principles, protocols and procedures.* New York, NY: Guilford Press.

Shapiro, F. (2018). *Eye movement desensitization and reprocessing: Basic principles, protocols, and procedures* (3rd ed.). New York, NY: Guilford Press.

Twombly, J. (2005). EMDR processing with dissociative identity disorder, DDNOS, and ego states. In R. Shapiro (Ed.), *EMDR solutions* (pp. 88–120). New York, NY: W. W. Norton.

van der Hart, O., Nijenhuis, E., & Steele, K. (2006). *The haunted self: Structural dissociation and the treatment of chronic traumatization.* New York, NY: W. W. Norton.

4

EMDR With Avoidance

Every psychological defense has an element of avoidance, in that the purpose of the defense is to protect the individual by minimizing or excluding from awareness of a realization, a disturbing memory, or a "trauma-reliving" part of self. It makes sense, both theoretically and practically, to think of this type of avoidance as a separate mental action from actual activation of the trauma "reliving." An avoidance defense contains dysfunctional positive affect of relief or containment, in contrast to the dysfunctional negative affect of the material that is being avoided. Both positive and negative affect distortions can be altered through focused sets of bilateral stimulation (BLS). All defenses contain an element of avoidance. That avoidance may be direct and conscious—a decision to not think of something, or not do something, on purpose. Alternatively, the avoidance may be much more subtle, and not particularly conscious. As mentioned in Chapter 2, Daniel Kahneman has documented a clear qualitative difference between what he calls "fast thinking" and "slow thinking." The former type of thinking is automatic and immediate, and is utilized in situations that require a rapid and expedient response. The latter type of thinking requires effort, but is more useful for situations that require careful evaluation of complex information. It seems, intuitively, that mental avoidance generally falls into the category of fast thinking; this makes sense, because rapid avoidance is often necessary as a response to an immediate threat. Richard Solomon and Lyman Wynne's research (1954) on avoidance learning with animals demonstrated this. Dogs were placed in an apparatus with a small light and an electrified floor, divided by a short barrier. The light would go on, and 10 seconds later the floor on one side, where the dog was, would be electrified and give the dog a painful shock. Every dog in his research quickly learned to immediately jump over the barrier to escape the shock each time the light went on. Then, after a random interval, a light would go on the other side of the barrier, and 10 seconds later, the floor on that side would be electrified. When this occurred, all the dogs quickly discovered that they could escape the shock by jumping back to the first side, which was no longer electrified. This type of escape behavior—learning to avoid by jumping—was quickly learned by the dogs and continued endlessly, with each repetition of the light, long after the time when the shock was disconnected. This is an example, not just metaphorical, of how avoidance responses occur internally—mentally—with many people. It is a reflexive response to threatening situations, thoughts, feelings, or stimuli—a deliberate, or automatic, shifting of awareness when a thought, perception, or feeling is uncomfortable—for example, changing the subject if a conversation is headed toward conflict, deliberately pulling awareness away from a disturbing memory, avoiding eye contact with an annoying coworker, lighting a cigarette during times of high stress, and procrastinating with regard to the cleaning up of a messy desk or closet. In each of these situations, the avoidance mental action or behavior brings a brief moment of relief. After an avoidance defense has been established, it is not about fear, but about relief. Relief from discomfort is the reinforcer that maintains the avoidance behavior. If the dogs in Solomon and Wynne's experiments could talk, after they had learned the automatic jumping behavior, we can guess that they might say, when the light goes on for the hundredth time, "I'm not afraid! I know what to do!" These features of avoidance—that it is quick, automatic, does not involve very much contemplation, and is strengthened (reinforced) by positive feelings of relief—can perpetuate avoidance behaviors long past the time when these behaviors are adaptive.

As was illustrated by the case described in Chapter 3, the combination of focused sets of BLS with mental actions or behaviors of avoidance can be therapeutically productive. An avoidance urge is the conscious manifestation of an implicit (nonconscious) memory of repeated times when avoidance resulted in containment of intense disturbance. At a feeling level, it is as though the emergence of the avoided trauma memory is unacceptably unpleasant. When this urge to avoid is activated, by simply being acknowledged in a therapy session, repeated sets of BLS allow information regarding present safety to alter and reconsolidate this implicit avoidance memory. Sets of BLS facilitate this reconsolidation by containing the emergence of sympathetic arousal, enhancing associational networks, and probably compelling "slow thinking," so that the person can relinquish more easily the relief affect of avoidance, and directly examine whether continuing avoidance is consistent with larger life goals.

EXAMPLE: THE LEVEL OF URGE TO AVOID (0–10) METHOD OF TARGETING AVOIDANCE

"Karl," a man in his mid-50s, initiated therapy following what could be called a severe "narcissistic injury." As he reported to me in our first sessions, he had spent much of his adult life focused on his own needs, particularly his need to be seen by others as superior—in intelligence, in his financial earning power, and in his achievement in his career. He had been very successful in work that had required him to be a hard-nosed, extremely aggressive negotiator. Our first session of therapy occurred at the end of what he described as "the worst year" of his life. Within a relatively short period of time, he had had a series of set-backs in his work, filed for bankruptcy, moved in disgrace from one part of the United States to another part, had a heart attack, and went to court with his ex-wife over child-support payments. In addition, he was currently having ongoing intense angry outbursts with his present wife and their young children. Although he initially came to therapy at his wife's insistence, he was able to see within the first few sessions how therapy could be personally useful for him. He stated that he wanted to regain his previous self-esteem. We spent some time in discussion about what that would mean. He was able to see that his previous self-concept, of being entitled, superior, and easily angered, was not something he needed to return to. He realized that this way of thinking had earned the enmity of others, rather than their respect. Rather, a better goal would be to learn a new way of living that would involve better connections with other people. As part of this, he became highly motivated to learn how to control his inappropriate anger. He liked this idea of learning to be a man who was not so difficult, and his wife, who was able to see his good qualities, was also very supportive of this idea.

With all this in mind, we set our goal for therapy to "work on the anger." He was easily able to identify many recent triggers for his angry episodes. I asked him to bring up one of the recent memories, notice how he felt in his body when he was so angry, and, "Take that feeling back to when you were a kid. What do you get? It doesn't even have to make sense. Just notice the time and the place that that feeling takes you to." This Affect Bridge (Watkins & Watkins, 1998) tracked directly back to times growing up in a rural area of Europe. His father would beat him severely if he failed to meet his father's expectations regarding behavior on their farm or in school. When these early situations of physical abuse were targeted with eye movement desensitization and reprocessing (EMDR), over the course of several sessions, he was able to view what occurred with much more of an adult perspective, with emotional distance, and process both his unresolved, previously unspoken feelings of anger toward his father, and also the underlying and intense feelings of unworthiness that had been the residue of these incidents.

Moreover, he was able to spontaneously realize that his behavior within his family, and previously in his business, had actually been a behavioral reen-actment of what had occurred with his father. His wife, children, and others had been put in the role of little victims, and himself in the role of the big bully who was in control. It was mentioned in Chapter 2 that posttraumatic stress disorder (PTSD) sometimes is manifested not only in flashback images, cognitions, emotions, and sensations but also in behavioral reenactments of trauma, and his behavior was an example of this. He had been behaving in certain negative ways, "on automatic pilot," and then had had enormous regret afterward. These behavioral elements of Karl's posttraumatic stress were resolved along with the visual, cognitive, and affective elements. Following these sessions, he reported that he was much more easily able to be the calm and loving person he wanted to be with his family members, and they recognized and appreciated this positive change.

The transcripted session, which follows, occurred following this work and just after the start of a new job. His new position was in his old line of work, where he had had occupational skills and a work history, but with new partners. At the time of the transcripted session, he had taken on the task of resuming tough negotiations during phone calls to people in other parts of the United States. He came to my office at 11 a.m. on a Monday, very frustrated with himself. He had just looked at the phone on his desk all morning, stuck in a state of inertia with regard to a series of important phone calls that he had to make. He asked, "Can EMDR help with this?" I thought perhaps it was worth a try. His structure of personality parts, at the start of this session, is illustrated in Figure 4.1.

We targeted the most disturbing image from that morning—sitting in his chair at work just looking at his phone, unable to get himself mobilized to make the calls. This is a verbatim transcript beginning about 10 minutes into that session. Where "[EM]" appears in the text, that is a moment when I said, "Notice that," "Stay with that," or "Think of that," accompanied by a set of 20 to 30 eye movement sweeps.

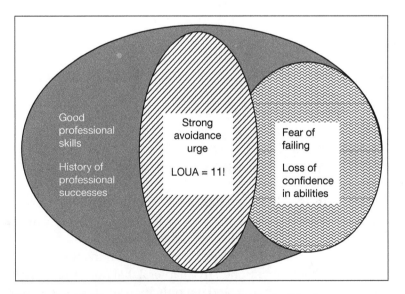

Figure 4.1 Karl's personality structure at the start of the transcripted session, showing his avoidance defense.
LOUA, level of urge to avoid.

Karl: I was grinding my teeth all weekend, thinking about the calls I have to make today. What if I have to be an SOB to be successful in this business? My family likes how I am now (much less angry temper), but I'm not sure it is such a good thing. I have to make these calls, but I just looked at my phone this morning. I just sat there, doing nothing! I'm afraid I'm going to wimp out, or maybe lose my temper again, and just screw it up. Maybe I've lost my edge and now I'm just lazy.

Therapist: As you are at your desk, looking at the phone, with that thought, "Maybe I've lost my edge and now I'm just lazy," what is the emotion you are feeling?

Karl: Fear, I guess. But more than that—the main thing when I look at my desk is—I don't want to make any calls!!

Because it was clear from his answer that he had a strong avoidance urge with regard to the phone calls, I shifted from the standard EMDR Phase 3 assessment steps to the protocol for targeting an avoidance defense. What follows is one way to set up the targeting of avoidance.

Therapist: So, looking at your desk and the telephone, and you haven't made any calls, here's a question. How much, 0–10, do you not want to make the first phone call right now—that is, just put it off until later, or do something else—with 10 the most urge to not call and 0 none of that urge at all? **(Karl: [Laughs] Eleven.)** *Where do you feel that Eleven?* **(Karl: In my gut.)** *Stay with that. Just be aware of looking at the phone on your desk and how much you don't want to call right now.* **[EM]** *That's right. Just think of that.*

This particular procedure for targeting avoidance is somewhat simpler than the EMDR Phase 3 steps for targeting a traumatic memory. Basically, the client is asked for a representative visual image of the avoidance (in this case, the phone on the desk), a 0 to 10 measure of the intensity of the avoidance urge, the location of that number in physical sensations, and then, the request, "Follow my fingers."

Karl: Each of those phone calls is to someone who wants to push me as far as he can. That makes the blood rise in my head. And I don't want to get angry. But maybe that is the only approach these guys understand. [EM] Anymore, I don't like to get into arguments with people. [EM] I've always approached business as an adversarial process. I see now that I burned some bridges with that. [EM] I don't know why, I just don't have any desire to call these guys and solve the problems. [EM] I should want to. My partners and my

family are counting on me. [EM] I'm tired of always having to solve other people's problems. These are problems that were caused by that guy in _____ (another state), not me. [EM] He left me with these problems and I don't know _____ law and I don't want to goof it up. But I could probably get it done. [EM] My gut was churned up all weekend, thinking about these calls. What a waste of energy. [EM]

Karl appeared at this point to have shifted in the intensity of his avoidance urge, so I went back to target. When you use this method of targeting avoidance, the reaccessing of the target occurs differently than when you are working with trauma. With this method, the therapist asks the exact same question that began the processing, with the emphasis on the words "right now" in order to draw the client's attention to the changing intensity of the avoidance.

Therapists who are learning about this method sometimes ask, "How do you know when to go back to target?" I think it is useful to go back when there are some indications, even minimal, that a shift has occurred in the client's need for avoidance. There are two reasons to go back to target more frequently. One, of course, is to check to see that useful processing of the avoidance urge is taking place. But also, it is important for the client to recognize the shift in this avoidance defense, and that recognition sometimes will only occur when the client does an inner assessment of the intensity of that urge. I do not think there is much downside to going back to target too frequently. Actually, when I asked Karl about the intensity of his avoidance, 0 to 10, he ignored my question, and just kept on processing, which was fine.

BACK TO TARGET

Therapist: Go back again to this question we started with. When you look at your desk, right now, in your mind, and see the phone there, and you haven't made the calls yet, 0–10, right now, how much do you not want *to make the first call?*

Karl: If I decide to call, it would be a way of letting go of the stress. [EM] I'm not afraid to talk to people, the most they can do is say "No." [EM] I am afraid of failing, but even if it fails it won't be of my doing. Some parts of this deal are out of my control. [EM] It's silly the pressure I put on myself. I want to make the call! [EM] Fear of losing my temper is just an excuse. The real reason I didn't want to call is because I didn't want to fail. [EM] I'm feeling a lot less stress right now. I know how to do this! I don't know why I project I will fail. [EM] I shouldn't take it so personally. I am going to go back and make those phone calls. [EM]

BACK TO TARGET

Therapist: Right now, again, think of your desk. How strong is the urge, right now, to not call?

Karl: Zero. I'm looking forward to calling and getting it moving again.

Therapist: How true, 1–7, does that statement feel, "I trust myself to stay cool, and get things done, effectively, right when they need to be done"?

Karl: Seven! No problem! [EM]

He was able to go directly back to his office that day and make these calls successfully. When he discontinued therapy a month later, he was reporting no further instances of inappropriate anger. He felt he was once again in the rhythm of his work, and was no longer avoiding any aspect of his new job.

EXAMPLE: THE "WHAT'S GOOD ABOUT . . .?" METHOD FOR TARGETING AN AVOIDANCE DEFENSE

"Janie," a professional woman in her late 20s, came to therapy following the accidental death of a close friend of about the same age. Over several sessions, she was able to recognize the importance of not stuffing her feelings of shock and sadness, but instead letting herself grieve for the loss of her friend. As these sessions continued, she realized that she had also pushed away sadness regarding other losses—particularly relationships with men that had initially seemed to be lasting, but then went sour.

One day, as we were discussing these previous relationships, she said, "I wonder if I was sexually abused growing up." She didn't know who it might have been, but she just had a vague sense that it had happened. Between sessions, she talked to her mother about it, but this conversation was not very helpful, in that she thought her mother was nervous and evasive about the issue.

Then, 2 weeks later, at the start of a session, she reported that she had had an important realization. Her personality structure at the start of this session is illustrated in Figure 4.2. The transcript of that session is as follows:

Janie: I used to think I didn't know who it was but now I'm sure it was Uncle _____.

Therapist: Do you feel sure?

Janie: Yes.

Therapist: Do you also have some memory pictures of it, even fragments?

Janie: No, none at all.

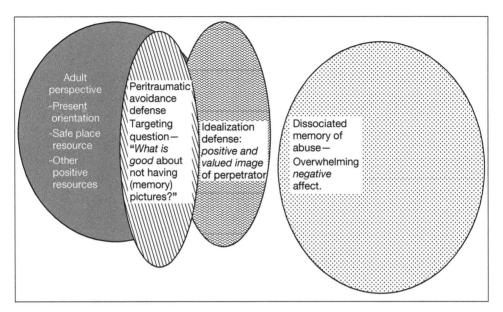

Figure 4.2 Janie's personality structure showing avoidance and idealization defenses.

I was not being skeptical with her when I asked if she was sure. She had not been sure the previous week. The lack of memory pictures might raise questions regarding the accuracy of her conclusion, but it might also indicate a different clinical picture. Trauma memories are sometimes dysfunctionally stored with different elements of the memory—behavior, affect, sensation, and knowledge (the BASK elements; Braun, 1988)—stored separately and dissociated from each other. A person might have sensations of abuse without knowledge of what those sensations are about. Or a person might have knowledge that a trauma occurred, but no memory pictures. Or pictures but no affect. With Janie, I wondered if perhaps an avoidance defense might be preventing full access to a traumatic memory, and so, to further explore this possibility, I asked the following question.

> *Therapist: This may be an odd question, but just see if there is an answer. Do you have a sense that in your mind somewhere, in a place you can't access, you do have memory pictures, or does it feel like there just aren't any pictures to find?*

Janie: I know the pictures are there. I just can't get to them.

This answer suggested the possibility that the memory pictures might exist in a dissociated part of her personality, and an avoidance defense might be in place with regard to that part. This is an example of how a defense need not be a conscious decision, but instead a long-standing aspect of the person's personality structure, established in childhood, that now is an obstacle to therapy. To check out this possibility, I asked her a question to bring any *positive affect* possibly connected with an avoidance defense to the center of her awareness.

> *Therapist: Here's a question.* What's good *about* not *having the pictures?*

> **Janie: If I had the pictures in my mind then it would be more real.**

> *Therapist: Can you stay with that?* **(Client nods, Yes.) [EM]**

> **Janie: Not having the pictures all these years, especially when I was a child, kept me away from knowing that Mom and Dad were not there for me. [EM]**

She is crying now, but she is able to continue.

> **I can picture myself today saying to my mother, "I needed you!" [EM]**

> **I picture her saying, "I didn't know." But I think my mother *did* know, and didn't want to see it. [EM] I am going back and forth in time right now. I'm thinking of the people in my life who have really cared. It's only a few people and they are not in my family. [EM]**

She seemed to be feeling a little less intensity of emotion at this point, so we went back to target, by asking the same question we started with, with the emphasis on the words "right now."

BACK TO TARGET

> *Therapist: Go back again to this question: What's good* right now *about not having pictures?*

> **Janie: I always thought of him (Uncle _____) as someone who was really kind to me, really there for me, and made me feel special. All the time growing up, I thought I could go to him. I thought he cared. If I have these pictures it would show that he didn't care. [EM] If I don't have the pictures, I don't have to face the fact that men, and sometimes women too, have not cared about me—for me. They just wanted something. [EM]**

> *Therapist: So go back again now to this question: What's good, right now, about not having those pictures?*

> **Janie: It is hard to admit . . . I *don't want* to admit that most of my relationships in my life, in my adult life, have been remote and on the surface. [EM] I pick men who don't want to care that deeply. I hear**

their sweet words and I respond. [EM] My mother gives me those sweet words too sometimes. She says, "You can tell me anything." But when I tried to talk to her about how someone had done something to me when I was a child, the first thing she said was, "It couldn't have been anyone in your father's family." [EM]

Of course, we could have paused the processing at this point and gone into a lengthy discussion of the implications of her mother's response. But those implications appeared to be clear to her, and so we simply went back to target.

Therapist: Go back again to this question. Right now, what's good about not having those pictures?

Janie: When it happened . . . I think I remember! . . . I *did* try to tell!! I can't remember for sure . . . but I think I did! [EM] I am picturing myself back then, when the abuse was happening. It is not a memory picture, I don't think—just something I'm picturing. But it's different right now. Whenever I have thought of this up until now, I see me as upset, but now I don't see me as upset—I'm more cut off from it all. [EM] I'm not so scared, but I am waiting for him to be done. [EM] For some reason, this makes me believe it happened a lot. It didn't just happen once. [EM] I see myself on the bed but looking away so I don't see him. [EM] I think that is why I don't have memory pictures. [EM] It is happening but I am pretending that it's not happening. [EM] That is why I won't look at him. [EM]

Because we were nearing the end of the session, I asked her a question that can be useful in eliciting an interim positive self-referencing cognition from a client—one the client can feel good about as she leaves the session.

Therapist: What are you figuring out here today that helps you?

Janie: I see why I didn't want to look at him. And it didn't just happen once. I didn't know that before. It also helps to know that I did something to help myself at the time so it wasn't so bad. I feel more sad, but also more connected—that's how it feels right now. Also, I feel totally exhausted. This is enough for today!

Janie's statement, that she feels "more sad" at the end of this session, illustrates a shift in feeling that often accompanies therapy progress. A client may enter therapy with intense feelings of anxiety, helplessness, or shame, and in the process of therapy those emotions diminish, but are sometimes replaced by sadness. The feelings of anxiety (in a safe therapy situation) or shame (when there was no shameful behavior) are distortions. There is a mismatch between what the person is experiencing and the realities of past and present. These distortions can be targeted and removed in successful therapy. The sadness, on the other hand, is about something real—the real losses of an earlier time in life. It is sometimes useful to explain this sequence of emotions to clients, especially if the client is feeling intense sadness or grief following realization of the losses of his or her childhood.

Figure 4.3 shows Janie's ego-state structure at the end of this session. As you can see, her situation with regard to these memories is not yet resolved. However, she now has coconscious access to the difficult memories, and during the subsequent 2 months of weekly sessions, she was able to resolve the issues relating to her uncle, as well as ancillary issues related to the abuse.

Janie's case illustrates how avoidance defenses can occur in a wide variety of ways. Since avoidance defenses can prevent full access to traumatic memories, clients may not be fully aware of those defenses, or the memories the defenses cover, at the start of therapy. Therapists should therefore be alert to signs of possible avoidance in the client's presentation.

Another example: A man in his late 50s recently remarried and was having current tension in his new relationship. He was not very interested in sex, and this issue was frustrating and embarrassing to both him and his wife. He regarded his disinterest as a significant problem and even had checked with his physician regarding his testosterone levels, which were normal. He could not identify any prior life experience that might be related to this problem.

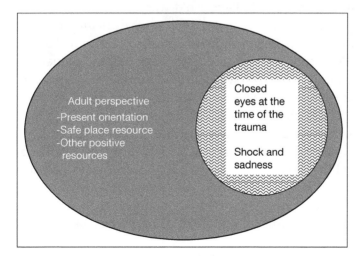

Figure 4.3 Janie's personality structure, with regard to this memory, at the end of her transcripted session.

Resolution of this issue occurred following direct targeting of his avoidance, which went as follows:

Therapist: Get a picture in your mind—it's Friday night—you and your wife are in bed, and it's still not too late in the evening. As you are lying there, you could turn one way, and start something, or you could just roll over the other way, and go to sleep. Here is a question. As you are lying there, and you haven't decided yet, how strong, 0–10, is the urge to just roll over and go to sleep?

Client: It's a 10!

He located that 10 in his physical sensations. We then did several sets of eye movements with him holding in mind his strong avoidance urge, and what he got to fairly quickly was an incident that had occurred when he was 9 years old. He laughed when he told me about it, as if it was just a trivial, inconsequential childhood event. His mother had caught him with some pornographic magazines, and she was very angry. She punished him by putting alkaline drain cleaner on his genitals, which was terribly painful and humiliating. As we continued to explore this incident, with sets of eye movement, he became increasingly aware of feelings of fear, anger at his mother, and disgust regarding his own body. We continued processing, using standard EMDR procedures, to the point of him fully realizing the impact of this previously minimized memory, as well as other similar events from childhood. He was able to see the connections with his present dilemma. He shared this information with his wife, and following some good discussions, they were both able to lighten up and progress toward exploring and enjoying their physical relationship.

Avoidance issues can come up at the beginning, in the middle, or toward the conclusion of therapy. A 33-year-old woman, married, with two children, ages 9 and 11, came to therapy to deal with some difficult problems in her workplace. A coworker was causing numerous stresses. I trust that her report regarding this difficult coworker was accurate, since that individual was later fired. In my client's initial sessions, we identified representative troubling situations at work. These situations carried specific negative cognitions: "I can't say what I really feel," and (when strong frustration would occur with the coworker) "I don't deserve to have good things in my life." These unhappy beliefs about self tracked back to incidents from childhood, where appropriate self-assertion was punished and the client's aspirations for higher education were discouraged by her father. Representative childhood incidents were identified and successfully processed with standard EMDR methods, and this resulted directly in the client having a much easier time at work, even though the coworker continued for a while to be difficult.

Following this work, I asked the client, "What's left?" She said that she "hated" her weight. She had begun gaining weight at the time of her marriage 12 years earlier, and she had been approximately 55 pounds overweight (according to some norms that she had found online) for the past 6 years. She said that she was getting "nice" pressure from her husband to lose weight, which was an annoyance, but also matched some pressure she felt within herself. Her eating habits were described as "normal"—that is, moderate portions, not many sweets. She identified her biggest obstacle as, "I hate exercise!" She was frustrated with herself for having this attitude, but the attitude persisted nevertheless (Figure 4.4).

The following is a transcript of the session (copied verbatim from a video recording) where we targeted her ego-dystonic avoidance of exercising. Readers who are familiar with A. J. Popky's EMDR-related method for treating unwanted urges will recognize, in the following, elements of Popky's Desensitization of Triggers and Urges Reprocessing (DeTUR; 1994; 2005) approach. Specifically, we first identify and "install" the resource of a positive day in the future, when the problem of hating exercise has been solved. Then, we target a situation that represents this problem, using the LOUA method.

> **Cassie: Before I had children, I used to work out. Now exercise is work. I don't like to sweat. And then I get so angry at myself: "Oh, stop feeling sorry for yourself! Just lose the weight!" I really want to lose the weight, but I don't want to have to work at it. I have the treadmill— top of the line. I just look at it. I want to be skinny. Why can't it just happen!? But I know that is not a good way to think. When I think of all this, I just feel tired!**

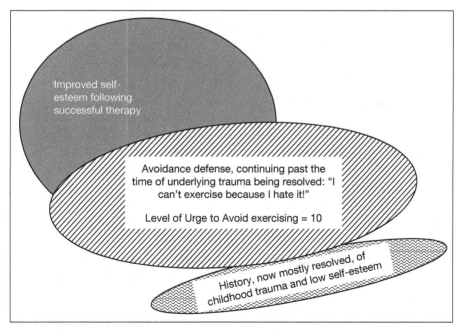

Figure 4.4 Cassie's ego-state structure at the start of her transcripted session.

Therapist: Can you get a mental picture of a day in the future when you no longer have this problem—it is no longer any problem at all? What would be going on, on that day, that would be different from this week?

Cassie: I'd work out and enjoy it. . . . I'd feel better about myself. My husband would like it, although it might scare him if I got too thin! I wouldn't have guilt for taking time for me. Clothes would fit—I would have a really beautiful blue dress to wear when we go out to a party at my work.

I remember enjoying being on an exercise machine, a stair climber. It would be nice to do that again. That body shape—flat stomach, pants that are not too tight.

I stopped going to the gym around the time of getting married. He (husband) assumed I would be at home after work, and that continued when we had our daughter about 2 years later. If I went to the gym, back then, I would feel guilty, not taking care of our daughter, not being around. It was also the money to pay for the gym membership. I see now that money wasn't that important—I don't have to live all the time like I'm deprived!

Therapist: Bring to mind a picture that represents the problem you have in your life today, with not exercising. What picture represents that? (**Cassie: The treadmill. It is just sitting there in the corner.**) *Right now, as you are standing in front of the treadmill, here is a question: How much, 0–10, do you not want to go over and work out on the treadmill for a few minutes?* (**Cassie: 10!**) *Where is that 10 in your body?* (**Cassie: I feel it all over. Maybe in my stomach.**) *Can you just stay with that? Just hold in mind how much you don't want to get on the treadmill, along with that feeling, all over, and especially in your stomach, and follow my fingers.* **[EM]**

Cassie: I feel like a failure. It is like, exercise is not my idea! [EM] I want to just walk away. I need to escape. [EM] Right before you stopped moving your fingers, and asked me what do I get, I had the same feeling that I had when I was having all that trouble at work. [EM] It's like the Nordic track is everything I can't have. How did that happen? Why did the Nordic track mean that to me?! [EM] It isn't just the Nordic track but it's exercise in general. It is all right there. [EM] It is a sense of "lack." There is not enough money, not enough of everything. There is nothing more to say. That is just how it is. This big machine is just a symbol.

Therapist: Go back once again to what we started with. You're standing in front of the Nordic track. What do you get now when you think of that?

(Cassie: It's just a Nordic track! [EM] It's not that I want to get on it, but it's just an exercise machine.) [EM] *So as you're standing there in front of the exercise machine how strong right now is that urge to just walk away and go do something else?* (Cassie: Seven.) *Talk about that seven.* (Cassie: It is just a machine. It's not going to do anything to me. [EM] It's not going to suck my soul out.) [EM]

Therapist: So go back to it again. What do you get now?

Cassie: Five! I can see myself getting on it. . . . But I would rather not. I would have to put on my running shoes, my outfit. [EM] I don't have any *"fat clothes"* to work out in, and that would cost more money. [EM] Why can't I get clothes? They make fat workout clothes. That feels exciting to do that. I want new running shoes too. [EM] Maybe then I could work out! [EM] I'm really confused how I came to think that way. The Nordic track seemed like a beast. So do I need to know why it became such a symbol? [EM] I don't know why I thought of it that way, but I don't have to be afraid to just use it for exercise. Somehow exercise became symbolic of everything I thought I couldn't have. It was one thing after another. At work, trouble getting along with _____ (husband), the situation with _____ (another family member)! One thing after another! Everything I couldn't have.

Therapist: So think once again of the Nordic track, right now, with all this in mind, and what do you get?

Cassie: It's like a 3. When we're done here today, I'm going to call _____ (husband), and then we will go together to get exercise clothes and we will both begin exercising, today! We both need to do this. We have the money for the clothes. And we both have enough time to do it. We can make time if we want to. [EM] I think I am also realizing I've been angry at him about this, about being too worried about money. [EM] I can challenge him. It isn't just about money for running clothes. It is that we don't have to live with the constant feeling of deprivation all the time. [EM] We both grew up with that, but we don't have to live with that anymore.

Therapist: So go back again to be standing in front of the Nordic track, and right now, how much, 0 to 10, you want to just go do something else?

Cassie: Not very strong, maybe a 2. I could go do something else and then come back and exercise. [EM] It feels like I want to just leave the session right now and go home and exercise! (*Therapist: Let's go back to it again. What do you get now?*) It is something I like to do, and want to do, and it is just an exercise machine. [EM] I am on the machine, and I like the feel of working my body. [EM] I am looking forward to it. *(Therapist: So, as you're standing in front of the machine, is there any urge at all to go do something else, or put it off until later?)* No. I'm excited about the idea of shopping for a new outfit to go with my fat body (smiles) and then going home and getting my body working again. I think _____ (husband) will go along with this, but whether he does or not, I know I can just go ahead and do what I need to do.

At the time of finishing therapy, 2 months later, this client had lost 5 pounds, and, moreover, was enjoying working out several times a week after work. Her case provides a good illustration of how, oftentimes, positive outcomes in therapy involve more than simply resolving traumatic experience. In her case, a self-defeating avoidance behavior had persisted even though it was no longer necessary—the circumstances of deprivation were mostly absent from her life, and the childhood memories of unworthiness had been resolved.

These are a few basic examples of how an avoidance urge can be targeted and resolved using adaptive information processing (AIP) methods. When the client's defensive structure is more complex, and dissociative disconnection between personality parts makes the situation more complicated, the targeting of avoidance defenses must be planned strategically, always bearing in mind the primary importance of maintaining the client's orientation to the emotional safety of the present. But even in these more complex situations, the same basic principles apply. Sometimes the only point of entry into a dysfunctionally stored memory network is an avoidance defense, and focused targeting on the positive elements of avoidance will reduce the intensity of the avoidance, leading to therapeutic access to, and targeting of, any remaining disturbing posttraumatic memory material.

AVOIDANCE DEFENSES WITHIN THE INTERNAL FAMILY SYSTEMS MODEL

Within internal family systems (IFS; Schwartz, 1995), a different vocabulary and different interventions are proposed to help clients who have strong habits of avoiding certain thoughts, feelings, and traumatic memories. These interventions can contribute substantially to the treatment of Complex PTSD and can be very usefully and strategically combined with AIP methods using sets of BLS. In the early sessions of therapy, Schwartz first discusses with a client a "language of parts," emphasizing that personality parts (separate states of mind that emerge at different times) are intrinsic to the human condition. Then, if the client is showing some type of avoidance behavior, Schwartz might ask the client to identify the part that is avoiding, and ask if that part would be willing to "step back one step" to allow direct therapeutic access to the part holding posttraumatic emotional disturbance. If the avoidant part is reluctant to do this, it can be helpful, then, to ask that part, "What are you afraid would happen if you did step back?" The fears of that part, such as the fear of being overwhelmed, can then be brought into the discussion. Schwartz also suggests another very useful intervention, which is to ask if the part that is reliving the trauma is willing to agree in advance to not overwhelm, if the avoidant part is willing to "step back." This is a kind of negotiation. If the trauma-reliving part agrees to not overwhelm, that agreement can generally be relied upon, and this can go a long way toward reducing the determination of the avoidant part to prevent emergence of the traumatic material. If the trauma-reliving part does *not* agree to this stipulation, the same question can be asked, "What are you afraid would happen if you did agree?" Often there are issues of distrust and mutual fear between the parts that need to be resolved through inner dialogue before this agreement can be obtained. Sets of BLS can be very helpful at each stage of this procedure in reducing the emotional investment held by the defensive part, and the fears that either of these parts may have with regard to each other. This reduction in mutual fear makes possible and facilitates the healing dialogue between parts. The use of BLS to facilitate therapeutic inner dialogue will be discussed further in Chapter 11, and Chapters 14 to 17.

INSTALLING AVOIDANCE AS A RESOURCE

In the previous examples, avoidance behavior was a problem in itself, and also prevented full access to unresolved disturbing life events. Through the use of EMDR-related procedures, the avoidance impulses were weakened, revealing the underlying memories and feelings, which then became available for processing.

Another aspect of avoidance is that it can be strengthened and utilized as a resource for a person who has *far too little psychological defense and far too much posttraumatic affect*. For example, a man came to therapy the day after a life-threatening auto accident. He had been driving on a mountain road and lost control of his vehicle, crashed against a guardrail, and then veered back across the road into another lane of traffic. For a split second, as his car was swerving, he was in the path of a large truck bearing down at high speed. His car was not hit, but was totally destroyed when it went into a ditch and hit some large rocks. His airbag deployed, and he was not badly injured, but was extremely shaken emotionally.

He was driven to our therapy appointment by his girlfriend who had encouraged him to get some psychotherapy for what had happened. At the start of our session, he told me that he had not slept all night, because every time he closed his eyes, he once again had the terrifying image of the truck coming toward him at high speed. As he gave this description, he was clearly very distressed. He was able to calm down to some extent through tossing a pillow back and forth, and then some breathing exercises. He said, though, that the image was still there in his mind in a very threatening way. In order to help him regain emotional control, through the creation of an avoidance resource, I said the following.

> *Therapist: Can you do this right now? Just a few minutes ago, we walked from my waiting room, up some stairs, by a hallway, and into this office. As we came through the hallway, you could see some other doors, to other offices in this building. Those are offices of other therapists here. Can you imagine that way down the hall, in another one of those offices, there is a little TV set (I held my hands about 4 inches apart), and on that little TV, behind that closed door, there is a video playing of that truck. That TV is playing down in that other office, but here's a question. What's good about being here in this room, right now, instead of in that other room down the hall?*

Client: I don't have to look at it!

I asked him to do a very brief set of BLS—tapping his own knees, alternating left and right, four times. Then, I asked him the same question again:

> *Therapist: Right now, at this moment, what else is good about being here in this room instead of that one?*

Client: If I wanted to, I could just go there, and knock on the door, and then go and unplug the TV.

This imagery, along with the question, "What's good about _____ (the avoidance)?" was helpful for him in gaining a sense of control over this flashing memory. Beginning with the image of the TV in the other room—still playing the image of the accident—he was then able to go on and use the recent events protocol (Shapiro, 1995) to get significant relief from the emotional residue of this accident. In the weeks that followed, he was able to completely resolve this particular memory (while also underlining a valuable lesson about driving more safely in the mountains).

Another example of an avoidance resource: A woman in her 60s was feeling overwhelmed by a powerful visual memory image, previously dissociated, from a sexual assault when she was 16 years old. She said, **"When you say the number '16,' it is happening all over again. It is awful!"** To help her gain more of a feeling of control over this flashback, I held up my hand as if I was holding something between two fingers, and said, *"See if you can put that memory image on an imaginary black and white photograph that I have in my hand, here."* Then I got out of my chair, and walked over to a far wall in my room, saying, *"Now, I am going to tape this small black and white photograph to the wall."* Then I went back and sat down in front of her again and said, "As you are looking at me right now, and you're not looking at that photograph right now, and you can't really see the place on the wall where I taped the photograph, what is good about just looking at me?" The targeting question, "What's good about _____ (the avoidance behavior)?" is very useful, not only—as previously described—for reducing the intensity of an avoidance defense when that defense is too strong, but also for the opposite purpose—strengthening avoidance is a resource when the client lacks emotional protection with regard to a posttraumatic intrusion. This client recognized that the purpose of my question was to help her strengthen her sense of emotional control, and that was the result. In a way that was similar to the previous example, this woman said, **"If I am looking at you, I don't have to look at that."** She had previously had successful EMDR sessions, and so I then asked her to simply hold in mind what she had just said, and follow my fingers for brief sets of BLS. With the buffer of her avoidance resource, we were able to continue with the sets of BLS, with the result that her anxiety and her feeling of loss of control with regard to this image diminished substantially, and we were then able to continue processing this particular memory, successfully, using standard EMDR Phases 3 to 7.

CONSTRUCTIVE AVOIDANCE

Carol Forgash is a highly experienced and creative EMDR therapist who has developed several ideas and interventions that are useful in the treatment of Complex PTSD. One of these is constructive avoidance (as described in Forgash & Knipe, 2007). With this approach, the client is asked to create, in imagination, imagery that will be useful in being able to cope with a situation that would otherwise be overwhelming. This method can be useful for a person who has begun but not completed therapy for overwhelming traumatic experiences. In other words, although therapeutic progress is occurring, there may be many unresolved memories that are much closer to the surface, due to the previous therapy. It can occur, at this midpoint of therapy, that a stressor arises that is unavoidable and highly triggering of the unresolved traumatic material. For example, a client who was orally abused as a child, and was progressing in her work in resolving these memories, suddenly and unexpectedly needed to have oral surgery—a root canal—to remove an abscess causing intense pain. She was terrified as she anticipated having to go through this surgery. It was all too triggering. It was very helpful for her to create constructive avoidance imagery.

> Therapist: If someone asked if you are planning to take your children (her actual children) with you to the root canal surgery, you would, of course, say, "No, they have to be in school." Would it be possible for you to also leave the children inside at home? These little children we have been talking about, that are inside, have

healthy teeth. It is only your adult tooth that needs this dental work. So the inner children don't have to be involved with it.

Then we created detailed imagery of a nice place where all the children could go while her adult self underwent the root canal work. The nice place had interesting videos, treats and snacks, and a kind, safe adult who could watch over all the children. The children could play, or watch a video, or take a nap—anything they wanted to do. It was just an imaginary place, but we elaborately created many details, and used sets of BLS to strengthen the positive feelings connected with each element of this imagery. The client also visualized how she actually anticipated it would be when she went to the doctor for the root canal work, going through it like watching a movie, pausing and focusing with sets of BLS on any moment of anxiety. For each difficult part, I said, "That may be one of the children who thought she was supposed to come with you to the oral surgeon's office. Just let her know that she can go back to the fun place, where she's completely safe, and you will let her know everything that happened, after the surgery is finished." She was able to go through the root canal surgery without being triggered by her memories.

So, in general, the "What's good about _____?" intervention can be used to weaken an avoidance defense that is already in place within the person's personality structure, and is preventing healing access to trauma. The same words can be used for a very different purpose—building the person's awareness of the relief of avoidance, so that more control can be gained over overwhelming memory material (Knipe, 1999). In the first instance, the client's larger goals are being frustrated by an avoidance defense, and targeting diminishes the power of that defense, revealing disturbing memories that can then be treated. In the second instance, the client's goals are different—the purpose of the intervention is to build increased protection to guard the client against the threat of being overwhelmed by disturbing memory. In both instances, sets of BLS are being utilized to move the client out of a distorted experience into one that is a step closer to adaptive resolution.

REFERENCES

Braun, B. (1988). The BASK model of dissociation: Part II-treatment. *Dissociation,* 1(2), 16–23.

Forgash, C., & Knipe, J. (2007). Integrating EMDR and ego state treatment for clients with trauma disorders. In C. Forgash & M. Copeley, *Healing the heart of trauma and dissociation* (pp. 1–90). New York, NY: Springer Publishing.

Knipe, J. (1999, Fall). Strengthening affect tolerance and adult perspective through construction of imagined dissociative avoidance. *EMDR International Association Newsletter,* 4(2), 10, 25.

Popky, A. J. (2005). DeTUR, an urge reduction protocol for addictions and sdysfunctional behaviors. In R. Shapiro (Ed.), *EMDR solutions* (pp. 167–188). New York, NY: W. W. Norton.

Schwartz, R. (1995). *Internal family systems therapy.* New York, NY: Guilford Press.

Solomon, R. L., & Wynne, L. C. (1954). Traumatic avoidance learning: The principles of anxiety conservation and partial irreversibility. *Psychological Review, 61,* 353–385. doi:10.1037/h0054540

Watkins, J. G., & Watkins, H. H. (1998). *Ego states: Theory and therapy.* New York, NY: W. W. Norton.

5

Targeting Idealization Defenses

Posttraumatic stress, whether big T or little t, is a distortion of perception. Something terrible happened in the past, and today, feelings—anxiety, helplessness—erupt into the person's consciousness, even though there is currently no current danger that warrants such intense feelings. The standard eight phases of eye movement desensitization and reprocessing (EMDR), with targeted sets of bilateral stimulation (BLS), have the reliable effect of moving this distorted perception to clarity and objectively accurate understanding of past and present realities. The past is now recognized as "over," and the posttraumatic distortion has been removed.

Experience can also be distorted in a positive direction, and these types of distortions are also often amenable to resolution through processing with sets of BLS. Of course, many of the happy experiences of life—and the memories of those events—are not distorted. Childhood times of being happy and free and times of being valued and loved by others—these are often the basis for positive resources, which are positive memories a person can have in his or her life today. For adults, the birth of a child, a marriage to a beloved sweetheart, graduation from school, and even unusual events like winning the lottery—occasions like these can have an immediate impact of intense good feeling, and even euphoria. And then, with time, the intensely positive impact shifts—we could say that processing occurs—so that the memory of these events, still positive, is now more subdued, and these positive recollections take their place within the individual's life narrative. Just as occurs with negative traumatization, overwhelmingly positive events are sometimes at variance (happily!) with the person's expectations and self-concept. The lottery winner might be unable, at first, to fully "take in" the reality of his good fortune, and might have an initial reaction of "I can't believe it!" But, as with negative events, something happy is likely to be processed over a period of time. The good news can "sink in" so that, a year later, it has become a resolved memory, still happy, but now taking its place as a real event within the person's life story. We all enjoy having and then integrating these positive experiences when we can.

The hypothesis stated here is that a chronic distortion of perception can occur when an intense positive experience remains unprocessed *and* is somehow a solution to a problem with unresolved trauma. This occurs when the experience, positive within itself, *has the additional positive effect of enabling the person to contain or avoid significant emotional disturbance.* The positive experience allows the person to shift awareness away from something that is upsetting to something that is pleasant. When this happens, the result can be what we might call an idealization defense—a positive experience that is not only positive in itself but also a means of avoiding a problem in the person's emotions. A corollary of this hypothesis is that this "problem-solving" aspect of a positive experience is necessary for the positive experience or memory to become a dysfunctional defense—major positive occurrences, no matter how positive, do not, in themselves, result in an irrational and self-defeating fixation on a behavior or distorted image.

EMDR therapy targets and resolves the dysfunctionally stored memories that are the basis of an individual's psychopathology (F. Shapiro, 1995, 2018). Typically, this means focusing EMDR procedures on specific disturbing memories. However, for *some* clients, at least *some* of the time, the only point of entry into the dysfunctional memory network will be an idealization defense—a behavior, or an image of self or others, that contains positive affect. Within the network itself, there may be many images that contain negative affect; however, these images are inaccessible, because the individual has learned, through life experience, to contain this disturbing memory material by quickly and automatically thinking of something positive. The idealization defense itself may be highly available for targeting and processing with sets of BLS, because the person is directly experiencing this defensive state of mind in the present, during the therapy session. In a way that is similar to what occurs with avoidance defenses, the targeting of idealization is likely to weaken the emotional investment in the idealized image, revealing underlying disturbing material that, in turn, can be processed in the standard EMDR way.

We can define idealization as a particular distortion in perception—someone or something, in the present or in the past, is viewed more positively than is factually justified. Idealization *can* be healthy and part of a good relationship (e.g., seeing the best in other people and ignoring their minor shortcomings). It is very normal, and probably very adaptive, for young children to idealize their parents, family members, community, school, and so on. However, many adults enter therapy with problems that include significant, unrealistic idealization—of others, or of self, or of a behavior—and that overvaluation stands in the way of seeing the events of life accurately. In these instances, idealization may be an obstacle to achieving therapy goals. The concept of an idealization defense is a broad category that includes narcissistic disorders, addictive disorders, impulse disorders, failures of willpower, fetishes, and unrealistically positive perception of others, of institutions, or of beliefs. Something troubling is pushed from awareness by means of a distorted, overly positive, highly valued perception or image. This can occur in a way that is not particularly problematic for the individual, as in the case of a person who had unhappy experiences in childhood, and then, in adult life, works to create positive and satisfying adult relationships, in part as a compensation for what occurred earlier.

Very often, however, an idealization defense can be a barrier to achieving therapy goals; specifically, it can be an obstacle to standard EMDR trauma processing. That is, emotional investment in an overly positive image can prevent the client from having full access to and knowledge of traumatic experience. For example, one client said to me, early in her therapy, "I had such a happy childhood! I talk to my friends, and hear about how it was for them when they were growing up, and it sounds awful. I am so lucky!" Later the client became aware of memories, previously completely dissociated, of how her older brother had sexually abused her and her sister. And in her case, the initial highly valued positive image of her brother, and her family, both of which proved later to be inconsistent with the reality of what occurred, had prevented her from realizing what had truly happened. An idealization defense may be initially created when the child's natural inclination to idealize caretakers and family combines with the child's need to *not be aware* of abuse or mistreatment (as a way of avoiding the pain of the abuse and/or as an adaptation to the perpetrator). Often, along with distortion of the image of the abuser, there is irrational shame about self ("I don't know why. I just always feel like I am a bad person."). The idealization image—of parents or family members—is highly valued, and in order to protect that image from contamination by traumatic events, those events can become entirely dissociated. This idealized image may be strongly and automatically sustained because it protects the individual from being aware of painful events. It is a defense—a blocking of intrusions of disturbing memories and feelings (usually quickly activated and nonconscious).

As a child grows up, this solution, which provides some emotional protection during childhood, may become a significant problem in itself. The child-grown-up may continue the same type of misperception of self or others as the interpersonal distortions of childhood continue. When idealization is a protection against awareness of disturbing memories, the cherished positive image often is impervious to change, logic, or disconfirming events. This can lead to problems in current interactions with other people, and even with the perpetrator.

Similarly, idealization can occur with regard to religious beliefs, political affiliations, a geographic region, a profession, or a workplace. A combat veteran of Afghanistan had severe posttraumatic stress disorder (PTSD) following a series of incidents in which his commanding officer made unwise decisions. In his therapy, this man was working on his PTSD from a combat incident, and he was stuck, vehemently and irrationally blaming himself for deaths and injuries—consequences that had resulted from one of the commander's decisions. He was able to resolve the feelings of guilt connected with these memories only after coming to recognize that his strong sense of idealization of the officer was not entirely deserved. Disinvesting from this overly valued positive image then allowed him to see the commander, see his own actions, and see the awful situations more clearly, although with great sadness.

An overly inflated perception of *self* (often together with devaluation of others) can be a problem in a similar way. Some people persist with a distorted self-congratulatory attitude because it has a defensive function—it may push away threatening doubts and fears about self, which often have their origin (frequently without the person's full awareness) in early childhood experiences of parental disengagement, emotional abandonment, or hypercriticism. Knipe (1998b, 2002; Knipe, Manfield and Snyker, 1998) described a course of EMDR treatment for a man with a narcissistic personality style. In this case, a self-image of entitlement and superiority to others had caused great disruption in this man's primary relationship and in his work situation. In his therapy, he was able to identify critical experiences that had been the basis for his overly positive self-concept. He was able to see that this false image of self had served a purpose during his growing up years—it had blunted the pain of his father's disapproval, his parents' chronic arguing, and his competitive alienation with his older brother. These negative experiences became available for EMDR targeting only after we first targeted representative early examples of the intense positive feelings of sssuperiority and being "more loved" (than father or brother) in his mother's eyes. His case was complex, and the course of therapy involved many more elements than simply targeting his positive affect states. However, over a 3-year course of therapy, he was able to shift his identification from a self-definition of superiority to a more realistic and grounded sense of self. In addition, with this more realistic perspective, his relationships significantly improved.

Additional examples of treating narcissistic personality style with EMDR can be found in Mosquera and Knipe (2015). Here are some other examples, just to give a wider picture of how this approach can be used. "Steve," a man in his late 40s, came to therapy initially due to conflicts in a close relationship. Both he and his live-in woman friend wanted to form a more lasting partnership, but they would often argue in a certain pattern—she would complain that he was far too reactive to minor criticisms, and his complaint was that she was not sufficiently appreciative of his financial and professional success as well as his other positive qualities. When these fights would occur, Steve would withdraw into silence—in his mind, his withdrawal was due to the necessity of protecting himself from hurt, but she would say that he was just sulking and pouting. During 2 months of weekly therapy sessions, he came to be more aware of how his need to be recognized as special and superior had significantly contributed to the tension in the relationship. He had had a very isolated and lonely childhood, feeling emotionally distant from his preoccupied parents and often picked on by older siblings. It seems, though, that he was able to perform well in school, and the identity of performance and achievement became his compensation for other unhappy family experiences. He had learned, basically, "If I achieve, I am safe. If other people don't see and recognize my achievements, I am nothing." Thus, any lapse from total recognition and appreciation by others, especially his partner, was experienced inaccurately as an accusation, "You are nothing," and this was the personality structure that was driving his emotional reactivity during their arguments.

These insights were helpful to him, and he felt very positive about seeing this issue more clearly. We were able to target, with EMDR, moments of his girlfriend's criticism, with the result that he was no longer emotionally reactive, and, moreover, he was able to see that her honest feedback to him was part of their healthy relationship. This progress in therapy opened up a new issue. He felt a little disoriented in realizing that the woman he was with truly was offering him something he had never fully experienced before—a loving relationship. It was at this moment in the therapy that he received a job offer for a position with substantially increased salary and prestige, in a different part of the United States, near where his family of origin still lived. His work in therapy had brought him to the point of realizing that he was at a crossroads: should he stay to explore and develop the potential of a loving relationship, or should he accept the job and become, in the eyes of his family, an outstanding success, thereby rectifying the times of lonely childhood rejection? Tough choice for him! We used Robin Shapiro's two-handed interweave method (2005), placing each side of the dilemma in a hand, and then combining an awareness of the emotional "weight" in each hand with repeated sets of BLS. This sharpened his understanding of the issue, but also intensified his conflict. He very much wanted to stay and continue to actualize the potential of his current relationship. *And,* he very much wanted to take the job offer—in many ways it fulfilled his strongly felt lifelong ambitions.

It was helpful for him to utilize the following intervention, in order to explore the possibility that an idealization defense—idealization of a new life with great success—was preventing resolution of his internal conflict. I said to Steve,

> *Therapist: See if you can get an image in your mind. Let's say you take the job, and now, 6 months later, things have worked out beautifully. It's really going just the way you hoped it would. Get an image in your mind right now that really incorporates all of the good things that are happening if you take the job, and it goes really well.*

> **Steve: I can get a picture of that! (Pause.) It is Saturday morning, and I'm feeling good about how the week has gone. I'm getting good feedback from everybody. They love my work! I'm driving on the Interstate in the new convertible I just bought. It's a** _____ (very expensive brand of car). **The top is down. I'm driving to the starting place for a 10K that I will be running in, and I feel pretty good that I will place pretty high, at least for my age group.**

Therapist: When you think of that right now, does it give you a good feeling? **(Steve: Yes. Definitely.)** *Where is that good feeling in your body?* **(Steve: In my chest. I guess in my legs too.)** *Can you just stay with that image, and be there, driving to the race?* **(Steve: Yes.)** *Stay with that.* **[EM]** *And what do you get now?*

Steve: I'm running in the race, and I'm loving it! *(Therapist: Stay with that.)* **[EM] I'm feeling really good after the race—I ran a good race.** *(Therapist: Stay with that.)* **[EM] I'm driving home now, feeling pretty good.** *(Therapist: Stay with that.)* **[EM] I'm just doing things around the house now, with the rest of the afternoon.** *(Therapist: Stay with that.)* **[EM] It's evening now, and I have a date with someone good-looking that I met at work.** *(Therapist: Stay with that.)* **[EM] That feels kind of bad.** *(Therapist: Stay with that.)* **[EM] Even if she's great, I will never have the same thing with her that I have now with _____ (the woman he is currently with).** *(Therapist: Stay with that.)* **[EM] It doesn't feel good.**

Therapist: Go back again and think of the image we started with, when you're in your nice convertible, going to the race. When you think about that again right now, what comes into your mind? What do you get now?

Steve: It all feels kind of shallow. It feels like plastic! *(Therapist: Stay with that.)* **[EM] The things I would have there would only be things.** *(Therapist: Stay with that.)* **[EM] I think my father wouldn't be too impressed even if he saw my car. I can just picture him saying something negative.** *(Therapist: Stay with that.)* **[EM] The appeal of the whole thing is much less now.** *(Therapist: Stay with that.)* **[EM]**

In the weeks that followed, he decided, without much hesitation, to stay in his current job and, especially, in his current relationship. He discontinued therapy 6 weeks later, still feeling resolved about his decision.

When doing this type of exploration, it is important for the therapist to be very aware of the client's emotional vulnerability. The discussion of issues of self-centeredness potentially can trigger intense feelings of shame in the client, and so the therapist may need to focus clearly and empathetically on how this particular defense was created, very understandably, as a response to childhood stresses. However, if there is sufficient trust, the client may be able to bring up a current example of a self-centered behavior, together with the associated positive affect that is the goal of this behavior. This behavior and positive affect, then, can be the focus of targeting with sets of BLS. With focused targeting on a positive memory or image associated with the defensive behavior, the defense will tend to weaken. Most clients experience a sense of relief when they are able to let go of a defensive behavior in this way. And present-day examples can either be targeted in themselves, or can be used to bridge to events in the past that set in motion the person's self-concept of entitlement or superiority.

Self-idealization defenses can occur in many forms—superiority, immunity to the usual rules of life that apply to others, lack of empathy for others, to name a few. With sufficient trust in the therapy relationship, key memories of the origins of idealized entitlement can be accessed with questions like, "When was it you first realized that you were smarter than other kids? Is that a nice memory? Can you just get a picture of it? When you think of it, where is that good feeling in your physical sensations?" Or, "Do you remember when you first realized that you didn't have to follow the same rules as everybody else?" Or, "Was there a time, maybe when someone else was crying, or having a hard time, and you thought, with some relief, 'It's not my problem.'?" Each memory, then, of an original situation where idealization first occurred can be a target for intervention and processing of the dysfunctional level of positive affect (LOPA; Knipe, 1998b, 2005, 2010) maintaining the strength of the defense.

The therapist needs to choose words sensitively and carefully in discussing the client's self-idealization defense so as to ensure that the client does not feel shamed or attacked. Also, the therapist needs to be on the alert for any countertransferential reaction to the client's self-statements when speaking from the entitled part. This entitled, superior "False Self" (Kohut, 1971) is typically very fragile, a thin veneer covering feelings of emptiness and often-enormous self-doubts.

With continuing sets of BLS, focused on representative positive memories of discovering and using this defense, and especially with trust in the positive regard of the therapist, the person can come to a more realistic, and even more comfortable, sense of self. These are often individuals whose histories include long periods of inadequate engagement and mirroring by significant others. A destructive double lesson was learned: "My inner needs and feelings don't count, and I must be exemplary and perfect to have connection with my caretakers." Investment in a narcissistic false self is intrinsically stress-producing for the individual. It is hard work to live the life of a narcissist—there must be a continual focus on creating a certain idealized impression in other people, and getting those other people to act the way they "should," often accompanied by a lack of real connection with those other people, and even with one's true self. The defense can give a sense of entitlement and superiority with regard to other people, but these attitudes do not meet a deep need for connection, and are meager compensation.

Investment in an overly positive image of self can dominate a person's sense of self, or can simply be a state of mind that sometimes arises, to varying degrees, in certain specific circumstances. Whether the investment is a lot or a little, gradually, in therapy, there can be a shift from emotional investment in the "False Self" to being comfortable in simply being one's "real self." The positive feelings that anchor the "False Self" originated in times when the self idealization effectively contained emotional disturbance, and the emotional investment in this image can be reduced through a focus on those times, and the positive feelings of those times, with sets of BLS. The illusion is given up, and there is a trade-off for this loss in an increased sense of groundedness and coherence within the self, as well as an opening for real connection with other people. A person can come to accept,

"I'm not wonderful, and actually that's okay, *and it is a relief to know* that I'm not terrible. It's okay for me to just be who I am." It is rewarding for the individual to discover simple permission to be human, and to be aware of the humanness of others. Therapy with these clients is, by necessity, slow and gradual.

The same general approach can be used when the idealized distortion is of another person (e.g., ex-partner, parents, children; Knipe, 2005), or of institutions, things, or actions (i.e., cathexes; Knipe, 2010).

There are other situations in which inappropriate idealization of another person (a partner, an ex-partner, a family member, or others) is problematic (Mosquera and Knipe, 2017). Here are some other examples of the use of the LOPA procedure, taken from session videos and case notes.

A woman in her late 50s came to therapy because her 25-year-old son was a source of constant stress to her. He was addicted to drugs and alcohol, he had lied to her many times, and he had stolen several very valuable items from her house. These problems had begun in his early teenage years. She had offered many times to pay for his substance abuse treatment, but he was not interested, and in fact was scornful of her efforts. It helped her to target her memory images of the most positive times with him—when he was much younger. With these sessions, she did not stop loving him, and she did not stop being alert for opportunities to truly help him, but she did develop more perspective regarding what was possible and what was not possible for her to do. She reported that this work made her "sadder but wiser" in that it gave her a needed perspective on how to think and feel about this ongoing relationship.

"Craig," a man in his mid-30s, came to therapy with chronic depression and very low self-esteem, which he attributed directly to the breakup, 4 years earlier, of his 9-year marriage. We targeted painful incidents from his marriage, and it became clear that, within this relationship, combat-related PTSD had contributed substantially to his ongoing problems with anger, as well as staying distant in the relationship. His wife had sought a divorce following several years of attempting to cope with his critical attitude and his long periods of silent withdrawal. Using standard EMDR, Craig was able to work through several situations that carried the theme of guilt—guilt that had been appropriate within the context of his marriage, but inappropriate with regard to horrible combat situations, where he had witnessed deaths that had occurred in the course of military action. Following this work, he was able to have some good conversations with his ex-wife, but in the intervening years, she had developed a new relationship, and it was sad for him to fully realize his marriage was really over. This work was successful, though, in helping him put these events in the past, with a new realization of his own worth, that he could be "okay" as a person. As therapy was winding down, he began a new relationship— something he had not wanted to attempt previously.

Then, about 4 months later, he called for an additional appointment. He had been dating a woman he met at work, "Louise," and he had felt that his life was taking a new and very positive direction. However, in the days before his phone call to me, "Louise" unexpectedly told him that she wanted to "begin seeing other people." He asked her if she had already started spending time with someone else, and she replied, "No," but he thought she was lying.

He arrived at this session feeling very bad and disappointed following this rejection. The structure of what he was experiencing at the start of this session is illustrated in Figure 5.1. As we began, he said, "Maybe I will never be able to make it with anybody." He had had previous success in using EMDR, and wanted to know if it could somehow help him with his present painful feelings. We used the LOPA method to help with this situation. This is a verbatim transcript of the last 30 minutes of this first session and the first 30 minutes of the next.

Therapist: Can you think of the nicest moment with her? The time you remember with the most intense positive feeling? I know there is probably some sadness too, when you think of that. But just get a picture in your mind that represents the good feeling you still have about her. . . . Can you get a picture like that? [**Craig: Yes.**] *Is it a positive feeling, when you think of that right now?* [**Craig: Yes.**] *Where do you feel that positive feeling in your physical sensations?* [**Craig: Here in my chest.**] *0–10, how intense is that feeling of "I can't let her go"?* [**Craig: It's a 10. It's a feeling of total joy, of really being loved.**] *Stay with that, and follow my fingers.* [**EM**]

Craig: Blue bedspread, her beautiful eyes . . . [EM] . . . Joy, that I was with her, meant to be with her . . . [EM] . . . I wonder what the next chapter in my life will be . . . [EM] . . . Without her, something is missing . . . [EM] . . . I just can't believe she doesn't want that too.

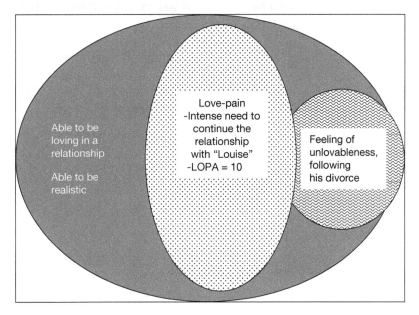

Figure 5.1 Targeting an unwanted feeling of idealization of another person, after being rejected in a relationship.
LOPA, level of positive affect.

At this point, we went back to target. With this method, as with avoidance, it is advantageous to go back to target more frequently than is typical when targeting traumatic memories. It is useful, not only for the therapist, but also for the client, to see how the positive affect investment in the initial image has shifted.

> *Therapist: Think again of that nicest moment. How intense now is the feeling of "I can't let her go," 0–10?*
>
> **Craig: It's less, 6–7. I can't blame Louise. She just is who she is . . . [EM] . . . I didn't stay with it (laughs). I was thinking about what I have to do at my office this afternoon.**

Is this an avoidance response? Or is this a distraction? Or is it connected somehow in a chain of associations?—That was not clear, but we simply went back to target to find out.

> *Therapist: So go back again and think of that nicest moment. What do you get now?*
>
> **Craig: Still her eyes, the room with blue, peace, joy, comfortable . . . [EM] . . . There was nothing wrong with that moment! It was really good when it was good . . . [EM] . . . I feel lighter . . . [EM] . . . (laughs) I was thinking of a woman who used to work in my office. . . . Hmm! . . . Hmm! . . . [EM] . . . I still can be alive and aware.**
>
> *Therapist: We're just about out of time, but go back again. What number do you get now, when you think of that nicest moment?*
>
> **Craig: It's still there. Maybe a 4–5. But it doesn't feel so desperate.**

At the start of our next session, 6 days later, Craig gave me a report of what had happened in the previous days. In the first 5 minutes or so, he said,

> **Well, I went home, took down her picture. . . .**
>
> **I really thought I could let my guard down with her. . . .**
>
> **I guess I heard what I wanted to hear. . . .**
>
> **What I wanted was more than she wanted. . . .**
>
> **I wrote her a letter, but I may not send it.**

He was feeling much less shock, less intensity of the painful feelings. I suggested, and he agreed, to check on our work by picking up where we left off the previous session.

Therapist: Today, when you think of the nicest moment with her, how intense is that feeling, "I can't let her go," 0 to 10?

Craig: I'm hearing the question differently today, with two answers. Do I want to hold on to her, or to an ideal? I want the *ideal* of her! That is still a 3–4. [EM]

His use of the word "ideal" was spontaneous. I had not used the word "idealization" with him. Due to repeated targeting with sets of BLS, his emotional investment in the idealized image of Louise was diminishing, and he was gaining an increased felt sense of how the reality of this relationship was different from the ideal. This particular insight frequently occurs as part of the healing process for people who have been rejected in a love relationship. Craig was still in love with the person *he had thought* Louise was. This was a very helpful insight. He was still in love with a person who did not actually exist, at least in the way he needed for her to exist. This illustrates how rational understanding of an emotional problem often is not sufficient for full comprehensive healing. If we were totally rational human beings, we would shift our feelings easily when learning that a beloved partner has actually been lying and pretending to care. We could say, "Well, with this new information, I don't love that person anymore!" But feelings do not seem to shift that way. Perhaps, in some instances, that is a good thing, giving resilience and stability to relationships. However, love and other feelings often continue on at times even though those feelings are no longer realistically tenable. Craig's case shows how targeting these feelings with sets of BLS can be very helpful in shifting the painful emotions so that they are less intense, as well as congruent with the objective facts of the situation.

Craig: I can still remember that image of Louise, to know what I need in a woman. I can be grateful to her for that . . . [EM] . . . How will I trust again? [EM]

This is an important question. We could have stopped the processing and had a discussion about, "How can you know if another person is trustworthy? How can you decide that? How can you determine that?" Instead, we just initiate another set of eye movements, and he answers his own question.

I knew what I knew . . . I just didn't want to see it.

Therapist: Go back again to the nicest moment. What do you get now?

Craig: At that moment, I was confident we had a future. [EM] It's a 3 now. I still feel empty, but not as intense. [EM] There are more people I haven't met! [EM] It's okay.

Therapist: Go back again. What do you get now?

Craig: It's still a 3. I'm just reflecting on how good the good stuff was. [EM] I wish she hadn't lied. [EM]

You can see here the *healing dialogue* between parts, facilitated by sets of eye movements. On the one hand, the part that still carries affection for the idealized image of Louise is "reflecting on how good the good stuff was," while another part is aware of facts that contradict this image. In his case, the healing dialogue happened naturally, as we proceeded through channels of information with sets of BLS. Later, in Chapter 17, a case example will be presented in which internal healing dialogue was facilitated with specific cognitive interweaves.

Craig: Maybe I'll learn a lesson, about my pattern. [EM] I know more now about what to look for. [EM] She didn't want to introduce me to her sister, like I wasn't quite acceptable.

Therapist: Go back again. What do you get?

Client: It's a 2, maybe a 1. I still miss that feeling. [EM] (Tears begin, but also smiling while he is crying.) Every time I come in here—do you want to make me cry!?

He is crying, and smiling, and it seems like it is just part of his release. I say, "Stay with that," and we do another set of eye movements.

Craig: Actually, it feels good to be able to cry. I see that I was desperate, and that made me not see. I can be whole, not desperate. [EM] There is still a little bit there, but I think I just want to let it linger for a while.

By the next session, he was feeling quite a bit better. The work had shifted his perspective in that he could see the loss of this relationship more objectively, with much less painful emotion, similar to the previous processing he had done with his war experiences and his troubled marriage. His therapy ended a few weeks after this, but I ran into him a year later—he was volunteering at a local Veterans Affairs (VA) outpatient center, and we had a chance to talk. He said he was in a new relationship at that point, and he said with cautious optimism that he thought this one would be more lasting.

The earlier session occurred shortly after Craig's rejection experience, but the dilemma of unresolved idealization of another person can continue unresolved for years. A woman who had divorced her husband 5 years earlier because of his numerous, unrepentant affairs was still highly apprehensive about the possibility of running into him with his new wife in a restaurant or in line at a movie theater. When a representative image of this fear was targeted, it became clear that the underlying source of the problem was that she was still grieving the loss of the relationship. As in the previous example, she was mourning the loss of the relationship she *thought* she had had, prior to learning of her husband's extramarital behavior. She was still emotionally invested in an image of a cherished relationship with *that* man—the ideal husband who would always love her and never betray her. In spite of what she knew, "objectively," about her ex-husband and her marriage now ended, she was still, in her emotions, attached to the idealized marriage that might have been. She had married at a young age, partially as a solution to the problems of a highly stressful family of origin, and also as a way to put aside her anxiety regarding being able to independently support herself as an adult. Ironically, at the time of her therapy, she had a good job and was able to be economically self-sufficient. In spite of this, though, her idealization of her husband and her now-ended marital status had continued on, unexamined, driving her fear of going out in public. We targeted this idealization, using the LOPA method, and she was able to see the reality of her situation more clearly. Following this work, she was able to fully let go of her regrets about the loss of her first marriage as well as her previous fears. She said, "If I run into him, *he's* the one who should be nervous!"

Idealization is often part of the clinical picture for couples in marriage counseling. One or both partners may be invested in an ideal of how the other person is supposed to be, and then arguing and fighting occur when one or both fail to live up to the other's idealized image. Also, idealization, combined with denial, can be a hidden obstacle to seeing and resolving core problems with couples. For example, a professional woman in her late 30s was repeatedly the recipient of intense drunken rage from her husband, and yet she remained in the marriage because, "He really does love me." She was continually troubled and disoriented by the ongoing situation and her indecisiveness. Her memories of good and loving times with him were still with her. She was highly invested in an image of him as a good partner, and this investment prevented her from seeing that his alcohol problem had worsened and become intolerable over the years. In her therapy, she targeted the positive feelings connected with memories from many years earlier, of when he had been much more of a loving friend and partner. This resulted in her seeing, at a deeper level, how her present relationship with him had changed and was no longer acceptable. Seeing the situation with more clarity, she attempted to find ways to save the marriage; however, after several months, with sadness, she initiated a separation. During the next year, her husband began going regularly to a 12-step program and stopped drinking. When I had my last contact with her, they had begun meeting, cautiously, to evaluate whether there was a chance of resuming their relationship on a basis that was more acceptable.

Mosquera and Knipe (2017) have described therapy procedures that can be useful in assisting clients who are ambivalent about leaving a partner in spite of that partner having been repeatedly abusive and physically violent. It is widely recognized that intimate partner violence (IPV) is a significant problem in our society—contributing to intense distress, danger, and even life threat for many women. Tjaden and Thoennes (2000) surveyed a large sample of women in the United States during the 1990s, and found that 25% had been sexually or physically assaulted by a partner, or dating partner, at some time in the past. Violence within a relationship is the leading cause of injury to women, more than car accidents, muggings, and rapes combined (Krug, Dahlberg, Mercy, Zwi, & Lozano, 2002).

Many women who come to therapy seeking a means to escape this type of situation *will not have any illusions* regarding the dangers of their relationship, that is, there will not be an issue of dysfunctional and distorted idealization with regard to their partner. The primary issue for these individuals is how to leave this relationship—perhaps create an action plan—while maintaining their own personal safety. There may be many obstacles to escape: fear of retaliation by the perpetrator if escape is attempted, financial dependence, lack of confidence in police, intense feelings of self-blame (after having repeatedly been blamed by the perpetrator), and learned helplessness (Ford, 2009; Royle & Kerr, 2010; Seligman, 1975; Walker, 1979; Williams & Poijula, 2013).

A subset of victims of IPV may present with a different initial clinical picture—intense ambivalence regarding whether to stay or go, in spite of the repeated violence within the relationship (Murray, 2008). For these individuals, ambivalence based on inappropriate idealization of the abusive partner may be a significant issue—one that can be addressed in therapy. In other words, the idealized image of the other may be highly valued in itself, and may also be blocking full conscious access to memories of disturbing abusive incidents. Because of this blockage, the client is not able to target and resolve those incidents, and take those incidents into account in making decisions about whether to continue or end the relationship. The client suffering from this type of ambivalent conflict is *blocked* in being able to develop adaptive resolution (i.e., a more accurate perception of both past events and the present nature of the relationship; Figure 5.2).

"If I had any sense I would get out right now! This is an impossible relationship. I am an idiot if I stay with him one minute longer!"

The LOPA procedure can be very helpful in assisting a client in resolving dysfunctional idealization of another person, in the context of IPV. The specific steps in this procedure are as follows:

- Be sure the client is able to glimpse that the high emotional investment in another person is problematic, and give permission for therapy to proceed to help the client relinquish that investment.
- Identify a specific memory image that contains positive emotion and represents the distorted idealized affect: "Is there a 'best moment,' a time you can remember when this relationship was very fulfilling and satisfying? Is there a good feeling connected with that time?" or "Is there a particularly pleasant memory that represents your feeling of love for _____? [or 'represents your wish to never let that person go?' or '. . . represents your wish to hang on to this relationship?']."

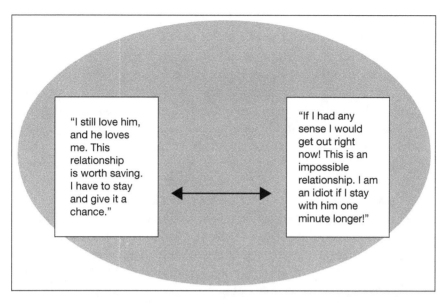

Figure 5.2 The ambivalent conflict between internal personality parts that can occur in a victim of intimate partner violence. The two poles of the conflict may be coconscious and simultaneously available in the client's awareness, or they may be partially or fully dissociated from each other, and alternate in the person's conscious awareness.

- If the client is unable to think of a purely positive memory but is able to identify a memory image with both positive and negative affect, the instruction from the therapist can be, "I know that when you think of that time, you have mixed feelings, but would you be able to briefly put the negative feelings aside, and simply focus on the positive feelings that still are there when you think of that time?"
- When this "best moment" is identified, the therapist can ask for associated positive cognitions—not only positive self-referencing cognitions (i.e., "I am a lovable person") but also other referencing positive cognitions (i.e., "He gives me safety and protection," or "He loves me in a way that no one else ever has"). These positive cognitions about the other person can be regarded as important elements of the targeted positive memory image.
- The intensity of positive feeling associated with this representative memory can then be put on a 0 to 10 LOPA scale (Knipe, 1998a, 2005, 2014), and that feeling can be located in physical sensations.
- Then, memory image, positive cognitions, and associated sensations can be held in mind while sets of BLS are initiated.
- As processing continues through repeated sets of BLS, the intensity of positive feelings regarding the "best moment" memory is likely to become less (consistent with the reality of the situation) and access to underlying disturbing information may increase. In most cases, this disturbing information will process by simply proceeding with

additional sets of BLS (although if more therapeutic power is needed, EMDR Phases 3–7 can be effectively used).

- Even if negative information arises, it is typically useful to continue to "go back to target" by asking the client to repeatedly think again of the "best moment" and report what the LOPA score is, "right now." By emphasizing the words *right now,* the client is assisted in seeing that the positive investment in the idealization is diminishing. The emergence of negative information during this procedure does not automatically mean that the dysfunctional positive information has been processed. For this reason, the original "best moment" should continue to be targeted until the LOPA score is down to a level that indicates an absence of idealized distortion. This is not a rote formulaic procedure, but one that requires the judgment of the clinician. But the outcome is typically a large reduction or elimination in idealizing distortions.

- The goal of this procedure is not, of course, to end the relationship in all cases. That may or may not be the most desirable outcome, and, ultimately, that must be the decision of the client. The typical result of this procedure, though, is a relinquishment of the idealization defense, resulting in a more realistic perception of healthy options and choices, and, in many cases, an increase in the courage and determination to make whatever decisions are necessary.

Here are some additional examples of questions the therapist can ask to identify targets for idealization processing.

- **(For a client who is in therapy to learn to better control his angry outbursts) "When were you really able to effectively control a situation by getting angry? What was good about discovering you could do that?"**
- **"When did you first experience that good feeling of being really special and better than other people? Right now, do you get some good feelings when you remember that time?"**
- **"You are telling me that, down deep, you never want to stop just being a kid—not so worried about adult responsibilities. When did you first discover the good feeling of thinking that way? When was the happiest time that you can remember, connected with that way of thinking?"**
- **"Can you think of a time when you lied about something, and you didn't get caught? It really worked out! You clearly got away with it, and figured out—Hey! This is a way sometimes to avoid being in trouble. Can you hold that in mind—the positive feeling that went with that?"**
- **"Think of being with a group of people, and be aware of that need you have told me about—the need to always be the center of**

attention. When was it that you *really were* the center of everyone's attention and it felt very good?"

- (For a client who was referred for therapy by a judge, following his arrest for breaking a restraining order and illegally entering his ex-wife's house) "You are telling me that you are thinking about driving by your ex-wife's house tonight, just to see if her new boyfriend's car is in the driveway. That is something you *have a strong urge* to do. How strong, 0–10, with 10 the most, is your desire to do that?"

The following transcript illustrates this type of targeting of a self-centered trait that is self-defeating. "Dave" entered therapy after his wife insisted that he go to therapy as a condition for her remaining in the marriage. Both he and his wife had professional educations, and she was employed full time; he, however, had had a checkered work history and was unemployed at the time of beginning therapy. His wife had been in her own therapy and had gained a new perspective; previously, she had been responsible for nearly all shopping, cooking, cleaning, and other household tasks, but now, with her increased self-respect and improved assertion skills, she was telling Dave that he had to take on his share of responsibilities in their relationship. In the home, Dave had shown many passive-aggressive behaviors, and had been manipulative with his wife in order to get her to do maintenance tasks (primarily passive-aggressive behaviors—e.g., just simply not doing tasks he had agreed to do) and guilt trips (e.g., criticizing her for complaining when he did not follow through on an agreement). She was no longer as vulnerable to these manipulations; paradoxically, as a result, the marriage was in a crisis.

Initially, he was in therapy only reluctantly; during the first few sessions, however, he became more comfortable in being open and talking about his point of view regarding the problems in his marriage. He stated that his wife was "prickly," overly critical, and that her affection for him was "too conditional." When I confronted him with questions about how he might also be contributing to the marriage conflicts, he did not get overtly defensive, but said, "Well, I'll have to think about that." Further probing hit a wall, though, as he passively, but insistently, avoided exploration of this possibility.

There was, in fact, much about Dave that was very likable. He could not be described as a narcissistic personality, but he did have some narcissistic traits, in that he was invested in an idealized and somewhat distorted sense of self as a person who should not ever have to grow up. He had a blind spot for how his unreliability and his self-destructive habit of avoiding responsibilities had created problems both at home and at work.

At first he was reluctant to use EMDR procedures to help with his marriage situation—in part because he still carried some resentment about how EMDR (with another therapist) had been so helpful to his wife, enabling her to be more assertive! He did agree, after some discussion, to target a representative recent argument, but he found it very difficult to describe details of how the argument had started, how it escalated, and so on. He was able to get a visual image of the "worst part," but it was hard for him to identify a self-referencing negative cognition (NC) that went with that image. His focus was on NCs about his wife! Nevertheless, we were able to work with the very minimal self-referencing NC: "It still bothers me." When we used EMDR to target a specific argument, the processing helped to some degree in reducing his frustration and tension, but we did not have the usual result of clarification or resolution of the issue. The main obstacle seemed to be that he simply had a strongly held belief in his own innocence in causing these difficulties, and that belief was blocking his ability to objectively see the situation and do some effective problem solving. This blocking belief, which was never explicitly stated but was evident indirectly in many ways, was, "I'm okay, no matter what I do, and if someone else thinks I have faults, I can just tune them out." In spite of his investment in this belief, though, and even though therapy was proceeding at a snail's pace, he said he was getting benefit from being able to "just talk about things."

Then, after 2 months of therapy, one day he came to a session wanting to tell about an argument that had happened over the weekend. He had been out shopping on Saturday, and came home to find his wife crouched down on the floor of their bathroom, cleaning up a toilet that had overflown. When she saw him standing in the bathroom door, she said, with irritation, "Did you know this happened before you left?" This confrontation on her part was reasonable, given his past behavior, but in this case it was inaccurate, because he had not in fact known of the problem with the toilet before he went shopping. When she said this, he was indignant at the false accusation; he shut the bathroom door without speaking and went to the TV room to sit in his comfortable chair. He was still feeling some of this indignation as he told me of this incident. When he described sitting in front of the TV, there was a bit of a smile on his face. I asked him about this. . . .

> *Therapist: When you sat down to watch TV, was there a comfortable feeling connected with that? You looked like you had an okay feeling when you told me about it.*

> **Dave: Yes, I guess so. I know she won't bother me there.**

> *Therapist: Just think of it again now. Where is that good feeling in your body when you think of that right now?*

> **Dave: It's in my stomach and a little bit in my chest. It's a feeling of "I can just watch TV. I'm okay. No problem."**

Therapist: Can you be aware of that feeling right now, in your stomach and chest, and that sense of being okay, and . . . take that back to when you were a kid? Just see where that takes you. It doesn't have to make sense. Just notice what memory comes up, when you think of that.

Dave: (Long pause.) Ahh. . . . Yes. I'm thinking of a time when I was with the puppies!

The Affect Bridge (Watkins & Watkins, 1998) connected his present-day feeling of "okayness" and comfort with a memory of puppies. The memory situation was from about age 4 to 5. It was Saturday morning, and at his house everyone was supposed to be working. He was supposed to be up in his room cleaning up his toys. Instead, he crawled into the back of a doghouse where there were new puppies, and he lay there, with the puppies playing and jumping all over him, while his parents were very worried and calling for him (he estimated for about 20 minutes). Finally, his mother looked in and saw him through the doghouse door, and she was smiling. He told me that this image, of his mother's smiling face, was very positive for him. He said that it gave him feelings of "She loves me. I'm special." We used the LOPA procedure with this image and its positive affect. Very quickly, after only three or four sets of BLS, he began to see his father's face behind his mother's face, and his father was not happy! We continued from there, processing the more disturbing channels of this memory, with the result that he was able to see, by the end of this session, that this is how he grew up. In his mother's eyes, he could do no wrong, and was totally lovable, no matter what. In his father's eyes, he was very often a disappointment. Dave had grown up, then, with two very different and competing self-concepts, one from his mother and one from his father. He wanted the total acceptance he had received from his mother, and he had been angry and frustrated in his life when other people did not give him this total acceptance, because the alternative way of thinking about himself was as a person who was hugely disappointing and inadequate.

To his credit, following this session, he saw the irrationality of thinking this way and went home to his wife to explain to her this new understanding. In the weeks that followed, he reported that he was finding it much easier to simply take on normal household responsibilities. He would remind himself of what he learned in this session each time he would be tempted to avoid a task he had agreed to. His wife recognized this change, and was very happy about it. She actually called and left a message on my voice mail saying, "He is 1000% better!"

Shortly after this session, he ended a period of unemployment. In his new job, he was sent to another state for a training program. New trainees were divided up into teams to accomplish certain tasks, with the goal of learning to work cooperatively with each other. During this training, he noticed that there were several instances of him attempting to get other trainees to do some work that legitimately should have been done by him. This was a resurgence of the old problem—of feeling entitled to get out of work, even if he did it in a way that was manipulative and sneaky.

The following week, when he returned to therapy, he disclosed this "relapse," and he agreed to use it as an LOPA target in order to get a better understanding of what had happened. I asked him to describe the details of what occurred in the training program, and then, once again, to do an Affect Bridge to see if there was an additional associated feeder memory for this behavior pattern of avoidance of work. Figure 5.3 illustrates the structure of his personality parts at the start of this session. He allowed me to video this session, and the transcript follows.

IDENTIFYING THE PROBLEM IN THE PRESENT

Dave: (At the training program) We were all around a U-shaped table. I just saw myself trying to push the work across the table, and I said to myself, "Here you go, trying this back door!" It was a pity-poor-me type of thing—"Come on, Jerry, you do it. You are my friend, good buddy." Trying to coerce him into doing it for me, instead of me doing it.

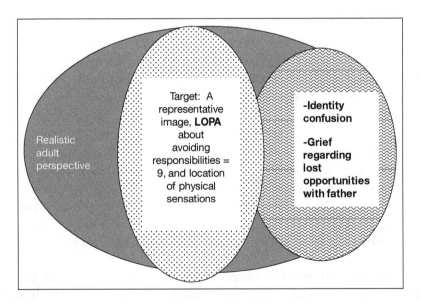

Figure 5.3 Targeting idealization of a self-defeating personality trait (entitlement, avoidance of responsibility).
LOPA, level of positive affect.

Therapist: You have done some good work on this—what you call, "hiding" from taking responsibility. (**Dave: Yes.**) *What happened in _____ (the training program) shows that there is still a little bit of the old stuff. Let's figure out a way to get to it. You did say, in that meeting, to Jerry, "Can't you do this, Jerry?" And so you tried it out a little bit. There is just a little bit, a shadow of what was there before. Dave, I want to ask you some focused questions about it.* (**Dave: Okay.**)

Affect Bridge to a Feeder Memory

Therapist: See if you can remember something. See if you can go back in your thoughts to find a time when you were really able to find that kind of comfort in "hiding." Hiding and getting out of doing something that, in some sense, you should have coped with. Was there ever a time when it really worked out, or paid off, and you got away with getting out of some work? Can you think of a time like that?

Dave: (Long pause.) Ah, yes. . . . We owned some property along a river. Some friends of mine came out. We had a little trailer house, before we built the house. My dad comes out and was going to work on the place, and I wanted to go with my friends and do some things. It was that withdrawal thing, that hiding-type thing. Hiding.

Therapist: So that's something you can remember pretty clearly? (**Dave: Yes.**) *Let your mind go back to it now, and, in fact, did you go with your friends that day?* (**Dave: Yes.**) *Do you remember the feeling you had, the positive aspect of being able to get away and get off with your friends? Can you think of that right now? As you look at it, you may see it with a different perspective that comes from your more recent work, but if you can, just put that aside for now and focus on what you can remember as being positive about that . . . when you got off with your friends and you didn't stay and work, and you got away with it. Bring to mind a picture that really represents the positive feeling of comfort at getting away, and getting out of that work. What picture do you get?*

LOPA PROCEDURES

Dave: There's a place on the little river there by the property where they fixed a rope, and there were about six or eight of us, and we were just swinging out on the rope. We were just swinging around, feeling real free and all our cares were gone and whatever . . . the world didn't exist for a while there. Just a real relaxing situation, a bunch of guys going out having a good time.

Therapist: So think of that right now. Just really be there if you can, and let yourself enjoy that. Let yourself really enjoy being there again, and when you let yourself think of that and enjoy that right now, think of the numbers 0–10, and how intense a positive feeling of enjoyment and comfort do you feel right now, when you think of that? (**Dave: It's a good 8 or 9.**) *Hold in mind swimming, and swinging on that rope with your buddies, and where do you feel that positive feeling in your body right now?—The aspect of that that's positive, where do you feel that in your body?*

Dave: In my stomach, and chest. It's one of those gut kind of feelings . . . feeling free, like in all the commercials for Coca Cola, or Pepsi commercials. They make you feel good about seeing the children, and doing things—it's that kind of good feeling. *(Therapist: If you put words with that good feeling, what would the words be?)* **Unrestrained juvenilism!—To me, it's just being a kid. I still remember a show Robin Williams did, about, "Don't ever grow up boys, hold on to that one part of your person, be a kid and have fun." And that's kind of what I've tried to keep in mind at times. I still want—part of me just wants to be a kid. When you're a little kid there's no responsibility, no stress, no pressure, just running in the yard with the puppies, having fun, playing, not having to worry about things, laughing uncontrollably. That's kind of how it was that day at the river for a while. Just a bunch of guys, cutting up—unrestrained juvenilism!**

Therapist: Hold that in mind, Dave, that free feeling, that unrestrained juvenilism and "I get to be a kid with no responsibilities," that nice pleasant feeling in your stomach and your chest. And can you just hold in mind that picture, swinging on those ropes, with your buddies that day, and follow my fingers? Just stay with that. That's right. That's good. **[EM]**

Halfway through this first set of eye movements, Dave abruptly moved his head back half an inch, while saying, "Hmm." This appeared to be a shift in ego states, from enjoyment of the image we started with, to more disturbing material.

Therapist: Okay. Now just let it go for a moment. Just come back into the room. . . . Okay, now go back into it again. What do you get now?

Dave: It was escape. It was hiding . . . I was trying to find myself through other people. I was trying to have fun with those guys, and hoping that they could tell me *who I was,* **or help me find out who I was. Maybe I could see myself through them—the type of people they were, their personalities, the way they did things. Those were the people I hung around with so that was who I was.**

Therapist: Can you think of that? Just stay with that. **[EM]** *Go back again to this image of that day when your dad wanted you to help him and you got off with your buddies, and you were swinging on those ropes. And when you think of being there, swimming and swinging on the ropes, check into that feeling of comfort, that feeling of getting away, and what would you say with regard to that right now, 0–10, how much of that comfort do you have right at this moment?* **(Dave: . . . about a 2.)** *What's different, when you look at it again?* **(Dave: Responsibility! I was running from things. Hiding.)** *Can you stay with that? Just be aware of that.* **[EM]**

Dave: I never thought I could match up to my father's expectations of me, and that was a lot of what I was feeling that day. *(Therapist: Just stay with that.)* **[EM] I wasn't scared to be around my dad, necessarily, but I just didn't know my role with him, at that time. [EM] He gave me a lot of latitude, and when I think about it, I was harder on myself than he was, on me. I just didn't know how to stand up and be a man with him. (Tears.) I didn't know how to *be* a man around him. So, I did the hiding routine . . . and that's what I was doing, running away with the friends and staying a kid and not wanting to grow up.**

Therapist: Stay with that. You are doing some good work today. Stay with that. **[EM]** *Go back into it again. What do you get now?*

Dave: If I had just been more aware of reality . . . my dad would have accepted me, there was no problem there. I didn't know how to *be with him*, to *accept him*. I wish we had seen each other more eye to eye, on a man-to-man type basis. I wish I would have had more of those times when I was younger, with him.

INTERWEAVE TO FACILITATE HEALING OF AN UNFINISHED RELATIONSHIP

At the time of this session, Dave's father had been dead for several years. And yet, it was clear that Dave had quite a bit of unfinished business with his father. For situations like this, in which an important relationship is unfinished, but the other person has died, the following intervention can be quite helpful. We could think of it as an internal healing dialogue between the client's self and his internal representation of his father, with accompanying slow eye movements, to help contain any fear that might be connected with this dialogue. Many clients who have gone through this procedure have said that it feels as though they are actually having a healing conversation with the other person, even though that other person is no longer available.

Therapist: Let's do something right now. See if you can do this. If you were given 2 or 3 minutes, to talk to your dad right now, and to see him in front of you and to be in his presence right now, just 2 or 3 minutes, would that be enough time? What would you want to say to him? What would you want to tell him?

Dave: That I wished we'd had more quality time when I was younger, that I wish he would have met _____ (his wife) and gotten to know her.

Therapist: Just visualize being with your dad and talking with him, and just talk with him in your mind right now. You don't even have to say any words out loud, because you can see him right in front of you. (**Dave: Oh, yeah.**) *And just follow my fingers and go ahead and talk with him right now and tell him everything you really want him to know. . . . If there's anything you regret, let him know that, like on that day you went swimming. Just let him know.*

While Dave is silently visualizing this conversation, I am asking him to follow my fingers in another long (40-second) **[EM]** set, the purpose of which is to help him strongly connect with his image of his father, without interference from overwhelming fear or guilt.

Dave: He's forgiven me. *Think of that.* **[EM]**

Therapist: You are figuring out some things here. Would you say that is true? **[Dave: Oh, yes.]** *When you think of that day, when you got away with something, can you let your mind go back to it again right now? Summarize for yourself what you're figuring out. What are you figuring out?*

Dave: I was only fooling myself. I was cheating myself and I wasn't living life. I was play-acting, not really engaging with people. I was there physically, but not with them emotionally. I was staying in a shell. I was hiding from my dad. I can see now, he was wanting us to have a better relationship, even a friendship, and get to know each other. He was very patient about it.

Return to the problem situation in the present.

Therapist: You are seeing a lot of things about this memory, of this particular day when you were 17. (**Dave: Oh yes.**) *Is there a connection, Dave, between the feeling this boy had in getting out of some work and getting away with something, and what you were feeling in _____ when you tried to pass some work across the table?* (**Dave: Oh yes.**) *What's the connection?* (**Dave: Running from responsibility, and not engaging in life!**) *Is it helpful for you to see this connection?* (**Dave: Oh, yes, very much so.**) *Stay with that.*

[EM] *If that starts to come up for you again, like you're tempted a little bit to get out of some work, what do you want to remember right at that moment?*

Dave: To take that responsibility, to be part of life, don't withdraw and hide! Engage with people and the situation.

This issue remained resolved for Dave after this session. He reported that life actually seemed easier when he simply took on responsibilities, instead of strategizing about how to get out of necessary work. He ended therapy 4 weeks after that, when he was relocated with his job to another state, but I contacted him 8 years later, just to be sure that I still had his permission to discuss this session in workshops (he previously had given me written permission), and to include his case in my writing. He said that that would be fine, and went on to say that he remembered these sessions as an important turning point. He also said that both his work life and his marriage had gone very well since the time of his therapy.

In speaking to Dave during this session, I used his language of "hiding" instead of the words—perhaps more accurate—"avoidance of responsibility." I used his word to ensure that he would know that I was not trying to shame him through this discussion of his "bad habit." Self-idealization, like all defenses, is a way the individual has learned to protect the self from painful emotions, and those individuals who reveal this potentially embarrassing information deserve acknowledgment for their commitment and taking their own therapy very seriously.

How is this method—the targeting of idealization defenses—different from the procedures of resource development and installation (RDI; Kiessling, 2003; Leeds, 2002; Wildwind, 1995)? Both types of procedures target images that contain positive affect. The difference might be clarified with an example. One client said, "I always was happy when I was with my Uncle John. I remember a time when he picked me up from school, and when I told him that I had just gotten an 'A' on a test, he took me out to get some ice cream." We used this client's memory image of being with her safe and caring uncle to help her install the resource of an awareness of her own lovableness and worthiness. With sets of BLS, her good feeling about herself initially increased, but then, with continued sets, she became aware of a painful contrast between the loving attention of her uncle and the indifference her parents showed regarding her school achievement. The nice times with her uncle were doubly valued because they took some of the sting out of the disappointment she felt at home. When RDI is taught in the EMDR standard training, the instruction is to use short sets of BLS, in order to prevent the initially positive memory image from "going negative." This linkage to negative material is often very difficult to predict. There are many examples of how it can occur—the remembered safety of going to a church may be linked to oppressive religious teachings—the memory of loving times with someone now deceased may quickly turn to grief. A therapist can be aware of these possibilities, and cautiously use short sets when the purpose in the therapy is to develop a positive image as a resource, as well as longer sets when the purpose is to access possible unresolved trauma material beneath the defense.

The examples in this chapter illustrate how idealization defenses can be targeted in a nondissociative clinical population. In Chapter 17, additional procedures will be described for targeting dysfunctional idealization in a client with a dissociative personality structure. Many clients with Complex PTSD and/or a dissociative condition have issues of "attachment to the perpetrator" (1998). This is a phenomena that very frequently—perhaps universally—underlies the origins of dissociation, and in this later chapter, EMDR-related procedures will be described that can be quite helpful in resolving idealizing distortions, and in facilitating personality integration, in clients with initially separate identities.

REFERENCES

Ford, J. D. (2009). *Posttraumatic stress disorder: Scientific and professional dimensions.* New York, NY: Elsevier.

Kiessling, R. (2003, September). *Integrating resource installation strategies into your EMDR practice.* Paper presented at the 2003 EMDR International Association conference, Denver, CO.

Knipe, J. (1998a). Blocking beliefs questionnaire. *EMDR International Association Newsletter, Winter, 6*(1), 5–6.

Knipe, J. (1998b). It was a golden time: Healing narcissistic vulnerability. In P. Manfield (Ed.), *Extending EMDR* (pp. 232–255). New York, NY: W. W. Norton.

Knipe, J., Manfield, P., & Snyker, E. (1998). *The use of EMDR with narcissistic and avoidance disorders.* Presentation at EMDR International Association Annual Conference, Baltimore, MD.

Knipe, J. (2002, June). A tool for working with dissociative clients. *EMDRIA Newsletter, 7*(2), 14–16.

Knipe, J. (2005). Targeting positive affect to clear the pain of unrequited love: Codependence, avoidance and procrastination. In R. Shapiro (Ed.), *EMDR solutions* (pp. 189–211). New York, NY: W. W. Norton.

Knipe, J. (2010, October 3). *Invited keynote address, the use of AIP therapy methods with dissociative symptoms and Complex PTSD.* EMDR International Association annual conference, Minneapolis, MN.

Knipe, J. (2014). *EMDR toolbox: Theory and treatment of Complex PTSD and dissociation.* New York, NY: Springer Publishing.

Kohut, H. (1971). *The analysis of the self: A systematic approach to the psychoanalytic treatment of narcissistic personality disorder.* New York, NY: International Universities Press.

Krug, E. G., Dahlberg, L. L., Mercy, J. A., Zwi, A. B., & Lozano, R. (2002). *World report on violence and health.* Geneva, Switzerland: World Health Organization.

Leeds, A. (2002). A prototype EMDR protocol for identifying and installing resources. In F. Shapiro (Ed.), *Part two training manual*. Pacific Grove, CA: EMDR Institute.

Mosquera, D., & Knipe, J. (2015). Understanding and treating narcissism with EMDR therapy. *Journal of EMDR Practice and Research, 9*(1), 46–63. doi:10.1891/1933-3196.9.1.46

Mosquera, D., & Knipe, J. (2017). Idealization and maladaptive positive responses. EMDR therapy for women who are ambivalent about leaving an abusive partner. *Journal of EMDR Practice and Research, 11*(1), 54–66. doi:10.1891/1933-3196.11.1.54

Murray, S. (2008). "Why doesn't she just leave?": Belonging, disruption and domestic violence. *Women's Studies International Forum, 31*(1), 65–72.

Ross, C. (1998, Spring). The problem of attachment to the perpetrator. *Inner Voices*. Available at *Sanctuary for the Abused*. http://abusesanctuary.blogspot. com/2006/09/problem-of- attachment-to-perpetrator.html

Royle, L., & Kerr, C. (2010). *Integrating EMDR into your practice*. New York, NY: Springer Publishing.

Seligman, M. E. P. (1975). *Helplessness: On depression, development, and death*. San Francisco, CA: W.H. Freeman.

Shapiro, F. (1995). *Eye movement desensitization and reprocessing: Basic principles, protocols and procedures*. New York, NY: Guilford Press.

Shapiro, R. (Ed.). (2005). The two-hand interweave. In *EMDR solutions* (pp. 160–166). New York, NY: W. W. Norton.

Tjaden, P., & Thoennes, N. (2000). *Extent, nature, and consequences of intimate partner violence* (NCJ No. 181867). Washington, DC: National Institute of Justice. Retrieved from http://www.ojp.usdoj.gov/nij

Walker, L. (1979). *The battered woman syndrome* (3rd ed.). New York, NY: Springer Publishing.

Watkins, J. G., & Watkins, H. H. (1998). *Ego states: Theory and therapy*. New York, NY: W. W. Norton.

Wildwind, L. (1995). *EMDR in the treatment of depression*. Presentation at the EMDR network annual meeting, Sunnyvale, CA.

Williams, M. B., & Poijula, S. (2013). *The PTSD workbook: Simple, effective techniques for overcoming traumatic stress symptoms* (2nd ed.). Oakland, CA: New Harbinger.

6

Treating Addictive Disorders With Adaptive Information Processing Methods

We can think of addiction broadly as any recurring behavior pattern that results each time in a short-term immediate positive feeling, but has large dysfunctional or destructive consequences over a larger time frame. Addictions often function as defenses and incorporate both avoidance affect (i.e., positive feelings of escape or relief from troubling feelings) and the positive affect of defensive idealization (i.e., unrealistic overvaluation of an image, concept, action, or part of self). Even for the therapist who does not specialize in working with addictive disorders, an understanding of addiction-targeting procedures can be valuable, because many problematic behaviors of clients—so-called "bad habits"—follow an addictive pattern. Most therapists have in their practice individuals who are struggling with "behavioral" addictions, such as pornography, video games, addictive gambling, or addictive procrastination. With some minor modifications, the same therapy procedures can be utilized, as an element of treatment of both addictive behavior patterns and problems with substances.

Several eye movement desensitization and reprocessing (EMDR)-related methods exist for working with addictions, and each has its relative advantages, based on the client's clinical presentation. Desensitization of Triggers and Urges Reprocessing (DeTUR; Popky, 1994, 2005) was the first method to be developed and was originally conceptualized as an urge-reduction protocol that could be used as an element of a comprehensive treatment plan for an addictive disorder. Popky's method basically involves three specific phases: (a) identify and install important positive resources, such as resourcefulness, worthiness, effectiveness, and particularly a positive image of a day in the future, after the person has become free of the addiction; (b) desensitize the urge affect (measured on a 0–10 level of urge [LOU] scale) associated with situational triggers to use; and (c) once the LOU reaches zero urge, for each situational trigger, combine the image of that trigger, now desensitized, with the positive body sensations of the addiction-free day in the future. There are several case study reports (Abel and O'Brian, 2010, 2014; Bae, Han, & Kim, 2015; Bae & Kim, 2012; Cox & Howard, 2007) and a small number of controlled studies (Franklin, 2015; Hase, Schallmayer, & Sack, 2008; Marich, 2009, 2010) providing empirical support for Popky's method. Also, there is evidence that Popky's protocol contributes significantly when added to other programs of treatment of addicted individuals. That is, a comparison between treatment as usual (TAU) and TAU + Popky's procedure, for addicted patients, showed greater reduction in a range of psychiatric symptoms (Carletto et al. 2017). Many experienced EMDR therapists have reported, over the course of many years, that these procedures are effective with people suffering from addictive disorders and impulse control disorders. Knipe, 1998a referenced Popky in describing the treatment of a man in his 50s who strongly identified with an overly idealized, narcissistic self-image. In this man's treatment, Popky's concepts of working with addictive disorders were extended to other types of defenses: the LOU measure was modified to become the level of urge to avoid (LOUA) to assess the strength of this client's avoidance defenses, and the level of positive affect (LOPA; 0–10) procedure was used to measure this man's actual emotional investment in a dysfunctional positive feeling regarding his imagined superiority. Each of these measures was linked with representative memory images, which then were the focus of sets of bilateral stimulation (BLS). Through these procedures, this man was able to relinquish his avoidance defenses and also reduce and resolve the positive affect that was at the core of his narcissistic self-image. The treatment of a person with narcissistic traits has much in common with treatment for addictive disorders, in that both typically involve a part of the personality that is focused on satisfaction of one's own needs while neglecting concerns regarding attachment to others as well as interpersonal responsibilities.

In 2008, Hase and colleagues contributed the concept of an addiction memory (originally defined by Boening, 2001), which is a nonconscious, implicit memory, with craving for a substance as its conscious manifestation. Hase's contribution is very important in that it points out that much of the substrate of memory that drives addictive behavior is implicit and nonconscious. Most addictive states of mind have an aspect that is automatic, and therefore not under direct conscious control. The craving to use, and the memory of the positive feelings after using, can be accessible to the individual, but are generally not very powerfully influenced by cognitive use of "willpower" to alter the addictive behavior. To varying degrees in different individuals, an addiction memory can take on characteristics of a dissociated part of the personality. A person might report, with sincerity, that he or she is very highly motivated to no longer have the addiction. However, later, an addictive state of mind or addictive part will exert control in response to certain situational triggers or disturbing feelings. It is as though there is a part of the personality that only wants to drink, or only wants to smoke, and does not care about the needs and concerns of the person as a whole. This is the disruptive effect of a partially dissociated, partially nonconscious addiction memory. Specific images that bring up this addiction memory—images of moments of craving or memories of relapse—can be targeted directly with sets of BLS, with the likely result that dysfunctional affect will reduce in intensity. More recently, Miller has also developed an EMDR-related method of treating addictions and impulse disorders (2010, 2011), and his approach proposes the use of somewhat different language (e.g., "Feeling States" instead of Hase's addiction memory, or Knipe's LOPA method, based on the concept of a separate ego state that contains dysfunctional positive affect). As with the other methods, the Feeling-State Therapy approach targets, on a 0 to 10 scale, the positive affect that occurs when a person engages in addictive behavior. One hypothesis of Miller's model is that this type of targeting is sufficient for resolving the addiction. In his view, it is not necessary to focus on triggering situations, urges, and ways that addictive behaviors function to suppress or avoid disturbing feelings or memories.

These methods differ not only in the procedures they use, but also in the overall model each has of how addictive disorders begin, and how these behaviors continue, even in the face of strong negative consequences. For example, within the Feeling-State model, it is hypothesized that the sole cause of an addictive disorder is an experience of euphoria in connection with the initial time or times the addiction behavior occurred. This may be true for some addicted individuals; however, in contrast to this perspective, it is important to take into account how, in many cases, adverse childhood experiences are highly correlated with the development of drug and alcohol dependence (Brown, 2013; Felitti et al., 1998). Guo, Hawkins, Hill, and Abbott (2001) in a review found evidence for many ways in which a child's environment predicts a higher likelihood of later alcohol dependence—extreme poverty, parental alcoholism, high levels of family conflict, alcohol dependence within the family, and lack of training for "refusal skills." These findings suggest that addictive disorders do not develop in isolation, but are more likely to develop in connection with difficult childhood stresses. The addictive behavior is a "solution" that is triggered in various ways by external or internal reminders of difficult times. For the majority of people with addictions, it may be unrealistic to separate the immediate positive affect of an addiction from the negative memories and feelings the addictive behavior defends against. Both may be part of the same package of unresolved memory material.

This raises the question: Why do some people develop an addiction, while others from a similar background do not? A partial answer comes from studies that show that certain personality characteristics in children of both sexes at age 11 (high scores on measures of novelty seeking, harm avoidance, and reward dependence) were predictive of chronic alcohol dependence (as assessed by medical records, arrests for driving under the influence (DUI) of alcohol, and treatment for alcohol dependence) at age 27 (Cloninger, Sigvardsson, & Bohman, 1998). A certain neurological marker of vulnerability to chronic alcohol dependence (the P3 component of long-latency event-related potentials [ERPs]) may be partially genetically determined (Begleiter & Porjesz, 1988). Studies comparing concordance rates for alcohol dependence between identical versus fraternal twins have determined a genetic vulnerability to alcohol dependence, especially with regard to development of severe and chronic alcoholism in males (Cloninger, Bohman, & Sigvardsson, 1981). However, these correlational studies also show that the variance accounted for by genetics is lower than other factors—the environmental influences. In other words, many people with this genetic vulnerability do not in fact develop an alcohol problem. Each client is different, of course, and it is important for the therapist to have both a general theoretical overview of addictive conditions and a specific understanding, for each unique client, of the structure of that person's addiction within his or her overall personality.

The hypothesis stated here is that chronic substance addiction often begins with the specific positive biochemical effect of the chemical *combined with* a lessening of posttraumatic disturbance—which then leads, over time, to the creation of a strong, situation-specific urge, and often an addictive part of self. And, it is worth noting that so-called "behavioral addictions" are in fact often linked to internally produced substances—the addictive behavior may result in a surge of dopamine and/or endorphins—strongly increasing positive affect. Thus, the "buzz" associated with an addictive behavior may be due to either externally derived substances, or endogenous chemicals, or both.

For some people, this "buzz" is only an isolated positive experience, without great importance, but for others it may be a powerful solution to a problem in their feelings. The latter individuals would be much more vulnerable to developing an alcohol dependency or an addictive disorder. In those cases, the substance, or the behavioral addiction, facilitates containment of disturbance—an ego state shift away from posttraumatic memory material into a state of lower sympathetic arousal. This is the way the addictive behavior or part is serving a defensive purpose. The therapist needs to know when, in the client's history, the addictive behavior began—and what disturbance did the addictive behavior alleviate? In other words, an addictive substance may initially be viewed as a nice thing!—"Wow! I really like getting high on pot! And when I feel bad because mom and dad are fighting, and I go do pot with my buddies, I feel a lot better! And also, I have all these new buddies!" The addictive behavior may have started out as a positive solution to a problem, but as time passed, it became a bigger problem in itself. This process is illustrated in Figure 6.1.

The sequence of events that creates an addictive disorder can be conceptualized as follows. A person has some type of trauma situation—big T or

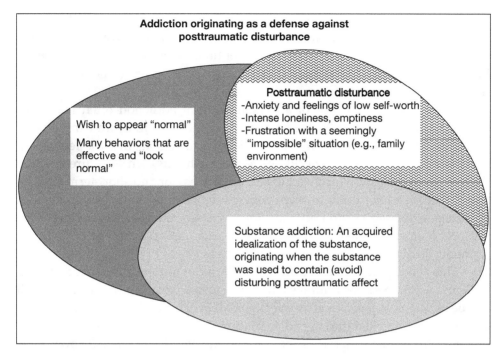

Figure 6.1 Substance addictions are often substance-assisted avoidance. With repetition, the addictive behavior may acquire an idealized (unrealistically positive) subjective value to the person.

little t—traumas of commission or traumas of omission (e.g., family conflict, parental disinterest, or neglect at home). As a result, there are posttraumatic symptoms—memory images, feelings, or negative beliefs about self. At a certain point in time, influenced by peers, media, or addicted family members, the person uses a substance, and this behavior is a solution to a problem. Drugs, alcohol, and/or an addictive pattern of behavior gives relief; with repeated occurrences, the person develops an addiction memory—a craving in response to certain situational or internal triggers. Once this occurs, other behaviors are developed to protect and maintain the addiction. For example, a cigarette smoker will have to have an elevated awareness of where and with whom smoking is permitted. An alcohol-dependent person may attempt to hide his or her level of usage, and may be distracted, at work and in relationships, by the planning of when to have the next drink. Life gets more difficult for a person with an addiction, and the difficulties increase for those substances that are illegal. A chronic illegal addiction can consume the major part of a person's time and energy. There will be certain situations (triggers) that signal an opportunity to use, resulting in a strong urge to use, and culminating in the highly charged positive experience of using, which then reinforces the behavior of using. After the positive feeling wanes, the cycle may continue with fear, regret, or shame about self; this, in turn, contributes to the person being more vulnerable to the next occurrence of a trigger. Or a person may go through a period of particular stress, and the shift into the addicted behavior pattern will initially relieve that stress, and then—perhaps the next day—amplify it. With repetition, the addiction memory will be increasingly linked with memory images, past and present, which then initiate these behavior sequences.

The ego-state structure of a person with an addiction often resembles Figure 6.2. There are unresolved traumas of various kinds, and there is an addictive defense that partially or completely protects against the feelings of posttraumatic disturbance. The addictive defense has its own structure, of situations triggering urges, which lead to addictive behavior and short-term positive affect; then, at a later point in time, perhaps the next day, they lead to feelings of shame, helplessness, and anxiety. As this cycle repeats and continues, the person becomes increasingly vulnerable to each new occurrence of a trigger situation, leading to a downward negative cycle.

This is one pattern, but a different pattern can also be observed, as shown in Figure 6.3. Sometimes traumas will not be identifiable, but the addiction will still be very strong, perhaps after effective EMDR or other therapy with early life events, or perhaps just due to earlier traumas being resolved in the process of living. With this pattern, it is as though the addiction has a life of its own, even after the reasons for the original development of the addiction are resolved.

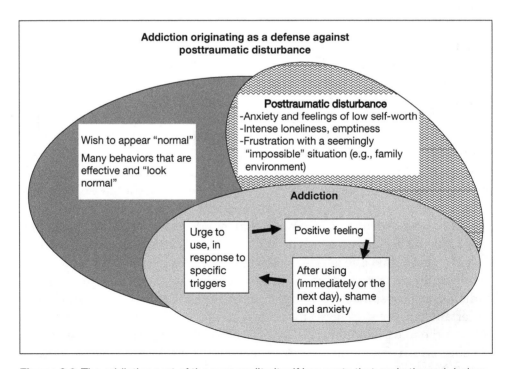

Figure 6.2 The addictive part of the personality itself has parts that cycle through being triggered, using, having a positive feeling, then having negative feelings and negative self-assessment, and finally leading to vulnerability to subsequent triggers.

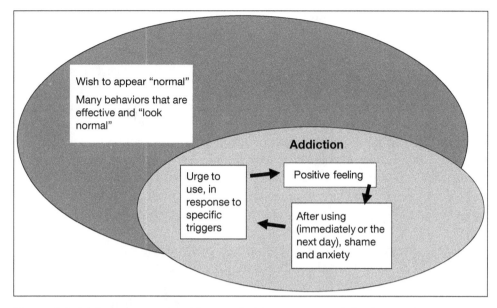

Figure 6.3 Addictive ego state *without* underlying trauma, *or following resolution* of underlying posttraumatic disturbance.

In 12-step programs, it is often said that addictions are "progressive." The recovering alcoholic who has been in sobriety for only a short time might aspire to be able to simply once again have the original high/rush or the "all is quiet in my head" experience. He might say to himself, "When I had my first drink, it was great. Maybe I can go back to just having one drink, and feeling that good feeling again, without it being a problem." It seems, though, that that is not how it works (although there are rare exceptions). A person who has been addicted, or alcohol dependent, usually cannot just "push the reset button" on the addiction. Addictions generally get worse. Typically, if a person who is chronically addicted has a period of sobriety, and then the addictive behavior resumes, he or she is in jeopardy of quickly returning to using at his or her previous high level, with destructive and often catastrophic results.

In addition to these issues, an addictive disorder will make more likely the occurrence of additional traumas (e.g., loss of employment, loss of relationships, other humiliations resulting in diminished self-esteem), which in turn can lead to an increase in using and contribute to a downward spiral.

Use of an addictive substance can initially be a "solution" in a number of different ways. It can be a way of regulating emotions—a high level of anxiety can be taken down to a level that is more comfortable. It also can be a way to escape the memories that created that anxiety. Sometimes, however, in contrast, an addiction can be a way to *access* feelings and memories. There are people who cannot get in touch with their sadness (e.g., regarding the death of a loved one) until they have had several drinks. One woman I saw in therapy years ago drank excessively because, in her words, "Dad didn't usually pay much attention to me, except when he was drinking. That is when we would have some nice conversations. I think I like to drink, in my life now, because it makes me feel close to Dad, even though he died several years ago." It was helpful for her to recognize this connection, and, in therapy, find other ways of comfortably connecting with the memory of her father.

Another example of how alcohol allows access to feelings: Some people have chronic, intense anger, which is bottled up at all times, except when the individual is drinking—which, of course, can be a dangerous problem for any people nearby. However, consistent with the phrase, "In vino, veritas," the individual may experience this anger as a release—"Now, I get to say what I really feel!" Of course, by breaking through this personal problem of their own anger suppression, they may be creating many new problems both for themselves and for others.

Furthermore, drinking and other addictions can be a way of compensating for losses. "I've had a hard day—I'm going to get drunk tonight." Or, "I've had a hard life. . . ." It can be a way of evening the balance of the scales. Another variation on this theme: "I'm a loser, so I might as well just drink (or use drugs). Nothing to lose." And, of course, addictions can be a way to find and keep social connections, which can be valuable for anyone, but particularly for an adolescent with low self-esteem and/or insufficient family support and connection.

In addition to substance addictions, there are many examples of behavioral addictions: eating addictions, such as compulsive eating or bulimia; and compulsive shopping, as in the case of people who max out credit cards for things they do not need. Sexual addictions often occur in the context of an attachment disorder, as a way to experience sexual release without having to risk true intimacy with another person (Carnes, 1989). Television addiction can be a significant problem. Oftentimes, a couple receiving marriage counseling will have a TV addiction as a hidden contributor to their communication problems. Relationships need conversation in order to be maintained, but if one person or the other just watches TV all night, and then goes right to bed, every night, their relationship will become more distant. Excessive TV can be a cause, as well as an effect, of dysfunctional communication. The same may be true of video games or social media involvement.

Elsewhere (Knipe, 2005), a case has been described in which a procrastination problem was conceptualized as an addictive disorder and was targeted successfully with EMDR. Procrastination is a learned avoidance and may be conceptualized as an addiction to "putting things off." It is also similar to other addictions in that it is a way of not facing something that is disturbing or difficult; the next day, however, there is often damage to self-esteem and feelings of self-efficacy when the person looks once again at the closet not having been cleaned, the messy desk, the bills that have not been paid, and so on.

All of the behaviors listed earlier can have a place in a life that is normally functional; however, the behavior becomes an addictive problem when it becomes overly idealized (unrealistically overvalued) and used as a repeated means of avoiding unpleasant feeling, and when it becomes destructive to relationships, workplace functioning, finances, and so on. An addictive pattern of behavior, if allowed to become chronic, will increasingly crowd out and displace other aspects of a "normal" life.

In general, then, it is hypothesized here that addictions continue because there is an addiction-focused part of the personality (often partially dissociated) that manifests in consciousness as a craving (the conscious portion of an implicit addiction memory), and which, in turn, serves to contain or avoid some type of emotional disturbance. In other words, substance addictions usually can be conceptualized as avoidance behavior, and, more often than not, reflect an ongoing conflict between personality parts. Additionally, it adds to the picture to also think of addiction as an example of dysfunctional idealization—of excessive positive emotional investment—in a self-harming behavior. This overvaluation results directly from specific memories of previously seeking and then doing the addictive behavior, and by this means getting both the drug effect and a shift of consciousness away from emotional disturbance. The strong urge can be activated by situational triggers and also by strong posttraumatic disturbance that urgently requires containment. The pull of this urge can often override "willpower."

This is not to say that cognitive aspects of recovery are unimportant—clients' confidence and predictions of their own success for recovery following inpatient treatment are highly correlated with actual success in recovery (Ilgen, McKellar, & Tiet, 2005). And some people are able to stop addictive behavior through strong personal determination and the power of will. But for people with chronic addictions, willpower alone generally will be insufficient to resolve the underlying unfinished debate between the addiction part and the part that does not want the addiction. In 12-step programs, the power of the group is used to effectively bolster the determination of the individual, while also greatly reducing the element of shame connected with the addiction. (It is easier to let go of the inappropriate shame if everyone else in the group also has the same problem.) With EMDR-related methods, we can add additional therapeutic power by directly targeting the addiction itself. All of these interventions can work together to give the addicted person the best shot at recovery.

In working with addictive disorders, background/treatment planning and preparation (EMDR Phases 1 and 2) are particularly important, prior to targeting the dysfunctional memory networks maintaining the addiction. One issue that often comes up in treatment planning is: Which do you target first, past traumas, present triggers to use, or images of the anticipated future?

Clearing out old traumas can definitely be helpful to a person struggling with addiction (Brown, Gilman, Goodman, Adler-Tapia, & Freng, 2015). Working with individuals convicted of a drug-related offense, and referred by the drug court to a drug education program, found that the addition of EMDR sessions to TAU increased the likelihood that participants would complete that program; completion of this type of program is correlated with significantly lower recidivism. At the same time, it is important to realize that, if old disturbing memories are targeted with a person who is still using, or is fragile in his or her sobriety, the work might destabilize the person and result in an increase in the addictive urges. And, to add to the complexity, if the present triggers or positive affect states are the first target, there is a different consideration that must be monitored—processing can go, perhaps unexpectedly, to old memories that are highly emotionally charged and potentially overwhelming. Many addicted clients are in despair regarding the future, and hope—an essential emotion for recovery—is lacking. If EMDR targeting begins with anticipated images in the future, processing will often tend to be more emotionally safe. Hofmann (2009) and Adler-Tapia (2012) have both proposed detailed procedures for resolving feared or dysfunctional events in the future before working with very disturbing issues from the past or the present. Triggers in the present or anticipated triggering stresses in the future may be safer places to start; then these situations, once processed, can serve as empowering resources for the person in working with emotionally charged memory images from the more distant past.

The DeTUR model also focuses on the future, with the recommendation that treatment begin with installation of imagined images of a positive future time when the person no longer has the addiction. This procedure can help the client discover not only a feeling of hope, but also the positive physical sensations that will accompany a new lifestyle of sobriety. These sensations often are an important element in recovery, because they counter (i.e., reciprocally inhibit; Wolpe, 1958) the dysfunctional positive sensations that the person may have, or anticipate, in connection with the addictive behavior.

Hase et al. (2008) recommends a certain approach for treating chronic addictions—an approach of maximizing emotional safety by starting with targeting the addiction memory, accessed by thinking of either a moment of craving or a recent relapse. His research with chronic alcoholics shows evidence that this approach significantly reduces both the craving for alcohol (following treatment and at 1-month follow-up) and relapse rate (at 1-month and 6-month follow-ups), relative to controls.

It is important in the initial history taking that past relapses be explored—information about times when the client tried, unsuccessfully, to quit the addiction. These times are traumas, often involving humiliation, and they can be targeted directly using standard EMDR. Generally, with a client who identifies an addictive problem, it is important to assess the level of motivation (LOM) to quit, using a scale, 0 to 100, with 100 the most. Sometimes though, a client will give a number that is lower than his or her actual motivation, because the client has failed to quit so many times, and does not want to be defeated again. This is a kind of blocking belief ("I can't beat my addiction!") that can be challenged when the person experiences a clear drop in his or her LOU to use and/or in the emotional loading of a positive addictive state. In my practice, I assume that therapeutic interventions are worth trying with clients who have a score on this LOM scale above 50. In order for therapy to be successful, the person's internal motivation is essential—it usually is not enough to be in therapy, or go to 12-step groups, in order to comply with external pressure; this issue often needs to be sorted out in the early stages of therapy.

People who try to quit smoking may relapse up to 30 times before succeeding (this is the average; Reuters, 2016). EMDR may be very helpful in stopping smoking, but at the start of therapy, the individual may be weighed down by past unsuccessful attempts, and have the inaccurate negative cognition, "My addiction is bigger than I am. I will never be able to stop." Targeting memories of relapse can be particularly useful in identifying hidden triggers, or hidden longing for euphoric states, that were driving the relapse.

Blocking beliefs often interfere with a person's attempts to break free of an addiction, and sometimes these beliefs will not be totally apparent in the client's presentation. A Blocking Beliefs Questionnaire (BBQ; Knipe, 1998b) can be useful in identifying such beliefs. These obstacles to quitting can then be targeted and resolved in various ways.

Figure 6.4 shows the BBQ. Items on this questionnaire are in the form of self-referencing statements, which then are evaluated on the same 1 to 7 Validity of Cognition Scale that is used in EMDR Phase 3. This questionnaire is not numerically scored, but is filled out by the client, and then can serve as the basis of discussion between the client and therapist. It is important that the client fill in the space at the top of the questionnaire, "Problem I want to solve_____." All of the items in the questionnaire relate to this identified problem. It is best for the client to describe the problem in a way that clearly leads to a specific outcome. For issues of addiction, the problem statement might be, "I want to stop smoking, but I can't seem to do it." If possible, vague statements, in identifying the problem ("I have a smoking problem"), should be made more goal directed and behaviorally specific.

Very often, blocking beliefs with a high score (generally 4 or above) will indicate an internal conflict between different states of mind, or perhaps even between separate personality parts, each with their own agenda. For some clients, simply identifying the blocking belief will be sufficient for them to overcome it, and proceed with the other steps (described below) to effectively resolve their addiction. For others, more discussion may be necessary. For example, a client might give a score of 6 or 7 for the item, "I've had this problem so long, I never could completely solve it." The therapist might then ask, "If you did solve this problem, and it really was no longer a problem, would that be okay with you?" If the client says "Yes" to this question, the therapist can simply say "Think of that." And initiate a set of BLS. For many clients, this question is likely to significantly shift that particular blocking belief so that it is much less of an obstacle. If the client says "No" to this question, that would strongly indicate

Name _____   Date ____/____/____

PROBLEM I WANT TO SOLVE _____

Please rate each statement on a scale from 1 = "feels completely untrue" to 7 = "feels completely true."

1.	I'm embarrassed that I have this problem.	1	2	3	4	5	6	7
2.	I'm not sure I want to get over this problem.	1	2	3	4	5	6	7
3.	If I solve this problem, I will feel deprived.	1	2	3	4	5	6	7
4	I don't have the strength or the will power to get over this problem.	1	2	3	4	5	6	7
5.	If I really talk about this problem, something bad will happen.	1	2	3	4	5	6	7
6.	This is a problem that can only be solved by someone else.	1	2	3	4	5	6	7
7.	If I ever solve this problem, I will lose a part of who I really am.	1	2	3	4	5	6	7
8.	I don't want to think about this problem anymore.	1	2	3	4	5	6	7
9.	I should solve this problem, but I don't always do what I should.	1	2	3	4	5	6	7
10.	I like people who have this problem better than people who don't.	1	2	3	4	5	6	7
11.	It could be dangerous for me to get over this problem.	1	2	3	4	5	6	7
12.	When I try to think about this problem, I can't keep my mind on it	1	2	3	4	5	6	7
13.	I say I want to solve this problem, but never do.	1	2	3	4	5	6	7
14.	It could be bad for someone else for me to get over this problem.	1	2	3	4	5	6	7
15.	If I get over this problem, I can never go back to having it again	1	2	3	4	5	6	7
16.	I don't deserve to get over this problem.	1	2	3	4	5	6	7
17.	This problem is bigger than I am.	1	2	3	4	5	6	7

(continued)

18.	If I got over this problem, it would go against my values.	1	2	3	4	5	6	7
19.	Someone in my life hates this problem.	1	2	3	4	5	6	7
20.	There are some good things about having this problem.	1	2	3	4	5	6	7
21.	Frankly, I don't have a problem.	1	2	3	4	5	6	7
22.	I've had this problem so long, I could never completely solve it.	1	2	3	4	5	6	7
23.	I have to wait to solve this problem.	1	2	3	4	5	6	7
24.	If I solve this problem, I could lose a lot.	1	2	3	4	5	6	7
25.	If I solve this problem, it will be mainly for someone else.	1	2	3	4	5	6	7

Figure 6.4 Blocking Beliefs Questionnaire (Knipe, 1998b).

some type of unfinished internal discussion or dialogue within the client, and it is likely to be helpful to identify this issue, and then perhaps proceed with an internal healing dialogue, as described in Chapter 14.

The BBQ can also be used to identify and target dysfunctional beliefs that arise with other problems, in addition to addictive disorders.

Another related obstacle might be any negative experience previously associated with 12-step programs. When an addicted person enters psychotherapy, a commonly encountered attitude is, "If my therapist tells me I have to go to a 12-step group, I'm quitting this therapy!" With sufficient rapport, and compassion from the therapist, this self-destructive attitude of avoidance can be worked with, using standard EMDR or some of the avoidance-targeting methods described in Chapter 4. For example, the therapist might say, "When you visualize actually arriving in your car outside an Alcoholics Anoymous meeting location, how much, 0 to 10, do you just want to get back in your car and go home?" Or, "As you visualize walking in the door of the meeting room and imagine seeing the other participants, what is your negative thought about them? What is your negative thought about yourself? What other thought about yourself, that is more positive, would you like to have instead at that moment? As you visualize the other people at the AA meeting, how true, on a scale of 1 to 7, does that more positive thought about yourself feel? What is the emotion you are experiencing as you are standing there in the doorway? 0 to 10, how strong is that emotion? Where do you feel that in your body?" And then, the therapeutic processing can continue with focused sets of BLS sets of BLS. A client might be asked to "run a movie" in imagery, regarding attendance at a 12-step meeting, from start to finish, and every moment of aprehension or avoidance in that movie can become a target, with the ultimate goal of running the entire movie without disturbance or avoidance.

And with regard to the interaction between Alcoholics Anonymous and psychotherapy, it is important to note that therapy itself sometimes can be used as an avoidance defense. A person might say, "Yes, I'm still drinking, but at least I'm going to therapy!" What the individual really needs to do is stop drinking, and the peer support of 12-step programs may be crucial, perhaps more crucial than therapy, in the person's recovery.

Generally, with a client who identifies an addictive problem, it is important to assess the LOM to quit, using a scale, 0 to 100, with 100 the most. Sometimes though, a client will give a number that is lower than his or her actual motivation, because the client has failed to quit so many times and does not want to be defeated again. This is a kind of blocking belief (e.g., "I can't defeat my addiction!") that can be challenged or even neutralized when the person experiences a clear drop in his or her LOU to use and/or in the emotional loading of a positive addictive state. In my practice, I assume that therapeutic interventions are worth trying with clients who have a score on this scale above 50. In order for the therapy to be successful, the person's internal motivation is essential—it usually is not enough to be in therapy, or go to 12-step groups, in order to comply with external pressure; this issue often needs to be sorted out in the early stages of therapy.

An important step in preparation is the installation of needed positive resources (Popky, 1994, 2005). For example, feelings of empowerment: "When did you really want to do something, and you set your mind on it, and you did it? When did that happen? Can you get a picture of that?" Another important resource is worthiness: "When in your life have you really known your own worth? Perhaps it was when you were with someone who held you in high regard. Or maybe it was when you had pride in an accomplishment. When was that?" With regard to worthiness, it is useful sometimes to ask the client, "Could you accept yourself completely, even if you never get over this addiction?" This may seem like an odd question, but it is often useful for the client to separate concerns regarding self-worth from treatment for the addictive disorder. This is a tricky issue, because if a person has an ongoing addiction problem, that problem may be bringing ruin to his or her life. But sometimes a person has an addictive disorder and is thinking, **"If I keep having this addiction, that proves I'm a bad person. If I were a good person, I could quit."** Often you will see this dichotomous way of thinking with smokers. The therapist can say to the client, "There are many fine people in this world who smoke. And there are many real jerks who don't smoke! The issue here it is not *whether you are a worthy person*. It is just that, if you continue smoking, you will get one package of results, and if you stop smoking, you will get another package of results. So the question is, which package would you prefer? This isn't about your worth—it's just about smoking." If the client is able to get this distinction, it makes all of the targeting much less complicated.

For many clients, a positive goal state resource (Popky, 2005) is often even more important in the therapy than identifying triggers and positive affect states, because this resource "pulls" the individual into becoming addiction free, while providing some compensation for the feeling of deprivation that may come when the addictive behavior is discontinued. The therapist asks, "Can you think of a day in the future when you no longer have this addiction? What good things would be part of your life on that day that you don't have today because you still have the addiction?" Then, whatever the client says in response to this question, the therapist can make a list of the good things. It can be money, self-respect, health, energy, the opportunity to see children or grandchildren graduate from school, a feeling of "wholeness" without secrets, and so on. From this list, therapist and client construct a positive visual image of the day in the future when the addictive problem is gone. "What would be good about that day when there is no longer a craving for that drink after work? Or, . . . that extra piece of cheesecake?" "What would be good about that day when you don't even think about cigarettes anymore?"

In this future image, it is not just that the client is no longer doing the addictive behavior—it is that the client no longer has an *interest* in doing it. As a reference point, the therapist can ask the client to think of something about which he or she has *absolutely no* interest. For example, a smoker might have no interest in ever trying heroin or methamphetamines. Or, the therapist might say, "If someone asked you this afternoon to go bungee jumping, would you be interested in that?" Most clients would say "No!" If the client likes bungee jumping, something else can be found. It is helpful for the client to have the sense of feeling "no interest." That "no-interest" feeling is an essential element of the "day in the future" image, and we can strengthen the felt reality and positive feelings associated with this image with sets of BLS. Popky suggests "anchoring" (Bandler & Grinder, 1976) these positive body sensations by tapping on the client's hand. I have found it useful to install these positive feelings by asking clients to use alternating hand taps on their own shoulders—a modified "butterfly hug" (Artigas, Jarero, Mauer, López Cano, & Alcalá, 2000)—while thinking of and enjoying what would be positive about that day in the future. This strengthens the associational connection between the tapping and the positive body sensations that will be part of full resolution and sobriety. And then, during later processing, an alternative method of BLS—eye movements, hand taps by the therapist, alternating tones, or alternating buzzers—can be used, in order to differentiate resource installation from processing of urges.

Generally, the primary triggers to use need to be identified. A trigger is a situation, thought, feeling, or memory that elicits an urge, or a high likelihood of using. There may be just a few triggers, or dozens, and the triggers may be logically inconsistent with each other. A standard joke in AA circles is, "My team just won—I'm going to go get drunk!—My team just lost—I'm going to go get drunk!" There may be primary triggers that frequently occur in the person's current life, and other, more hidden triggers that might emerge only after a person has stopped using. For example, an individual in sobriety might say, "Gee, I haven't had a drink in 6 months. That wasn't too hard. Maybe I'm not really an alcoholic. Maybe I can go back into that bar again and see all my friends." And then once the person is in the bar there may be a flood of images and smells that are triggers for an urge to drink. This is known in Alcoholics Anonymous as "stinkin' thinkin'"—the way rationalization, during sobriety, can be intense and in the service of the part of self that just wants to continue drinking. This illustrates two issues: (a) the importance of identifying hidden triggers and (b) the frequent importance of using a parts model, or an ego-state model, in working with people who are substance dependent.

Also, for many addicted individuals, it is important to identify the anticipated positive experience that occurs when the person acts on urges—the feeling of actually doing the addictive behavior (Knipe, 2005; Miller, 2010). The client can be asked, "When you have that urge, what is the feeling, or the state of mind that you are seeking with the urge?" Sometimes, when I am working with a person who wants to stop smoking, I will suggest that he or she try a "healthy cigarette" right there in the office. I demonstrate a "healthy cigarette" first, by holding my hand to my mouth, looking at the ceiling, taking a very satisfying deep breath, and slowly letting that breath out. This action, in itself, gives a pleasant calm feeling (a feeling that is independent of, but can be mistaken for, a direct effect of the nicotine). Then the client is asked to do the same, and enjoy the sensations of vividly imagining intake of smoke. As the client continues to experience this exercise, we will do several sets of BLS. This procedure targets the specific positive feeling that occurs when smoking, but without the specific nicotine effect. The urge, or pull, of this feeling can then be desensitized. These steps can heighten the client's awareness of how much of the positive feeling associated with smoking is actually not intrinsic to smoking. Typically, after this exercise, the client will report a lessening of an urge for an actual cigarette.

For some clients, it may be more efficient to target, with BLS, the positive affect states that occur during the addictive behavior rather than the many triggers that are driving addictive urges. For example, in Chapter 15, a case from 2007 is described (Veronica) in which the targeting of urges was initially tried, but with only limited success. This client was able to break through and resolve an addictive behavior (excessive consumption of sugar drinks) through targeting the high positive affect held within a separate child part—a part that was still living in trauma time, and using the addictive behavior as a way to cope with traumas that were long over. Once the adult client was able to look at her childhood self with compassion and see the connection between the addictive behavior and trauma, this client was able to permanently let go of the addiction.

The approach—of identifying and targeting positive affect states that are serving a defensive purpose—can be fairly straightforward for some clients, but more difficult for others. Because an addiction memory is an implicit memory, partially outside of conscious awareness, verbal labeling of the addictive positive affect state may be difficult for some people. For example, a woman in her

50s, recently diagnosed with emphysema, came to therapy to try to eliminate her habit of smoking nearly two packs a day. Actually, her motivation to stop smoking was not very high—she said it was only about a "10 to 20" on the 0 to 100 LOM scale. A period of 6 months elapsed from the time of her visit with the doctor to the time of calling for an appointment for therapy. It became clear early in our sessions that this reluctance was due to the fact that she was using cigarettes to facilitate dissociation from extremely troubling childhood memories, as well as related memories from her adult life. At the beginning of therapy, she reported that she would sometimes light one cigarette, leave it in the ashtray burning, and then light another without any awareness of the first. It was only after nearly 2 years of treatment, focused on resolving horrible events of her childhood and helping her begin to integrate her dissociative personality structure, that she was able to stop smoking entirely. Once the larger personality issues were moving toward resolution, she was able to relinquish the smoking, which had served as a defense against feelings originating in her early life—feelings of being abused, frequently shamed, and overly controlled by her parents.

When the time came in therapy to target her smoking, she was able to easily tell me the main trigger situations for the behavior, but was unable to identify any LOU, or positive feeling, connected with these triggers. She was able to benefit from the Popky's method through the use of a slight modification. I asked her, "As you think of fixing dinner (a trigger), and you really imagine being there, what is the probability, 0% to 100%, that you will light up a cigarette?" She was easily able to answer this question (it was initially 100%!), although without a felt sense of urge in her body sensations, or anticipation of any positive feeling connected with a cigarette. We then proceeded with sets of BLS, and her probability score for that specific trigger situation went down to zero. During subsequent weeks, we proceeded with three other triggers in the same way. It was very useful for her to reaccess the "day in the future" resource following the successful work with each trigger. Following these sessions, she reported that she had stopped smoking completely. A year later, her husband came for a brief episode of therapy with me; and during our discussions, he verified that she truly had discontinued smoking. This is an example of how smoking behavior, associated with triggers, can be desensitized, even if the affective element of the urges is partially or completely dissociated.

Within an addictive person's memory networks, triggers and urges are often linked through association to positive affect states, and vice versa. The experience of an urge usually contains anticipation of a positive feeling, associated with using. In the process of desensitizing a particular trigger, channels of memory information will emerge and be resolved; these channels will usually include the salient positive feelings that occur while using. Conversely, the identification of a euphoric, addiction-related feeling will typically be related to specific triggering events. With addictions we should look for the best and safest target of opportunity—if the positive affect state is readily available, and there is sufficient emotional stability, target the state. If the positive state is difficult to verbalize, or not so obvious, and the urges related to situational triggers are quite accessible, target those, and listen for the emergence of core positive affect as processing goes through channels. Either approach can work quite well, though I think the advantage goes to targeting the urges associated with specific situational triggers, as opposed to a verbally identified positive affect state, since the urge is a more immediate experience, as opposed to a concept introduced by the therapist, which is one step removed from the immediate experience. With this caveat in mind, a good guideline is to be ready to use either approach; if one is not entirely successful, use the other. In other words, if all the triggers are desensitized, but the person is still using, or tempted, look for hidden positive states connected with using. If all the identified positive states are apparently resolved, but the person is continuing to use, or has urges, look for hidden triggers!

Oftentimes, an addiction may be driven by several separate motivations. Figures 6.5 to 6.7 show how a therapist can use the hands to illustrate, for a client, the complexity that occurs oftentimes in resolving an addictive disorder. An addiction may be held in place, in spite of its destructive effects on a person's life, by multiple factors, which might include avoidance of disturbing memories, avoidance of other trauma-related material, euphoric feelings, the use of the addictive behavior to facilitate dissociation, identification of self with the addictive behavior, helplessness about quitting, and many other factors that together create a web that traps the individual in a behavior that is ongoing and self-destructive. The clenched fingers in Figure 6.5 provide a way of illustrating this complexity. As therapy proceeds, the grip of the addiction begins to weaken (Figure 6.6). Finally, with successful targeting of each of these elements, the addiction is broken (Figure 6.7). This simple metaphor, using the hands, has been useful to many clients in helping them understand the multiple ways that their addictive disorder maintains its grip.

The following transcript illustrates how each of these EMDR-related protocols is related to each other and overlap. The transcript is taken verbatim from a video recording of a therapy session that occurred in 2005. The structure of the session follows Popky's DeTUR protocol—it occurred prior to the development of the CravEx and Feeling-State approaches. However, within this session, both the importance of targeting the situational trigger and the importance of processing addiction memories can be seen. I am grateful to the woman in this session for her generous permission to write about her experience.

"Hunaida" was a therapist, age 35, in a developing country. I was a trainer and she was a participant in trainings organized by the EMDR Humanitarian Assistance Program (now called Trauma Recovery). The training, and this session, took place in an area of the world with frequent and ongoing traumatization for many of the people who live there. In the training, I had mentioned how

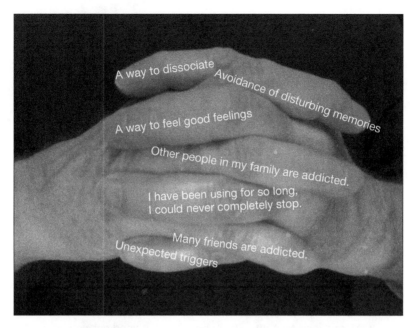

Figure 6.5 Clenched fingers can symbolize the many separate factors (dysfunctional channels of information) that maintain the tight hold of an addictive disorder.

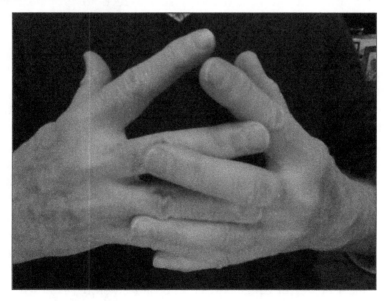

Figure 6.6 During the process of recovery, the addiction begins to loosen its grip.

the Popky's DeTUR protocol could be used to treat a smoking addiction. This therapist contacted me during a break and stated that she was determined to stop smoking, and she requested a session to begin work on this. I agreed on the condition that she follow up this session and complete any necessary ongoing

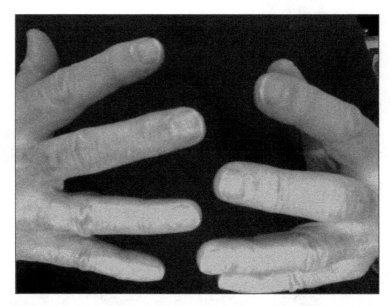

Figure 6.7 Finally, the grip is released, though vigilance may be needed for a long time after the person has obtained sobriety—the hands may remain in close proximity.

work with a local EMDR-trained therapist. I agreed to provide continuing consultation to her therapist by email, as needed. She agreed to this plan.

Hunaida had begun smoking at age 21, and up until approximately a month before this session, she had been a very heavy smoker. In the days before our session, she had been able to cut down her smoking to approximately 10 cigarettes per day, through determination and willpower, but she had not been able to reduce the usage below that. She had many positives that were potentially helpful in her effort to quit. She was not using smoking to dissociate or to contain unresolved posttraumatic disturbance. In addition, she had arranged her social environment to support her goal of quitting—she had told several friends that she would try to stop smoking on the day of our session!

This session occurred late in the afternoon after the last day of the EMDR training program. The following transcript illustrates several elements of Popky's approach, particularly the identification and installation of the "day in the future" positive goal state resource, and then the identification and targeting of the most powerful triggering situation for smoking. Following Popky's protocol, I asked Hunaida for a representative visual image of this trigger, a 0 to 10 score for an associated LOU to smoke, and the location of the urge in body sensations. For the following transcript, as was the case for the transcripts in Chapters 4 and 5, [EM] indicates where I have said to her, "Notice that," or "Stay with that," or "Think of that," combined with a set of 20 to 30 sweeps of eye movements.

Hunaida: Whenever I have a cold, I have a lot of coughing, not like normal people, and always I have problems with my throat and my lungs, and it stays for a long time, and I don't like it. (Coughs.)

Therapist: What would you like to have happen here? What would even surprise you, something really good?

Hunaida: A feeling or an incident? No more do I want to smoke. I don't want to have this urge that I need to put this between my fingers and smoke.

Therapist: You'd like to have something happen so you don't have the urge to smoke anymore?

Hunaida: Yes. When I have the triggers, it's very strong.

Therapist: I'm going to ask you some focused questions, and just answer whatever is true. **(Hunaida: Okay.)** *What would you say your motivation is right now? Let's say 100 is that quitting smoking is extremely important to you and 0 is no motivation at all.*

Hunaida: You know, I *need* to stop. I *want* to stop. Let's say 90 out of 100!

Therapist: Okay. As you said, you know you need *to stop but how much do you* want *to stop? . . . because they are different.* **(Hunaida: I *want* to stop.)** *Good.*

Development of the Positive Goal State

Therapist: So, I am going to ask, then, for you to think of a day in the future when you have stopped smoking completely. And think of it this way: It's not just that you are not smoking anymore; you don't even have an interest *any more.*

Hunaida: Oh, I don't have an interest to smoke.

Therapist: Yes, you remember that once you were a smoker but you don't think of it now. It was a long time ago, and you just don't think about smoking anymore.

If someone said to you, in the middle of the day, "Let's go get drunk right now," you would probably say, "I don't want to do that." **(Hunaida: That's right.)** *And so what I am saying is—realize what the* feeling *is of not having an interest at all in something. In other words, some people have horrible problems with other addictions, but you don't. So, that's a model for you, of what it would mean to not have any interest at all in smoking.* **(Hunaida: Ahh, yes, okay.)** *That is what I am saying. That is an interesting idea. Just think of that.* **[EM]**

Hunaida: I'm trying to feel that day in the future. *(Therapist: Let's talk about that day.)* **I'm trying to find a situation. . . .**

I'm staying in the house with my children and I am not smoking. My children are healthy. I am healthy. I'm not coughing. I'm having a very nice time drinking coffee, without having that urge, or having that interest to go and get a cigarette. And I can see the pack of cigarettes in front of me and I'm not touching it. *(Therapist: Okay.)* **I need to go to that place.**

Therapist: So you are in that house, with your children. It's healthy for you. It's healthy for your children. **[Hunaida: I'm doing it also for my children. (Cough.)]** *And you are having a nice cup of coffee. And on this day in the future, you are breathing very easily, it's not like the cough you are having right now.*

Hunaida: And another reason for stopping cigarettes is—I play sports a lot and I am on a volleyball team, and when I work hard, I feel like my breath is going to stop, and I am ashamed of that feeling. I am ashamed.

Therapist: So, that's a good reason to want to stop smoking. And can you imagine playing volleyball, and you have so much breath that you never get out of breath, such good energy all the time? **[Hunaida: Yes, very good.]** *Let's say you are in your house, and you are having a cup of coffee, and today is a day when later you are going to play volleyball. And you're just thinking about it as you are having your cup of coffee. And you feel healthy. And you are breathing easily and deeply, and it feels good. And you can remember, just thinking about it, you can realize that when you play volleyball these days you have lots of energy and it's really fun. You can do things now that you couldn't do before when you were out of breath. So, just kind of be in this picture and enjoy it. What else is there that would make it even more positive?*

Hunaida: More positive? The breath. I need my breath not only in volleyball but in other sports. I need to stop smoking because— when I win, I don't want to be breathing so hard.

Therapist: So go back again to this day in the future when you've stopped smoking, and you're not interested in cigarettes any more. Someone else might talk about smoking, but you don't have an interest in it any more. So, just try to imagine being at the table with your coffee, and your children are there, and you can see that they have lots of energy too because the air is fresh, and they are healthy, and you are breathing so easily. I know right now you are having trouble breathing, but just imagine that in this picture, you're thinking that later today, you are going to do some aerobics and some jogging. And it's so nice when you can run as fast as the wind, and it's terrific, and you never get out of breath. It just feels so good, and it's like . . . a real pleasure to be able to do that. So, let yourself enjoy that right now, and just kind of step into that picture so that it's bright and clear, and with colors, and you can see it like you are there. And, is that a nice picture? Are you able to enjoy that right now? (**Hunaida: Yes.**) *So, really enjoy that. And just tap your shoulders back and forth. Stay with the nice feelings. That's good. How does that feel?* (**Hunaida: Good.**) *Now, notice where that good feeling is in your physical sensations.* (**Hunaida: In my heart.**) *Notice that. Just enjoy that. That's good.*

Just really enjoy being there, feeling so healthy. That's good. This feeling is there as a resource for you. (**Hunaida: Yes.**) *So now we are going to shift. Put that resource over here on the shelf.*

Finding the Most Powerful Trigger

Therapist: And now, what is the most powerful trigger for smoking for you?

Hunaida: The most powerful?

Therapist: Maybe you can think of four or five, but just pick the biggest one.

Hunaida: The biggest one, I can't determine. Today I tried so much . . . with the coffee.

Therapist: So, coffee is a trigger for you.

Hunaida: Yes, it is. I pushed it and I pushed it but I couldn't control it. It still is a trigger. And, lunch, after lunch was so hard! And when I enter my home . . . that is a very big trigger!

Therapist: So these are three different triggers.

Hunaida: And parties! And trips! Whenever I am happy, I love cigarettes.

Therapist: You know, before we stop today, since we only have this 1 hour to work, I will go over some things that you can do on your own, that will help you with all these triggers. And I'm glad you will be able to keep working on it with _____ (an experienced, local EMDR therapist).

Hunaida: Yes. The biggest trigger I maybe can say is when I am in a restaurant. In the restaurant, I love to smoke.

Therapist: So let's start with that. What we will be doing here will take the urge down, but this is not a test of your goodness as a human being. (**Hunaida: Yes.**) *This is a no-failure approach. We're going to work on something to help you with the urge, but then after you leave here, in the next day, or the next hour, if something happens and you smoke, that doesn't mean you are a terrible person. This is only about smoking.*

Hunaida: Yes. It doesn't mean I am bad. But it does affect me. I want to be strong, and then the weakness appears. But whatever happens, I *do* accept myself even if I never stop smoking. I accept myself.

Therapist: Okay. That's good. So now, get a picture of being in a restaurant, and have it be a particular restaurant. Have it be in the restaurant where you always go.

Hunaida: *In all*! I smoke in all, but there are one or two . . . I always go there. I will pick the one where I am noticed by everybody, that I am smoking, and I don't like that. . . so I need to pick that one. I pick that one.

Therapist: So be there right now. Get a picture of being there. Have it be that you have cigarettes. **(Hunaida: Okay.)** *And they are right there on the table.* **(Hunaida: Okay.)** *With a lighter.* **(Hunaida: Okay.)** *What else is there?*

Hunaida: There is a friend there, who always goes with me.

Therapist: Your friend is there and you're having a good time? **(Hunaida: Okay.)** *Be there now, and have a clear picture in your mind so that you are really there, and having a good time talking and joking, and the cigarettes are right there. So, here is my question, with the cigarettes right there, how much (0 to 10), when you think of that, do you have an urge to smoke?* **[Hunaida closes her eyes and bows down her head at this point.]** *As if I didn't know.*

Hunaida: Ten! [Ironic laughing.] My hand starts moving. I want to take it.

Therapist: Yes, I understand. So, be aware of the 10, where do you feel that 10 in your physical sensations, right now, when you are right there at the table with your friend?

Hunaida: My heart is going: Bump, bump, bump, and my hand wants to touch it.

Therapist: Okay. Now scan through, and see if there are any other sensations that go along with that. See what else there is.

Hunaida: I don't know exactly. Maybe *all of me* wants to smoke.

Targeting the Choice Point—The Moment Just Before Beginning the Addictive Action

Therapist: Just be aware of that. And, the friend is there and the cigarettes are there and the ashtray is there, the lighter is there, and you are having a good time, you are talking, and it's a 10, and your hand wants to go pick up the cigarette, and you feel it in your heart. Just stay with that. You haven't chosen to do it yet. You haven't reached for it yet, you just want to. Just be aware of how much you want to and follow my fingers. That's good. **[EM]** *And now go back to the same moment, you haven't chosen it yet, the cigarettes are there. What do you get now? Might not change. . . .*

Hunaida (with her left hand grasping her right hand): Yes, yes. I didn't pick them. I was struggling not to, I was struggling not to take them. *(Therapist: Think of that.)* **[EM]** *(Therapist: Just stay with that.)* **I pushed the cigarettes into the corner, so as not to see them anymore.** *(Therapist: Stay with that.)* **[EM] I went and bought hot chocolate. Always at that restaurant, we have to have hot chocolate. Hot chocolate is what I have. And I sat down.**

Therapist: So now, go, do this, go back again to the picture we started with— before you pushed the cigarettes away. They are still there. You haven't chosen yet. You are talking with your friend. **(Hunaida: I can imagine it.)** *And now, right when you imagine it, use the numbers (0 to 10). How strong is the urge?*

Hunaida: It is less. It doesn't feel like it's as much anymore. Ten to seven.

Therapist: What's different?

Hunaida's awareness of her hand expresses a coconscious but separate smoker part of the personality.

Hunaida: What's different is . . . my hand. Before my hand was here, and I was holding my hand to keep it from moving, but now I'm sitting like this (more upright) and I am feeling a little bit free of my hand picking the pack of cigarettes. *(Therapist: Notice that difference. Notice how that is different and better.)* **Yes, I feel more comfortable.**

Therapist: Stay with that. **[EM]** *Good, now take another deep breath. What do you get now? What comes into your mind right now?*

Hunaida: I still can see the same picture. The pack of cigarettes is in front of me, and the lighter. But, we're having a good time, with my friend, talking about people going out and in, in and out; we're having a good time. *(Therapist: You have lots of things to say about everybody.)* **Yes.**

Therapist: Just think of that. **[EM]** *What comes into your mind now?*

Hunaida: What came into my mind? Someone my friend loves comes into the front of the restaurant and she's so happy. I'm so happy for her.

Therapist: Think of that. **[EM]** *What do you get now?*

Hunaida: About the same scene? He said hello. And he went out, but we continued having a good time . . . and I forgot the cigarettes! [Laughs.]

Therapist: You forgot to smoke! **(Hunaida: Yes!)** *Think of that.* **[EM]**

Therapist: You're sitting down with your friend. You are laughing, the cigarettes are there, what do you get now?

Hunaida: I put the pack of cigarettes in my bag, and the lighter. And the ashtray, I used to bring it from the table next to me, I put the ashtray back to the table so as to get rid of it.

Therapist: Think of that. **[EM]** *So go back again to the picture we started with, the cigarettes are still there on the table, the lighter is there, the ashtray is there. You're talking back and forth with your friend, 0 to 10, right now . . .*

Hunaida: It is a 5. It is 5. I know if I am in this situation right now I would have put them in my bag. I would have thrown them there.

Therapist: Think of that. **[EM]** *It's still a 5 not a 0. Talk about that 5.*

Hunaida: The 5 means I still want to smoke but it isn't that same urge. It's relaxed a bit.

Therapist: Notice the difference. **[EM]** *Take a deep breath. Go back to it again. What do you get now?*

Hunaida: What do I get now? I feel, like I don't want to smoke. I haven't the urge to smoke. Right now, I feel that.

Therapist: Notice how that feels. Notice how that feels. **[EM]**

Hunaida: I don't know. Maybe it's less. It's less than before. But still, there is something. I'm not going to lie. *(Therapist: No, don't lie.)*

Processing continues in this way, as we move through channels of memory information driving the smoking urge. These channels are experienced by the client as feelings, as nonverbal—difficult to express in words. Five minutes later, the LOU score has dropped even further.

Therapist: It was a 10, then a 7, and now, a 3. What's different from when we started?

Hunaida: *The urge*. It's as if it is a close friend of mine that should be with me. I'm not separated from it at all. I always have a pack of cigarettes in my bag and at home, in a drawer and on a table. But now,

I feel that I will not put it in my bag. I will not take it with me to the restaurant. [EM] This situation has given me a lot of strength.

Therapist: Do you mean what we are doing here right now?

Hunaida: Yes, yes! Given me a lot of strength. I am trying to imagine myself tonight. I'm going to meet my friend. I'm going from here to the restaurant, to that restaurant where I *always* smoke . . . and I will do my best.

Therapist: Just think of that. Just think of how it will really be. [**EM**]

Hunaida: We are sitting without cigarettes and my friend asks me, "Don't you want to smoke?" I tell her, I've stopped smoking! She is looking at me. [Hunaida makes a face.]

Therapist: So she is looking at you that way? Think of that. [**EM**] *It seems like something is happening here that will make it easier to actually not smoke. But notice that there still may be a little bit of urge there.*

Hunaida: There is. I am not going to lie.

Therapist: Don't lie. Even though, in the restaurant, you might not smoke, you still might have the urge. You might think, "Oh, I want to but I can't." So, go back again and see what is still there. Even though you chose not to smoke, how much urge is still there?

Hunaida: If a pack of cigarettes is in front of me, if it's in front of me, I can tell you it's still a 3.

Therapist: Tell me about that "3."

Hunaida (looking at her hand): It's like I want to. . . . No! . . . I want to. . . . No! . . . I want to. . . . *Stop it!* Don't smoke. Finished. It's *me* that is preventing my hand to go. . . . But my hand is much easier now.

Therapist: Just notice that urge that's still there. Stay with that. [**EM**]

Hunaida: When I think of the urge, it goes from 2 to 1 now. It is less, but I can't say it is a zero. Because I feel that it is *still in me*. If I say it is a zero, that means maybe I'm lying to myself. Because it is still in me.

Therapist: Stay with that. [**EM**] *That's good.*

Therapist: So if you are true with yourself, what do you get?

Hunaida: How much is the urge? [*Therapist: Yes.*] **Trying to go back to the restaurant where the box of cigarettes is in front of me, part of me is saying, "Yes it is down," but part of me is saying, "Don't lie to yourself. It's still there. There is something."**

Therapist: It couldn't be true that this could be so easy. **(Hunaida: Yes.)** [EM]

Two minutes later . . .

Hunaida: It might be zero (said with hesitation).

Therapist: So it may be zero, but it might not be zero?

Hunaida: With a pack of cigarettes in front of me? (*Therapist: Yes.*) **It might be zero.** (*Therapist: It might be zero but it might not be zero?*) **(Long pause, then laughing.) It's a half!**

Therapist: Okay. Stay with that. [EM]

Interweave to Assist the Client in Disconnecting Smoking From Other Positive Experiences

Therapist: Can you think of all the lovely times you've had, smoking in that restaurant? Just think of all the lovely times you've had . . . smoking in that restaurant. Think of how nice that was, to smoke. Just let yourself really enjoy that.

Hunaida: Hmm. I love it. [Long pause.] I feel like it's in the past.

Therapist: Stay with that. [EM]

Hunaida: I feel like—I am born now. The smoker has passed away and the new one has come. I'm sitting in the same restaurant without cigarettes.

Therapist: Stay with that. [EM] *Is there even a little trace of urge?*

Hunaida: No. None. None whatsoever.

Therapist: So it feels like a total zero?

Hunaida: Yes, total zero.

This zero was very different, and much stronger, than the previous "zero." I asked her to linger for another set of eye movements on the feeling of being completely without urge for cigarettes, just to help her place this feeling more clearly in the memory. Then I asked her to access the physical sensations of the positive goal state by just doing the alternating taps on her shoulders. This tapping tends to bring up the positive feelings of the "day in the future" resource, even without naming this resource. These positive feelings, then, are strengthened as a new association to the previously powerful smoking trigger.

> *Therapist: Just realize, this is what total zero feels like.* [EM] *In the restaurant, see the pack of cigarettes in front of you, hold that picture in your mind and again, tap your shoulders, and just be there. Just enjoy being there.* (**Alternating shoulder taps.**)

> *Therapist: That's good. That's good. What would you say that you are seeing today? You may be surprised to be able to see something.*

> **Hunaida: You mean what happened today? I'm going to say . . . I'm going to open my mouth and say [Laughs.]—I was thinking of the pictures, and I was into it, and I was completely into it, and I feel much stronger. I feel strong and free of something that was holding me.**

> *Therapist: Just think of that.* [EM]

Installation of the Positive Cognition, and an Interweave to Help the Client Generalize to Other Triggers

> *Therapist: Right now, just let yourself go through all the other triggers, just think of them. You don't have to make yourself feel any particular way but just think of that feeling—I am strong. And think of as many triggers as you can think of right now.* [EM] *That's good. And what are you getting?*

> **Hunaida: I feel like I can do the same in those other situations, the same as I did in the restaurant.**

> *Therapist: Good. And again, think of those. Think of each one. Pause with each one so you can really get a sense of how you can be strong in that situation.* [EM] *That's good.*

> **Hunaida: Okay. [Nods head.] I can be strong. I *am* strong.**

> *Therapist: Stay with that.* [EM] *So, is this a good stopping point for today?* (**Hunaida: Yes.**)

The next day, I returned to the United States, but later learned that Hunaida had gone to see the local therapist about 3 weeks after our session, and in that time had not had a single cigarette. When I returned to this same location 1 year later, to do another EMDR training, I enquired and found that she was having only one cigarette per week, while having coffee with a neighbor. In 2013,

8 years after our session, I contacted Hunaida by email to ask her permission to include her transcript in this chapter. She was glad to give permission, and said, "The session we had was very helpful, and if we had had additional sessions, I'm sure I could have stopped completely at that time." With a sense of empowerment and self-respect, she told me of how she had "divorced cigarettes" (i.e., permanently quit smoking) on a specific exact date, 2 years after our session.

The protocol used in this session was the DeTUR method, although there was also an interweave at the end of the session to help her generalize this work to many associated feeling states—the "lovely times" she had had smoking with friends in restaurants. This intervention built on the empowering experience of noticing that her LOU score, to the restaurant trigger, had gone to zero. Apparently, this helped her disconnect the linkage between the positive good times and the specific behavior of smoking. This linkage was weakened further when she went on to combine her emerging positive cognition, "I am strong," with many other triggering situations in her life.

Later, in Chapter 15, the course of therapy for "Veronica" will be presented. Her case illustrates how, with a client with a dissociative personality structure, targeting of urges connected to situational triggers is not always sufficient for resolving an addictive behavior. In her case, we use the LOPA method (previously described in Chapter 5) to resolve a child part's very strong positive affect, which was driving a self-destructive addictive behavior.

REFERENCES

Abel, N. J., & O'Brien, J. M. (2010). EMDR treatment of comorbid PTSD and alcohol dependence: A case example. *Journal of EMDR Practice & Research, 4*(2), 50–59. New York, NY: Springer Publishing. doi:10.1891/1933-3196.4.2.50

Abel, N., & O'Brien, J. (2014). Treating addictions with EMDR therapy and stages of change. New York, NY: Springer Publishing.

Adler-Tapia, R. (2012). *Child psychotherapy: Integrating developmental theory into clinical practice* (p. 81). New York, NY: Springer Publishing.

Artigas, L., Jarero, I., Mauer, M., López Cano, T., & Alcalá, N. (2000, September). *EMDR and traumatic stress after natural disasters: Integrative treatment protocol and the butterfly hug.* Poster presented at the EMDRIA Conference, Toronto, Ontario, Canada.

Bae, H., Han, C., & Kim, D. (2015, March). Desensitization of triggers and urge reprocessing for pathological gambling: A case series. *Journal of Gambling Studies, 31*(1), 331–342. doi:10.1007/s10899-013-9422-5

Bae, H., & Kim, D. (2012). Desensitization of triggers and urge reprocessing for an adolescent with Internet addiction disorder. *Journal of EMDR Research and Practice, 6*(2), 73–81. doi:10.1891/1933-3196.6.2.73

Bandler, R., & Grinder, J. (1976). *Patterns of the hypnotic techniques of Milton H. Erickson, M.D* (Vol. 1). Cupertino, CA: Meta Publications.

Begleiter, H., & Porjesz, B. (1988). Potential biological markers in individuals at high risk for developing alcoholism. *Alcoholism: Clinical and Experimental Research, 12*, 488–493. doi:10.1111/j.1530-0277.1988.tb00231.x

Boening, J. A. (2001). Neurobiology of an addiction memory. *Journal of Neural Transmission, 108*(6), 755–765. doi:10.1007/s007020170050

Brown, S. (2013). *The adverse childhood experiences (ACE) study, addiction, and the role of EMDR.* EMDRIA Annual Conference, Austin, TX.

Brown, S., Gilman, S. G., Goodman, E. G., Adler-Tapia, R., & Freng, S. (2015). Integrated trauma treatment in drug court: Combining EMDR therapy and seeking safety. *Journal of EMDR Practice and Research, 9*, 123–136. doi:10.1891/1933-3196.9.3.123

Carletto, S., Oliva, F., Barnato, M., Antonelli, T., Cardia, A., Mazzaferro, P., . . . Pagani, M. (2017). EMDR as add-on treatment for psychiatric and traumatic symptoms in patients with substance use disorder. *Frontiers in Psychology, 8*, 2333. doi:10.3389/fpsyg.2017.02333

Carnes, P. (1989). *Contrary to love: Helping the sexual addict.* Minneapolis, MN: CompCare Publications.

Cloninger, C. R., Bohman, M., & Sigvardsson, S. (1981). Inheritance of alcohol abuse: Cross-fostering analysis of adopted men. *Archives of General Psychiatry, 36*, 861–868. doi:10.1001/archpsyc.1981.01780330019001

Cloninger, C. R., Sigvardsson, S., & Bohman, M. (1998). Childhood personality predicts alcohol abuse in young adults. *Alcoholism: Clinical and Experimental Research, 12*(4), 494–505. doi:10.1111/j.1530-0277.1988.tb00232.x

Cox, R. P., & Howard, M. D. (2007). Utilization of EMDR in the treatment of sexual addiction. *Sexual Addiction & Compulsivity, 14*(1), 1–20. doi:10.1080/10720160601011299

Felitti, V. J., Anda, R. F., Nordenberg, D., Williamson, D. F., Spitz, A. M., Edwards, V., . . . Marks, J. S. (1998). Relationship of childhood abuse and household dysfunction to many of the leading causes of death in adults: The adverse childhood experiences (ACE) study. *American Journal of Preventive Medicine, 14*, 245–258. doi:10.1016/S0749-3797(98)00017-8

Franklin, J. L. (2015). *The effectiveness of EMDR therapy on clients with addictions* (Theses, Dissertations, and Projects). Retrieved from https://scholarworks.smith.edu/theses/921 (No. 921)

Guo, J., Hawkins, J. D., Hill, K. G., & Abbott, R. D. (2001). Childhood and adolescent predictors of alcohol abuse and dependence in young adulthood. *Journal of Studies on Alcohol, 62*(6), 753–762. doi:10.15288/jsa.2001.62.754

Hase, M., Schallmayer, S., & Sack, M. (2008). EMDR reprocessing of the addiction memory: Pretreatment, posttreatment, and 1-month follow-up. *Journal of EMDR Practice and Research, 2*(3), 170–179. doi:10.1891/1933-3196.2.3.170

Hofmann, A. (2009). The inverted EMDR standard protocol for unstable complex post-traumatic stress disorder. In M. Luber (Ed.), *EMDR scripted protocols: Special populations* (pp. 313–328). New York, NY: Springer Publishing.

Ilgen, M., McKellar, J., & Tiet, Q. (2005). Abstinence self-efficacy and abstinence 1 year after substance use disorder treatment. *Journal of Consulting and Clinical Psychology, 73*(6), 1175–1180. doi:10.1037/0022-006x.73.6.1175

Knipe, J. (1998b). Blocking beliefs questionnaire. EMDR *International Association Newsletter, Winter, 7*(4),5–6).

Knipe, J. (2005). Targeting positive affect to clear the pain of unrequited love: Codependence, avoidance and procrastination. In R. Shapiro (Ed.), *EMDR solutions* (pp. 189–211). New York, NY: W. W. Norton.

Marich, J. (2009). EMDR in the addiction continuing care process case study of a cross-addicted female's treatment and recovery. *Journal of EMDR Practice and Research, 3*(2), 98–106. doi:10.1891/1933-3196.3.2.98

Marich, J. (2010). Eye movement desensitization and reprocessing in addiction continuing care: A phenomenological study of women in recovery. *Psychology of Addictive Behaviors, 24*(3), 498–507. doi:10.1037/a0018574

Miller, R. (2010). The feeling-state theory of impulse-control disorders and the impulse-control disorder protocol. *Traumatology, 16*(3), 2–10. doi:10.1177/1534765610365912

Miller, R. (2011). *Breaking impulse-control disorders: A new theory and protocol for compulsions*. EMDRIA Annual Conference, Anaheim, CA.

Popky, A. J. (1994). *EMDR protocol for smoking and other addictions*. Presentation at the annual meeting of the EMDR Network, Sunnyvale, CA.

Popky, A. J. (2005). DeTUR, an urge reduction protocol for addictions and dysfunctional behaviors. In R. Shapiro (Ed.), *EMDR solutions* (pp. 167–188). New York, NY: W. W. Norton.

Reuters, Health News. (2016, June 21). Smokers may try to quit 30 times before it sticks, *Reuters*. Retrieved from www.reuters.com/article/us-health-smoking-quit-attempts-idUSKCN0Z72PL

Wolpe, J. (1958). *Psychotherapy by reciprocal inhibition*. Stanford, CA: Stanford University Press.

III

An Adaptive Information Processing Model for Treating Dissociative Personality Structure

7

Treating Dissociation Within an Adaptive Information Processing Model

THE ORIGINS OF DISSOCIATION

We all have parts within our personalities—separate states of mind that are able to engage in the tasks of daily living (such as cooking, cleaning, working, or sleeping)—parts that have various ways of connecting with others, parts that seek meaning and purpose, and parts that react to danger with behaviors of self-protection. By definition, dissociative individuals, of course, have separate parts of the personality, but to an extent, that is true of everyone. What is different and unique for people who are dissociative is that, typically, some of their parts are extreme adaptations to threatening circumstances of the past. As part of adaptation, these parts may have created impaired conscious access between parts, or conflictual relationships between parts, or virtually no access at all.

The first time I observed dissociation was in 1981. I was struggling as a new therapist to get my skills up to speed and working in a partial hospitalization per day treatment program. I had heard about dissociation in my graduate training—it was described as an extremely rare condition, and I might not see such a person at any time during my entire career. I was working with a 23-year-old woman who was seeking help for chronic depression. She was intellectually capable, but socially isolated, marginally employed, and felt that life was passing her by. There was a "little girl" quality to her voice. She told me that much of her low self-esteem had originated in her early teens when her body did not go through the usual changes of puberty. She still had a prepuberty body appearance and had not yet initiated menstruation. Her doctor had been unable to find a cause for this problem. Her parents had separated when she was 10, and she had been very close to her father prior to that time. During divorce proceedings, she, at age 12, was coerced by her mother to go onto the witness stand and deliberately lie about her father. In our therapy session, as she was telling me this, initially in a rather unemotional way, her face suddenly had a terrified look. She leapt out of her chair, went out the door of my office, and headed down a long hallway, sobbing intensely. I raced after her, finding her at the end of the hall, lying in a fetal position. We came back to my office and sat down. I asked her, with surprise and alarm, "What just happened?" She replied, "What do you mean?" She had no memory of what had just occurred. My internal reaction was, "You gotta be kidding!" I kept this thought to myself, however, and I later realized that if I had been more aware of what was going on with my client, and also more aware of dissociation in general, I would have been much better able to help her.

This was my introduction to dissociation. This client had been living with her mother, and had had virtually no contact with her father in the intervening 11 years. Until this session, she had dissociated a very guilty 12-year-old child-hood part that had harmed her beloved father. We went on from there, and I think she benefited from her therapy in spite of my naïveté and inexperience. As therapy proceeded, she was able to allow herself to openly realize that she did not have to adapt to her mother's intense hatred of her father, but instead she could acknowledge her feelings of guilt, the horrible feelings of the loss of her father, and her anger regarding her mother's pressure on her to lie. As she did this work, she actually took on more of an appearance of a 23-year-old woman, and she was happily surprised to begin menstruation! It is as though her development resumed following these realizations. She was able during this time to have a frank talk with her mother about what had happened, and initiate contacts with her father, which were welcomed by him. We learn from our clients, and this client taught me a lot. One particular lesson was the importance of learning to recognize dissociation, as well as learning how dissociative disorders "make sense" in the context of a client's difficult life history. In therapy, this type of conceptual understanding is often a crucial "tool" in helping clients come to an understanding of their own normality.

An understanding of dissociation begins with the recognition that human personalities—dissociative and nondissociative—universally have parts. Sometimes, the structure of these parts involves amnesiac separation as well as significant conflicts between parts, and these conflicts, in turn, often cause significant emotional problems (Forgash & Knipe, 2007, 2012). One implication of this larger conceptualization—a "parts" model—is that many troubled people, previously regarded as untreatable, can now be potentially helped through appropriate therapy interventions aimed at (a) resolving the internal dysfunctional mental states that maintain dissociative separation between parts and (b) resolving the incongruities between parts. The list of people now more potentially treatable would include those who might be described (insensitively) as "crazy," or "not ready to change," or even "lazy" (terms that do not appear in the diagnostic manual). With the recognition of the central importance of ego-state conflicts and dissociative processes, we can now see that many people who were thought to be outside of the purview of psychotherapy can actually benefit greatly, particularly with therapy that is informed by specific theoretical models of dissociation and eye movement desensitization and reprocessing (EMDR)-related methods of information processing. In connection with this, it is interesting to note that in the 1980s, following the introduction of the diagnosis of posttraumatic stress disorder (PTSD), this condition was regarded by many therapists as intractable. Unfortunately, at that time, many clients were told, even by well-meaning therapists, that they "just have to live with it." Still today, it can be heard when a TV newscaster is reporting on a terrorist incident or kidnapping, or victims of a natural disaster, "These people will never get over this." We know now, with strong scientific evidence (Bisson et al., 2013; Bradley, Greene, Russ, Dutra, & Westen, 2005; Davidson & Parker, 2001; Maxfield & Hyer, 2002; Rodenburg, Benjamin, de Roos, Meijer, & Stams, 2009; Seidler & Wagner, 2006), that for the great majority of clearly remembered disturbing memories, this is untrue. This fact can justify skepticism when other groups of clients are described as untreatable with psychotherapy.

Dissociation can happen in degrees. There can be a complete lack of awareness between personality parts, or one part may be partially aware of another part: "I am me, and there is another presence here with me." Very often, there is fear and phobic avoidance regarding this other presence. The word "haunting" can aptly describe this experience. Some dissociative clients have described it as like having noisy neighbors in an apartment—something is going on in the other side of the wall, but it might be better to not know what it is! Additionally, a dissociative person may be aware to some degree of separate, incongruent, and conflictual self-states, but attempt to hide these parts from being detected by others.

It is unfortunate that there has been a kind of "sibling rivalry" between EMDR-related methods and cognitive-behavioral methods of treatment for trauma-related conditions, including dissociative disorders. It is as though, in our field of psychotherapy, there is a kind of dissociative disorder, with some clinicians taking on one identity and others, another. In time, through listening and dialogue, integration of approaches is bound to occur, incorporating from each what is valuable. And, consistent with that understanding, a thesis of this book is that a conceptual/cognitive understanding of dissociation is necessary for both the therapist and the dissociative client. It is necessary for the therapist, because such an understanding gives an overview of the client's dysfunction and the appropriate and safe path to healing. For the client, a cognitive overview is necessary, not only for the earlier reasons, but also because a cognitive understanding of one's own difficulties can serve as a container for disturbing affect that may need to be accessed before it can be healed during the course of treatment. Many dissociative clients carry a deep shame about self, and it can be very useful for those clients to have an understanding of how the separation of the self into dissociative parts is not a personal flaw but was the inevitable result of a very nonengaging and/or abusive early environment. A discussion between client and therapist of how cognitive models apply to the individual case are often important as a preliminary step to prepare that client for the arduous and potentially destabilizing work of trauma processing. Specifically, it is frequently crucial for clients to know how dissociated parts can develop as "normal" adaptations to difficult childhood experiences, to know the different categories of parts that can occur, and to be able to visualize how the path of therapy can lead to realization of the client's goals.

For a child growing up in an environment of early, frequent, and severely neglectful nonengagement and trauma, the creation of separate first-person identities is an understandable adaptation. When the adults responsible for caretaking are also the sources of enormous stress for the child, there are consequences in terms of the encoding, neurologically, of the child's concept of self, concept of others, and basic assumptions regarding the essential safety (versus danger) of social interactions. Colin Ross, the developer of Trauma Model Therapy (Ross & Halpern, 2009), has been writing about the origins and treatment of dissociative disorders for over 30 years. In his view,

> The fundamental driver of dissociation . . . is the problem of attachment to the perpetrator. In order to survive, the child must attach to the person who is hurting (her). There is no escape and no other option. In order to maintain the attachment systems up and running, they cannot be contaminated by the traumatic information coming in through the senses; that reality must be dissociated. What difference does this model make and therapy? The focus of therapy is not on the content of the memories—the target is the ambivalent attachment. (Ross, 1997)

On the surface, this statement may appear to challenge the basic premise of the Adaptive Information Processing (AIP) model of EMDR—the hypothesis that most emotional problems originate in dysfunctionally stored posttraumatic memories. However, there is in fact no basic contradiction between these approaches. The kind of ambivalence that Ross describes originates when the child experiences a "near-impossible" situation—the need for connection and nurturance conflicts directly with the need for avoidance of harm and pain— and consequently a split in identity is the only available solution. One client was describing her memory of helplessness and painful abuse at the hands of a caretaker, and said "I had no way out! But then I found a solution. I wasn't there!" *Someone else* was there—a new part of self that took the abuse. In this way, the attachment to the perpetrator could be protected, and not compromised by the dissociated memories of horrible mistreatment.

In order to describe the origins of dissociative personality structure, it is necessary to first describe the ways in which an integrated identity develops under conditions that are "good enough" (Winnicott,1956). During *normal* development in infancy, a baby begins to integrate different modalities of experience: visual, kinesthetic, motor, and affective experience. Faces are associated with the satisfaction of needs. The eyes are coordinated with the movement of the hand. Inborn action systems take form in accordance with the conditions of the child's environment. Intense learning is occurring from the beginning of life.

However, later, these early learnings may not be recognized as memories. Most people, if asked "What is your earliest memory?" will report some recollection from 2½ to 4 years of age, because generally that is when the brain matures sufficiently to store memories as visual images. However, if prior to this time a child experiences an event that has a high emotional impact, that may also be stored visually. Most experienced therapists have had clients who have reported clear visual memories from the first 18 months of life. The clarity of these memories often suggests that they are accurate, although, of course, there is usually no way to verify this. If these very early memory images are disturbing to the individual, they generally can be targeted and resolved using standard procedures. The issue of the memory's validity does not have to be an impediment to processing—the troubled feelings the person is having in his or her present life, in connection with the memory, are the EMDR target in these instances.

During this early time, before most memories are encoded visually, there is learning that takes place in attachment experiences with caretakers, and this learning forms a major part of the foundation of later personality development (Main, 1996). We can think of the attachment style—child or adult—as an individual's characteristic way of answering three basic questions—What kind of person am I, in what kind of world, with what kind of people? (Bowlby, 1988). The answer that a child develops, very early, with regard to these questions will tend to be an adaptation and will reflect the interaction patterns between that child and the first caretaker. If the caretaker is tuned in, reliably mirrors the child's affect and the child's experience, and responds contingently to the child's expressions of needs (i.e., crying), the child will begin to internalize the repeated characteristics of this interaction. Internal representations of "other" and "self-as-separate-from-other" will begin to form. The "good enough" parent (Winnicott, 1956) will teach internal affect regulation through first providing external regulation—empathetically soothing when sympathetic arousal is too high, and by creating happy moments and shared play when the baby's affect is too low. It is fun for parents, as well as relatives and neighbors, to enjoy bringing out positive affect in a baby, getting the smile, and enjoying the giggles. This is a very happy experience for most adults.

If appropriate bonding continues with "good enough" emotional safety and consistency, the child then develops a sense of *Self* within a safe place in the world. With these ongoing experiences, the child is likely to develop an orientation of secure attachment. Figure 7.1 illustrates how parental attunement and parental regulation of a baby's affect create in the infant the beginning of a sense of self, a beginning of affect regulation skills, and a positive general feeling about relationships with others. Schore (2001, 2012) describes the ways early attachment learning takes place through eye contact between parent and child. Through the eyes, and through simultaneous mutual activation of certain right hemisphere functions (e.g., the parent speaking with a soothing, prosaic tone, or softly singing a lullaby), parent and child can enter into a very pleasant synchrony. This type of interaction reduces sympathetic arousal, while increasing positive feelings, in both. Mutual gazing creates positive feelings, but initially, the intensity of these feelings may be more than the baby is used to; when this occurs, the baby can look away, while the parent's eyes remain available. Then, when the baby is ready, eye contact can be resumed. This is one of the ways that baby can begin to learn self-regulation of affect. Also, since these interactions never go perfectly, a baby with a less-than-perfect, but "good enough" parent will have opportunities to learn that disruptions in a relationship can be repaired. For example, if a baby pulls his or her mother's hair, and the mother makes a sound of pain, the baby might pull away. But then, if the mother's loving eyes remain available, the connection can be resumed, strengthening the important lesson that a rupture in a relationship can be repaired.

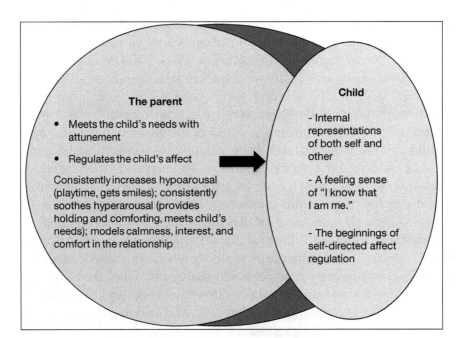

Figure 7.1 With appropriate attachment experiences, the child is able to develop an initial sense of self.

There are many genetically prepared processes that contribute to the creation of a strong bond between parent and child, which is so obviously necessary for the survival of the individual and the species. Many of these processes are nonconscious. For example, a parent is drawn to the eyes of a baby, and the baby seeks the eyes of the parent. This in itself is soothing for both; when the mutual gazing occurs, the pupils of the infant's eyes expand. The sight of a baby's wide eyes then can evoke a similar pupillary response in the parent. This response occurs nonconsciously for nearly all women, and for most men who have a history of being caretakers for their children. And this is but one of many examples of how attachment bonding, when it goes well, is the result of an automatic neurological interface between parent and child. A fuller description of the specifics of how this fascinating process occurs can be found in Schore (2012, pp. 118–151).

When attachment experiences go well, the result for the child is the beginning of an integrated sense of Self, which then can provide resilience in the face of later traumatic experiences. How, exactly, does an experience of Self develop? Demassio, writing in *Self Comes to Mind* (2010), describes Self as a process that can be viewed from two vantage points: Self as *observer* of one's own experience and Self as *knower, with a first-person identity*—the felt sense of "I know what is me and what is mine, and what is not me and what is not mine." This felt sense—a sense of ownership of one's own experience—is an implicit (nonconscious) memory of preverbal interactive experiences with caretakers, and it is the foundation of a cognitive/verbal experience, which comes later, that we can call "self-concept." Demassio has noted that "Self" is phylogenetically more advanced than "mind." Mind involves consciousness of the actions necessary for survival, but the development of Self requires ongoing interactions with the "other"—the child learns that Self and other both exist, and exist separately. Self, then, initially takes the form of the child's core dyadic interactions, and this becomes a problem if the caretaker, on whom the child totally depends, is a source of abuse, harm, or pain. This is why, if significant neglectful nonengagement or abuse occurs early in the parent–child relationship, that maltreatment may impair a child's ability to form a coherent, unified sense of Self. If incidents of chronic and repeated parental misattunement and/or abuse occur, inborn defensive action systems of anger and escape from harm will be activated in the child. However, the child must also regard the caretaker as the source of supplies necessary for survival. If these circumstances occur early in life, frequently, and with severity, it will be necessary, as an adaptation, for the child to create separate self-states—separate personality parts. The formation of a single core identity, active continuously, will simply not be possible because of the contradictory demands of that child's environment. The strong intrinsic impulse to remain attached to the (neglectful, abusive) caretaker will be expressed in a part of the personality focused on adaptation. This attachment-focused part may be protected and maintained by dissociating the memories of abuse. Or the memories of abuse may only be partially dissociated, with the result that the child is likely to exhibit some type of defense to weaken the strength of the memories of maltreatment—for example, defenses of avoidance, minimization, idealization of the perpetrator, or defensive self-shaming—so that some degree of attachment to the perpetrating "caretaker" can be preserved. For these children, then, development of separate self-states may proceed along separate tracks, as indicated in Figure 7.2. In many situations, this adaptation is facilitated if the child learns to have an amnesiac separation—a lack of coconsciousness—between parts. The adaptive part's task of looking normal cannot afford interference from flashing memory images of abuse or neglect.

There are many reasons why a parent might not provide a baby with "good enough" early attachment experiences. The mother or father may be unavailable, due to death, illness, physical disability, immaturity, addiction, narcissism, or the burden of too much to do. One unfortunate pattern occurs when the arrival of the child activates, in a parent, previously dormant posttraumatic stress from the parent's own childhood. For example, a mother may have been traumatized in her family while growing up and have learned, as an adaptation to that trauma, to ignore, or even be scornful of, any feelings or experiences of her "inner child" self. The mother may dislike, within herself, her fears, her feelings of inadequacy, her need at times to be spontaneous and playful, or her need for comfort and support. In this situation, the arrival of a baby daughter may stimulate in the mother intense confusion and conflicted emotions, along with the positive feelings that also may be occurring. These inner fears and conflicts can

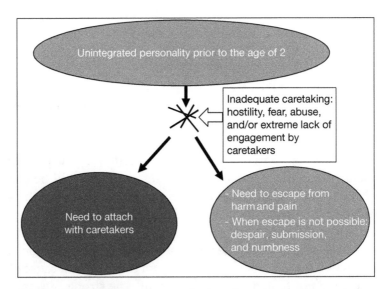

Figure 7.2 Early and severe neglect or abuse by caretakers can impair normal development of self and lead instead to the development of separate self-states to separately meet the child's needs for attachment and for self-protection.

quite easily be projected inappropriately onto an infant daughter. The normal crying of a baby may be misinterpreted, at a feeling level, as an angry accusation from the baby—"You are not a good mother." The mother's ambivalence may result, in spite of her best intentions, in inconsistent and inadequate caretaking of baby. Another pattern—the parent may have an attitude of "All my life, I have never been able to count on love from anyone. Now, I have this wonderful baby, who will always love me!" This is a very nice feeling, one that can backfire later when the baby has long nights of irreconcilable crying due to teething or colic, or, later, when the child starts to enjoy independence/individuation behaviors. These dysfunctional characteristics of a caretaker can be present by degrees—just a little bit, or in a way that has a devastating influence on the child's developing internal working model (IWM; Liotti, 1992, 2004, 2006) of relationships.

Consistent with this picture, a child with an insecure, disorganized attachment style is likely to have parents (one or two) who are, to some extent, dissociative (Barach, 1991; Egeland & Susman-Stillman, 1996). A young child whose parents have dissociated parts will be compelled to develop separate and different adaptation styles, not only for each parent, but also for each part of each parent; the task, for the child, of organizing these adaptations is formidable. In addition, a child growing up in this type of environment is much more likely to be emotionally insecure, just simply due to the increased stress and the complex strategies necessary to cope with that stress. If parental behaviors with a baby are erratic and frightening or frustrating of the baby's intrinsic attachment needs, the infant is more likely to develop, during the first two years of life, an insecure, disorganized attachment style (Beebe, et al, 2012). The child might exhibit a cycling through successive behavior patterns, sometimes focused on connection with caretakers, sometimes focused on avoiding pain and danger, but with little possibility to integrate those responses, and often showing behavior that is an ambivalent mix of contradictory impulses (e.g., smiling while whimpering, or approaching a parent with back turned). In many ways, deficits and deficiencies in a child's early interactions with caretakers—"traumas of omission"—lay the groundwork for the development of a dissociative personality structure. As a child in this unfortunate environment grows up, that individual will be more vulnerable to being overwhelmed by specific "traumas of commission." And, concurrently, psychological defenses are likely to develop—mental actions that have the function of protecting the conscious self from posttraumatic affect.

Exactly what is the mechanism by which dissociative disorders develop? In 1997, Putnam and Trickett noted that relatively little information was available regarding this question, except for the assumption that severe traumatic events were somehow involved. That same year, Ogawa, Sroufe, Weinfield, Carlson, and Egeland (1997) published the results of a longitudinal study that showed observed parental nonengagement—together with insecure, disorganized attachment behaviors in 2-year-old children—predicted clinically significant scores on the Dissociative Experiences Scale (DES scores >30;

Carlson et al., 1993) at age 19. Moreover, and surprisingly, early measures of disordered attachment were far more correlated with DES scores at age 19 than were measures of childhood abuse—that is, chronicity, severity, or age of onset of abuse (a correlation of $r = 0.58$ between age 19 DES score and measures of early misattunement, accounting for 34% of variance, versus a correlation of $r = 0.25$ between age 19 DES score and an index of abuse history, accounting for 6% of variance). A score above 30 on the DES at age 19 is not, by itself, a sufficient evidence of a dissociative disorder, but it may indicate vulnerability to dissociative separation of parts. These results of Ogawa and colleagues were later confirmed in another longitudinal study (Dutra & Lyons-Ruth, 2005). A parallel finding was observed in studies of cortisol levels in children. Children who are securely attached, as a group, do not show unusual elevations in cortisol levels (Spangler & Grossmann, 1993). However, clinically significant parental depression during a child's first 2 years predicts significantly elevated cortisol at age 4½ (Essex, Klein, Cho, & Kalin, 2002) and at age 7 (Ashman, Dawson, Panagiotides, Yamada, & Wilkinson, 2002), indicating impaired regulation of fearful arousal in these children. Lyons-Ruth and colleagues (Dutra, Bureau, Holmes, Lyubchik, & Lyons-Ruth, 2009) identified two types of parental interaction patterns with young children that significantly correlated with dissociative symptoms at age 19: a "hostile/self-referential" pattern and a "helpless/fearful" pattern of behavior. The first pattern tended to occur with mothers who themselves had had a history of receiving or witnessing physical violence, and the second pattern tended to occur with mothers who had been sexually victimized. These two patterns are hypothesized to be linked in that both might contribute to a parent being unduly influenced by his or her own life history and, consequently, unresponsive to a child's intrinsic attachment cues, resulting in the child being repeatedly "shut out" of opportunities for interaction. The child may develop "learned helplessness" (Seligman & Maier, 1976) regarding the fulfillment of attachment needs, that is, the child might partially or wholly stop giving attention to forming connection with others. A consistent pattern of hostility on the part of the parent, or fearfulness that prevents soothing interaction—both of these situations, if repeated—present the child with a problem for which there is no good solution. There is only the bad solution of creating separate senses of self—personality parts formed to meet separate attachment and self-defense needs (Liotti, 1992).

Repeated frightening behavior (hostility, or excessive fear) on the part of a caretaker can lead to a conditioned response in the child of sympathetic arousal (struggling, distress), which then can become a highly potentiated response to the caretaker. If, for the infant, sympathetic arousal becomes more and more associated with contact with the parent, this arousal will be accompanied by excessive (hypermetabolic) right brain activation. In extreme situations, if sympathetic activation is ongoing and unremitting, this excessive activation can lead to neurological cell damage or even cell death (Schore, 2001). For children who have this type of frequent fear, and frequent frustration of attachment needs in interaction with caretakers, there is another neural impulse that is increasingly likely to occur—the switch to hypoarousal—dorsal vagal parasympathetic activation (disengagement, passivity, submission, a flattening of affect and energy), which allows for lowered neurological metabolism and cell survival under conditions of extreme and repeated stress (Schore, 2012). The unfortunate result when these conditions repeat during infancy is a learned tendency on the part of the child to quickly activate dissociative numbness in response to perceived threat. This is doubly damaging. Not only is the child learning a dysfunctional response to threat—one of numbness and helplessness instead of active coping and integration of experience—but that child is also not learning positive affect regulation skills. Instead, the child is likely to develop a dysfunctional internal working memory (IWM; Liotti, 1992) of how to experience relationships. The child's intrinsic need for the parent to lovingly witness his or her experience and affect (Whitmer, 2001) is frustrated. The child's need for a parent's loving eyes is unfulfilled. If contradictions such as these characterize the childhood environment, then separate self-states are likely to develop. Many years later, in the person's present adult life, these different self-states may still exist, overlap, and be coconscious to some extent, or the states may be totally amnesiac with regard to each other—that is, conscious access between states may be limited or absent. It would not be accurate to say, in these instances, that the personality is fragmented, because the word "fragmented" implies that the parts once were unified. More typically, the person may never have had a fully coherent single sense of self to begin with, because early attachment failures with caretakers prevented the emergence of a single sense of self.

Early learnings, even those not recognized later in life as memories, are retained and influential within the personality. An infant does not typically have the capacity in the frontal lobes to easily develop visual memory images, but patterns of emotional regulation, and even nonverbal appraisals of self and others, may be acquired during this time. The right brain matures much faster and more extensively than the left during the first 2 years, and the right brain typically cannot hold conscious, semantic memories. Instead, the memories are implicit and procedural—and deep (Schore, 2012). Trauma and neglect, occurring preverbally and perpetrated by caretakers, may often be "remembered" not as an identified memory, but as a set of assumptions about relationships. Within the child-grown-up, these assumptions may then be projected onto adult relationships or form the basis of assumptions about life itself; for example, the attitudes, "People can't be trusted," or "There is no such thing as a safe place in this world," or "No one cares about me," or "I just don't like to be with other people—I always feel that they don't like me!" And we can include another grim example: "Life is solitary, poor, nasty, brutish and short" (from the philosopher, Hobbes, 1651/1929!). Perhaps the adult who believes, "Everyone is out to get me!" is remembering a time, early in life, when that was an accurate perception. Early traumatic events—traumas of omission or commission—may set in motion attitudes and assumptions that become the individual's "map of the world," or, at least, the map of the interpersonal world the individual lives in. And that person may be still using that map at age 40 to negotiate and try to cope with interpersonal relationships.

When these unfortunate events occur, development of a unified self may be impaired, and this can be the beginning of what later develops into a dissociative personality structure in the adult. The adult client with this type of history may behave and think in ways that are confusing and stressful to both the client and other people. Specifically, the dysfunctional IWM may be projected onto others, distorting those relationships and contributing in many ways to adult reenactments of the damaging interactions of childhood. In therapy, these dysfunctional attachment experiences may be evident in the transference, and it is very important for the therapists working with dissociative disorders to be aware of the many ways that countertransference can occur, particularly through projective identification (i.e., the client projects a negative image onto the therapist, and the therapist, because of his or her own personality makeup and history, begins acting in a way that validates the projection; e.g., this can happen with projected anger, frustration, sexual interest, and fears regarding therapist competence).

The residue of an unsafe early environment can be rectified through later positive experiences (including effective therapy); conversely, a safe early environment can be overridden by extensive later trauma. But the norm is for infantile interpersonal experience to form, in many ways, the template for approaching later relationships.

The separate parts of self, in a dissociative adult, may have certain relationship patterns that have a resemblance to relationships within a dysfunctional family. The parts may never communicate with each other, or be indifferent to each other, or be afraid of each other, or hate each other, or have a dominance/ submission relationship with each other, or have an idealization/denigration relationship with each other. Each dissociative person's unique structure of parts, developed as an adaptation to the childhood environment, is likely to have a certain stability, even though the threats and the deprivations of childhood are no longer there. As described in Chapter 1, this separation of the self into dissociated parts is a third category of damage (along with dysfunctionally stored traumatic memory and psychological defense) that can result from a difficult early environment. As will be described in Chapter 14, for each category of damage, sets of bilateral stimulation, focused on representative memory images, can be an important element in the treatment of Complex PTSD and dissociative separation of self-states.

REFERENCES

Ashman, S. B., Dawson, G., Panagiotides, H., Yamada, E., & Wilkinson, C. W. (2002). Stress hormone levels of children of depressed mothers. *Development and Psychopathology, 14,* 333–349. doi:10.1017/S0954579402002080

Andrade, J., Kavanagh, D., & Baddeley, A. (1997). Eye movements and visual imagery: A working memory approach to the treatment of posttraumatic stress disorder. *British Journal of Clinical Psychology, 36*(2), 209–223. doi:10.1111/j.2044-8260.1997.tb01408.x

Barach, P. M. (1991). Multiple personality disorder as an attachment disorder. *Dissociation, 4*(3), 117–123. Retrieved from https://scholarsbank.uoregon.edu/xmlui/bitstream/handle/1794/1448/Diss_4_3_2_OCR_rev.pdf?sequence=4&isAllowed=y

Beebe, B., Lachmann, F., Markese, S., Buck, K., Bahrick, L., Chen, H., . . . Jaffe, J. (2012). On the origins of disorganized attachment and internal working models: Paper II. An empirical microanalysis of 4-month mother–infant interaction. *Psychoanalytic Dialogues, 22,* 352–374. doi:10.1080/10481885.2012.679606

Bisson, J. I., Roberts, N. P., Andrew M., Cooper R., Lewis C. (2013). *Psychological therapies for chronic post-traumatic stress disorder (PTSD) in adults.* Cochrane Database of Systematic Reviews, Issue 12. Art. No.: CD003388. DOI: 10.1002/14651858. CD003388.pub4

Bowlby, J. (1988). *A secure base: Parent-child attachment and healthy human development.* New York, NY: Basic Books.

Bradley, R., Greene, J., Russ, E., Dutra, L., & Westen, D. (2005). A multidimensional meta-analysis of psychotherapy for PTSD. *American Journal of Psychiatry, 162,* 214–227. doi:10.1176/appi.ajp.162.2.214

Carlson, E. B., Putnam, F. W., Ross, C. A., Torem, M., Coons, P., Dill, D., . . . Braun, B. G. (1993). Validity of the dissociative experiences scale in screening for multiple personality disorder: A multicenter study. *American Journal of Psychiatry, 150,* 1030–1036. doi:10.1176/ajp.150.7.1030

Davidson, P. R., & Parker, K. C. H. (2001). Eye movement desensitization and reprocessing (EMDR): A meta-analysis. *Journal of Consulting and Clinical Psychology, 69,* 305–316. doi:I0.1037//0022-006X.69.2.305

Demassio, A. (2010). *Self comes to mind.* New York, NY: Pantheon.

Dutra, L., Bureau, J., Holmes, B., Lyubchik, A., & Lyons-Ruth, K. (2009). Quality of early care and childhood trauma: A prospective study of developmental pathways to dissociation. *The Journal of Nervous and Mental Disease, 197*(6), 383–390. doi:10.1097/NMD.0b013e3181a653b7

Dutra, L., & Lyons-Ruth, K. (2005). Maltreatment, maternal and child psychopathology, and quality of early care as predictors of adolescent dissociation. Presented at the Biennial Meeting of the Society for Research in Child Development, Atlanta, GA.

Egeland, B., & Susman-Stillman, A. (1996). Dissociation as a mediator of child abuse across generations. *Child Abuse and Neglect, 20*(11), 1123–1132. doi:10.1016/0145-2134(96)00102-0

Essex, M. J., Klein, M. H., Cho, E., & Kalin, N. H. (2002). Maternal stress beginning in infancy may sensitize children to later stress exposure: Effects on cortisol and behavior. *Biological Psychiatry, 52,* 776–784. doi:10.1016/s0006-3223(02)01553-6

Forgash, C., & Knipe, J. (2007). Integrating EMDR and ego state treatment for clients with trauma disorders. In C. Forgash & M. Copeley (Eds.), *Healing the heart of trauma with EMDR and ego state therapy* (pp. 1–55). New York, NY: Springer Publishing.

Forgash, C., & Knipe, J. (2012). Integrating EMDR and ego state treatment for clients with trauma disorders. *Journal of EMDR Practice and Research, 6*(3), 120–128. doi:10.1891/1933-3196.6.3.120

Hobbes, T. (1929). *Leviathan, or the matter, forme, and power of a commonwealth, ecclesiasticall and civil.* London, UK: Oxford University Press. (Originally published 1651)

Liotti, G. (1992). Disorganized/disoriented attachment in the etiology of the dissociative disorders. *Dissociation: Progress in the Dissociative Disorders, 5*(4), 196–204. doi:10.1037/0033-3204.41.4.472

Liotti, G. (2004). Trauma, dissociation and disorganized attachment: Three strands of a single braid. *Psychotherapy: Theory, Practice, Research, Training, 41*(4), 55–74. doi:10.1037/0033-3204.41.4.472

Liotti, G. (2006). A model of dissociation based on attachment theory. *Journal of Trauma and Dissociation, 7*(4), 55–74. doi:10.1300/j229v07n04_04

Main, M. (1996). Introduction to the special section on attachment and psychopathology: 2. Overview of the field of attachment. *Journal of Consulting and Clinical Psychology, 64*(2), 237–243. doi:10.1037//0022-006x.64.2.237

Maxfield, L., & Hyer, L. A. (2002). The relationship between efficacy and methodology in studies investigating EMDR treatment of PTSD. *Journal of Clinical Psychology, 58,* 23–41. doi:10.1002/jclp.1127

Ogawa, J. R., Sroufe, L. A., Weinfield, N. S., Carlson, E., & Egeland, B. (1997). Development and the fragmented self: A longitudinal study of dissociative symptomatology in a non-clinical sample. *Development and Psychopathology, 4,* 855–879. doi:10.1017/s0954579497001478

Putnam, F. W., & Trickett, P. K. (1997). Psychobiological effects of sexual abuse: A longitudinal study. *Annals of the New York Academy of Sciences, 821,* 150–159. doi:10.1111/j.1749-6632.1997.tb48276.x

Rodenburg, R., Benjamin, A., de Roos, C., Meijer, A. M., & Stams, G. J. (2009). Efficacy of EMDR in children: A meta-analysis. *Clinical Psychology Review, 29,* 599–606. doi:10.1016/j.cpr.2009.06.008

Ross, C. (1997, February), The problem of attachment to the perpetrator. *Many Voices, IX*(1), 6–7. ISSN:1042-2277

Ross, C., & Halpern, N. (2009). *Trauma model therapy*. Richardson, TX: Manitou Communications.

Schore, A. N. (2001). Effects of a secure attachment relationship on right brain development, affect regulation, and infant mental health. *Infant Mental Health Journal*, *22*(1–2), 7–66. doi:10.1002/1097-0355(200101/04)22:1<7::AID-IMHJ2>3.0.CO;2-N

Schore, A. N. (2012). *The science of the art of psychotherapy*. New York, NY: W. W. Norton.

Seidler, G. H., & Wagner, F. E. (2006). Comparing the efficacy of EMDR and trauma-focused cognitive-behavioral therapy in the treatment of PTSD: A meta-analytic study. *Psychological Medicine*, *36*, 1515–1522. doi:10.1017/s0033291706007963

Seligman, M. E. P., & Maier, S. F. (1976). Learned helplessness: Theory and evidence. *Journal of Experimental Psychology: General*, *105*(1), 3–46. http://dx.doi.org/10.1037/0096-3445.105.1.3

Spangler, G., & Grossmann, K. E. (1993). Biobehavioral organization in securely and insecurely attached infants. *Child Development*, *64*, 1439–1450. doi:10.2307/1131544

Whitmer, G. (2001). On the nature of dissociation. *Psychoanal Quarterly*, *70*, 807–837.

Winnicott, D. W. (1956). Primary maternal preoccupation. In *Collected Papers, Through Paediatrics to Psychoanalysis* (pp. 300–305). London: Tavistock Publications.

8

The Basic Framework for the Preparation Phase

For the dissociative client, therapy must begin and proceed with cautious vigilance regarding the client's ability to maintain a sense of safety and orientation to the present. A client may initially have a great fear, or reluctance, to disclose, or to consciously access, personal information, memories, attitudes, emotions, physical sensations, and other mental actions. The barrier to disclosing may be between client and therapist—fear of the therapist's judgment—or within the client—impaired access to parts of self, due to internal fear. Much information may not be consciously known, initially, to the client's apparently normal part (ANP). To the extent possible, it will be important to establish with the client a beginning *contract for therapy*: an exploration with the client of what the hoped-for result of successful therapy might be. For example, the therapist might say, "What if you come into therapy here, and as some time passes you realize that this therapy has been very helpful. On a day in the future, you might think, as you leave my office, 'This therapy really has worked, the way I hoped it would! I'm glad I got into therapy.' Here is a question: How would you know? What do you suppose you would be noticing, or thinking about, if you said that to yourself?" The client's answers to this question will provide a cognitive understanding, on the part of both the client and therapist—a beginning framework and direction for how therapy can proceed to achieve the client's stated goals. The identification of therapy goals is important, not only to structure treatment planning and therapy sessions, but also to help the client impose some increased clarity on the confusing push and pull of separate internal self-states. When I am providing consultation to eye movement desensitization and reprocessing (EMDR) therapists regarding their difficult cases, a frequently occurring issue is one of incomplete identification of therapy goals.

As sessions continue, additional elements of the client's clinical picture are likely to become more evident. Personality parts that previously were hidden will emerge, and these parts may have very different agendas for therapy than those of the ANP. The goals for therapy may need to be redefined. There may be disagreement between parts regarding therapy goals, but general goals can usually be found that the whole personality system can *allow*, and not block.

There are many therapeutic interventions that can help the dissociative client untangle the confusing, often contradictory, structure of internal parts. Over 100 years ago, Janet (1907/1965) proposed basic guidelines for working with people who show behavior patterns that he called hysteria and what we can recognize, from his case descriptions, as probable Complex posttraumatic stress disorder (Complex PTSD). These guidelines are now generally accepted as necessary within several different models of treatment for dissociative conditions (Herman, 1997; van der Hart, Nijenhuis & Steele, 2006; van der Hart et al., 2013). Within these guidelines, stabilization must precede processing of trauma-related material, which in turn must occur before integration of separate personality parts is possible. It makes sense that stabilization must precede the potentially destabilizing work with traumatic memories and their sequelae (Figure 8.1). In addition, integration of the personality—putting the parts of self back together into a unified identity that realizes the difference between the traumatic past and the safer present—can only happen when most of the disturbance and

Stabilization

- Reduction of phobia of attachment (with therapist) and reduction of phobia of attachment loss
- Self-soothing skills
- An attitude of "I can be bigger than my memories."
- Overview of treatment plan; treatment preparation
- Reduction of "therapy-interfering behaviors"

Processing of trauma-related material

- Processing of memories of traumatic events—memories that are experienced as "relivings"
- Processing of trauma-related actions (overt and covert)
- Processing of conflicts and phobias between parts
- Processing distorted perceptions of the present; distorted predictions of the future

Integration of previously dissociated parts

- Coconsciousness between parts, with a continuous life narrative
- Synthesis of previously dissociated parts
- In this phase of therapy, there may be a need for new skills (e.g., assertion, conflict resolution)

Figure 8.1 Phase-oriented treatment is necessary for dissociative clients.

"relivings" held within the separate dissociated parts has been desensitized and resolved. Typically, of course, therapy does not proceed right through this sequence: one, two, three! Stabilization is usually necessary prior to trauma work; following the trauma work, there is very often a need to return again to stabilization before treating additional trauma. As the traumatic "relivings" of the past are realized, desensitized, and synthesized, positive momentum in the therapy is created. For some clients, major progress toward personality integration can occur spontaneously following trauma resolution, because then the dissociative separation between parts—necessary to contain disturbing affect—is no longer necessary. For other clients, the separation between parts may continue even after extensive, successful trauma work. In these cases, continuation of separate internal identities may indicate that those parts are continuing to have a narcissistic investment in separation, and/or this may be a sign that there is hidden unfinished traumatic experience held by one part or another.

Janet's formulation of the necessity of these three phases, for work with clients with complex traumatization, makes perfect sense; in practice, however, there is often a mixing of the phases. Many of the particular procedures described later that are part of the preparation phase also indirectly address and begin to provide processing for trauma. If a client is asked, "How much, 0 to 10, do you not want to think about that disturbing memory?" is this part of preparation, or is it the beginning of the trauma-processing phase? If a therapist gathers information on a client's history of sexual assault, and the client is able, perhaps with difficulty, to describe the history, is this Janet Phase 1 or Phase 2? This is really an academic question that does not need to have an impact on what actually occurs within therapy sessions. Janet's phases provide a useful guideline, but one that should be accompanied by the therapist closely tracking the client's needs and experience. Perhaps the most important element of preparation for clients with complex traumatization is the therapist's accurate, well-communicated empathy with regard to the client's experience, moment to moment. This therapist characteristic, along with an attitude of positive regard for the client, is essential (Truax & Carkhuff, 1967) in creating a relationship of mutual trust in which therapeutic movement can occur. This feeling of trust in the therapist is a significant contributor to an important element of the trauma-processing phase—the client's ability to achieve dual attention—simultaneous awareness of present safety while accessing past trauma.

The eight phases of EMDR therapy do not contradict Janet's phases, but provide a different perspective. The EMDR phases can be integrated with Janet's three phases, as indicated in Figure 8.2. A major advantage of EMDR in healing trauma-reliving self-states is that EMDR focuses on only one specific memory at a time, or even one isolated fragment of one memory. This is potentially helpful for clients who are vulnerable to a nonproductive type of affect bridging (Watkins & Watkins, 1998)—being carried, without control, through a chain of associations from one disturbing memory image to another, and then to another, and so on—there is a danger that the sum of all the disturbances from all the

Stabilization
- EMDR Phase 1: History-taking, treatment planning
- EMDR Phase 2: Treatment preparation
- EMDR Phase 7: Closure

Processing of trauma-related material
- EMDR Phases 3 and 4: Target assessment and desensitization/reprocessing
- EMDR Phase 6: Body scan (and processing any remaining sensations from the trauma memory)

Integration of previously dissociated parts
- EMDR Phase 5: Installation
- EMDR Phase 8: Reevaluation

Figure 8.2 Janet's three phases overlap with the EMDR eight phases. However, with EMDR, the target of therapy is a specific memory, not a dissociated part.
EMDR, eye movement desensitization and reprocessing.

opened memories might be overwhelming. The client's experience would be one of opening up all the doors to all the disturbing memories, without resolution. For clients who are especially vulnerable to being emotionally overwhelmed by this type of chained affect bridging, a negative outcome can often be avoided by "tightening" the focus within EMDR Phases 3 and 4. That is, the client can begin processing with a single memory, or even a memory fragment, and then after every set of bilateral stimulation (BLS), there can be the instruction, "Okay, now, go back again to the exact memory image we started with. What do you get now?" If, following sets of BLS, the client cannot access the initial image, that probably indicates that therapeutic processing has occurred; if this is the case, or if the image is now less accessible, vague or fuzzy, that probably indicates the question can be, "What do you get when you *try* to see that exact image again?" In other words, the processing/reprocessing element of the usual EMDR procedure is prevented and replaced by a repeated focus on processing only a specific memory image. This is similar to Shapiro's original EMD procedure (F. Shapiro, 1989). Whether or not this "tightening" procedure is used, EMDR, in general, has the advantage of being specifically focused on discrete pieces of memory, in a way that can be very helpful to a client in containing potentially overwhelming amounts of posttraumatic affect.

When a dissociative client is in EMDR therapy (or any type of psychotherapy), a chief danger is *dissociative abreaction*—the abrupt switch from the part of self that is oriented to the safety of the present to another part of self that is having an intense "trauma-reliving" experience. Many dissociative clients, while in the part of self that is oriented, have some degree of awareness of trauma-related inner experiences (feelings, memories, or childhood parts), but the oriented part has a phobic avoidance of these dysfunctionally stored elements. In order for traumatic memories to be healed and integrated, they must first be fully accessed, and therein lies the problem. As discussed previously, the oriented, "apparently normal" part may have significant avoidance defenses, many of which are involuntary, and these defenses stand in the way of full access to "trauma-reliving" parts. An additional concern is the danger that, if and when the client is able to access the traumatic material, he or she would be overwhelmed by it, and would be vulnerable to a dissociative abreaction. If this were to occur, it would not be a therapeutic experience. The person might still have his or her eyes open, but the person would not be with the therapist anymore—he or she would be in a reliving experience of a horrible moment in the past, without the resource of present safety.

As discussed in Chapter 1, a necessary condition for the effectiveness of EMDR procedures is dual attention, the simultaneous awareness of present safety in the therapist's office and the traumatic memory material. It is very helpful for the client to have a positive attitude of, "I am bigger than my problems. I have troubling old memories. I may have an addiction. I have anxiety and depression. But these experiences don't have to define me." This attitude is difficult to achieve for many highly traumatized individuals; therefore, extensive preparation prior to trauma processing is often required. A firm grounding in present orientation and emotional safety is extremely important prior to attempting trauma work. This grounding can often be facilitated through specific stabilization procedures. Here are a few examples—asking the client to:

- Simply be aware of the sensations of breathing in and out
- Asking the client to "locate a space" in the right arm, the left arm, the right leg, the left leg, the abdomen, the chest, and so on
- Listen to and simply being aware of muffled sounds in the therapy building
- Respond to simple questions regarding the therapy office—"How many tissue boxes do I have in this room?"
- Get out a chair and walk with the therapist to the other side of the room, and then back again, and then to the other side, and back, and so on
- Answer simple arithmetic problems—"What is 5 plus 7? Minus 3?"

Procedures such as these can be very helpful in assisting a client to remain oriented to the safety of the therapist's office.

When therapy has reached the trauma processing phase, the therapist must be aware of the delicate balance involved in accessing traumatic disturbance, "just enough" so that that disturbance is processed and resolved in a way that remains under control. In the EMDR introductory trainings, there is a metaphor of, "If you are driving through a long tunnel, keep your foot on the accelerator!" In other words, trust the process and continue sets of BLS during EMDR Phase

4 even if the client is experiencing an emotional abreaction, so long as the client reports change and progression in his or her experience with continuing BLS sets. This is good advice for working with clients who are able to maintain orientation to the present while working with an old memory. However, for dissociative clients, this metaphor may not be the way to go. The primary guideline, instead, is to make sure that therapy, and processing of dysfunctional information, continues in the appropriate direction—the direction of healing, but slowly enough that the continuation of dual attention is not too difficult for the client. In working with dissociative clients, slow is fast (Kluft & Fine, 1993). There are several metaphors that can be useful in explaining this to clients. One is the image of driving down a mountain road that has many twists and turns. The issue, in this driving situation, is not how fast you can go, but whether you have control. It may be necessary at times to slow down, to watch for sharp turns in the road, and even, at times, to come to a temporary stop. The main point, in working with highly traumatized clients, is to start from a place of present orientation and safety and access traumatic material in a titrated way, slowly if necessary, in a way that facilitates ongoing positive momentum in the therapy. For those who live in colder climates, there is another automobile metaphor: driving in the wintertime from one town to another on an icy road. You know where you are going—the other town—but you have to also pay very close attention to what is immediately in front of you and whether you are remaining in control. Otherwise, you could easily end up in the ditch. This is how trauma processing often is with a very highly dissociative client. Constant attentiveness to the client's emotional safety on the part of the therapist is a high priority.

Mindfulness is a term used to describe a calm, attentive state that can serve as an effective buffer against intrusions of posttraumatic memory disturbance. Initially, to be mindful is to simply be aware of ongoing experience, with a commitment "to reside as best one can from moment to moment in awareness with an open heart, a spacious, non-judging, non-reactive mind, and without trying to get anywhere" (Kabat-Zinn, 2003). And from this commitment, over time, mindfulness can become an important resource, a skill in managing and directing one's own awareness to immediate experience. Ongoing practice with meditation and with yoga has been shown to create skill with self-calming (as well as resting changes in EEG and increased cortical volume [S. Shapiro & Walsh, 2003]). Self-soothing procedures can be more difficult for a person who is experiencing a high level of intrusions from disturbing memory, and so for clients with Complex PTSD, the initial learning of these methods may be the focus of several therapy sessions, and/or a yoga class or a structured ongoing meditation group. Mindfulness skills are also taught within skills training groups that are part of the cognitively oriented treatment for borderline personality disorder: Dialectical Behavior Therapy (DBT; Linehan, 1993).

Within the community of EMDR therapists, a variety of procedures of resource installation and development (e.g., Gonzales & Mosquera, 2012;

Kiessling, 2003; Korn & Leeds, 2002; Leeds, 2002; Popky, 1994; Schmidt, 2004, 2009; van der Hart, Groenendijk, Gonzalez, Mosquera, & Solomon, 2013; Wildwind, 1995) have been proposed as a means of bringing positive and adaptive attributes and feelings to the center of awareness, so that the client will be emotionally fortified in preparation for accessing posttraumatic disturbance. Similarly, therapists working and writing within the Theory of the Structural Dissociation of the Personality (TSDP) have provided a number of very helpful procedures and exercises that can be carried out individually or in a group setting, guided by a therapist, to enhance self-reflective skills, inner feelings of safety, time management, improved coping with emotionally triggering situations, and maintenance of appropriate interpersonal boundaries (Boon, Steele, & van der Hart, 2011).

Another very useful preparation procedure, especially for clients who have inadequate attachment experiences early in life and/or repeated trauma, is the Early Trauma Protocol (ETP) developed by Katie O'Shea (2009). The specific procedures within this protocol assist the client in exploring more fully any issues of damaging parental nonengagement and maltreatment that may have occurred preverbally. In addition, the ETP also includes an "affect resetting" procedure, which is designed to correct distortions in the client's affective reactivity, and return the client's neurologically based affect system to its "original factory condition." The core affects of human beings each have an adaptive function. Fear is an unconditioned response to imminent danger and pain, or other harm. Shame (emotional shutdown, a search in the mind for personal transgressions) is an intrinsic response to situations where interest or excitement is suddenly untenable, often because that excitement violated an individual's own moral code, or resulted in being caught by someone else. These and other affects have a purpose; however, in many clients with an extensive trauma history, these affects arise in a way that has nothing to do with these purposes, or the immediate situation. For example, a person with PTSD may feel fear when thinking of a traumatic event, even though there is no immediate danger. As will be discussed in Chapter 12, shame often is part of a client's clinical picture even though that affect often makes no logical sense in terms of either the client's present situation or his or her history. O'Shea's Affect Resetting procedure is one of desensitizing key words—such as fear, rage, anger, shame, and panic/grief (core affective states; Panksepp, 1998)—that are initially emotionally charged in themselves and are often linked directly to traumatic memory material. Clients who undergo "resetting" in this way, during the preparation phase, tend to have greater resilience when they later target traumatic memory material—either specific memories or trauma-reliving parts.

As illustrated in Figure 8.3, the enhancement of positive mental actions and realizations can be very helpful and give the client a sense of being larger than his or her own pathology. This type of shift toward increased empowerment is therapeutic in itself, but for highly traumatized individuals, resource

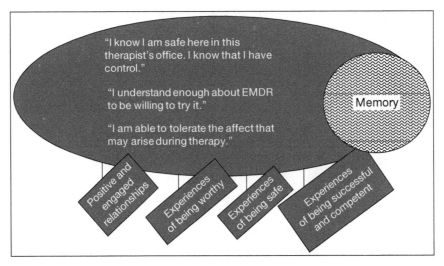

Figure 8.3 Resource installation during EMDR preparation phase: Positive memory networks can be enhanced and brought to the center of consciousness to facilitate the functioning of the natural information processing system.
EMDR, eye movement desensitization and reprocessing.

installation alone is usually not sufficient to provide comprehensive therapy. It is also necessary to use this "installed" sense of empowerment as a platform for direct treatment of unfinished disturbing memories. In addition to the positive qualities shown in Figure 8.3, consistent ongoing ability to maintain orientation to the safety of the therapist's office, even while accessing traumatic material, is a crucial resource for many clients with a dissociative vulnerability. Specific procedures for installing this crucial resource will be discussed in detail in Chapter 13 and illustrated in Chapters 15 and 16.

REFERENCES

Boon, S., Steele, K., & van der Hart, O. (2011). *Coping with trauma-related dissociation*. New York, NY: W. W. Norton.

Gonzales, A., & Mosquera, D. (Eds.). (2012). *EMDR and dissociation: The progressive approach*. Charleston, SC: Editors.

Herman, J. L. (1997). *Trauma and recovery*. New York, NY: Basic Books.

Janet, P. (1907). *The major symptoms of hysteria*. London, UK/New York, NY: Macmillan. (Reprint of 1920 edition, 1965, New York, NY: Hafner).

Kabat-Zinn, J. (2003). Mindfulness-based interventions in context: Past, present, and future. *Clinical Psychology: Science and Practice, 10*(2), 144–156. doi:10.1093/clipsy.bpg016

Kiessling, R. (2003, September). *Integrating resource installation strategies into your EMDR practice.* Paper presented at the 2003 EMDR International Association conference, Denver, CO.

Kluft, R. P., & Fine, C. G. (1993). *Clinical perspectives on multiple personality disorder.* Washington, DC: American Psychiatric Press.

Korn, D. L., & Leeds, A. M. (2002). Preliminary evidence of efficacy for EMDR resource development and installation in the stabilization phase of treatment of complex posttraumatic stress disorder. *Journal of Clinical Psychology, 58*(12), 1465–1487. doi:10.1002/jclp.10099

Leeds, A. (2002). A prototype EMDR protocol for identifying and installing resources. In F. Shapiro (Ed.), *Part two training manual.* Pacific Grove, CA: EMDR Institute.

Linehan, M. M. (1993). *Cognitive-behavioral treatment of borderline personality disorder.* New York, NY: Guilford Press.

O'Shea, K. (2009). The EMDR early trauma protocol. In R. Shapiro (Ed.), *EMDR solutions* (Vol. 2, pp. 313–334). New York, NY: W. W. Norton.

Panksepp, J. (1998). *Affective neuroscience: The foundations of human and animal emotions.* New York, NY: Oxford University Press.

Popky, A. J. (1994). *EMDR protocol for smoking and other addictions.* Presentation at the annual meeting of the EMDR Network, Sunnyvale, CA.

Schmidt, S. J. (2004). Developmental needs meeting strategy: A new treatment approach applied to dissociative identity disorder. *Journal of Trauma and Dissociation, 5*(4), 55–78. doi:10.1002/jclp.10099

Schmidt, S. J. (2009). *The developmental needs meeting strategy: An ego state therapy for healing adults with childhood trauma and attachment wounds.* San Antonio, TX: Developmental Needs Meeting Strategy Institute.

Shapiro, F. (1989). Efficacy of the eye movement desensitization procedure in the treatment of traumatic memories. *Journal of Traumatic Stress Studies, 2,* 199–223. doi:10.1002/jts.2490020207

Shapiro, S., & Walsh, M. (2003). An analysis of recent meditation research and suggestions for future directions. *The Humanistic Psychologist, 31*(2–3), 86–114. doi:10.1080/08873267.2003.9986927

Truax, C. B., & Carkhuff, R. R. (1967). *Toward effective counseling and psychotherapy.* Chicago, IL: Aldine.

van der Hart, O., Groenendijk, M., Gonzalez, A., Mosquera, D., & Solomon, R. (2013). Dissociation of the personality and EMDR therapy in complex trauma-related disorders: Applications in the stabilization phase. *Journal of EMDR Practice and Research, 7*(2), 81–94. doi:10.1891/1933-3196.7.2.81

Van der Hart, O., Groenendijk, M., Gonzalez, A. Mosquera, D. & Solomon, R. M. (2014). Dissociation of the personality and EMDR therapy in complex trauma-related disorders: Applications in Phases 2 and 3 treatment. *Journal of EMDR Practice and Research, 8*(1), 33. doi:10.1891/1933-3196.8.1.33

van der Hart, O., Nijenhuis, E., & Steele, K. (2006). *The haunted self: Structural dissociation and the treatment of chronic traumatization.* New York, NY: W. W. Norton.

Watkins, J. G., & Watkins, H. H. (1998). *Ego states: Theory and therapy.* New York, NY: W. W. Norton.

Wildwind, L. (1995). *EMDR in the treatment of depression.* Presentation at the EMDR Network annual meeting, Sunnyvale, CA.

9

Preparation: The Language of Ovals

The complex connections between issues of attachment and dissociation into parts can often be communicated to clients using a "language" of ovals. These ovals, drawn on paper during a therapy session, represent (from a psychological/experiential perspective) the client's self-states or parts and (from a neurological perspective) complex memory networks. These parts are created through repeated experiences with a similar theme. In addition, these parts have characteristic relationships with each other within the person's overall personality. They may be dissociated from each other or have various roles with regard to each other.

Beginning in Chapter 1, images of ovals were used to describe different configurations of personality structure. Similarly, drawn pictures of ovals can be used to represent the development of both positive and dysfunctional attachment patterns and the connection between dysfunctional patterns and structural dissociation within the personality. The use of this method of communication, through ovals, is especially useful for those clients who are initially frightened of the idea that they have separate parts of self, some of which may be dissociated. One client, when I began speaking to her of the different places that were evident in her own personality structure, said to me, with alarm, "I'm not a multiple, am I?" She did not have full dissociative identity disorder (DID), but had seen many TV shows and movies that depicted DID with overdramatization, giving her the impression that separate dissociated parts were something weird and unacceptable. The use of ovals language was helpful to her in clarifying that she was a normal person who had to adapt, as a child, to a very abnormal environment.

In 1995, Landry Wildwind, an excellent and creative eye movement desensitization and reprocessing (EMDR) therapist, presented some ideas on how to treat chronic depression with EMDR-related methods. I have used and extended Wildwind's approach, finding it very useful not only with depressed clients but also with clients with dissociated parts and dysfunctional attachment styles. With a client who has already disclosed some information indicating insufficient parental engagement, and traumatic events in his or her family of origin, I often will get out a piece of paper and some colored pens and draw a series of ovals to represent the dilemma of a child growing up in a dysfunctional family. The type of drawing that results is shown in Figure 9.1.

I generally talk to the client in the following way, while making the drawing, beginning at the top.

> *I'm going to draw something here that we can use as a basis for discussion. First, here is a picture of how it is supposed to go, when things go well between a parent and a child.* (Two ovals are drawn in the upper corners of the paper, one enclosing the word "parent," and the other oval containing the word "child.") *A parent sees the needs of the child and responds with affection, empathy, and mirroring.* (An arrow is drawn from the parent oval to the child oval.) *In this way, a bond is created that gives the child a safe place to grow up.* (A larger circle is drawn that encompasses the smaller ovals.) *This is how it is supposed to go.*
>
> *From what you have told me, this is not exactly the situation you had growing up. You had a parent, and you were a child.* (Two additional parent and child ovals

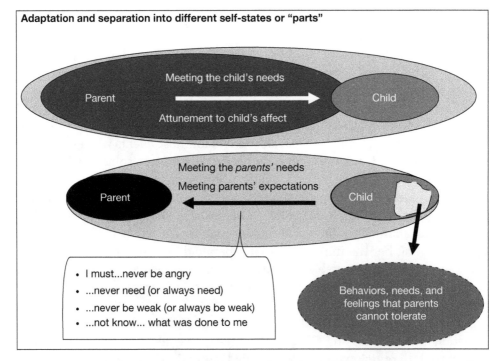

Figure 9.1 A drawing that can be made for a client who developed separate personality parts in order to adapt to incomplete or inadequate parental engagement.

are drawn, down the page.) *But this positive situation, of loving attunement, was not occurring in the way you needed, and so what I think you did—perhaps intuitively—you tell me—is you found ways to meet your parent's needs.* (An arrow is drawn from the child oval to the parent oval) *and that created enough of a bond for you to survive.* (A smaller circle is drawn around these ovals.)

Now, there were parts of who you were as a child that could not exist within the connection you had with your parent. These were parts of you that one or both of your parents ignored, or could not connect with, or could not tolerate. (A separate oval, with a dotted border, is drawn outside of the parent-bond circle.) *For example, maybe your parents couldn't handle you being angry, or you speaking truthfully to them about something, and you had to adapt to that.*

So here is a question. (Therapist points to the arrow that goes from child to parent.) *What was this arrow? What did you need to do to meet your parent's needs in order to have a connection?*

When this method is used, the therapist makes a list of all the ways the client as a child had to adapt to the parent's needs in order to maintain connection, while disregarding his or her own needs. To illustrate, Figure 9.2 shows my case notes (upper left corner) and the actual responses (written on the right) from a man in his early 30s, in therapy for treatment of depression. I had not previously known that this client had been sexually abused, and I think that the

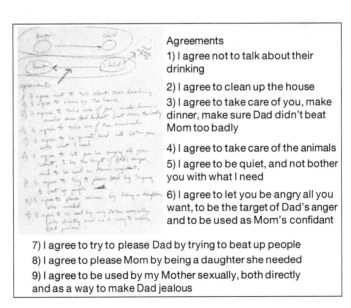

Agreements

1) I agree not to talk about their drinking

2) I agree to clean up the house

3) I agree to take care of you, make dinner, make sure Dad didn't beat Mom too badly

4) I agree to take care of the animals

5) I agree to be quiet, and not bother you with what I need

6) I agree to let you be angry all you want, to be the target of Dad's anger and to be used as Mom's confidant

7) I agree to try to please Dad by trying to beat up people

8) I agree to please Mom by being a daughter she needed

9) I agree to be used by my Mother sexually, both directly and as a way to make Dad jealous

Figure 9.2 Example: Session notes from a client in treatment for a depressive disorder.

structure of this method made it easier for him to disclose this information. For this client, the "agreements," the ways of connecting with parents by meeting parents' needs—each of these translated directly into an EMDR target.

It is very useful to have these ovals on a piece of paper, so that in subsequent sessions the therapist or client can point to different places on the page while discussing the different adaptations or parts within the client. Figure 9.3 illustrates how, in a dysfunctional childhood environment, the "normal, acceptable" self-state(s) may become differentiated from aspects of the child (emotions, perceptions, needs, memories, etc.) that are unacceptable to the child's caretakers.

ATTACHMENT TO THE PERPETRATOR

There is a related factor that, for children in a dysfunctional environment, also contributes to the development of separate self-states. Ross (1998 Ross & Halpern, 2009) has described "the locus of control shift," a phenomenon that tends to occur, primarily in young children, when a child experiences an uncontrollable and highly disturbing event. The child, influenced by his or her normal childhood egocentricity—that is, an assumption of being at the center of his or her own, personal universe—will search the mind to find a way or ways of explaining the horrible event in terms of his or her own causal agency. This can occur

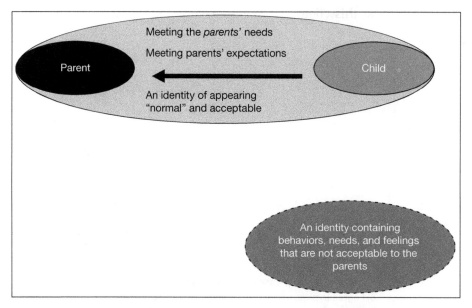

Figure 9.3 Ovals to show how parts may develop separately. Some parts are visible to the parent and appear "normal," while other aspects of the child—the characteristics and needs that are not attended to or tolerated—exist outside of the bond with the parent.

for traumatic events that are apart from any difficulty in a family situation. For example, in Turkey, following the 1999 Marmara earthquake, therapists working with children there reported that many of these children would be frightened that they had caused the earthquake by some misbehavior (S. Yurtsever, personal communication, 2001). Another example: Sadly, adult survivors of sexual assault will very often feel ashamed afterward, and perhaps even not report the crime to police. This does not make sense. The perpetrator should be ashamed, but frequently the victim will be plagued by thoughts of, "I shouldn't have been walking in that park," "I should have had better locks on my door." For many adults, and particularly for children, the "locus of control shift" functions to defend against a full awareness of the fear and actual fact of helplessness during the time of a trauma, while also functioning to preserve a positive, valued image of the world as ultimately controllable ("if only I hadn't . . .").

The locus of control shift, then, frequently occurs when a child is abused or severely neglected by a caretaker. A split in self may occur. With abuse or severe neglect, defensive systems of anger and escape from harm are activated, but also the child has a natural inclination to idealize the caretaker, and must regard the caretaker as the source of supplies necessary for survival. Ross has speculated, based on his clinical experience with such cases, that this type of split is present in every clinical case of DID, and in fact is the origin of dissociation for those people suffering from this problem. If the child is able to fully dissociate the memory of the abuse experience, a positive image of the perpetrating caretaker can be preserved. More commonly, though, the abuse may only be partially dissociated and minimized (e.g., "I have vague memory pictures, but I'm not sure it really happened." Or, "Yes it happened, but it didn't bother me"). In this type of situation, the client may have had a strong feeling of shame about Self—"It's better to be a bad kid with a good parent than a good kid with a bad parent." Children in this unfortunate situation will often think hard to create a narrative in which the perpetrator is still a "good parent," if only in the child's mind.

This is very similar to the Stockholm syndrome (Jameson, 2010), which is when an individual, who has been captured by another person and isolated from outside contact, comes to identify with and have affection for his or her captor, in an unconscious act of self-preservation. Children, especially very young children, tend to believe what they are told by adults, even if it is absurd. ("You caused me to abuse you. You asked for it.") The beliefs of captors are often incorporated in this way into the individual's perception of his or her circumstances. In each of these instances, the need—based on the imperative of survival—to remain connected to a caretaker, even an abusive caretaker, overrides and takes priority over what the child knows from direct experience.

As the child grows up in this unfortunate environment, a type of split within the Self is likely to occur, with an adaptive part becoming increasingly focused on the importance of appearing normal in order to maintain connection with other people in general, and another part of Self remaining hidden, with continuing "right now reliving" of traumatic events and the childhood identity. This can result in the personality structure that the structural dissociation theorists (van der Hart, Nijenhuis, & Steele, 2006) refer to as primary dissociation—one apparently normal part (ANP) and one emotional part (EP; Figure 9.4).

If the child's world includes different environments requiring very different adaptations, separate ANPs may develop. For example, if it is sadly "normal" for a child to have to submit to physical or sexual abuse within the family, and then appear as a different kind of "normal" when he or she goes to school the next day, separate personality parts are likely to be created to adapt to these widely different circumstances. The EP, holding the traumatic reliving, or qualities that are unacceptable in either environment, may be isolated in a separate part (Figure 9.5).

It is intrinsic to this situation that avoidance develops between an ANP and the EP or EPs in order to block disruptive intrusions from EPs into ANP. As mentioned earlier, ANPs and EPs all function for the benefit of the individual, but have very different agendas. As described in Chapter 2, a single traumatic memory is a piece of unexperienced experience. A life event was so overwhelming and disturbing that the processing of that event was interrupted and unfinished. An EP is made of such events, and the unfinished memories held by each EP push for expression, seeking completion of the incomplete, unresolved traumatic experiences. An ANP, though, has the task of appearing normal and acceptable; thus, disruptive intrusions of posttraumatic images and feelings

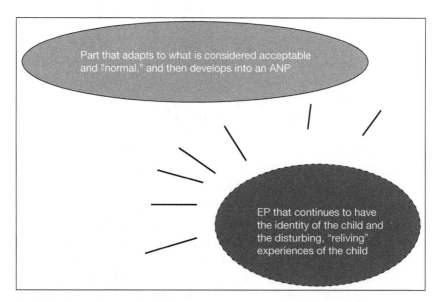

Figure 9.4 Then, as the child grows up. . . .
ANP, apparently normal part; EP, emotional part.

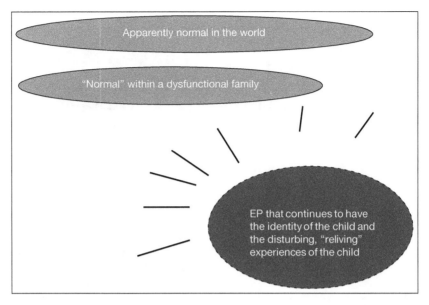

Figure 9.5 Different adaptive parts may develop as responses to different situations.
EP, emotional part.

from EP are unwelcome. For EMDR therapists, working with the tools of the Adaptive Information Processing (AIP) model, it makes sense to think of this type of avoidance as a defense, amenable to therapeutic processing, using the methods described previously in Chapters 3 and 4. Similarly, idealization, as described in Chapter 5, may also serve a defensive function (Figure 9.6).

These personality patterns are being described in their simplest form, in order to show how different types of personality structures can be created and then develop. Of course, the clinical picture is often more complicated, with many dissociated self-states intruding into awareness and experiencing some degree of "reliving" of the traumatic past. In addition, the clinical picture usually includes defensive actions that began and are maintained in order to protect the functioning of the ANP or ANPs. This more complicated situation involving several ANPs, several EPs, and several defenses is illustrated in Figure 9.7.

This method of using these ovals to describe different types of personality structures can also be applied to other types of situations. If, during childhood, meeting the parent's needs does not reliably result in connection with the parent (e.g., with a parent who is always "zoned out" or completely uninvolved), a child might automatically fall back on a more primitive means of connection, one that occurs with many mammals: connection by fighting, in order to gain control and power in a dominance hierarchy, as illustrated in Figure 9.8.

For a child who has been unable to form a coherent sense of self, fighting with the parent can provide an identity—a self-definition of being "independent," and in control, although with the cost of also being "bad." One client

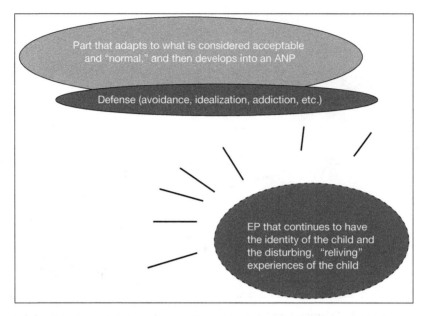

Figure 9.6 To maintain stability of the ANP, defenses (avoidance, idealization, shame, addiction, etc.) may develop.

ANP, apparently normal part; EP, emotional part.

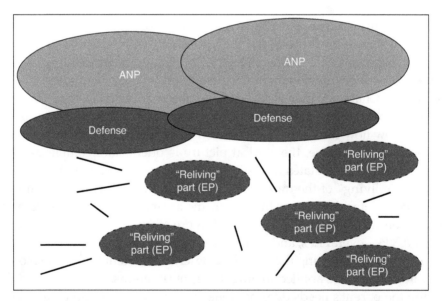

Figure 9.7 There can be many ANPs, many EPs, and many defenses.

ANP, apparently normal part; EP, emotional part.

told me, "My father was gone, and most of the time, it was like, to my mother, I didn't exist. When I fought with her, that proved how bad I was, but at least I existed." Another client, coming to therapy for help with a problem of uncontrolled anger, said, "When I was 8 or 9, my father used to beat me with a hose,

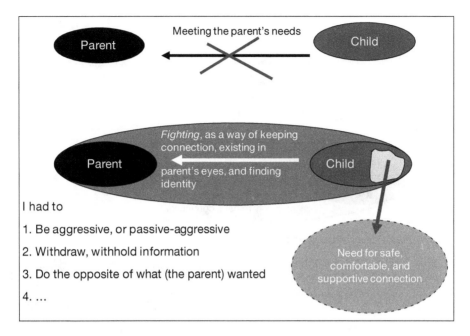

Figure 9.8 If meeting parent's needs does not result in connection, another means of connection for the child is to attempt to win/fight/dominate.

sometimes for nothing. When I was 15, I was big, and one time when he started in, I took the hose from him, and beat him with it. He never tried anything after that." For this client, fighting back in this way redefined the nature of his relationship with his father in a way that increased safety, although at the price of increased alienation.

Another variation (Figure 9.9) is the situation where the client had a highly narcissistic parent, who was so focused on his or her own needs that the child was not very much in the parent's awareness, except when conforming to the parent's idealized image of how the child should be. In the Greek myth, Narcissus was a beautiful man who was loved by many other people. However, Narcissus had a terrible flaw. He would not allow himself to be warmed by the love of other people. When the gods on Mount Olympus saw that this was occurring, even with true and deep love from another, the gods punished Narcissus by putting him in the same bind that others had experienced, with him. He was made to fall in love with his own reflection in a pool of water. The reflection could not feel his love, and he withered and died at the side of the water.

This expresses a dilemma of the child of a narcissistic parent. The child's natural need to attach, by expressing love and helping the parent to feel loved, is frustrated. The child in this situation often has to become a "narcissistic object," an appendage of the parent's identity, in order to have some semblance of connection. With this situation, there may be great efforts to live up to the parent's ideal, along with hidden, dissociated feelings of intense loneliness and unworthiness when that idealized goal is not achieved. A child growing up with this

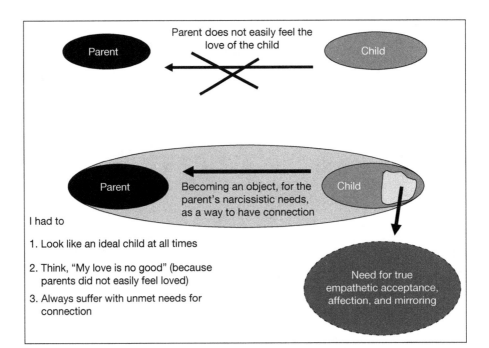

Figure 9.9 Children naturally idealize parents and need to know that their parents feel loved. But narcissistic parents sometimes have trouble feeling the love of others, even the love of their own children. When this occurs, a child may attempt to be a "narcissistic object"—a child who is ideal in every way, in order to have connection.

situation may have the distorted impression that his or her love is inadequate, because the parent, in his or her narcissism, was not open to receiving the child's loving feelings, expressed normally and directly (Figure 9.10).

A child may need to develop different adaptations to different caretakers. This may not only occur following a divorce, but also can occur when the parents' marriage remains intact and the parents have very different expectations of the child. The case of Dave in Chapter 5 is an illustration of this general type of situation.

And, if the parent is dissociative, with different parts, often the child will need to develop separate adaptations to each of these presentations by the parent. One example of this general situation is illustrated in Figure 9.11. A client in therapy for treatment of a dissociative disorder drew the picture in Figure 9.12, illustrating how she had to develop many parts within herself—some adult parts, some child parts—to adapt to the many parts within her mother.

The use of ovals is not a rote procedure, but it is a flexible means of giving both client and therapist a communication language for how the client's separate parts developed as a natural and normal adaptation to his or her childhood environment. This language can then be used in subsequent sessions to discuss specific parts, and relationships between parts, by simply pointing to places on

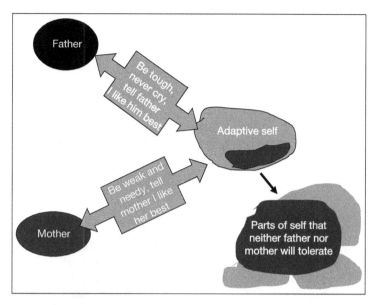

Figure 9.10 Different adaptive ego states may form with different caretakers . . .

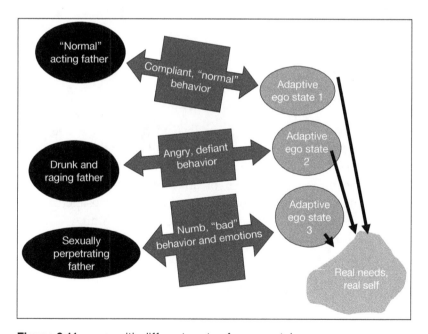

Figure 9.11 . . . or with different parts of one caretaker.

the paper. Also, when the client's personality structure can be depicted visually, the very complex nature of that structure is simplified to a great extent. The ovals, then, can provide a cognitive platform for the use of AIP trauma processing procedures, such as the "Loving Eyes" method and the method of Back-of-the-Head Scale/Constant Installation of Present Orientation and Safety

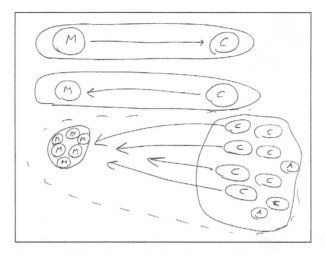

Figure 9.12 Drawing made by a 41-year-old woman
with DID, showing how she had to develop many
internal parts—child parts and adult parts—to adapt
to the many parts of her dissociative mother.
DID, dissociative identity disorder.

(BHS/CIPOS), which will be described and illustrated in Chapters 11, 13, 15, and 16.

REFERENCES

Jameson, C. (2010). The short step from love to hypnosis: A reconsideration of the Stockholm syndrome. *Journal for Cultural Research, 14*(4), 337–355. doi:10.1080/14797581003765309

Ross, C. (1998, Spring). The problem of attachment to the perpetrator. *Inner Voices.* Available at *Sanctuary for the Abused.* http://abusesanctuary.blogspot.com/2006/09/problem-of-attachment-to-perpetrator.html

Ross, C., & Halpern, N. (2009). *Trauma model therapy.* Richardson, TX: Manitou Communications.

van der Hart, O., Nijenhuis, E., & Steele, K. (2006). *The haunted self: Structural dissociation and the treatment of chronic traumatization.* New York, NY: W. W. Norton.

10

Preparation: Drawings

DRAWINGS BY CLIENTS

Clients with dissociative personality structure can sometimes feel disoriented as they begin to fully realize their own internal system of parts. If a drawing can be made with the parts represented on one sheet of paper, this, for many clients, can give a sense of containment and control. The method is to simply ask the client to draw a "map" that shows important information about his or her inner experience—"Can you draw a picture of what you are experiencing right now?" The "map" may be a representation of all known elements of the client's personality structure or, more often, may be an image depicting the parts that are involved in remembering a particular emotionally charged incident. These maps can be open ended, with the client able to freely draw in a way that is highly expressive, or the therapist can suggest a particular structure for what to put on the page. It is important that the client knows that this is not an art contest! Scribbles or circles on the page to represent parts or feelings are okay. In my office, I keep a stack of white paper and colored pens; quite often, I will ask a client to make a picture of some kind that represents what we are talking about in the session. Very often, a picture like this is easily worth 1,000 words! Some drawings made by clients in treatment for Complex posttraumatic stress disorder (Complex PTSD) are shown in Figures 10.1 to 10.7.

In Figure 10.1, four separate personality parts are represented. A little baby part holds memories of very early sexual abuse by her father, and that image fills the head of a terrified 3-year-old part who is anticipating more abuse. The shadow represents a part in total despair, in a fetal position, following the abuse. And the larger head represents the adult self who is helplessly suffering with intrusions from the other parts. This picture was very evocative and told more about the client's inner experience than could easily be conveyed just through verbal description. A drawing like this can facilitate the therapist and client talking more extensively and productively about the client's inner world.

Figure 10.2 was made after a client said to me, "It's always the same. When I look straight ahead, all the parts are always in the same place." I asked her if

Figure 10.1 A 55-year-old woman client's drawing of her personality parts.

Figure 10.2 Drawing made by a client who said, "It is always the same," with specific parts always located in the same place in her visual field.

she could draw a picture of this, and as she made this drawing, she described each part and the relationships between the parts. The face in the upper right corner, for this client, initially felt like a constant threatening presence, always ready to criticize and find fault with her in a brutal way. As therapy proceeded, it became clear that this part was originally created in imitation of an actual perpetrator during her childhood. Other figures in this drawing had very specific meanings to this client, and this "map" of her internal world was a great help to her in containing her posttraumatic affect and helpful to me in planning the sequence of therapy interventions.

Figure 10.3 was drawn by a client who experienced torture as a child, with multiple perpetrators. It conveys the terror of these experiences in a very vivid way.

Figure 10.4 was drawn when a client said to me, with great emphasis, *"I wish you could know* what it is like to be me right now!" I handed her a blank sheet of

Figure 10.3 Client drawing: A memory of the eyes of perpetrators who were hurting her.

Figure 10.4 Client drawing: Her experience of inner chaos, with many shouting, angry parts. Putting the parts on a single piece of paper allowed her to develop some emotional distance from the chaos, and also enabled her to express and share this complex experience.

paper, and she made this drawing, with a red marking pen, very quickly, in only 7 or 8 minutes. Again, it is a vivid expression of her inner world, with many talking voices, loud noises, much confusion, and chaos. This is an experience that can occur when many internal dissociative barriers suddenly break down, and many of the parts of the dissociative personality are talking, but not listening. It helped this client to make this drawing. By putting this chaos on a piece of paper, where both the client and I could simply look at it, the separate voices became more of a single noisy collage, and the client was able to become more calm. And, again, the drawing gave me important information about the client's inner world.

Figure 10.5 was made by a client attempting to express how one part of her had control of the voice and had the privilege of being "out," and other parts were stuck behind a "wall," unable to gain "airtime," because the part that was out refused to relinquish control. You can see the big ears on some of the unhappy internal parts as they listen in frustration to what is being said. This picture represents a situation that often happens in the treatment of dissociative conditions. A part is out and does not want to give up the voice because that part has enormous fear that if it goes back inside, it will never be able to come out again—it will be in a situation of permanent exile. If a child part will not allow an adult part to come back at the end of a therapy session, it can be a significant problem—the child may be stuck in a very disturbing "trauma time," the child cannot drive the car home, another client may be in the waiting room scheduled for the next hour, and so on. If this occurs, often it can be quite useful for the therapist to persuasively reassure the child part, "Don't worry! You will not be forgotten! When we begin our next session, I will remember to ask you to come out again, I promise." Later, in Chapter 16, the treatment of a dissociative combat veteran will be described, including a moment in a session when the younger part—a "soldier" emotional part (EP)—refuses to give up control to the present-oriented apparently normal part (ANP). For this session, there was no

Figure 10.5 Client drawing: One personality part is "out," but is jealously keeping other parts behind a "wall."

time pressure, and the ANP and EP both remained "out," coconscious of each other, and were able to engage in a productive therapeutic dialogue.

These last two pictures (Figures 10.6 and 10.7) are from a session with a dissociative client in which we were working on her deep feeling of shame about herself.

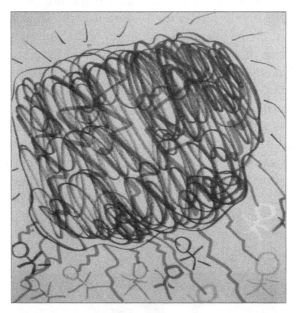

Figure 10.6 Drawing made by a dissociative client at the beginning of a session, in response to the question, "What does shame look like, to you, right now?"

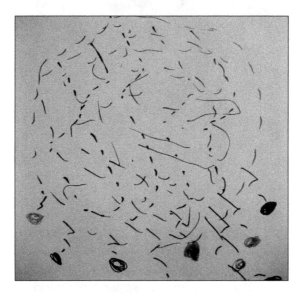

Figure 10.7 Drawing made by the same client, in response to the question—"What does shame look like, right now?"—at the end of the same session.

During this session, we were targeting a particular event that was the origin of her chronic feeling of "badness." These pictures illustrate a way for clients to express and recognize their own progress, in addition to the usual numerical measures that are used in EMDR, the 0 to 10 Subjective Units of Disturbance score, and the 1 to 7 Validity of Cognition (VOC) score. At the beginning of the session, I asked the client if she could make a drawing (Figure 10.6) of "what shame looks like." Figure 10.7 is the drawing she made at the end of the same session, in response to the same question. It is easy to see that the second drawing is more positive, although it still has small smudges indicating that there still are remaining traces of the shame feeling. Nevertheless, these pictures were helpful to this client in providing additional visual evidence of her therapeutic progress.

Figure 10.8 is a sculpture that a client brought in one day. We had been focusing on the strong avoidance need of her "adult" self—an ANP—with regard to a very young child EP that was still "reliving" sexual abuse by her father. This sculpture was therapeutically useful for the client to do, and useful for me as well, by providing more information about her internal struggle with avoidance versus acceptance of her inner child. As you can see, the "adult" part is pushing the "child" out of her heart, and neither is very happy

Figure 10.8 Cardboard sculpture made by a client between sessions, to express ANP's phobic avoidance of a child EP.

ANP, apparently normal part; EP, emotional part.

about it. She made this sculpture after she had already done some initial work toward understanding her strong urge to not think of the child, but that urge, and the associated memories, still remained. We used this sculpture to target and resolve the ANP's remaining avoidance defense.

These are the ways for clients to communicate visually and nonverbally. The use of colored pens to make drawings like this can be especially useful for dissociative clients with child parts, because children like to draw. The child parts, who initially might be quite reluctant to be involved in the therapy process, can sometimes become enthusiastic about participation through the use of drawings like this. In addition, a picture provides a kind of vocabulary, in visual images, of the attitudes and characteristics of different personality parts and relationships between parts. As mentioned previously, a drawing of internal parts can facilitate internal dialogue—for example, "When this part says she still wants to go on as if the abuse never happened, what does this part have to say?"

THE DISSOCIATIVE TABLE, OR CONFERENCE ROOM METHOD

This approach, first developed by George Fraser (1991, 2003), is another means of using a drawing to help a client safely identify, access, describe, and gain protective emotional distance from highly volatile trauma-reliving parts, as well as help the client understand the relationships between those parts. The conference room imagery can be introduced to clients during the preparation phase, before specific therapy work to process traumatic events or reintegrate trauma-reliving parts. EMDR therapists Sandra Paulsen (1995) and Kathy Martin (2010) have written and presented excellent information on how to integrate the dissociative table with AIP procedures. I will be describing here some specific ways in which I have adapted this method to help clients who have different personality parts that hold identities that are incongruent or in conflict with each other. These parts may be mostly aware of each other, or partially dissociated, and the relationships between parts can variously be characterized as phobically avoidant, angry, dominant/submissive, indifferent, or unaware. The activation of these different parts, in different situations and circumstances, creates a lack of coherence and consistency in the individual's behavior, which is often confusing to the person and intrinsically related to the problems that person is bringing to therapy.

This method is generally used after a particularly troubling memory or a trauma-reliving personality part has been identified. It can be introduced to a client in the following way:

Therapist: See if you can use your imagination to think of a room—it's an imaginary room—with large comfortable chairs. The chairs are around a table (therapist draws a large rectangular table, with three-quarter rectangles, representing chairs, around the table). Can you just use your imagination right now and think of a very comfortable room like that?

And on the wall there is a large TV screen (therapist draws another rectangle on one side of the table).

Depending on the client's ability to stay present through this procedure, the screen might be blank, or have an ongoing movie, or a still picture, or a black-and-white still picture taken from far away.

And now, can you visualize yourself just walking into that room? And go ahead now, and sit down in one of those nice chairs. That's good.

This request will typically access the client's ANP. The next step is to bring other parts into the room (i.e., other parts that may be involved in a particular memory are placed into other three-sided rectangle "chairs"). This step, in itself, facilitates a lessening of dissociative distance between parts; for that reason, it can be the beginning of personality integration. The way that other parts are identified will depend in part on the issue that is the client's focus. For example, if the client is an adult, and the focus of a therapy session is on resolving an incident of childhood sexual abuse by the father, at age 8, the therapist might suggest the following:

Look over now at the doorway of this comfortable room, and in the doorway, see an 8-year-old girl that is you. Just watch as she comes into the room and sits in one of the other comfortable chairs. Notice what she looks like—you know what a little girl that age looks like—just see her as she goes over and sits there in another chair.

For some clients, this imagery might bring up too much affect; in these cases, the dissociative table can be used in other ways that provide more containment. A 35-year-old woman—a survivor of childhood sexual abuse—was aware of her own dissociative personality structure, but was also very frightened of her own child parts. Later in her therapy, she was able to use the dissociative table in a way that was empowering for her, but in the beginning, her ANP had enormous fear of even thinking of her child EPs. We proceeded in the following way (see Figure 10.9), in order to help her be less fearful regarding her own personality structure and also to introduce dissociative table imagery to her in a less threatening way. The following procedure helped her gain more understanding of her own contradictory emotional responses, and why they had been so confusing to her.

I described for her the 0 to 10 Subjective Units of Disturbance Scale (SUDS), and then asked if she could think of something that, on this scale, was disturbing, but no more than a 1, 2, or 3. She said,

Client: "Yes, I can. When I was driving here today, I noticed that someone had thrown a bag of trash on the side of the road, and it

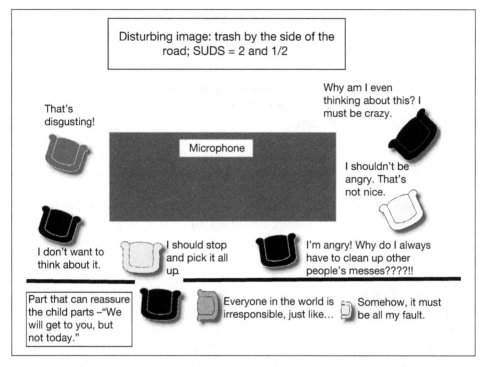

Figure 10.9 Dissociative table imagery, with a low-SUDS target.
SUDS, Subjective Units of Disturbance Scale.

scattered all over. When I think of that right now, it bothers me—that's about 2 and a half."

She was able to visualize the general structure of the dissociative table quite easily. We put her memory picture of the trash by the side of the road on the TV screen. Before we proceeded any further, I drew a three-quarter rectangle facing the screen (representing a chair) and asked if there was a part of her that could stand guard for this session to make sure that we would stay focused *only on the disturbance from the trash*. Also (assuming her childhood parts were listening in the background), I said,

> *Therapist: We can talk during this session about this mild disturbance you're feeling, and that can be a way of preparation for working in future sessions with some of the bigger situations that still feel like too much to think of. If there are little parts of you that are listening right now, I'd like to ask them to allow the work today to go forward, with them watching, if they want to, but not overwhelming you with the feelings they have. In this therapy, we will get to everything, but we have to do it one step at a time.*

I then asked the client, *"Do you think they heard me?"* She said, **"I think so. When you said that, I could feel myself relax a little bit, so maybe they were**

listening." It was important for both of us to acknowledge the presence of these child parts, and do so in a respectful manner, not just out of courtesy, but also for a very practical reason—if any of the child parts objected to this work, the work could be blocked.

We then went ahead in the following way, with the drawing of chairs, table, and TV screen already on a piece of paper, and the words, "Trash by the side of the road" on the screen.

> *Therapist: When you think of the trash, what is the first thing that comes into your mind?* **(Client: That's disgusting!)** *Okay. And now look at it again.*
>
> *When you look at it now, what is the second thing that comes into your mind?* **(Client: I don't want to think about it.)** *All right. And now look at it again, and what is the third thing that comes into your mind?* **(Client: I should stop and pick it all up.)**

We proceeded in this way with the client saying, with the next chair, **"I'm angry! Why do I always have to clean up other people's messes!?"** And then, **"I shouldn't be angry. That's not nice."** And then, **"Why am I even thinking about this? I must be crazy."** Because this particular client appeared to be vulnerable to being destabilized, I did not include sets of bilateral stimulation (BLS) following each of her responses. She benefited just by having her self-structure represented on the paper, where she could see all of the different parts and points of view. With other clients, I have used a similar structure and included one or more sets of BLS following each response, just to help the client reduce the sympathetic arousal connected with naming each of the parts.

This client was able, with the help of the dissociative table imagery, to contain the emergence of childhood parts. She was also able to see how her response to this simple, mildly disturbing situation activated many different points of view—the same basic themes that she had in her life with regard to much more disturbing posttraumatic material. It gave her a cognitive structure that later served as a method of containment, and a platform for the use of EMDR, in targeting specific memories that were much more disturbing.

Her initial use of the dissociative table helped in a major way for her to begin to understand why her thoughts and feelings about both present-day stresses and past events were so confusing and contradictory. She also was able to see that, for several of the parts, the beginning of an important dialogue was already occurring—for example, between the third and fourth chair and the fourth and fifth chair. It was very useful for her to take this dialogue further, resolving issues of inappropriate self-blame, and also anger, and then sadness, about how irresponsible people sometimes do things that hurt others. This was, of course, a major issue of her childhood as well, but by structuring this session in this way, she was able to put aside the childhood issues and have the experience of desensitization—processing a mild disturbance from two to three to less than one. This was an empowering resource for her in her continuing therapy, and she was ultimately able to use the same dissociative table structure to become more aware of each of the child parts within her, help those parts to reconcile with each other through empathetic dialogue, and successfully resolve traumatic experiences held by specific child EPs.

This method can be used when a particular memory image has been identified. For some clients who are already aware of the structure of their own parts, it can be appropriate for the therapist to simply ask the question, "When you think of that (the troubling memory), who is here?" Then, the therapist can request that parts that are linked with a traumatic event can come into the room and be in their chairs. Other clients might not be so aware of their own personality structure, but the separate ego states or parts might be evident from the client's general clinical presentation. Much confusion and emotional disturbance may be occurring due to internal parts that are not sufficiently aware of each other or are in conflict with each other. In a previous session, the client may have said, "Sometimes I just feel like an inadequate little 10-year-old!" which could indicate a younger part. Or maybe the client has talked about an internal critic—a presence who is always criticizing the core ANP. If it is likely that another part is somehow linked to a particular memory disturbance, the therapist can suggest that that part also enter the room with the table and sit in one of the other chairs. If the ANP is very frightened of another part, the Constant Installation of Present Orientation and Safety (CIPOS) procedures (described in Chapters 13, 15, and 16) can often be helpful, with the ANP glancing at the fearsome part for only a brief period of seconds, and then looking away. Sometimes, child parts are too frightened to be part of this process, but still want to be involved, and these parts can listen under the table, or just outside the door to the dissociative table room, or they can watch what is happening through an imagined closed-circuit TV. All of these variations on the dissociative table method should be done in a way that is empathetically respectful of the client's need for emotional safety.

If the client is able to maintain dual attention and a sense of emotional safety with the therapist, it can be very effective to do the Affect Bridge procedure from the chair with the most affect to a feeder memory, a memory of when that part originated. If the client is able to access this feeder memory, while still retaining present orientation and emotional safety, standard EMDR Phases 3 to 7 procedures can be used, and following this processing, the initial target—on the screen in the conference room—will likely be much less disturbing.

With the dissociative table method, the parts of self are represented by drawings on a page—just ink on paper—enabling the client to have a degree of protective distance from the affect held within those parts. This aspect of the method increases the client's sense of emotional safety and facilitates the client's being able to develop an overview of discrepant parts that exist internally.

Seeing the parts assembled, together, on a piece of paper, each with its own separate characteristic feelings and separate points of view, can help a client glimpse the fact that all these parts are elements of a single, unitary personality, which is his or her own. For clients who, at the start of therapy, feel fragmented, without a sense of a true "Self" (Schwartz, 1995), it is often helpful for the therapist to say,

> *You know what it is like to be in this chair. And you know what it is like to be in this chair. And even though it might be frightening to you, you also know what it might be like to be in this chair. It might be an interesting question for you to think about—"Which chair contains* the real you?"

> *Here is something to think about. The real you is the place within you from which you can see each of these chairs, and the states of mind that are in each chair. That's the real you.*

Or, if this is too threatening for the client, it can be helpful to say,

> *When you look at that image on the screen that represents the traumatic memory, what percentage of you is in each chair?*

If this second method is used, the "percentage" is likely to change when therapy proceeds successfully. It is often helpful to have one additional chair on the paper—a chair suggested by the therapist—containing a point of view about the traumatic incident that would express resolution of that incident, such as "It's really over now," or "I was just an innocent child and it wasn't my fault," or "I did the best I could with a difficult situation." The client might say, in the beginning, "There is nobody in that chair," but as the therapy proceeds, a larger "percentage of self" will probably be located there, validating the progress of the therapy.

With this method, the imagery of a comfortable room, table, and screen is useful, but not necessary. Any imagery can be used that the client is comfortable with. There can be a discussion between parts, sitting in a secluded and pleasant backyard (Figure 10.10), or in a beautiful meadow. Or the parts may all come together in the therapist's office. The main requirement is that the imagined meeting place, itself, is defined from the beginning as safe and comfortable.

This method can be useful even when there are only a few parts. Oftentimes, this imagery can be used with people who have an adult state that has one reaction to a trauma, and a child state that has a very different reaction (Figure 10.11). A very nice outcome, that occurs frequently, is that the adult self, through processing, comes to have a compassionate acceptance and a loving feeling toward the child self. This can be a very healing moment in therapy, facilitated by the dissociative table imagery.

Are drawings, sculptures, and tables such as these part of Janet's Phase 1, preparation, or Phase 2, processing? As was mentioned previously, it is here that

Figure 10.10 Some clients may have difficulty with imagery of a closed room. The "dissociative table" procedures can be done with any imagery that the client is comfortable with (e.g., chairs in a pleasant, private backyard on a warm, sunny day).

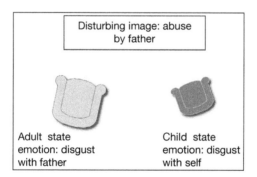

Figure 10.11 The dissociative table method can be used even if there are only two parts involved in a traumatic event.

Janet's original conceptualization of phases may break down, in that these and other methods both prepare for trauma resolution and are beginning that resolution. The line between the phases is blurred because effective therapy involves repeated vacillation between emotionally safe experiences and the titrated accessing of memory material that is disturbing. This blurring of Phases 1 and 2 will become even more evident in Chapters 11, 13 and 14, with discussions of the "Loving Eyes" procedure, the CIPOS method, the Internal Healing Dialogue (IHD) procedure, and case presentations to illustrate these interventions.

REFERENCES

Fraser, G. A. (1991). The dissociative table technique: A strategy for working with ego states in dissociative disorders and ego state therapy. *Dissociation*, 4(4), 205–213.

Fraser, G. A. (2003). Fraser's dissociative table technique revisited, revised: A strategy for working with ego states in dissociative disorders and ego state therapy. *Journal of Trauma & Dissociation*, 4(4), 5–28. doi:10.1300/j229v04n04_02

Martin, K. (2010, September/October). Fraser's dissociative table technique: A Phase 2 strategy. Presentation at the 15th EMDRIA Conference, Minneapolis, MN.

Paulsen, S. (1995). Eye movement desensitization and reprocessing: Its cautious use in the dissociative disorders. *Dissociation*, 8(1), 32–44.

Schwartz, R. (1995). *Internal family systems therapy*. New York, NY: Guilford Press.

11

Loving Eyes: "Looking" From One Part to Another

The Loving Eyes procedure, simply put, is asking an oriented part—typically the apparently normal part (ANP)—to form a visual image of an emotional part (EP)—a younger part that is experientially reliving a traumatic event. Often, there is phobic fear and avoidance maintaining the dissociative separation between parts like these (van der Hart, Nijenhuis, & Steele, 2006). An ANP may be phobic of an EP because of the potentially overwhelming disturbance or information the EP contains, and because of the disruptive influence of the EP on the main function of the ANP—doing the tasks of daily living while maintaining an appearance of normality. Conversely, EPs are often frightened of encountering the judgment and rejection of an ANP and hide themselves from being accessed by the ANP. These factors may be so intense as to prevent dual attention, thereby preventing the standard use of eye movement desensitization and reprocessing (EMDR).

SITUATIONS IN WHICH DUAL ATTENTION IS NOT INITIALLY POSSIBLE

When the EMDR standard procedures are being used with a disturbing memory (single incident, clearly remembered, and without dissociation), the client is simply asked to "Think of the event." The Phase 3 questions establish a baseline for the Subjective Units of Disturbance Scale (SUDS) and the associated visual image, cognitions, emotions, and sensations. These questions are very useful in bringing into awareness all of the major elements of the traumatic memory so that processing can be full and comprehensive. This works very reliably when the person is able to maintain dual attention—simultaneous awareness of both present safety and past trauma.

However, as stated earlier, this dual attention situation may be hard to achieve for many people with more complex traumatization. A person with a very difficult trauma history might simply begin to think of a trauma and be immediately flooded by overwhelming disturbance, putting him or her on the edge of losing orientation to the safety of the present. For this situation, the usual Phase 3 questions might not be appropriate.

For example, a man might be at the edge of a "dissociative cliff" when he begins to think of a sexual assault incident. He may be struggling to maintain orientation to the therapist's office. He is already very close to having too much disturbing information, and the Phase 3 questions would have the potential of bringing up even more. It would probably not be helpful or wise for the therapist to ask, "Can you get an image that represents this incident, or an image of the worst part? What is the negative thought you have about yourself when you think of that? What sensations are you feeling in your body when you think of that?" These are questions that, for many clients, are useful in setting up the target memory for processing. However, for other people who are highly vulnerable to emotional flooding, these questions might significantly disrupt the balance between awareness of past and present, and make dual attention impossible for the individual.

For this type of problem, the Loving Eyes procedure can be used to initiate processing in a way that is more gentle and less challenging to the client. With appropriate targeting, with bilateral stimulation (BLS), parts can (a) become more aware of each other; (b) begin to become less afraid of each other; and (c) through internal dialogue, guided by the therapist, soften their positions of fear or opposition to each other. The general effect of sets of BLS is to reduce sympathetic arousal and extend associational connections for whatever experience is at the center of consciousness. If a client is focusing on a conflict between internal parts, there may initially be a high level of fear. Focused sets of BLS can lessen the sympathetic arousal connected with this conflict, resulting in a lessening of fear and, in addition, sets of BLS can invite additional associations and information, which can be useful in reconciling the conflict. Both parts—ANP and EP—were initially formed with an adaptive purpose for the individual; therefore, adaptive resolution of the conflict between parts is nearly always possible if the phobic mutual fear can be contained, and therapeutic information processing can move forward. In other words, when sets of BLS are combined with the client's focused awareness of an internal conflict, this tends to invite new relevant information to enter into the conflictual dialogue between those parts. This can turn a frightened internal conflict into a healing conversation.

The term *Loving Eyes* describes the outcome of this procedure, but in a sense, we could also call it the "Clearing Out All the Obstacles to Loving Eyes" procedure! With a focus on internal dialogue, a client can come to realize that separate viewpoints or parts inside were each necessary adaptations to life difficulties, even though they may now be working at cross-purposes within the personality.

Think of two good friends talking about a topic of disagreement. If each clearly expresses his own point of view while also listening carefully and calmly to the viewpoint of the other, a healing resolution becomes more likely (or at least an "agree to disagree" resolution). In the end, one might say to the other, "I see why you feel that way," or "I see what you're going through." To "see" the problems of another conveys a message of understanding, and even acceptance. Mutual compassionate validation—"seeing" the other person's point of view—helps resolve conflicts and disagreements between people, and the same principle applies to conflicts between parts within an individual person. More basically, in many areas of life, a visual connection between individuals is intrinsically linked to attachment and connection. Poor eye contact, in an adult, may suggest some degree of guardedness or self-protective distancing in a relationship. One element of healthy attachment between babies and their caretakers is mutual eye contact—there is a predisposition for each to find the eyes of the other and maintain a mutually soothing and pleasant gaze (Schore, 2012). In many ways, eye contact is an essential element of connection.

In a way that is similar to what occurs when there is conflict between individual people, conflict between internal parts can be healed by a comprehensive conversation, an exchange of viewpoints, with not only talking but also empathetic listening. The Loving Eyes procedure is a means of helping clients develop, step by step, this type of healing connection, followed by conversation between initially conflicting dissociative parts. It is specifically useful in two opposite kinds of situations: when there is far *too much* fear (or anger, or despair) in the EP for the parts to be in direct contact and when there is *too little* communication of affect, initially, between parts, due to psychological defense or too much dissociative distance between the parts.

Previously (in Knipe, 2007, 2009), session transcripts were presented that illustrated this type of dialogue between parts, using targeted sets of BLS. This chapter and the remaining chapters in this book also contain case examples that illustrate variations on how this Loving Eyes procedure can be used to help parts initially make contact, then speak their separate points of view to each other, then engage in a dialogue that can create reconciliation of the conflict between the parts. To the degree that this healing dialogue results in closure and reconciliation, the path then opens to processing of all traumatic memory disturbance held by those parts, as well as integration of the personality.

STEPS IN THE LOVING EYES PROCEDURE

The Loving Eyes procedure, then, can be an alternative to the usual questions of EMDR Phase 3. The steps are as follows:

Step 1. Begin by helping the adult client (i.e., the present-oriented part of the personality) to have a strong sense of present orientation and safety in the therapist's office, and then ask that present-oriented part to visually witness the feared childhood event *as a separate person from the child*. For example, the therapist might say, "Sitting in this chair, the adult you are today, can you just look at that child? *You know what children that age look like. Can you just see this child?"*

Step 2. If the client says **"Yes,"** the therapist initiates eye movements with words that are open and permissive, such as "Just see this child. And when you see this child, just see whatever you see." The therapist's wording is open ended and conveys acceptance of the child, without judgment. This type of unconditional acceptance is probably what the child originally needed at the time of the traumatic event. It frequently occurs at this point that the adult ego state begins to experience the feelings of the child, and so the therapist must take care to ensure that these feelings are contained within the adult's sense of present safety. Sometimes, it is necessary to pause in this process, so that the client will stay oriented to present safety. The Constant Installation of Present Orientation and Safety (CIPOS) procedures described in Chapters 13 to 16 can also be added to assist the client in maintaining orientation to the present.

Step 3. It often occurs that the adult client initially has a nonaccepting reaction to this image of the childhood self. These negative reactions to the child represent defenses (specifically, avoidance, discussed in Chapter 4, and/or defensive shame, which will be discussed in Chapter 12), which remain in place in order to maintain dissociative distance from the painful affect that is held within the separate, frightened, child ego state. In some instances, this defense can be processed by simply asking the client to focus on the positive feelings associated with the defense. For example, the therapist might ask, "What's good about knowing that you today are *not* that child? What's good about knowing that you are not stupid (or weak, pathetic, powerless, naïve, etc.)?" In response to this question, the client might say something like, **"The person I am today—I can be strong (or assertive, or make good decisions, etc.)!"** Whatever the client's response, the therapist can then respond, "Think of that" and initiate a short set of BLS, in order to strengthen the client's positive self-statement as a resource. Very frequently, the avoidance urge/shaming response will lessen, and the resistance to compassionately seeing the child will likely diminish. The client may begin saying things like, **"I feel sorry for her,"** or **"She is really in a no-win situation."**

Step 4. When the client is able to freely see the child, the therapist may then ask, "When you look at that child, can you see the feelings behind the face? Usually, the client will acknowledge that the child's feelings can now be seen, and at this point, the adult part may begin to share (i.e., feel) the feelings of the traumatized child, but in a way that can be more easily tolerated. As sets of BLS continue, with sufficient continuing orientation to present safety, the fear of the child is likely to dissipate and positive feelings of connection and compassion for the child are likely to increase.

Step 5. As the client begins to speak of the child compassionately, the therapist can ask, "When you look at that child, how do *you* feel about the child?" This is an important question that often elicits a very powerful positive response. Even though this child part was previously feared and avoided, the client now may be surprised to discover the possibility, as an adult, of viewing this inner child with love and respect. The child part of the personality can then begin to experience this love and validation (which may be experienced by the adult as an inner relaxation).

Step 6. The question for the adult part can be raised, "Can she (the child part) hear you?" in order to strengthen the connection.

Step 7. Another question might be, "Is there anything that you know, as an adult, that would be helpful to that child? Something that child doesn't know?" Whatever the client answers to these questions, the therapist can respond by saying, "Stay with that," and then begin an additional set of eye movements. This internal dialogue typically continues, back and forth, facilitated by sets of BLS, to a point of healing resolution. Chapter 14 will describe some of the reasons for the effectiveness of this healing dialogue procedure, as well as additional information about how to present this procedure to a client.

Step 8. If the client says that the child is **"scared that we see him,"** or **"worried that we will criticize him for being afraid,"** then the shift can be back to the adult self with questions like, "Do you in fact, as an adult, looking at the child, feel critical of the child?" If the answer to this question is yes, it may be necessary to go back to Step 3, to help the adult part soften their fear, avoidance or angry rejection of that child. Interweaves of cognitive information about the realities of the child's life circumstances are often useful in softening the harshness of the critical adult's perspective (e.g., *Therapist:* "Do you think that child has it rough?").

EXAMPLE: LOVING EYES METHOD AS AN INTERVENTION WHEN THERE IS "TOO MUCH" DISTURBANCE

"Ronnie," a 43-year-old man, came to therapy following his arrest for physically assaulting his wife. Because he was very ashamed about his behavior, it was initially very difficult for him to access the state of mind he had been in during the assault. By the time of the fourth session, he was able to tell about the intense feelings of anger that would inappropriately come up in him. We used EMDR Phases 3 to 7 to target a present-day situation that had evoked strong "irritation." In that session, he was able to recognize that his anger had been covering other, more basic feelings of helplessness and unlovableness. He reported the next week that he had had better control over his anger, and he recognized that his wife was not deserving of this reaction; in spite of these cognitive insights, however, he still was feeling these emotions. I asked him to think of another triggering situation (he had several), and be aware of the anger in his body, and take that back into the past. He was able to do an Affect Bridge (Watkins & Watkins, 1998) to many events—anger in work situations, previous relationships, and within his family of origin. I asked him what his earliest memory of anger was, and he told me, with some difficulty, of a clear memory image from around the age of 2 to 3. He was in a bed at the house of a babysitter and crying while she changed his diaper. She shouted at him to stop crying, and when he could not do that, she pinched his testicles, very hard and painfully. Ronnie remembered the babysitter later telling his mother, "Your son was very bad today. I don't want him back here again." His mother, then, was also very angry at her son. He could not tell his parents what the babysitter had done. In the days after this incident, his parents could not find another babysitter, and so, as he remembered, his mother had to quit her job. He told me that after this incident both his father and his mother repeatedly blamed him for the loss of family income.

When my client described this incident, he was visibly shaken. To check on his state of mind, I asked him, "Right now, when you think of what happened, using those numbers, 0 to 10, how disturbing is it for you?" He said, "25! I'm really angry! I'd like to take a swing at somebody. It should never have happened!"

I asked him if he could put aside this memory for a moment, and return to just be aware of the quiet safety of my office. He was able to do this, "pretty much," by looking around my office, and by looking at a squirrel in a tree outside my window. We had previously developed imagery for a "safe and comfortable place," and also imagery for a "container" that could hold traumatic memories until we were ready to work on them, incident by incident. But he said, "I can't put this back in the container. It is too important." I asked him if he could remain aware of being safely in the present, while simply looking at this little boy that he was during this awful experience. He said, credibly, that he was able to do that. I then said to him, "With your awareness shifted away from that babysitter, just look at that boy, while it is happening. Just look at this child, and see whatever you see." With repeated sets of BLS, focused in this way, information processing of this event took place. He saw the terror of the child and the shame feelings of the child (since this babysitter was attempting, quite deliberately, to give the child shame feelings). He also processed feelings of how he felt later when his parents were angry at him. He even was able to visualize his adult self, talking to this boy, telling his inner child of his goodness and innocence. Since we had bypassed the usual EMDR Phase 3 steps, we had not preidentified a desired positive cognition (PC) about self; however, the following therapy process occurred at the end of the session. (**[EM]** in this transcript, taken from a video recording, indicates a set of eye movements.)

Therapist: What did you figure out here today?

Ronnie: That memory was so real! *(Therapist: How is it now?)* **I still remember it. But it feels like it's in the past.** *(Therapist: When you think of it again right now, is there any remaining feeling of being angry and helpless?)* **No. It's more sad now, for all those years of uncontrollable anger. [EM] Actually, I feel kind of peaceful. [EM] Can I have a tissue?** *(Therapist: This is hard, isn't it?)*

> **Ronnie nodded, "Yes," and then said: Yeah, but I want to get through it. I've been looking for years to find a way to get through it. Drugs don't help.** *(Therapist: Remember the first day you came in here? You didn't have a lot of hope that this was going to help you either.)* **No. Now I wonder how my job is going to contain me.** *(Therapist: What are you saying, exactly?)* **I'm working this service job now. I have so much more potential than that. But there has been fear about looking for something better.** *(Therapist: Is there a connection between this incident we're talking about and the fear you have had about looking for a better job?)* **Yes. I lived in a lot of confusion, and a lot of the confusion is starting to clear up, and I can see that I can control my anger a lot better now than I could before. Before I would just get outrageous. I wouldn't feel like I was good enough for a good job.** *(Therapist: So, is that shifting now?)* **Yeah, definitely. [EM]**

When I asked him about his SUDS level for this particular memory, at first he said, **"I have to say '1' because I can't say a zero, because it has been with me for such a long time."**

This appeared to be a blocking belief (Knipe, 1998b). Rather than dispute the logic of his statement, I simply asked him if it would be all right with him if all of his disturbance regarding this memory could be gone. When he said yes, we initiated another set of BLS.

> **Ronnie: It's just a trace now. I give it a .5.** *(Therapist: What is that trace about?)* **Because I can still physically feel it and I remember it. [EM] That pain is gone. I don't feel it now . . . I'd give it a 0 . . . I feel really calm right now.**

We were out of time and ended the session at this point. In his session the next week, he told me that this memory remained resolved. In addition, generalization had occurred—he said that it was strange, but very positive, to no longer get so irritated about little things. Ronnie's therapy with me ended, somewhat prematurely, a few weeks later when he relocated to a nearby state; once there, he was able to enroll in a training program that would qualify him for a better job. I later learned, from his wife, that he remained in this new location after the training was completed, and his wife soon after joined him there. This session allowed him to lay down a significant portion of his burden of anger and shame, be a better partner in his marriage, and feel significantly better about himself.

EXAMPLE: LOVING EYES AS AN INTERVENTION WHEN THERE IS "TOO LITTLE" DISTURBANCE

A second type of situation where dual attention may be absent is one when there is a strong defense in place that prevents the present-oriented part from realizing the extent of unresolved disturbance held by another part. Or, a variation—the part of the personality that is speaking in the therapist's office— may be unaware of the connections between a specific memory and current disturbing feelings and distorted perceptions. For either of these situations, in spite of this disconnect, the unresolved posttraumatic disturbance may show up intrusively in various ways. A client might report frequent nightmares with the same theme. A client might also have stronger than expected emotion when talking about a particular person from childhood. Or the client may simply express extreme dislike of self for having certain feelings without knowing why that dislike is there. As part of this picture, the client may be able to describe difficult events from childhood, but then minimize the impact of those events (e.g., "That just doesn't bother me," or "I really don't remember very much about that."). Of course, in the process of living, people do get over things. The natural information processing system of the mind can often fully resolve a disturbing memory in the absence of therapy. But for some clients, this may not be the case—unresolved disturbance may be buried deep. The posttraumatic emotions are still within the person and are having a distorting influence on the person's present life, but those emotions are not available to the part of the personality that is speaking in the therapist's office. A task of therapy, then, is to develop a thin thread of access to the place in the structure of the personality where the disturbance is held, and then widen that thread of connection into a channel of communication, so that a healing dialogue can occur.

For example, "Linda," a woman in her late 20s, came to therapy with several presenting problems, particularly low self-esteem and difficulty in being assertive and expressing her own needs in close relationships. She was able to use EMDR effectively, targeting a present-day assertion situation with her live-in boyfriend (i.e., with a negative cognition of "I can't say what I really feel" being replaced during the session with a PC of "I am able to easily say what I really feel, in a way that has complete respect for myself, and for him too."), and as a result, she reported becoming more comfortable in her ability to say "no," and in expressing her own needs.

In our first few sessions, before this EMDR work, we had discussed her family background, and I had asked her my usual intake questions, including a brief inquiry about whether she had any history of sexual abuse. She had said "no" to this question, but after this first EMDR session, she mentioned, almost casually, an additional piece of information—that her stepfather once had been sexually inappropriate with her. It was at night when she was 13 years old, and her mother walked in just as the stepfather, in her bedroom, was beginning inappropriate touching. She said, "It doesn't bother me that that happened. I know that's a big problem for a lot of people, but I don't have a lot of feelings about it. She divorced him right after that, and I was glad about that, because he was really hard to get along with." She also said that, except for a few words the next morning, after her stepfather was gone, she and her mother never spoke about it afterward. As we continued to talk about this incident, she said, "I don't want this to bother me, but maybe it does, because I really don't want to talk about it." She was telling me of her awareness of an avoidance defense, and we could have targeted that, using the procedures described in Chapters 3 and 4, but it seemed safe and possible and more useful to her if we were able to gently access this memory directly. I asked her if she could, first of all, be completely aware of being comfortable, safe, and tuned in to my office in the present, knowing that this incident happened long ago, 15 years in the past. And then, I asked her if she could, while maintaining this awareness, see this 13-year-old girl, "right when it is happening." She was able to do this and still maintain good awareness of the safe present. We then initiated sets of eye movements, with the beginning instruction, "Just look at her, and see what you see." During the next 15 minutes, what emerged was, first of all, seeing the terror of her younger self, pretending to be asleep, and then seeing the child's relief when her mother came into the room. She remembered her mother and stepfather fighting and arguing down the hall, her stepfather leaving that night, the brief conversation with her mother the next morning, and learning, "He won't be coming back." In this processing, she was able to speak from her adult self, and tell her younger self, "It wasn't your fault. There was nothing about you that made him do it." She was also able to recognize that, at the time of the incident, she needed to talk much more with her mother about what had happened, but she did not do so, because of nonverbal signals from her mother that the incident was not something that would be talked about. Her mother had died of cancer several years earlier, and it was hard for this young woman to realize that her mother had not been sufficiently available to her following this incident. In imagery, she was able to visualize talking to her mother, and put into words not only her unmet needs from age 13, but also her wish that her mother would have allowed much more conversation after this occurred. In subsequent sessions, Linda talked empathetically about how her mother had had her own emotional problems, and had been distracted and disengaged during this and other incidents. Linda had had to adapt to this situation by minimizing her own needs, and she was able to see how this adaptation, of always putting her own needs second, had carried into her current relationships. This insight, together with her EMDR work developing assertion skills, was very useful and empowering for her.

If a child receives an injunction from caretakers—"Talking about needs (or fears, or anger) is not allowed in this family!"—that child is likely to have a problem if a situation occurs that very naturally brings up these nonallowed needs or feelings. The child may adapt by putting a defense of avoidance or denial in place, causing problems in the present life of the child-grown-up, and also making those childhood incidents much less available for standard EMDR processing. For these clients, at the start of therapy, there may be an odd absence of emotion in connection with particular memories that might otherwise be expected to be disturbing. The posttraumatic emotion may still be present, but not consciously available, within the personality. The ego state or part holding the disowned feelings can sometimes be identified by asking the following type of question:

"When you were a child, was there ever a time that you were afraid? Most children, at one time or another, are afraid of something. Can you think of a time when *you* were afraid?" Or, "Was there ever a time when you were angry? When something happened that was unfair? You might not have told anybody about feeling that way, at the time, but can you remember a time like that?" Or, "Was there ever a time you really needed something, or really wanted something, and you just didn't get it? Was there ever a time you just had to live with the frustration of that?" With memories that are identified in this way, the Loving Eyes procedures can often be helpful in accessing and resolving disowned emotions.

The Loving Eyes method can be used flexibly across many clinical situations. A man in his 50s was very frustrated because he had had a lifelong problem of a hand tremor in many ordinary social situations. This was an embarrassment to him and had, for many years, been a significant and frustrating barrier to his wish to start a dating relationship. He first noticed this problem on his first date after his discharge from the Army, when he was 27. During his time of service, he had had a noncombat job, loading munitions for transport on aircraft. On one occasion, he mishandled a bomb, and watched it bump down a ramp, certain that it would explode any second, killing him and several other people. In fact, the bomb was not armed, and did not explode. When he told me of this incident, he said that it was not frightening to him—"It turned out okay."—even though he was exhibiting the hand tremor. We used the Loving Eyes procedures to focus on this incident, and he was able to see a connection between this problem and something that had occurred long before the incident with the bomb. During his growing up years, his father had told stories of how, during World War II, he had been on an Air Force plane, flying over the ocean, with two of four engines on fire, but his father had said proudly that he had been totally unafraid. My client had heard this story and had taken in the lesson that any and all fear was unacceptable, even in the most dangerous situations. At the end of this session, my client was able to see that the message in his father's story made him ill-equipped for handling a situation that had caused enormous fear in himself. He was able to give himself permission to have some nervousness in new situations, including dating. Consequently, through the use of EMDR and some role-playing, he was able to handle those situations much better. In addition, both his distress about his hand tremor and the actual tremor itself were significantly lessened.

Another example—A professional woman in her early 50s was leading a successful life in many ways, but she still often was troubled by bouts of self-criticism. She thought that her critical attitude toward herself was, "not neurotic, but justified," for several reasons, one of which was, "I don't make good decisions." She could identify many incidents in her family of origin that contributed to her negative feelings about herself, but she said, "I can't blame them." She went on to say, "My life got off to a bad start. I got pregnant when I was 17, and that made things really hard for a long time. I'm angry at myself about that."

Her statement, that she was angry at herself, indicated an unfinished discussion between internal parts. The "angry at self" part was in my office, and so to locate the other part of her, I asked her the question, "Can you look right now and see this 17-year-old girl who is about to go ahead, and let that boyfriend have sex? See exactly where she is, at that moment. Just look at her, there, and see what you see." She was able to create a clear visual picture of her younger self in that situation, and then combine sets of BLS with her image of herself at 17. At first, she had a very critical attitude toward her younger self, but as we continued with sets of BLS, with the consistent focus of "seeing" this young girl, this adult client began to soften her critical tone and she was able to see that his girl was not only inexperienced with boys, but also was yearning for a loving connection—something she was not receiving in her chaotic and self-involved family. At first—when I asked, "What could you say to her that would help?"—this client had a lecturing tone in talking to this younger self ("Don't be stupid! You should know better than to do that!"), but with a dialogue, back and forth over the course of the session, she was able to see this young girl much more compassionately, and this, in turn, helped her have a more forgiving attitude. She then was able to go on and successfully use standard EMDR processing for several other similar incidents that had been the basis for her self-criticism.

These Loving Eyes procedures, of visualization of a younger traumatized part, repeated sets of BLS while "seeing" the younger part, and then healing internal dialogue between parts, can often be easily integrated with the method of CIPOS, which will be described in Chapter 13. Loving Eyes procedures are also a precursor to the use of the Internal Healing Dialogue (IHD) method, described in Chapter 14, with a clinical example in Chapter 17.

REFERENCES

Knipe, J. (1998a, Winter). Blocking beliefs questionnaire. *EMDR International Association Newsletter, 7*(4), 5–6.

Knipe, J. (2007). Loving Eyes: Procedures to therapeutically reverse dissociative processes while preserving emotional safety. In C. Forgash & M. Copeley (Eds.), *Healing the heart of trauma and dissociation* (pp. 181–226). New York, NY: Springer Publishing.

Knipe, J. (2009). Shame is my safe place: Adaptive information processing methods of resolving chronic shame-based depression. In R. Shapiro (Ed.), *EMDR solutions II* (pp. 49–89). New York, NY: W. W. Norton.

Schore, A. N. (2012). *The science of the art of psychotherapy.* New York, NY: W. W. Norton.

van der Hart, O., Nijenhuis, E., & Steele, K. (2006). *The haunted self: Structural dissociation and the treatment of chronic traumatization.* New York, NY: W. W. Norton.

Watkins, J. G., & Watkins, H. H. (1998). *Ego states: Theory and therapy.* New York, NY: W. W. Norton.

12

Treating Defensive Shame

For many clients, shame is hidden beneath other aspects of a client's presentation, such as chronic anger, depression, substance dependence, or general social withdrawal (Bradshaw, 2005; Nathanson, 1992). And, for other clients, chronic shame is not at all hidden, but is a very visible part of the client's initial presentation in therapy. When a client comes into therapy with very low self-esteem—chronic feelings of helplessness or apathy—a lack of confidence and a self-definition of inadequacy, badness, unworthiness, or deficiency—and these qualities have little or no apparent basis in that person's abilities or behavior, the therapist should be alert to the possibility that the client's negative self-assessment is serving a defensive purpose. As described in Chapter 1, a defense is any mental action or behavior that has a function within the personality of preventing full conscious awareness of disturbance connected with trauma. Shame or self-blame does not feel very good. But, for a very young child, and even for some adults, a mental search for one's shortcomings may not feel as bad as the intense reliving of a horrible experience. This may be especially true, in the case of a child, if the traumatic experience was perpetrated by an adult who was in the role of caretaker. A child who is abused or severely neglected within the family is often compelled to search the mind for some way to blame the self. The underlying attitude (sometimes explicit but more often implicit and not articulated) is, "What happened has to be my fault! It can't be Mommy's fault or Daddy's fault. It must be that I am a bad kid with good parents. It can't be that I am a good child with bad parents—with parents who don't care about me." The latter idea would be too frightening for many young children to even contemplate. Self-blame is compelling because it protects the needed positive (though perhaps inaccurate) image of parents; in addition, self-blame allows the child to maintain an illusion of having had control over a situation that was uncontrollable. The child then may try to compensate for this imagined shamefulness in unrealistic ways: "I will try to be perfect, all the time. Maybe then they will like me and treat me better." Shame may become a primary element of the child's self-concept, and even be expressed then in acting out—"bad"—behaviors. In other words, the defensive function of shame may be strengthened, and the identity of shamefulness may be validated by actual unacceptable actions. Many decades later, in therapy, the client might say, "Of course I know that I am a shameful person. Look at all the bad things I've done!"

Silvan Tomkins (1991) and later Donald Nathanson (1992) have described shame as a basic affect—a neurological predisposition that is innate and constitutional, rather than learned. In this context, the innate, "wired-in" affect of shame has a positive purpose, in an evolutionary/survival sense. The purpose is to shut down other affects, such as excitement or interest, or even terror or anger, if those other affects become untenable or unsustainable. Shame can occur, of course, when a person realizes that he has behaved in a way that violates his own conscience, or if he is caught doing something wrong. If a person is doing something that is a violation of his or her own moral values, or is behaving in a way that is logistically untenable, or a dead-end somehow—interest in that something is clearly unsustainable and not going to go anywhere—that is when, automatically, shame is activated as an adaptive mechanism to block the inappropriate feelings of interest, and stop the person from doing what he is doing. It is a reflexive mechanism to immediately stop maladaptive interest and enthusiasm, "put on the brakes," and redirect and repair, as necessary. In this way, shame is adaptive in that it puts a stop to activities or involvements that will go nowhere; therefore, it is a way of conserving energy expenditure. But, as we know from the situations of many clients, shame (feelings and self-concept) can also be highly maladaptive. Shame can be impervious to logic, can be resistant to therapeutic intervention, and can also occur in ways that are, objectively speaking, totally unrelated in any way to moral transgression.

There is also a reciprocal relationship between shame and pride (i.e., defined here, not as healthy self-esteem but as unrealistic self-idealization, as described in Chapter 5). To illustrate, here is an example. For several years, I had an office a few miles from the U.S. Olympic Training Center in Colorado Springs, and one client wanted very much to gain a place on the Olympic cycling team. He was an excellent athlete, but the Olympics were two or three steps above his level and, realistically, out of reach. When he failed to make even the initial cut, it was a blow to his self-esteem. He was unduly critical of himself, trying to inventory all the things he should have done differently. We targeted his negative self-appraisal directly with eye movement desensitization and reprocessing (EMDR), and we also targeted (i.e., using the methods of Chapter 5 for resolving idealization defenses) the origins in his family of the high importance he had placed on his Olympic goal, with the result that he was able to face his sadness regarding the loss of his dream, and still know he was okay. This shift allowed him to direct his energy elsewhere, toward endeavors where he could have more success. In the end, it was sad for him, but also, in a sense, a good thing for him to realize what was possible and what was not possible. By the time of ending therapy, a few months later, he was feeling relief at no longer having the tension of trying to achieve an unreachable goal.

Several years ago, in a little novelties store, I saw an adhesive bumper sticker, which said, undoubtedly with sarcasm, "I feel so much better since I've given up hope!" Maybe a better way to express this idea is to recognize that some aspirations are self-defeating. In our work as therapists, we often work pretty hard to help our clients develop hope regarding their futures. However, it is also important to note that sometimes the most helpful therapeutic intervention may be to assist the client in relinquishing an emotional attachment to something unrealistic or unattainable. The problem of the man with the Olympic aspirations illustrates Nathanson's concept of shame as an affect that has a positive evolutionary purpose, to shut down interest—even *flatten* interest—in an image or activity that is unrealistic and unproductive (and possibly shift to one that is productive). Sometimes, in life, we encounter a "brick wall," where surrender to the realities of life is sadly necessary. If one is faced with a truly impossible situation, withdrawing further effort is adaptive. And this is the positive function of shame, as that term is defined by Nathanson. The whole experience of shame may include a search in the mind for, "What did I do wrong?"; a numbing of interest and excitement; a feeling of diminished, washed out energy; and certain body postures of lowered head and slumped shoulders.

Shame can be a verbally labeled negative identity or a thought the person has about self; it can also be a visceral experience. Clients have described this body experience as a pervasive loss of energy, while "knowing the evilness of you," of being unworthy, of surrendering or giving up. Very often, a client will say this feeling is "all over," that it is everywhere in the body and not just in a specific body location. One client said, "It feels like it is in my DNA!" (Knipe, 2009).

These physical sensations of shame seem similar to what Stephen Porges, the developer of Polyvagal Theory, has described as dorsal vagal parasympathetic activation. Within the Polyvagal Theory (Porges, 2007, 2009), different conditions in the environment activate different responses in the vagus nerve, the 10th cranial nerve, which regulates autonomic arousal. The vagus nerve extends from the brainstem to the abdomen, with connections to the heart, esophagus, lungs, and other organs. This nerve controls activation of the autonomic nervous system, and determines different affect states, in response to the individual's perception of different environmental conditions. Perceived safety activates the *ventral vagal parasympathetic* response and a feeling of calm and connection with others. This is the feeling of comfort that develops from being with other people who are easy to be with and emotionally safe. It also seems to be the feeling that occurs when a person is enjoying being in nature (Paulsen & Lanius, 2010). This is the feeling that EMDR therapists are attempting to facilitate in clients when they help clients develop a "safe place" or "comfortable place" resource.

In contrast, if a situation of danger is perceived, the response is *sympathetic arousal*, which is typically experienced as alarm, shock, fear, or anger. Sympathetic arousal involves increased tension in voluntary musculature, and a relative shutdown of blood flow to the digestive system, in preparation for responding to potential danger. Sympathetic activation is commonly thought of as the fight-or-flight response, but it also involves the type of freeze response that facilitates alertness to present danger. The ventral vagal parasympathetic response, if strongly established, can help an individual have resilience (i.e., inhibition of sympathetic response) in the face of threatening stimuli. This aspect of ventral vagal activation—the capacity of the ventral vagal system to override moderate levels of sympathetic arousal—appears to be the basis of the original systematic desensitization procedures (Wolpe, 1958), which taught anxious clients to first become deeply relaxed, and then systematically confront a hierarchy of initially threatening imagined phobic images.

Perceived impending death or physical immobilization activates the *parasympathetic dorsal vagal* response, a relative shutdown of body activity, physical energy, and even respiration. Dorsal vagal activation can be seen to overlap descriptively with Nathanson's concept of shame affect (i.e., an immediate flattening of untenable interest or excitement, together with a search in the mind for "What did I do wrong?"). It also overlaps with the phenomena of learned helplessness (Seligman & Maier, 1976), as when repeated inescapable pain directly causes a subsequent extinction of attentiveness to options and choices for escaping the pain. Dorsal vagal parasympathetic activation occurs in all mammals, as an intrinsic and automatic response to situations of impending death or being trapped and immobilized. The body goes into a mode of surrender—shutting down muscle tension and even slowing respiration, looking dead, feigning death. If a predator catches a little animal—for example, a fox catches a rabbit— the prey may look dead. This appearance and this body response is a last ditch survival mechanism. If the predator lays down the prey, which appears to be dead, for a moment, the prey might suddenly pop up, quickly shake, run away, and survive.

We frequently see this dorsal vagal parasympathetic response as an element of the posttraumatic stress disorder (PTSD) in our clients who have been abused by their caretakers. The intensity of this response may be related directly to the intensity of other affects that had to be quickly blocked, because, for various reasons, those other affects could not be sustained. For example, a woman in her late 40s, with very low self-esteem, had thought of herself, all her life, as a "depressive personality." She thought that she was a "low-energy" person who had trouble developing interests and commitments. Initially in therapy, as we were exploring the history of her depression, she told me, with great difficulty, about her history of sexual abuse by her father. Over time, she was more able to talk about, and then therapeutically work with, incidents of abuse. The first incident of abuse occurred when she was 6. Her father had left the family (my adult client thought because of an affair with another woman), but then changed his mind and told her and her mother that he would be returning. My client, at age 6, was not thinking at all about her father's infidelity or inconsistencies, but was simply very excited and happy that her father would once again be at home. A few days after his return, she wanted to just go and sit in his lap, and it was then that he began to touch her inappropriately. This little 6-year-old girl was stunned and (she later remembered) deeply ashamed. We could surmise that her self-shaming response—the shutdown of her normal 6-year-old child's interest and excitement—was extreme because of the necessity of bringing an immediate stop to her intense joy and happiness at the return of her father. All of these affective responses were occurring at a nonconscious level at the time of the incident, but the shame feeling continued after this incident, and had a very strong impact on her cognitive self-definition. Since in therapy she was able to clearly remember what had happened, and was also able to maintain dual attention (both past and present), we were able to successfully use standard EMDR Phases 3 to 8. She was able to move from a negative cognition (NC) of, "I'm just bad" to a fully true positive cognition (PC) of, "I know I am a good person (and I was an innocent child)."

In this example, the client remembered a specific incident that was identified as the origin of her adult feelings of shame. Clearly remembered memories of this kind can often be successfully targeted using standard EMDR. Within the Phase 3 steps, the NC expresses the shame about self, or the inappropriate attribution of responsibility for a traumatic event. The PC that answers the NC expresses a healthier and more realistic attitude toward the self, in the context of the remembered event. The typical result with targeting this type of well-remembered event, then, is a diminishing of shame. Shame (either directly felt, or in the form of self-attributions of badness, inferiority, inadequacy, stupidity, inappropriate responsibility, etc.) tends to be a feature of clients who, as young children, suffered abuse or severe neglect at the hands of caretakers. In the adult client, the negative feelings about self tend to come up very quickly—an example of overly reactive "fast thinking" (Kahneman, 2011), as described previously in Chapter 2.

If this direct targeting of a remembered event stalls, it can be due to a blocking belief (as described in Chapter 5). For example, a person might say, "I have known that I am not good enough since before my earliest memories. There's no way that this EMDR can change that." Or, "I don't want you to tell me that I'm a good person! That proves to me that you don't get it!" Statements like these indicate that there is a very strong investment in the negative definition of self. What is the source of this investment? In these instances, it is likely that other traumatic events, less available to consciousness, are driving the shame defense. In the adult client, negative self-referencing cognitions regarding childhood events may contain an element of absurdity. Some examples (and there are many more): "I should have known to not try to get Dad to stop hitting Mom, when he was drunk"; "I should have known not to let Daddy touch me in that way!"; "I should have known to lie to Daddy when he asked me where Mom was, when she went off with her boyfriend"; "I should have been able to figure out a way to get Mom to stop drinking"; "When I was 13, my brother (age 19), said I asked for it—he said I wanted it too. After a while, I gave in to it, because I couldn't get away from him. That makes me just as bad as he was."

Here is another example of the treatment of shame. A woman in her early 50s came to therapy with chronically low self-esteem. In one of our initial sessions she said, "I'm just a piece of shit! Those words feel like home." She was able to give me many pieces of "evidence" of her unworthiness, evidence that seemed irrationally critical of herself. This self-appraisal tracked back to several incidents from her childhood, the most troubling of which was a time, from age 7, when she remembered deliberately drowning a litter of kittens. She had been so happy to find the kittens in a barn, and was shocked when her beloved grandmother put the kittens in a bag, then took her—the 7-year-old granddaughter—to a nearby pond and angrily forced her to push the bag under the water. We targeted this incident directly, with the result that this client was able to look at her 7-year-old self with compassion and acceptance, and also have a forgiving attitude toward her grandmother. She said, "My grandmother had had a tough life. She had several miscarriages, and had to walk away from my grandfather, who drank and beat her. Maybe she was trying to teach me that sometimes you have to be tough." I do not know if this client's assessment of her grandmother's motivation was accurate or not, but this new understanding allowed her to keep some of the positive feelings for her grandmother, forgive her childhood self, and resolve this incident. This client was able to see, through this processing, that she had decided, that day, that she was entirely bad as a way to make sense of a horrible situation. Once she had this cognitive insight, and had come to see that her labeling of herself as bad, though irrational, made a kind of sad sense, it was much more possible for her to go back again and successfully target the confusion and feelings of fear and helplessness connected with this incident. This in turn helped her bring to mind other similar incidents that had occurred with both her grandmother and mother, and bring those to resolution also, with the end result that she was able to have more appreciation of the struggles she had as a child, as well as a clearer sense of her own worth in her present life.

These cases illustrate how shame feelings are often part of posttraumatic disturbance originating in childhood, especially when very positive feelings were abruptly and unexpectedly followed by shocking trauma caused by a valued other. Childhood-onset PTSD, very often, is at least as much a shame disorder, or a "shutdown" disorder, as it is an anxiety disorder.

When a child's early experience includes frequent instances of this type of dorsal vagal visceral "shutdown" reaction, even preverbally, it is then much more likely, as the child continues to grow up, that self-concepts will form around an affect of self-blame. The child may develop an irrational but pervasive cognitive identity of shamefulness, and this identity may be experienced directly, or may itself be covered by other feelings such as defensive blame toward others. Years later, the adult may have a dysfunctional interpersonal style that reflects the cognition: "I'm no good, but I have to always act so that others think I'm okay." Or that child-grown-up may walk into a therapist's office looking for help in alleviating a constant, horrible feeling of inadequacy or unworthiness—one that continues in a very irrational way. One clue that this latter situation may be occurring with your client is a "funny argument," where the client is giving evidence that "proves" how deficient the client is—"I did this wrong, and I did this wrong, and I was so insensitive when I talked to this person, and I am so stupid!" And so on. The therapist's natural reaction might be, "You really are being pretty rough on yourself. You do a good job at your work. You are kind to people. You are caring." An odd debate is occurring. The client is arguing about how bad he or she is, and the therapist is arguing how good the client is. In some instances, this pattern will happen when a client is trying to elicit positive feedback and complements from the therapist. But more often, there is an issue of the client carrying defensive shame. There may also be an issue between the therapist and client regarding projective identification. This debate should happen, not between therapist and client, but between client and client. The client has a part that is at least somewhat well oriented to present reality and wants to benefit from therapy, and another part that is stuck in shamefulness, originating in traumatic events. Usually, when this type of odd debate occurs, the client is unconsciously projecting his or her optimistic, self-validating part onto the therapist. This helps the client simplify internal struggles—"Am I okay? Or am I not okay?" The therapist is receiving the projection of the optimistic part; because the therapist believes that the client *is* basically okay, and the therapist begins verbalizing what was projected from the client. The client then has the opportunity to simplify his or her own internal struggle, and act out the self-shaming side of the debate through arguing, and sometimes in behavior. This can happen in many ways: "I am so bad—No, you're not." Or, "People are no damn good—People are basically good." These and many other similar polarities can be acted out in this way, stalling therapeutic progress until it becomes more clear that these are unresolved debates between internal parts of the client's personality.

Another variation of this problem is the situation of a client who is carrying an entrenched self-definition of badness, and who then gets in trouble for actually behaving in a way that is "bad." Individuals with this pattern will often come to therapy reluctantly, pushed by others, or by a court, in a way that feels, to the client, like an embarrassing confirmation of their feeling of badness. Psychological defenses may cover this embarrassment. This particular personality pattern may overlap with a narcissistic style, as described in Chapter 5, and elsewhere (Knipe, 1998; Mosquera and Knipe, 2015). In these instances, narcissism may cover shame, and shame may cover early childhood trauma with caretakers. For clients who are able to see the path that therapy might follow, and bravely persist in the process, each of these elements can be successfully targeted, in turn.

As previously mentioned, a child may have feelings of shame, notably self-defining thoughts of shame, following parental abuse or neglect because the shame about self allows the child to preserve a valued, idealized image of a "good enough" parent. This image may be factually inaccurate, but the child's need to maintain an attachment bond is a powerful factor in overriding all other considerations. Similarly, adult victims of sexual assault sometimes fall into feelings of shame about themselves in a way that is totally inaccurate and illogical, objectively speaking. This unfortunate self-shaming may function to maintain a desired positive image of something external to the self (e.g., an illusion of a "safe enough" world, where bad things can always be prevented, and where random, uncontrollable, and unpredictable horrible events do not occur). In cases of assault, the person who should be ashamed is the perpetrator, but often the victim has shame feelings that are very strong. For example, following an assault, the victim may have vehement thoughts of, "I shouldn't have been walking in that park. I should not have been wearing those clothes." Or, "I should have had three locks on my door, instead of just one." "I should have . . . I should have . . .!" This can also occur with combat veterans who help-lessly witnessed terrible things, and who may have intense, irrational blame of self afterward, even though the obvious objective truth is that they were not responsible for what happened. Or, as another example, a young child, follow-ing a natural disaster, might worry that he or she caused the earthquake (or the tsunami, or the tornado) by being disobedient, by not cleaning up the bedroom, and so on. In other words, there are many examples of how, sometimes, follow-ing a tragedy, a person will blame the self for something that really was not his or her own doing, as a way of pushing from awareness the full extent of that person's own powerlessness during a traumatic event.

Guilt and shame are very different, even though these words are some-times used interchangably, by some clients. Guilt is the appropriate response to the realization of having done something wrong, something that violates one's values. Shame is, "I am something wrong." Guilt is, "I made a mistake." Shame is, "I am a mistake"—it can be a pervasive identity.

An actual perpetrator of a crime (e.g., an assault, a theft, or anything else that was deliberately hurtful to another person) may be in therapy—perhaps voluntarily, perhaps following a court order—and in these instances, one goal of therapy will be to help that person realize and get in touch with his or her own guilt—not neurotic guilt, but true guilt about what the person has done. Along with realization of true guilt can come a desire to somehow rectify the harm that was caused and become a person with justified self-esteem.

This issue was underlined for me with a particular client. A woman in her 50s was in therapy for treatment of a lifelong feeling of unworthiness and bad-ness about herself. We were able to trace this feeling back to her family where she had been sexually abused; she was also treated badly in other ways by her parents and older siblings. Over the course of many sessions, we used standard EMDR to work through incidents one by one, and this work was very success-ful for her. She realized that the hurtful actions of others had not been her fault. She had not been a bad kid who had deserved all that bad treatment. And then one day, as this work was winding down, she came into a session and said, "I have to tell you what I did this week. I went down to the police station and turned myself in." For years and years she had been embezzling money from the organization she had been working for. She estimated that she had embezzled between $80,000 and $100,000. She was the person within the organization in charge of writing the checks, paying the bills, and keeping the books. She said she never would have been caught. But after the work she had done in her therapy, she wanted to turn herself in. She was arrested, convicted, sentenced to pay some restitution, and put on probation (since it was a first offense). And she was fired from her job. Nonetheless, she was content with that outcome! Her conscience was clear and was not bothering her anymore. Her case really shows the difference between guilt and shame. She came in to therapy with shame, and therapy brought her to guilt, which she then rectified in the way she needed to.

Shame affect may be intrinsically linked with the development of dissociative personality structure. Figure 12.1 illustrates how all children are born with certain action systems—potentials to develop certain mental actions and behaviors necessary for survival. For example, one inborn action system for nearly all children is the propensity for learning a language. Children have a readiness for language, and they acquire the language of their environment. This is a metaphor for how other action systems are actualized and shaped by the child's environment. Children come into the world with an inborn readiness to attach to their caretakers. Also, from the first days of life, children have an automatic response to pain and discomfort—crying as well as withdrawal from the source of the pain. Children have a readiness to learn to play,

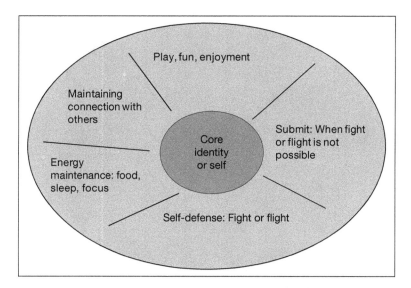

Figure 12.1 In a "good enough" childhood environment, inborn action systems will develop into behavioral response patterns that are relatively well integrated and under the control of a "core" or executive ego state, a Self.

have enjoyment, eat, and are able to focus attention. If the child's environment encourages all of these action systems to develop without conflict or interference from each other, what can then happen is the development of a core identity—a single unitary sense of Self—that manages thoughts and behaviors across many situations. As Self, the child can learn to manage which action systems and which behaviors will be implemented appropriately for each life situation.

However, if the child is abused or neglected by a caretaker, the action systems of attachment are put into direct conflict with the action systems of self-protection (as illustrated in Figure 12.2). The need to maintain connection is in conflict with the need to escape harm and pain. A child in this situation may be only able to develop a very weak sense of Self, or perhaps even an absence of a single sense of Self. Different self-states may have to develop independently to meet the different demands of the child's environment. This situation has been described by Colin Ross (1998; Ross and Halpern, 2009) as "the problem of attachment to the perpetrator." Ross speculates that this dilemma is a significant element in the origin of dissociative personality structure.

A child who is abused by a caretaker, then, has a significant obstacle to developing a secure, unitary identity. The connection with the caretaker must continue as a source of life's supplies: food, shelter, and warmth. And yet the child also needs to protect against physical pain and severe emotional distress. The child has no good choices, only some bad ones. The child might

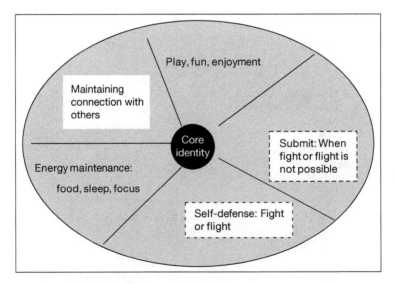

Figure 12.2 A child who is abused or neglected by a caretaker will have an impediment to forming a unified core identity. The innate need for comfortable connection will be incompatible with the innate need for self-protection.

find solutions, not as a conscious process, but just as something that unfolds automatically. The child might dissociate traumatic events entirely, thereby enabling a continuing attachment to a perpetrating caretaker. The attachment to the perpetrator can continue because the child does not have conscious awareness of what the perpetrator did. As a result, the individual may come into a therapist office many years later with a very low appraisal of his or her own worth, but not be aware, initially, of the abuse.

EMDR-related methods can be used to help a client first develop a *cognitive* understanding of the irrationality of his or her self-shaming NCs, and then to resolve the *body feelings* of "badness" that are often present, especially when abuse or neglect at the hands of caretakers occurred very early in life (Knipe, 2009, 2010). Chapter 17 is a detailed case example of how EMDR-related methods can be used to help a dissociative client whose primary symptom was intense shame about self.

REFERENCES

Bradshaw, J. (2005). *Healing the shame that binds you* (Rev. ed.). Deerfield Beach, FL: Health Communications.

Kahneman, D. (2011). *Thinking, fast and slow.* New York, NY: Farrar, Straus and Giroux.

Knipe, J. (1998). It was a golden time: Healing narcissistic vulnerability. In P. Manfield (Ed.), *Extending EMDR* (pp. 232–255). New York, NY: W. W. Norton.

Knipe, J. (2009). Shame is my safe place: Adaptive information processing methods of resolving chronic shame-based depression. In R. Shapiro (Ed.), *EMDR solutions* (Vol. II). New York, NY: W. W. Norton.

Knipe, J. (2010, October 3). *Invited keynote address, the use of AIP therapy methods with dissociative symptoms and Complex PTSD.* EMDR International Association Annual Conference, Minneapolis, MN.

Mosquera, D., & Knipe, J. (2015). Understanding and treating narcissism with EMDR therapy. *Journal of EMDR Practice and Research, 9*(1). 46–63. doi:10.1891/1933-3196.9.1.46

Nathanson, D. L. (1992). *Shame and pride: Affect, sex, and the birth of the self.* New York, NY: W. W. Norton.

Paulsen, S., & Lanius, U. (2010). *Towards an embodied self: The treatment of traumatic dissociation.* Presentation at the Annual EMDRIA Conference, Minneapolis, MN.

Porges, S. W. (2007). The polyvagal perspective. *Biological Psychology, 74,* 116–143. doi:10.1016/j.biopsycho.2006.06.009

Porges, S. W. (2009). The polyvegal theory: New insights into adaptive reactions of the autonomic nervous system. *Cleveland Clinic Journal of Medicine, 76*(Suppl. 2), S86–S90. doi:10.3949/ccjm.76.s2.17

Ross, C. (1998, Spring). The problem of attachment to the perpetrator. *Inner Voices.* Available at *Sanctuary for the Abused.* http://abusesanctuary.blogspot. com/2006/09/problem-of-attachment-to-perpetrator.html

Ross, C., & Halpern, N. (2009). *Trauma Model Therapy.* Richardson, TX: Manitou Communications.

Seligman, M. E. P., & Maier, S. F. (1976). Learned helplessness: Theory and evidence. *Journal of Experimental Psychology: General, 105*(1), 3–46. doi:10.1037/0096-3445.105.1.3

Tomkins, S. S. (1991). *Affect imagery consciousness volume III. The negative affects: Anger and fear.* New York, NY: Springer Publishing.

Wolpe, J. (1958). *Psychotherapy by reciprocal inhibition.* Stanford, CA: Stanford University Press.

13

The CIPOS Procedure

The method of Constant Installation of Present Orientation and Safety (CIPOS; Forgash & Knipe, 2001; Knipe, 2002, 2007a, 2010; Knipe & Snyker, 2000) is a procedure that can extend the healing power of eye movement desensitization and reprocessing (EMDR) to a much wider population of clients. It works on the principle that, by expanding and developing an individual's ability to remain oriented to the safety of the present situation, that person, then, is much more able to safely access and resolve highly disturbing memory material. As was described in earlier chapters, particularly Chapters 1 and 8, people who have a dissociative personality structure and/or who have unusually difficult troubling memories often have a vulnerability to dissociative abreaction—a very unpleasant "trauma-reliving" experience, together with loss of emotional safety when traumatic material is accessed. In other words, overwhelmingly disturbing memory material, perhaps previously dissociated, may begin to flood into that person's awareness, threatening to overwhelm his or her orientation to the safe present. If this occurs, the client's eyes might be open, but experientially, the client is not fully present. The person's thoughts may be totally in a "trauma world"—another time and place of unhappy and emotionally overwhelming life experiences. If this intrusion of posttraumatic material is allowed to continue in a session, it can be devastating to the client, damaging to the client's trust in the therapist, and misleading in that it can leave the client with a false impression that his or her emotional problems are hopelessly unresolvable. This, by definition, is an absence of dual attention. If standard EMDR procedures are attempted with a person in a dissociative abreaction, things are very likely to get worse. For example, it would not be wise to ask a highly disoriented client, who has lost access to present safety and is reliving a horrible moment of childhood abuse, "What is an image of the worst part?" The Phase 3 questions have the potential of inviting even more disturbing feelings, and the disoriented client may already have far too much. If the therapist pushes to obtain answers to the Phase 3 questions, and then initiates Phase 4 (sets of bilateral stimulation [BLS] while the client is immersed in the overwhelming event), even more disturbing material may be invited into awareness. BLS tends to facilitate integration of experience, break down dissociative separation between parts, and invite additional disturbing material to come into consciousness (Paulsen, 1995). For clients who are able to remain oriented while this occurs, BLS can bring into awareness all the elements that need to be healed and integrated. Each traumatic memory can be activated in the safe therapy office, allowing reconsolidation of that memory in a form that does not contain the previous disturbance (Ecker, Ticic, & Hulley, 2012). However, for those people who are much more vulnerable to losing orientation, these procedures can easily overwhelm, unless other safeguards are in place. Without sufficient dual attention, the memory can feel more real than the real situation the client is in. Trauma access without sufficient emotional safety is simply reliving the horrible events and not experiencing good therapy. Figure 13.1 illustrates how the client on the edge of a dissociative abreaction might feel, with feelings of fear, avoidance, and impending loss of control.

Many of the procedures described in earlier chapters—the strengthening of "safe place" and other resources, the targeting of avoidance, idealization, and shame defenses, the Loving Eyes procedure—can be used to help with this type of situation. With highly vulnerable clients, the CIPOS procedures can be integrated with those other methods, in order to help the client preserve emotional safety and orientation to the safe present, while allowing the successful processing of highly disturbing memory material. This procedure is not a replacement for the important preparation procedures described in Chapters 8 to 10, the methods of targeting and resolving defense described in Chapters 3 to 6, or the Loving Eyes procedures described in Chapter 11. These procedures have been described separately, for clarity, but most often they are used together in a way that is appropriate for the particular client.

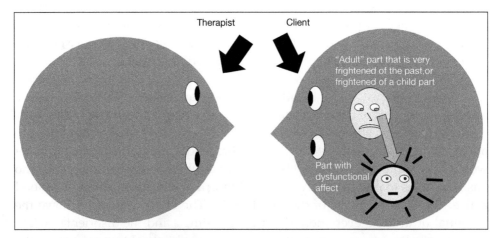

Figure 13.1 If the ANP or adult part of the personality is very frightened of the trauma-reliving EP, the BHS and the method of CIPOS can often be used to safely treat the EP. ANP, apparently normal part; BHS, Back-of-the-Head Scale; CIPOS, Constant Installation of Present Orientation and Safety; EP, emotional part.

The CIPOS intervention utilizes short-term memory (STM), which is a particular memory phenomenon that is easily observed and which overlaps substantially with another phenomenon, working memory (WM). WM is employed when a person is holding several pieces of information in consciousness at the same time, as when trying to multiply two double-digit numbers, or trying to look up a phone number while having a conversation. One of the theoretical explanations for how EMDR therapy (particularly EMDR Phase 4) is effective is that the sets of BLS overload WM, disrupting and loosening the stereotyped retrieval of disturbing memory material that is rigidly and dysfunctionally stored (de Jongh, Ernst, Marques, & Hornsveld, 2013). STM is a simpler phenomenon than WM—it is the memory trace that is retained in a place of conscious access for a period of seconds. For example, as you are reading these words, you might hear a sound—a car passing by outside, or the sound of an air conditioner or heater coming on—something that is inconsequential to you and easily ignored. But STM traces stay available to consciousness for a period of seconds. Following this period of seconds, STMs such as these "decay," and are no longer available. The period of seconds during which a memory is retained, prior to decay, tends to be from 3 to 30 seconds, depending on the complexity of the remembered sensations or information. For example, in one study (Peterson & Peterson, 1959), the availability of STM for retention of simple verbal information (three-letter trigrams, or nonsense combinations) was high after 3 seconds, moderate after 6 to 9 seconds, and very low after 15 seconds. The CIPOS procedure takes advantage of this STM phenomenon. When a dissociative person shifts from a state of present orientation into a state of thinking of a trauma, the STM of present orientation generally stays available for a period of 2 to 20 seconds (depending on the client's degree of vulnerability to dissociative abreaction), and can be much more easily reaccessed during that period.

As discussed in Chapter 2, an essential condition for the effectiveness of EMDR is the maintenance of dual attention: simultaneous orientation to present safety and access to disturbing posttraumatic memory material. Awareness of safety provides a critical element necessary for the reconsolidation and healing of posttraumatic "relivings." This type of dual attention is very difficult for many people who are receiving treatment for severe traumatization/dissociative personality structure. An individual may be quite oriented to the safety of the therapist's office, but when a disturbing memory is accessed, or when the present-oriented part of the personality is displaced by a trauma-reliving part, a dissociative "switch" may occur, and dual attention may be lost. The CIPOS intervention is designed to address this problem by giving the client a repeated experience of going into the traumatic material for only a brief period of seconds, and then coming back to orientation once again. With this method, both the intensity of the trauma memory, and any avoidance defense related to the memory, will both be softened, allowing easier and safer access by the client. The period of seconds is individualized for each client, and is short enough so that orientation to the present remains in STM, and is therefore much more available to return to as a place of safety. As the client goes into the traumatic memory for a few seconds, and then comes back, that client is engaged in a behavior that may have been very difficult previously. Many people with complex posttraumatic stress disorder (Complex PTSD) have said that they slide into trauma way too easily, without being able to stop themselves, down a "slippery slope" or pulled in as if in the power of a magnetic force. One client said, "I want to be here, but I am drawn there." Once orientation to the safe present has been lost, the return to orientation may be very difficult. A person might remain in the ongoing trauma state—in the trauma world—for hours, or even days. The CIPOS procedure is a way of helping clients learn to reduce their own catastrophic expectations regarding access of traumatic memories (Ecker, 2018), while also learning an important skill—the skill of more and more easily coming out of trauma and back to the present. And then, in turn, this skill can significantly fortify the person and enhance his or her ability to enter into the memory material again for therapeutic processing, opening the door to therapeutic resolution of that memory.

The CIPOS procedure is intrinsically linked to the use of the Back-of-the-Head Scale (BHS; Figure 13.2). The BHS is a way to measure, moment to moment, at the beginning of a session, and throughout a session if necessary, the extent to which a client is oriented to the safety of the present situation. The scale is necessary because oftentimes this information will not be readily available to the therapist by just looking at the client's face. There are clients who are able to appear totally present, even when they are not—they have learned to do this in their life as part of the skill set of the apparently normal part (ANP). And, conversely, a client might be sobbing intensely, and appear to be lost in a traumatic

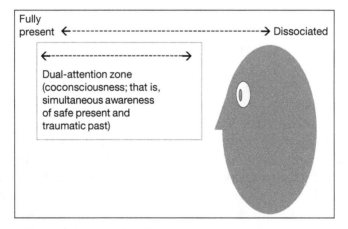

Figure 13.2 The BHS showing the zone of dual attention that is necessary for emotionally safe trauma processing.
BHS, Back-of-the-Head Scale.

memory, but in fact be totally oriented to the present, even while showing (and processing) such emotion. For those clients, the BHS will give a more accurate reading of the degree of their true present orientation.

This is the script for using the BHS.

> *Therapist: Think of a line that goes all the way from here (therapist holds up two index fingers about 14 inches—about 35 cm—in front of the person's face), running right from my fingers, to the back of your head. Let this point on the line (therapist moves fingers) mean that you are completely aware of being present here with me in this room, that you can easily listen to what I am saying and that you are not at all distracted by any other thoughts. Let the other place on the line, at the back of your head, mean that, even though your eyes are open, in your mind you are completely in a memory from the past. (Since even mentioning the trauma memory may, for some clients, create some additional loss of present orientation, I usually repeat the description of the scale, using a tone of voice that is calm and matter-of-fact.) The place out here (wiggle fingers) means you are completely present; the other place at the back of your head means you are in the memory. Point with your finger where you are on this line right at this moment.*

For many dissociative clients, the BHS can be thought of as a useful language, a way for the client to express and communicate a very important and familiar aspect of his or her mental life. One client said to me, **"I'm aware of when I am present, and when I am off daydreaming, or thinking of something upsetting, and missing what other people are saying. This line is very familiar to me. It helps to be able to talk about it."** Nearly always, clients are able to identify where they are on this line, at any given moment, even if they are in the most dissociated place, at the back of the head.

This line, then, is a way to assess whether the client is currently experiencing dual attention—that is, whether it is safe to proceed with trauma targeting using sets of BLS. For these highly vulnerable clients, usually it is necessary for the person to point to a position of at least 3 inches in front of the face in order for trauma-focused work to proceed. It is also important to listen to the clients' tone of voice when they tell where they are on this line. One client might point to a place 6 inches in front of the face and say, with a sad tone of voice, "I'm only this far out." Another client might point to the same place on the line, but say, with an upbeat tone, "I'm right here on the line!" The second client would be much more likely to be within the zone of readiness for processing.

The BHS can be used at any point in a therapy session—for the therapist to assess the degree of the client's orientation, for the therapist to bring the client's attention to the fact that he or she is oriented, and, oftentimes, as a way to bring the client back to orientation if there is too much drifting into traumatic reliving without sufficient balance between present and past.

The CIPOS method then can be used if the individual is within this zone of dual attention, with the following steps (Figure 13.3):

1. First of all, the client needs to understand why and how the CIPOS procedures might be useful. A preliminary step is often needed—addressing the client's long-standing phobic avoidance of the traumatic material. All of the preparation methods described in Chapters 8 to 10 can be helpful in containing and lessening the client's fear of his or her own memories. It can also be useful to focus on specific avoidance defenses, using the methods described in Chapters 3 and 4. Usually, these are avoidance urges originating in ANP.

2. Before using CIPOS, it helps to walk the client through each of the steps described later, explaining very concretely what will happen, step by step, culminating in the anticipated resolution of the painful and difficult memory. This usually can be done in a way that is credible and understood by the client. Also, the client can be asked to remember difficult events from the past that once were disturbing, but now are "just memories," simply events that are recalled without disturbance. These can serve as resources in giving validity to the therapist's assurance that the same result can occur with the memories that are still "hot." This type of information will, in itself, go a long way toward alleviating the client's anxiety about accessing trauma-laden parts.

3. Permission should be requested, and obtained, not only from the primary ANP but from all the other parts of the internal system before beginning to use the CIPOS method.

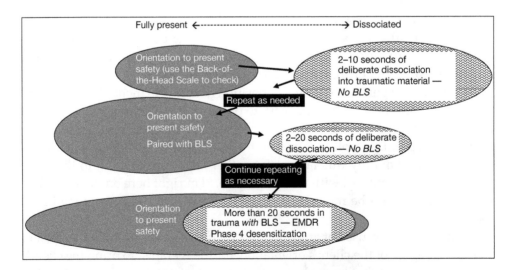

Figure 13.3 The method of CIPOS—sequence of procedures.

BLS, bilateral stimulation; CIPOS, Constant Installation of Present Orientation and Safety; EMDR, eye movement desensitization and reprocessing.

4. Especially for the initial uses of CIPOS, it is prudent to schedule a 90- to 120-minute session, if possible. This will allow plenty of time in the therapy session to make progress with both the remembered aspects of the memory and other elements that may have been dissociated.

5. Ensure the client is aware of "objective" reality (i.e., the present situation in the therapist's office, including the objective safety of that office). This cognitive orientation to present reality does not have to be accompanied by feelings of safety, but it should be clear in the client's intellectual understanding. In other words, proceed with CIPOS only when it is clear that the client knows that the therapist is "on the client's side," and not likely to judge, blame, or significantly misunderstand things that the parts of the client might say. This is, of course, important in any therapy work, but is particularly important because of the vulnerability created by the use of the CIPOS method.

6. Before accessing traumatic material, strengthen the client's present orientation by some or all of the following:

   • "Simple questions," such as "How many tissue boxes do I have in my room?", "Can you hear that car go by outside?", "See those two pictures over there on the wall? Which one do you like better?", "Do you think my plants need watering?", "Can you see the flaw in the design in this carpet?" If the client asks why the therapist is asking these odd questions, the reason can be explained—these questions are all designed to help the client remain oriented to the reality of the therapist's office.

   • When the client responds to these questions, the therapist says, "Notice that." Or, "Think of that," and initiates a short set of BLS to strengthen the client's present orientation. The purpose of this short set is to allow the client to linger on the realness of the present situation and strengthen that realness with BLS.

   • The therapist might say, "What's good about being here right now, instead of in that memory?" Whatever the client answers, install with BLS. Once, when I asked a client this question, he said, "That's a really dumb question!" Since that time, I often will introduce this question by acknowledging how "dumb" it is.

   • One particularly effective intervention is to have a game of "catch" with a pillow, a balled-up tissue, or a pen. It seems that it is just about impossible for a person to stay in the trance of a trauma-reliving experience while trying to follow the trajectory of a tossed object. Catching something requires an orientation to the present. It activates the orienting response. Playing "catch" in this way typically reorients a person within a matter of a few seconds, and this procedure is often very useful, in conjunction with the BHS, to demonstrate to a client his or her own ability to move back and forth on the BHS line.

- For many clients, simple arithmetic problems are reorienting, possibly because mathematics tends to be a function, for most people, of the verbal areas of the left hemisphere. Similarly, the client might be asked to do another physical action—for example, walk with the therapist from the chairs to the door of the office, and then back again to the chairs, and then back to the door, and then to the chairs, and so on. Reorientation is also likely to occur if the client holds a drop of water or an ice cube in the hand (Linehan, 1993), or alternately counts to 10 and hums a song (Gallo, 2007).
- The BHS can be used to assess whether the client is in the zone of dual attention (see Figure 13.2).

7. When present orientation is sufficiently established, the client can be asked if he or she is willing to go into a memory image for a very brief period of time (e.g., perhaps only 2 to 10 seconds), with the therapist keeping track of the time. For example,

Therapist: In a few moments—not yet—but in a few moments, would you be willing to close your eyes and go into that memory for just a few seconds— maybe just 8 seconds? I will keep track of the time on my watch (therapist holds up the hand with the watch to make this clear and concrete with the client). When the 8 seconds is over, I'll say, "Just open your eyes, and come back here into the room."

For some clients, 8 seconds is about the right length of time. For other clients, it is too long. It is just fine if a client wishes to have a shorter number of seconds, since the client probably has a good intuitive sense of how many seconds can be safely tolerated. Some clients will want to challenge themselves by taking on a larger number of seconds; it is important to tell these individuals that the main point of this procedure is not to prove how many seconds can be endured, but simply to get some practice at coming out of the reliving experience of the disturbing memory. With practice, the client can quickly develop this very useful ability.

This is essentially a carefully controlled dissociative process. It is also a paradoxical intervention which, in itself, can alter the attitude of the client's ANP toward the disturbing memory or dissociated part. Many clients have a belief, created through life experience, that either they can be in control or they are in an out-of-control dissociated state, but it is impossible to do both. This procedure is a way for the person to encounter and experience the "pull" of dissociated memories while still maintaining emotional control.

8. Immediately following the end of the agreed-upon period of seconds, the therapist instructs the client, using soothing but repetitive and

emphatic words, to "Come back into the room now," until the client's eyes open and they are looking out into the room again. When the client's eyes are open again, the therapist gives encouragement ("Good," or "That's right") and then resumes the CIPOS interventions, with statements like, "Where are you right now?" with the answers followed by short sets of BLS. It sometimes happens that the client gives an answer indicating that his or her awareness is still dominated by the traumatic memory (e.g., **"I'm with him!"**); in this instance, it is usually sufficient for the therapist to simply clarify by saying, "Where are you right now, *in actual fact*? Just look around the room. Is it reassuring to realize that you are really here?" The CIPOS interventions are continued in this way until the client is able to report, using the BHS, that he or she is once again oriented toward the present reality of the therapist's office. At this point, Step 5 can be repeated.

9. As this procedure continues, the client develops increasing ability to "stay present" as well as greater confidence and a sense of emotional control in confronting the disturbing memory. This opens the way to the use of the standard EMDR desensitization procedures, that is, of directly pairing BLS with traumatic material.

The CIPOS method can extend the healing power of EMDR to a much larger group of clients—those who are vulnerable to dissociative abreaction and/or are very frightened of traumatic material. This would include many clients suffering from Complex PTSD. When this method is being used, the therapist must monitor closely the client's ability to "come back" after the agreed-upon number of seconds. From my own experience, and many reports from colleagues, a prudent guideline for dissociative clients would be to use CIPOS only with those who can tolerate going into traumatic material for 2 or more seconds. If the client cannot go into the trauma memory for even 2 seconds without having trouble in coming back, this method should not be used. Throughout this procedure, listen for any report from the client expressing orientation to the present, empowerment in confronting the traumatic material, or insight regarding his or her own personality dynamics; when these reports occur, follow them with a brief (five to eight sweeps) set of BLS to strengthen the awareness of the positive affect of these reports. At every opportunity, acknowledge the client's increasing ability to return to the present orientation and safety more and more easily.

CIPOS can be used in a variety of situations. If parts of self are seated around a dissociative table (Fraser, 1991, 2003), some of those parts may be frightened to look at other parts. The part with fear might find it easier to begin by looking at the fearsome part for a brief period of seconds, and thereby overcome the fear, following the CIPOS steps. Many clients have remarked that when they are able to take a closer look at a frightening emotional part (EP)—such as an internal perpetrator-imitating part—they are able to see that this part is not the actual perpetrator, and realize, in some cases, that this part is simply a frightened or angry young child. CIPOS can also be used when a client is able to look at an image of his or her younger self, in the trauma situation, but is frightened of fully accessing the sensory memories of that child. In these instances, the client can be asked, "Would it be possible for you to go into the body of that child for just _____ seconds, and then go back to simply observing the child?" Another application of CIPOS can be when a client has fear of being aware of the body parts or sensations. For example, one client was frightened to be fully aware of her own hands, since this awareness linked to memories of what she had been forced to do during early childhood sexual abuse situations. Another client with dissociated parts was initially frightened to look into a mirror when she was in a child EP, and CIPOS was helpful to her in closing the gap between this child EP and her age-oriented ANP.

The Flash Technique (FT; P. Manfield, personal communication, 2018; Manfield, Lovett, Engel, & Manfield, 2017) is a promising EMDR-related method, which has a structure that is in some ways similar to CIPOS. FT involves identifying an overwhelmingly disturbing memory, and then instructing the client to "flash" on the memory—that is, access the memory for a brief millisecond— such a brief period of time that "You're not even sure that you thought of it." Manfield will even instruct the client, "During the flash, don't think of it," or simply ask that the client flash on the "intention" to think of the memory (P. Manfield, personal communication, 2018; Ecker, 2018). This procedure appears to assist clients in titrating the exposure in a way that does not activate a self-protective avoidance impulse. Some manageable abreactions are reported—that is, abreactions that occur while maintaining sufficient awareness of present safety—but these appear to be resolved relatively easily using standard EMDR procedures following FT procedures.

Manfield advises that this approach is not yet demonstrated to be safe and effective for clients with dissociative personality structure. The FT may prove to be a significant contribution to EMDR therapy for dissociative clients, and for nondissociative clients who have high fear regarding memory access. Experimental trials with random assignment experimental and control conditions will be necessary to support the present anecdotal reports. It seems, from the cases presented in the 2017 article, and from my own observations using FT, that these procedures have two potentially therapeutic results. They provide the client with the resource of an easier avoidance defense ("You don't need to think of it—just identify the memory, then just flash during sets of eye movements."). With FT, the new resource of "flashing" replaces the previous dysfunctional avoidance defense of, "I want to avoid thinking of this!" Both of these avoidance defenses are mental actions accompanied by positive affect of relief, safety, and containment, but the "flash" defense, for some clients, is less of an obstacle to processing the underlying traumatic material. And as noted by Ecker (2018), in some cases, FT targets and reconsolidates an implicit assumption driving an avoidance defense—an assumption of catastrophic results if the memory is accessed. This is similar to the disconfirming of an avoidance impulse when level of urge to avoid (LOUA) or CIPOS is used with clients who are vulnerable to dissociative switching. My observation (and this is confirmed by Manfield, 2018) is that the use of this, or any other, procedure targeting an avoidance defense reduces not only the intensity of the avoidance, but also simultaneously decreases the intensity of the underlying traumatic material.

For both FT and CIPOS, the primary therapeutic shift appears to be in affect, not in cognition. Initially, the individual has, to either a greater or lesser extent, an urge for relief and containment through avoidance. This urge is an affect and an implicit memory of one instance, or many instances of suppressing the memory through avoidance. As processing occurs with FT, as with LOUA and CIPOS, that processing is primarily at a feeling level, and the initial avoidance cognition—"I don't want to think of the traumatic memory!"—is simultaneously processed to adaptive resolution—"I am able to access this memory without losing safety." Therapeutic processing of the "trauma-reliving" element of the memory can then proceed unimpeded using standard EMDR.

Manfield (2018) reports that for some clients, he has been using a variation of Flash. The client is asked to "flash" for a fraction of a second on "not thinking of the memory." This appears to be similar to the procedure described in Chapter 3, of asking a client, "What's good about not thinking of that memory?" Both types of phrasing may be useful to an avoidant client, as ways of integrating present safety with an avoidance urge, and thereby re-consolidating and reducing the intensity of an avoidance response.

Chapter 14 will show the application of CIPOS that comes up most frequently in clinical practice—the situation of a dissociative client who, while in ANP, is experiencing an intense intrusion of posttraumatic affect from a separate, trauma-reliving EP. This chapter also describes the use of the LOPA procedure (described in Chapter 5) to treat a dissociative child part that is still invested in a defensive, self-destructive action that contains dysfunctional positive affect.

Chapter 16 describes the treatment of a highly dissociative Vietnam veteran. In his case, a trauma-reliving EP and an ANP that is highly avoidant of that EP are both viewed from the perspective of the present-oriented Self. In this case, the CIPOS procedures were used to help the ANP overcome fear of a trauma memory and the EP overcome fear of abandonment, resulting in reconciliation and apparent integration of these personality parts.

REFERENCES

de Jongh, A., Ernst, R., Marques, L., & Hornsveld, H. (2013). The impact of eye movements and tones on disturbing memories involving PTSD and other mental disorders. *Journal of Behavior Therapy and Experimental Psychiatry,* *44*(4), 477–483. doi:10.1016/j.jbtep.2013.07.002

Ecker, B. (2018). The flash technique in EMDR: How and why it works, Coherence Psychology Institute LLC, Retrieved from http://www.CoherenceInstitute.org

Ecker, B., Ticic, R., & Hulley, L. (2012). *Unlocking the emotional brain: Eliminating symptoms at their roots using memory reconsolidation.* New York, NY: Routledge.

Forgash, C., & Knipe, J. (2001). *Safety-focused EMDR/ego state treatment of dissociative disorders.* Paper presented at the EMDR International Association Annual Conference, Austin, TX.

Fraser, G. A. (1991). The dissociative table technique: A strategy for working with ego states in dissociative disorders and ego state therapy. *Dissociation, 4*(4), 205–213.

Fraser, G. A. (2003). Fraser's dissociative table technique revisited, revised: A strategy for working with ego states in dissociative disorders and ego state therapy. *Journal of Trauma & Dissociation, 4*(4), 5–28. doi:10.1300/J229v04n04_02

Gallo, F. (2007). *Energy tapping for trauma.* Oakland, CA: New Harbinger Publications.

Knipe, J. (2002, June). A tool for working with dissociative clients. *EMDRIA Newsletter, 7*(2), 14–16.

Knipe, J. (2007). Loving eyes: Procedures to therapeutically reverse dissociative processes while preserving emotional safety. In C. Forgash & M. Copeley (Eds.), *Healing the heart of trauma and dissociation.* New York, NY: Springer Publishing.

Knipe, J. (2010, October 3). *Invited keynote address, the use of AIP therapy methods with dissociative symptoms and Complex PTSD.* EMDR International Association Annual Conference, Minneapolis, MN.

Knipe, J., & Snyker, E. (2000). *The method of Constant Installation of Present Orientation and Safety.* Presentation at the EMDRIA Annual Conference, Montreal, Canada.

Linehan, M. M. (1993). *Cognitive-behavioral treatment of borderline personality disorder.* New York, NY: Guilford Press.

Manfield, P. (2018). Personal communication.

Manfield, P., Lovett, J., Engel, L., & Manfield, D. (2017). The flash technique in EMDR therapy: Four case examples. *Journal of EMDR Practice and Research, 11*(4), 195–205. doi:10.1891/1933-3196.11.4.195

Paulsen, S. (1995). Eye movement desensitization and reprocessing: Its cautious use in the dissociative disorders. *Dissociation, 8*(1), 32–44.

Peterson, L. R., & Peterson, M. J. (1959). Short-term retention of individual verbal items. *Journal of Experimental Psychology, 58*, 193–198. doi:10.1037/h0049234

14

The Persistence of Dissociative Personality Structure and the Internal Healing Dialogue (IHD) Procedure

Why does dissociative personality structure persist long past the time when it was adaptive as a means of coping within a difficult early environment? If human beings were completely logical, we might expect that dissociative adaptations to a difficult childhood would diminish or discontinue when that child grows up and escapes that stressful world. But, for most adult dissociative clients, the separation between parts has continued long past the childhood time when it was created, when it was needed, and when it was adaptive. Why is this? In other words, what factors maintain the dysfunctional separation between dissociated personality parts, even long after the person has grown up and has been living in the larger adult world, perhaps for decades? By definition, for individuals suffering from dissociative disorders, factors exist that are ongoing barriers to mutual awareness between parts, and once that awareness has been achieved in therapy, there are additional barriers to synthesis and merging of personality parts. To the extent that these barriers can be identified and therapeutically targeted, personality integration—typically the larger goal of therapy for an individual with a dissociative disorder—becomes much more possible.

Within the Theory of Structural Dissociation of the Personality (TSDP; van der Hart, Nijenhuis, & Steele, 2006, pp. 204–209), it is hypothesized that dissociative separation between identities or parts is maintained by a series of internal phobias—fear and avoidance that arise whenever there is a possibility or threat of coconscious connection between specific dissociated mental states. The apparently normal parts (ANPs) of the personality may have phobic fear of disruptive intrusions from emotional parts (EPs)—unpleasantly vivid trauma memories, emotional disturbance, and trauma-related mental actions. Virtually any type of mental action may have been tainted by association with traumatic events, and in the person's present life, those actions may now be phobically avoided. These feared mental actions may include behaviors (such as assertion, honest expression of feelings, accurate perception of past and present realities), and also include emotions (such as trust, hope, anger, shame, sexual arousal, and even fear itself). And the phobia-based distancing can go the other way. EPs of the personality may be afraid of the rejection and judgment of an ANP, and, as a result, these EPs may be angry, or "hiding," inaccessible to the ANP.

These types of internal phobias prevent contact and integration between personality parts, and if parts are known to each other, but still separate, there is likely to be an ongoing pattern of antagonistic relationships between them. For example, the client, as ANP, might have intrusive fears that originate in the unresolved trauma of an EP, and then have an additional anger/shame with regard to these fears—"I hate it when I get afraid like that!" Or the ANP may be frightened and angry about the disruption caused by the inner voice of an EP—"I always hear this voice inside, telling me I'm no good. I start to feel confident, and then that tears me down. I hate that voice! I wish it would just shut up and go away." Conversely, EPs may be angry at an ANP for keeping them in exile, never allowing them to "come out," and perhaps never even wanting to acknowledge their existence. These phobias, leading to internal conflict, are a primary factor in maintaining dissociative personality structure, long past the time when that structure was adaptive.

Unrealistic and inappropriate idealization, in various forms, may be an additional contributing factor maintaining dissociative disconnect between parts. Idealized (i.e., unrealistically positive) images are often pleasing within themselves and are valued for that reason. In addition, though, idealized images often serve a defensive purpose—one of preventing the emergence of disturbing, traumatic memories (as described in Chapter 5). Rigidity of personality structure can result when a certain part has the task of shutting out all threatening, reality-based information that might undermine an overvalued mental image. For example, one part may be highly invested in maintaining an unrealistically positive image of one's father, thus blocking conscious access to memories of maltreatment by the father. This creates an internal impasse, with resulting confusion and dysphoria on the part of the ANP. In other words, the ongoing dissociative disconnect between parts may be maintained because of an idealization defense, and, in addition, there may be dissociated parts that function to prevent an idealization defense from being tainted by certain realities and/or memories of traumatic experience.

Another element often maintaining separation between dissociative parts appears to be the phenomenon of Learned Helplessness. In a variety of research studies (e.g., Seligman and Maier, 1976), it was demonstrated that people, or animals, that are trapped in an inescapable place of repeated punishment are very likely to develop attitudes of helplessness and submission regarding their options after a period of time. In other words, it is hypothesized that repeated aversive experiences of helplessness diminish attention to, and awareness of, choices. This research is directly applicable to the situations of many clients with Complex posttraumatic stress disorder (PTSD), who grew up with ongoing, inescapable adversity. For these clients, their condition may have elements not only of sympathetic arousal, but also dorsal vagal parasympathetic activation (as described previously in Chapters 7 and 12), together with cognitive and visceral elements of self-shaming. Learned helplessness impairs not only hope but also the mental energy needed to reconcile the internal conflicts and incongruities of separate dissociated parts. If an infant's intrinsic attachment behaviors were repeatedly frustrated by nonresponsiveness or frightening behavior from caretakers, the infant may have developed a response of helplessness with regard to meeting attachment needs. The child's natural propensity to learn to attach to, and enjoy, other people may have been thwarted. Instead, separate self-states may have been developed as adaptations to the needs and stress-inducing behaviors of adults, as described in Chapter 7. If these events occurred preverbally, they may not be consciously accessible to the adult dissociative client living in today's world, but they may be a factor in perpetuating that client's internal structure of nonintegrated parts.

In a related way, defensive shame about self can be an obstacle to personality integration. One client, with a history of sexual abuse, said, "I can't let myself think of what might have happened. It makes me feel so ashamed!" Shame feelings frequently arise during therapy when an adult client is accessing memories of positive attachment to the perpetrator (Ross, 1998). The eye movement desensitization and reprocessing (EMDR) targeting of this type of shame defense was previously described in Chapter 12.

Blocking beliefs (such as those listed in Chapter 6) can stand in the way of personality integration. In general, blocking beliefs express a certain divide or unresolved discussion between personality parts (with ongoing conflict between different needs, different orientations, different agendas). One part holds the belief, while another part wishes to advance in therapy toward a desired goal.

For *some* dissociative clients, personality integration will occur spontaneously when the posttraumatic disturbance, held internally, within parts, is resolved and no longer overwhelming. For these clients, the need for protective dissociative distance between parts thereby becomes less needed. For example, in Chapter 15, the client, Veronica, shows this type of spontaneous integration at the end of a successful therapy session focused on resolving a posttraumatic distortion of a child EP.

For other clients, however, the dissociative distance between separate first-person identities is maintained even after significant trauma processing has occurred. The continued sense of separation between internal parts may continue due to hidden unresolved memories, hidden internal phobias, ongoing anger between parts, denial defenses, strong avoidance defenses, idealization defenses, and shame/helplessness defenses. It may not be clear to either the client or the therapist why this continuing dissociative separation is occurring, but the client may be very frustrated by this situation. In these circumstances, appropriately focused sets of bilateral stimulation (BLS) can be potentially quite helpful in identifying and therapeutically targeting barriers to personality integration, and safely lessening the dissociative distance between parts.

THE INTERNAL HEALING DIALOGUE PROCEDURE

What is being proposed here is an extension of the use of BLS to help dissociative clients who are frustrated by the persistence of dissociative separation between parts, even following significant therapeutic reprocessing of post-traumatic disturbance. A client may wish to achieve personality integration for many reasons—for example, to "finally know who I really am," to be able to live in the world authentically without hidden feelings or motives, to no longer have the confusion of being pulled in different directions by discrepant parts, and to be able to truly regard oneself as a "normal" person, with a deep sense of self-acceptance with regard to all of the adaptations that were necessary to cope with traumatic circumstances earlier in life.

Even if therapy has progressed to the point that now there is some degree of mutual access—simultaneous awareness, each part of the other—the parts may still have intensely different perspectives, and a variety of negative feelings with regard to each other. Internal healing dialogue (IHD) is used when the client has progressed to have sufficient orientation to the safety of the therapist's office, and is able to observe the internal parts that remain in some type of conflict or standoff. Using language from the Structural Theory of Dissociation (van der Hart et al., 2006), the client now has sufficiently elevated "mental level" and sufficient "presentification" to be able to know the experience of one part of Self, and then shift into knowing the experience of another separate part of Self. Using language from the Internal Family Systems model (Schwartz, 1995), the client is looking at internal personality parts from Self, and Self is assisting in a "leadership role," directing therapy toward personality integration.

The Back-of-the-Head Scale, described in Chapter 13, can be useful in assessing the client's ability to achieve this place of present orientation and safety. This is a place of mobilization of the client's natural, intrinsic Adaptive Information Processing (AIP) system. The therapist's role in using the IHD procedure is to exert a steady influence to help the client maintain orientation to present safety, and assist each of the conflicting parts in self-expression, and in listening (similar to what would happen in couple's therapy, when a therapist assists two separate people to improve their skills of respectful clear expression and active listening). For the great majority of dissociative clients, this type of healing internal conversation has been prevented in the past by impulses of fear, avoidance, anger, indifference, learned helplessness, and so on. The IHD between parts may initially be quite contentious, but nevertheless productive, because it can facilitate resolution of a lifelong dilemma. Often this is an internal conversation that never happened before!

IHD generally begins through use of Loving Eyes procedures, as described in Chapter 11. When Loving Eyes procedures are used directly, as described in that chapter, the ANP visualizes a child EP. In some instances, the ANP will have a compassionate and positive feeling as an immediate response, towards the EP child part. But just as often, the opposite will occur—some type of defensive process will emerge—for example, a fear of that child, denial of a traumatic event, a wish to avoid thinking of the child, or a shaming dislike of the child. The therapy session can then be devoted to processing (reducing the intensity of) whatever defensive action is occurring, and then resolving the underlying traumatic material.

The use of Loving Eyes in order to resolve an internal conflict involves suggesting to the client that he or she create a *representation of each side* of the conflict. The therapist must remain alert to whether the client is maintaining sufficient present orientation and safety when carrying out this task. The original developer of an EMDR-related method of integration of parts is Robin Shapiro. Her two-hand interweave procedure (Shapiro, 2005) involved the client placing one conflicting feeling, thought, choice, belief, or ego state in one hand, and another in the other hand, and then simply beginning sets of BLS, with the client reporting, after each set, any shift in emotion or perception of the parts. If information or feelings in one hand or the other is distressing, that distress can be targeted using the standard EMDR protocol. This method is very flexible in its application to a wide variety of clinical situations in which different mental states are incompatible or in conflict. It is very helpful to many clients—a direct perception of two hands can then serve as a reference point in speaking about two different personality parts. By placing each part in the client's own two hands, the implicit (perhaps subliminal) message is taken in—"These are both part of me."

Alternatively, the therapist may present his or her own hands, with palms facing the client, to represent the client's personality parts. A possible advantage of using the therapist's hands is to introduce dialogue interweaves—"One part of you says this (therapist wiggles left hand) and then, what if the other part of you would reply by saying . . . (therapist wiggles right hand)? What would this part (wiggle left hand) say in reply?" Other possibilities: The client or the therapist can make a drawing on a page showing separate ovals or scribbles to indicate the conflicting parts. Then, as the dialogue proceeds, the therapist or client can point to each of the places on the page to refer to each of the internal states. Dissociative table imagery (Fraser, 1991, 2003; described in Chapter 10) can be used, with a large imagined video screen on a wall to show visual memories, different chairs at a table to indicate the different parts, and a microphone that can be handed back and forth between the parts to reflect which part is speaking.

When the representation—hands, drawing, or dissociative table—has been established, and a visual memory image of the internal conflict or disagreement has been identified, then, with the memory image in mind, the therapist asks *one* of the two conflicting parts to express as clearly as is possible *that part's point of view* regarding the memory. For example, one part might say, "I don't know if it really happened. I don't think it really happened." Whatever is spoken by the client, the therapist initiates a set of BLS, with words like, "Notice that" or "Stay with that." Then, the focus is shifted and the other internal part/identity/ego state is asked, "What is your reply to that?" That part might say, "I don't want to think that it happened, but I have pictures in my mind of every detail. I think it did happen." This reply is then followed by an additional set of BLS. Then, the first ego state is asked to reply to the reply, and again this is followed by a set of BLS. Defenses may arise, and these can be targeted and resolved. Parts may have polarized in the past, and one or both may be rigid in adherence to a particular point of view. When this occurs (and it often does), there's often a fear of over-whelm or of loss of control that is driving the rigidity. This can be addressed in a number of ways; for example, "What are you afraid would happen if you gave validity to what that other part is saying?" Previously dissociated memories, held by one part or the other, may become apparent, and these can be the focus of processing. As this procedure continues, the typical result is a shift in per-spective, and a gradual reduction in the fear and antagonism that has prevented this internal dialogue in the past. The client is likely to become less frightened of continuing the dialogue, and more aware of contextual information that was previously unavailable to these conflicting parts. This is similar to what occurs in normal, trauma-focused EMDR when the client benefits by feeling less dis-turbance while becoming more aware of the larger context of a traumatic event.

Within the field of psychotherapy, it is hardly new to ask different, sepa-rate personality parts to talk to each other as a means of healing inner conflict and facilitating personality integration.

This approach has roots in psychoanalysis, and was further developed by Moreno (1969) in the context of psychodrama; it was also part of the "empty chair" method developed by Perls (1951; Polster & Polster, 1974) in the context of Gestalt Therapy. What do focused sets of BLS add? As described in Chapter 2, BLS, when paired with consciously held emotionally charged memory mate-rial, will tend to expand associational connections, reconsolidate the memory material to a form that is more consistent with past and present realities, reduce sympathetic arousal, reduce the "aliveness" and vividness of "reliving" aspects of the memory, create more emotional "distance" between Self-as-observer and the content of the memory, and assist the client in using productive and mindful "slow thinking" instead of reactive "fast thinking" to process the memory. Each of these BLS effects contributes to EMDR's well-documented effectiveness with disturbing trauma material. As described in Chapters 3–6 and in Chapter 12, focused sets of BLS can also facilitate the resolution of psychological defenses. *We can hypothesize that appropriately targeted sets of BLS can also contribute to the reduction of the mental actions (phobias, avoidances, and idealizations) that maintain entrenched differences and conflicts between dissociative personality parts. This resolution can, in turn, facilitate movement toward personality integration.*

As described in Chapter 9, a commonly observed example of conflicting internal parts, in the presenting picture of dissociative clients, is the "attachment to the perpetrator" problem (Ross, 1998). The client's "Adult" part may have fear, avoidance, anger, and/or shame with regard to a child part who suffered abuse at the hands of a caretaker. And parts can have parts. Within the child part, there may be one self-state that hates the perpetrator, while another self-state may be highly invested in continuing to idealize—think positively of—that perpetrator. This conflict in perspective—intense anger versus positive attachment—within the child EP may have previously blocked any internal discussion that could have resolved the actual reality of how the perpetrator was (back then) and is (even in the present). This conceptualization may be threatening to many clients, especially in the early stages of therapy, due to the "idealization of other" self-state being completely dissociated. Figure 14.1 shows ovals representing a possible personality structure for a client who has resolved ambivalence by dissociating the positive attachment to the perpetrator(s).

If the clinician suspects that a client has this complex dilemma, it is typically important to help the client discover this internal situation on his or her own, either (as Ross does) through cognitive restructuring/Socratic dialogue or during IHD procedures. If a therapist prematurely tries an interpretation—for example, "Perhaps, in addition to your hatred of your abusive father, you also have a positive attachment to him"—many clients will regard this interpretation

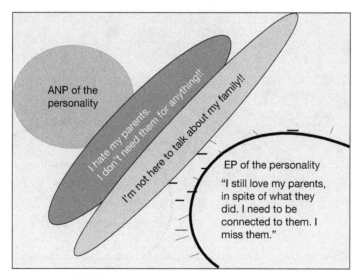

Figure 14.1 The client may present in therapy as a person who has strong negative feelings toward caretakers, and the other side of the ambivalent pole—continued affection for the caretakers—may be entirely dissociated.
ANP, apparently normal part; EP, emotional part.

as pretty lousy therapy, and may go looking for another therapist. The case example in Chapter 17 illustrates a more graded approach—specific ways of using the IHD procedures to help a client reach a full realization of a dissociated idealizing self-state. Once the client has this realization, the internal dialogue can proceed to help the client find resolution to the "attachment to the perpetrator" problem.

This split may take another form, as illustrated in Figure 14.2. The positive attachment may be held by a consciously available self-state, perhaps merged with the ANP, and the trauma memories and negative feelings toward the perpetrator may be entirely dissociated. In these instances, it is not unusual for the client to show not only a positive attitude toward the perpetrator, but also a tendency to irrationally take on excessive responsibility—even shame— for frustrations that occurred in the relationship with the perpetrator (Knipe, 2009). Again, premature interpretation of these dynamics by the therapist may be counterproductive. Strong idealization defenses may have been established very early, as a necessary element of the very young child's bonding with a parent. A client's idealization of this bond may be strongly entrenched because it has pushed from awareness memories of neglect, abandonment, and betrayal.

As the reader might imagine, there may be complexities, twists, and turns in the course of this dialogue, just as occurs when two adults are attempting a conversation to resolve a complex and emotion-laden disagreement. Emerging attitudes of intransigence of one or both parts may be grounded in initially hidden defensive processes and/or unresolved posttraumatic disturbance. The ANP

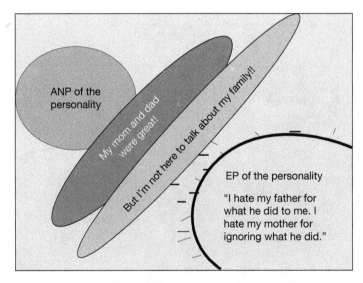

Figure 14.2 The client may present in therapy with strongly positive attitudes toward caretakers, even though there is a history (dissociated) of abuse or neglect. Initially in therapy, the other poll of the ambivalence—strongly negative feelings toward caretakers—may also be dissociated.
ANP, apparently normal part; EP, emotional part.

may have memories of intense and unwelcome intrusions of highly disturbing posttraumatic material, and this may be driving a very strong avoidance urge. There may be a lifelong conviction of shame about self ("I am just a bad person," or, as one person said, only half joking, "I just decided a long time ago that I have to accept that I'm guilty of everything!") along with an intense wish to continue a strong idealization of a perpetrator. There may be a strongly felt reluctance to really know the depths of grief regarding childhood abandonment. Hidden unfinished trauma material and/or defenses may be blocking the dialogue. Over the course of therapy, each of these elements can be targeted in turn as they arise, with vigilance of course, regarding the maintenance of present orientation and safety.

In several of the session transcripts in this book, this type of healing dialogue, facilitated by sets of BLS, can be seen. In Chapter 17, a therapy session is described that illustrates in detail the use of IHD procedures.

REFERENCES

Fraser, G. A. (1991). The dissociative table technique: A strategy for working with ego states in dissociative disorders and ego state therapy. *Dissociation*, 4(4), 205–213.

Fraser, G. A. (2003). Fraser's dissociative table technique revisited, revised: A strategy for working with ego states in dissociative disorders and ego state therapy. *Journal of Trauma & Dissociation*, 4(4), 5–28. doi:10.1300/j229v04n04_02

Knipe, J. (2009). Shame is my safe place: Adaptive information processing methods of resolving chronic shame-based depression. In R. Shapiro (Ed.), *EMDR solutions* (Vol. II). New York, NY: W.W. Norton.

Moreno, J. L. (1969). *Psychodrama volume 3: Action therapy and principles of practice.* Boston, MA: Beacon House.

Perls, F. (1951). *Gestalt therapy.* New York, NY: Julian Press.

Polster, E., & Polster, M. (1974). *Gestalt therapy integrated: Contours of theory and practice.* New York, NY: Vintage Books.

Ross, C. (1998, Spring). The problem of attachment to the perpetrator. *Inner Voices.* Available at *Sanctuary for the Abused.* http://abusesanctuary.blogspot.com/2006/09/problem-of-attachment-to-perpetrator.html

Schwartz, R. (1995). *Internal family systems therapy.* New York, NY: Guilford Press.

Shapiro, R. (2005). The two-hand interweave. In R. Shapiro (Ed.), *EMDR solutions* (pp. 160–166). New York, NY: W. W. Norton.

Seligman, M. E. P., & Maier, S. F. (1976). Learned helplessness: Theory and evidence. *Journal of Experimental Psychology: General, 105*(1), 3–46.

van der Hart, O., Nijenhuis, E., & Steele, K. (2006). *The haunted self: Structural dissociation and the treatment of chronic traumatization.* New York, NY: W. W. Norton.

IV

Case Examples

15

Veronica

- Constant Installation of Present Orientation and Safety (CIPOS) with a highly disturbing memory held by a dissociated part
- Level of Positive Affect (LOPA) procedure with a dissociated part that is emotionally invested in a dysfunctional action

This chapter describes two particular sessions in the course of therapy of a woman with a severe dissociative disorder. In the first of these sessions, we used the Constant Installation of Present Orientation and Safety (CIPOS) procedures to assist her, not only in targeting and resolving overwhelmingly difficult memory material, but also to facilitate therapeutic dialogue between separate parts of the personality. In a subsequent session, sets of bilateral stimulation (BLS) were also used to help her let go of an intense positive feeling—a psychological defense that was held by a young emotional part (EP), but was problematic for her apparently normal part (ANP). In both of these sessions, the healing effects of sets of BLS (i.e., a lessening of fear; an increase in realization of positive, reality-based information) were important in helping her resolve what previously had been a very difficult internal conflict.

Veronica was 58 years old when she first entered therapy with me in 2004, for treatment of depression and panic that had originated in a dissociative separation between her adult, "normal-appearing," part and child parts that were still reexperiencing sexual abuse by her father. Initially, the clinical picture included child parts of different ages that had had to cope in different ways with abuse that had occurred between the ages of infancy and 4½. There were two separate episodes to her therapy, the first one of which ended in 2007, and the second episode during 2009 to 2010. The earlier course of therapy was described in Forgash and Copeley's *Healing the Heart of Trauma and Dissociation With EMDR and Ego State Therapy*, Chapter 6, Loving Eyes (Knipe, 2007). The later episode of therapy, which was much briefer, is the focus of this chapter; it was also described during my presentation at the Eye Movement Desensitization and Reprocessing International Association (EMDRIA) conference in 2010. I am grateful to this generous client for her permission to describe her course of treatment and include, in the following section, a verbatim account from video recordings of the two particular sessions. She hopes that therapists who read of her journey, from painful feelings to recovery, will use her experiences to help their own clients.

Veronica had been in therapy for 22 years prior to our first session. She had worked with several skilled and compassionate therapists, and that therapy had been helpful to her. However, her condition had not been treated as a dissociative disorder; consequently, separation and avoidance between parts were continuing to erode her self-esteem, and also give her frequent feelings of panic and confusion about her own identity. During our initial 2004 to 2007 episode of therapy, she was able to successfully resolve issues of intense avoidance with regard to childhood EPs. She was then able to desensitize her fear regarding horrible images of abuse and then go on to eliminate panic attacks and significantly reduce her phobias of certain foods—foods that had reminded her in various ways of the oral abuse by her father.

Following this work, she said, "I am not afraid of him anymore. And that little part of me (whom she called 'Mimi') is with me now." It was at this point that we discontinued therapy sessions.

Fifteen months later, I received a call from her, requesting another appointment. Over the phone, she said, **"I'm still not afraid of my father. I still can think about that. When I was coming in, you asked me once what was the worst part, and we worked on that. I'm still okay with what we worked on. And Mimi and I are still together. But we never worked on the worst part of the worst part!"**

One result of our previous work had been an actual change in the activity of her saliva glands. She realized, during and following work with incidents of sexual abuse by her father, that she had had a lifelong sensation of dryness in her mouth. Following some intense eye movement desensitization and reprocessing (EMDR) sessions targeting oral abuse, she reported, with happiness and surprise, "I got my saliva back!" It appeared that, previously, she had had a nonconscious phobia of sensations of wetness in her mouth, and, following this work, that phobia was sufficiently reduced to allow her saliva glands to function. However, after she discontinued therapy, it became clear that this problem had not been fully resolved. Over the phone, she told me how, increasingly, she would feel ashamed, disgusted, and nauseous whenever she would be aware of saliva or other oral sensations. She said (with the viewpoint of the little girl inside), **"After it happened, all that badness went into my stomach and was inside me and I could never get rid of it!"** She related that these sensations and images were intense, sapping all her physical energy, and even, at times, blurring her vision. I was concerned about her ability to drive to my office, but she felt confident that she would be able to safely get to an additional therapy session, which we set up for 2 hours.

What had occurred with her, apparently, was that the good work she did, with remembered memory images, had invited other disturbing memory material that had previously been out of awareness. This is not an uncommon event in the treatment of individuals with dissociative personality structure. The initial work remains finished, but the success of that work invites additional memory information to come into consciousness. When this occurs, it is important the client understand that this in no way invalidates his or her previous work in the therapy. Sometimes, it is helpful for the therapist to get out the session notes from the previous work, so that the client can see that the work previously done, with particular memories and issues, remains done. It is as though all the little memories and internal parts have been watching the therapy process; some have had a successful resolution, whereas others are in the back waving their hands saying, "Me too! Me too!" Veronica was calling with the hope, based on the previous episode of treatment, that she would be able to resolve this remaining, very uncomfortable experience with wetness sensations in her mouth.

When we met, we just talked for a while, and she was easily able to become comfortable once again in the therapy situation. However, she said, "This feeling I get is really bad. It makes me want to throw up," and "When I start to really think of it, I just go away." When this dissociative response began to occur in the office, she was able to reorient herself fairly readily, within 10 seconds or so, but her vulnerability to begin to "go away" suggested that we should use the CIPOS method, rather than standard EMDR, to help her with this issue.

Figures 15.1 to 15.5 show the process of treating this memory material. The transcript for this session follows. I began the session by asking a question that simply identified the memory we would be working on, and then using

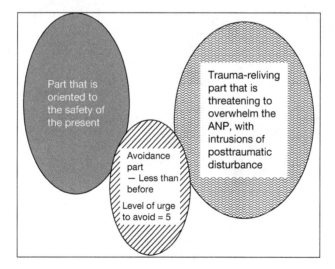

Figure 15.1 Veronica begins the session with a moderate amount of avoidance, but she is able to put this defense aside once it has been acknowledged.
ANP, apparently normal part.

the Back-of-the-Head Scale (BHS) to assess Veronica's degree of orientation to the present (vs. dissociation into this memory). In this transcript, where [BLS] appears, that is where I have said, "Think of that," or "Stay with that," and then initiated a set of BLS audio tones. When I ask Veronica to go into the traumatic material for a brief period of seconds without BLS, that is indicated by ***.

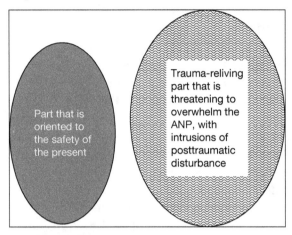

Figure 15.2 Without the avoidance, she is feeling very vulnerable; however, she is willing to proceed, and she is able to continue to be aware of the safety of the present (as assessed with the BHS).

ANP, apparently normal part; BHS, Back-of-the-Head Scale.

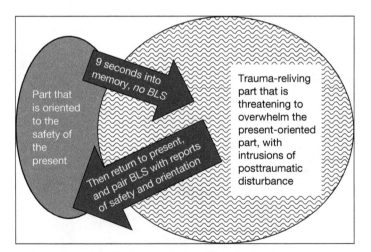

Figure 15.3 We begin the CIPOS procedure. She goes into the traumatic memory material for 9 seconds, and then attempts to come back to present orientation. Through a game of "catch" and some simple arithmetic problems, she is able to come back to being oriented to the present, as assessed by the BHS.

BHS, Back-of-the-Head Scale; BLS, bilateral stimulation; CIPOS, Constant Installation of Present Orientation and Safety.

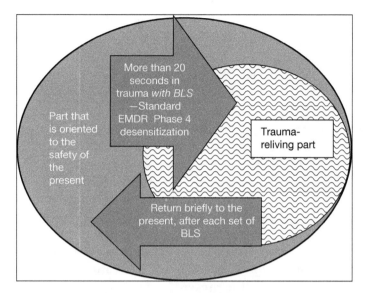

Figure 15.4 As we continue CIPOS, she becomes more able to come out of the trauma memory, which then actually gives her more ability to safely go back into this memory for a longer period of seconds. As this continues, the disturbance held within the memory diminishes.

BLS, bilateral stimulation; CIPOS, Constant Installation of Present Orientation and Safety; EMDR, eye movement desensitization and reprocessing.

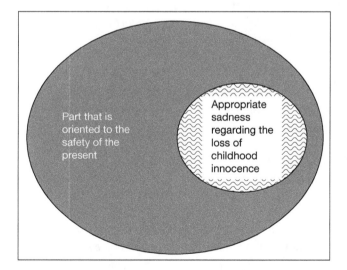

Figure 15.5 At the end of the session, the feelings of fear, avoidance, and lack of control are gone. Some sadness remains, because the abuse was in fact a very sad and tragic loss of childhood innocence.

Therapist: If I were to ask you to go in your mind to the hardest part—the worst part of the worst part of what your father did to you—would you know what I would be referring to? **(Veronica nods "Yes.")** *With regard to the worst part of the worst part, where are you on a line that goes from out here (therapist wiggles two fingers about 15 inches in front of client's face) where my fingers are, all the way to the back of your head? This place on the line (15 inches in front of face) means that you're completely present with me, and the other end of the line, at the back of your head, means that you are completely reliving this memory.* **(Veronica: Not remembering it, but reliving it.)** *Yes. So where are you on this line—just point with your finger where you are.* **(Veronica, pointing to the midpoint of the line: Right here.)** *So do this now. Let your little bear go back and forth here.* **(Veronica tosses a stuffed animal.)** *Good! Great! Here he comes!*

Now, check again, where are you on the line right now? **(Veronica points to a place on the line that is all the way out, indicating that she once again has a full awareness of the present.)**

Next, we begin the CIPOS procedures, as I ask her the question, *"What's different?"* Her answer is a resource of present orientation, and we install it with a set of BLS.

Therapist: What's different? **(Veronica: I'm really here with you, and I wasn't thinking about it.)** *Just pause for a moment and think about that difference. I am going to turn on the sounds now ([BLS] begins—alternating auditory tones) and just realize what is different about being out here.* **(Veronica: It doesn't feel as bad when I'm out here. Even when I am thinking of it, when I'm out here, it doesn't feel as bad.)** *Good. And just listen to the sounds, while you take some comfort in that.*

Therapist: Just think of how we could spend the time today. We have about an hour and an half. **(Veronica, with a sarcastic tone: What could we do?)** *We could talk about the worst part of the worst part. . . .* **(Veronica: Or?!!)** *Or we could talk about anything else!!* **(Veronica, smiling: Oh, let's talk about the worst part of the worst part!)**

Veronica's ability to joke about this indicates that she still has good access to the present, and the safety of our relationship. Nevertheless, she is verbalizing an avoidance wish, and so we shift our focus to this response.

Therapist: Okay, and I have asked this question before. Using numbers 0 to 10, how much do you not *want to think of the worst part of the worst part? How much do you not want to talk about it? How much would you rather talk about anything else?*

Veronica: Of course I'd rather talk about anything else, but I do want to get well, and I do want to feel better soon. So it's probably 50–50. It's probably about 5. Is that what you're asking, 0 to 10? Or is it a 7? You are talking about a 10? Okay. I really want to do it. I feel strong today.

Her words and the strength in her voice indicate that her avoidance impulse is not likely to be an impediment to direct processing of this traumatic material. Avoidance that is at a moderate level of intensity can often be put off to the side (Schwartz, 1995) to allow direct access to dissociated parts that are "burdened" by unpleasant feelings. Veronica's statement, that she is feeling strong, is a positive resource, and we go ahead and strengthen that resource with a set of BLS.

> *Therapist: Good. Just listen to the sounds while you think of that. Just notice that you feel strong today.* [BLS with alternating auditory tones]
>
> *Just say what you are thinking.* (**Veronica: It was really sad, what he did.**) *Stay with that.* [BLS] (**Veronica: I'm just thinking about me being so little and him being so big.**) *Stay with that.* [BLS tones]

Since she has begun accessing these potentially overwhelming memories of abuse, I check to see if the dual attention has been disrupted.

> *Therapist: Let me ask this question again. Where are you on the line right now?*

Veronica made a sad face and pointed to the front of her forehead. Once again, we played "catch" with her stuffed animal.

> **Veronica: Okay, now I'm back out.** (*Therapist: Where are you on the line, now?*) **Right here. (She pointed nearly all the way out to the therapist's fingers.)** (*Therapist: You were here. And now you are here. How do you know?*) **Because I feel different. I feel different. I don't feel hazy and foggy. And I don't feel like I'm in a dream.**

The game of "catch" helped her quickly regain orientation to the present, and so we are able to safely proceed with access to traumatic material for a brief period of seconds with no simultaneous BLS.

> *Therapist: And now, in a moment, I am going to ask you to do something. I'll ask you to close your eyes for 9 seconds, and go all the way into the worst part of the worst part.* (**Veronica closes her eyes.**) *** *I am keeping track right now on my watch, and continuing to talk, so you will know I'm still here. And as you go into the worst part of the worst part, notice what you notice when you're there. . . . Now open your eyes and come back here.* (**Veronica opens her eyes.**) *And can you hear the sound of that truck outside?*
>
> (**Veronica: Yes . . . but my eyes lose focus.**) *Is that from keeping your eyes shut?* (**Veronica: No . . . when I go back.**)

Her loss of ability to focus her eyes suggests a high degree of dissociation and possible loss of orientation to present safety. And so once again we use the BHS to assess her degree of dissociation.

So come back here, and now . . . where are you on the line right now? Just check and see. **(Veronica points to the place right in front of her face—not far enough out.)** *Okay, so let's just take more time now so that you can come out all the way.* **(Veronica, in a more quiet voice: How can I get out?)** *How about if you catch this pen?* **(Veronica: No. I don't want to. I can hardly see it.)**

Her visual distortion, having just gone into her trauma world, is now interfering with using a game of "catch" to help her reorient, so we use a different method.

Therapist: Okay. So, how about telling me how many fingers I am holding up? (Therapist holds up fingers.) Five . . . plus five **(Veronica: Equals 10),** *plus 2* **(Veronica: Twelve),** *minus 5* **(Veronica [laughs]: 7? That's hard.)**

Veronica (after a pause): I'm out!

Therapist: Now that you're out, isn't it kind of nice to know that you can do that? And that can give you confidence to be able to go back into that memory. **(Veronica: Yes.)** *Think of that. Just enjoy that feeling of "I can come back."* [BLS tones]

We are installing the "I can come back" positive resource.

Therapist: So knowing you can come back out, can you go back in for 10 seconds? **(Veronica: Yes.)** *I will keep track of the 10 seconds, and just notice whatever you notice. *** Now, open your eyes and come back. And how is it now?* **(Veronica: It's hard to come back. I'm supposed to be able to come right out, right?)** *No, not really. What we're doing here assumes that it is hard for you to come out. That's why we're going into it for such a short number of seconds— so that it is possible for you to come out, even if it is hard. Let's do this—see if you can catch this (a wadded-up tissue).* **(Veronica catches it, and we toss it back and forth twice.) (Veronica: I'm out!)** *So again now, 30 seconds ago you were still in, but now you are out. What's different? Just say what's different.* **(Veronica: I'm just aware of everything in the room. I don't feel hazy.)** *Where are you on the line right now?* **(Veronica points to a place near my fingers.)** *Almost all the way out. Okay. That's good. And here's a question. How do you know you're almost all the way out? Because you know that somehow.*

Veronica: Because my head is clear, my vision is better, and I am just aware of the sounds outside. When I go all the way in, I don't hear or think anything else except your voice, if you say something. I'm tuned in to your voice, but everything else isn't there. *(Therapist: So you're telling me how you know when you're out.)* **I know when I can hear everything, the cars, the plane, and I can see the trees, and I can see the office, the ugly picture (points), and the nice picture (laughs).**

Her description of how she knows she is "out" is a positive resource, which we then install.

> *Therapist: I am going to turn on the sounds again right now and you just notice that you are out right now, while you listen to the sounds. And notice what's good about being out right now, along with the sounds. You're doing great.* [BLS tones] **(Veronica: Yes. It was easier this time.)** *Is that kind of nice to realize?* **(Veronica: Yes.)** [BLS tones] *Just listen to the sounds while you realize it was easier this time. It is a nice thing—that you're able to come back like that. It is a good thing.*

Because Veronica appears to be more able now than at the beginning to access present safety, I ask a question to determine if dual attention is now a possibility for her.

> *Therapist: In a moment I am going to ask if you can do something. Can you right now have half your awareness here with me, so that you know for sure that you are entirely safe, you are living in today, and with the other half of your awareness, go and be in the worst part of the worst part, so that it's like a split screen on a television?* **(Veronica: Okay, I'll try.)** *Now, if you can't do it, you tell me. What happens when you try?* **(Veronica: I better not close my eyes. Because then I go all the way into it.)** *Okay, so keep your eyes open, because that way you know where you really are. So keep your eyes open and see if you can do it. Can you do it? I haven't turned on the sounds yet.* **(Veronica: Yes.)** *So I'm turning on the sounds now.* [BLS tones] *And what do you get? What do you get when you are both there and here? It's like you are there, you really are there, and you're really here.*

(Veronica: It's really scary.) *Yes, so come back here. Just come all the way here. Can you hear that crow out there (outside a window)?* **(Veronica: Yes. It's a "Grackler's Crow."**—She makes a sound to imitate the crow— **Sometimes they will answer me.)** *Now, when you're ready, go back into it. And what do you get? You can say anything at all about the worst part.* **(Veronica: It's disgusting.)** *Stay with that.* [BLS tones] *What do you get now?* **(Veronica: A kind of nauseous feeling. . . . And I feel so sorry for me, poor *little* me.)** *It's good to have compassion for yourself. This is sad, what happened.* **(Veronica: Yes. It's really sad.)** [BLS tones] **(I stayed in half-and-half that time.)** *Stay with that. That is a good ability to have.* [BLS tones] **(Veronica: It is harder to go back in than it was. It doesn't feel as intense. So I think I'm not doing it right. I wonder if I'm not doing it right. What do you think?)** *I think you're doing just fine. I think the fact that it doesn't feel as intense, now, means that this is getting resolved.* **(Veronica: It's easier to stay half-and-half.)** *Good. Go into it as far as you possibly can.*

Veronica: I'm less there. I'm more watching. And I pulled Mimi away. That's what I want to do. And I am watching him. [BLS tones] He's kind of creepy. *(Therapist: Where are you on the line?)* I'm out. When you said, "Where are you on that line?" I went ZING! I came right out, right to your fingers. *(Therapist: Is that a good thing that you're able to come right out?)* Yes. It's a lot easier to come out now than it was when we started. *(Therapist: Yes. Right. And that actually makes it easier for you to go back in, knowing you can easily come out. It can give you confidence going back into it, knowing you can come out. So, with that in mind, go back into it again. What do you get right now?)* It's like I put my foot in, but not my whole half in. Just enough to kick him if I have to! [BLS tones] *(Therapist: So from being all the way out, go back into the worst part of the worst part, and what do you get now?)* I'm just hazily there. Like I was just hazily out before. Now I'm just hazily there. It is more hazy. I can't go in as far. Do you want me to go in farther? Should I go in further?

Therapist: Go in as far as you can. But if you can't go in very far, that's okay. What happens when you try to go back into it? When you try to think of, as you said, that sensation in your mouth, and the texture of it? **(Veronica: I won't ever like to think about it. It's only normal that you don't want to think about that stuff.)** *That's right. I know it's hard for you to think of it. But, as we've said before, if you can think about it, on purpose, right now, that can help.* **(Veronica: Okay.)** *See if you can think about it right now, on purpose, and what do you notice about it?* **(Veronica: I am able to let go of some of it. It's like I have pushed some of it to the other side and some of it is still hanging on.)** *Okay, so let's get to what is left. When you go back to thinking of the worst part of the worst part of the texture, what do you get now?*

Veronica: Not having control and not being strong made it really scary because you're helpless, and you don't know what to do. You just wear yourself out, fighting. *(Therapist: Stay with that.)* [BLS tones]

Veronica: Who are you working with today? Who? Mimi or me? *(Therapist: Is there a difference?)* I don't know. *(Therapist: That's an interesting thing. Is Mimi here?)* Well, I'm playing with my bear (stuffed animal), and I'm kind of being a little smart-alecky. And yet I feel like *I'm* here. *(Therapist: So you, the grown-up, are here, and you, Mimi, are here. Is it possible that both of you are occupying the same exact body right now?)* Yes. *(Therapist: And that is something that is sort of new, but is it okay with you?)* Yes. . . . Hmm. *(Therapist: Is that interesting?)* It's *very* interesting. *(Therapist: I am going to turn on the sounds and just notice how it is for both of you to be together. You are you. And you are you.)* [BLS tones] It's hard to believe that a few years can mess up half a century. *(Therapist: Right. Stay with that.)* [BLS tones]

Veronica (talking to her child part): It's not there anymore. It's not there even a little bit. And he's gone and will never ever be around you again. *(Therapist: And what does Mimi say when she hears you say that?)*

Veronica (in child's voice): Are you sure?

Veronica (in her adult voice): Yes, I am positive. You have to trust me.

Therapist: You and Mimi just listen to the sounds now. [BLS tones] *What does Mimi say back to that, that you are asking her to trust you?*

Veronica (in child's voice): You have to promise that you won't get mad at me if I think or act silly. Do you promise just to love me like I am? *(Therapist: What do you say back? Be honest.)*

Veronica (in her adult voice): I hope I do. I'm going to try my best.

Therapist: Can she see your sincerity right now?

Veronica (adult voice): Yes. [BLS tones] **I'm going to do my best but I'm not perfect. And maybe someday I will forget and think you (the child, Mimi) are stupid, but it's really not you that is stupid. It's him, or the adult me doing something stupid. Because a 4- or a 5- or a 3-year-old, she can't do something stupid.**

Therapist: What does Mimi say when she hears you say that?

Veronica (in child voice): I feel better.

Veronica (in adult voice): I think it's mostly gone. I think it's gone. I think it's gone. *(Therapist: Stay with that. Just examine that. Be aware of that.)* [BLS tones] **I think I am more integrated with Mimi today.** [BLS tones]

Veronica (adult voice): It is not so much that I am taking Mimi into my heart. She is taking the grown-up me into her heart. When Mimi is here, I feel more like the real me. We're together. That feels real. That feels good.

Following the session, there was no return of the feelings of shame and fear previously connected with the oral sensations and images of "the worst part of the worst part." She was once again feeling very free and very positive about herself and her life. Because of her previous setback, however, just to be on the safe side, we set up an additional follow-up session for 1 week later. At our next meeting, she still was feeling very resolved about work from the previous session, and was no longer triggered by oral sensations. We met again

4 weeks later, and the work with the "worst-of-the-worst" remained done, but she had been to her physician, and there was an additional problem. She had been gaining weight significantly during the previous year, and her doctor had told her that she was prediabetic, and she was scheduled to retake a blood test (A1C test) to determine her baseline blood sugar levels. She knew the cause of her weight gain. She was drinking between *1 and 2 L* of soft drinks (usually caffeinated colas) each day. She told me, "I know I have to stop, or at least cut down, but I can't!"

She told me these things with a sense of being overwhelmed by the need to stop drinking these soft drinks, and without any apparent awareness of a possible connection between this problem and the previous session that had focused on sensations in her mouth. She seemed to regard it as simply a problem of an unwanted impulse.

We began by taking the approach of directly targeting the cola-drinking behavior, using Popky's Desensitization of Triggers and Urges Reprocessing (DeTUR) method (described in Chapter 6). First, we identified and installed positive resources of empowerment, feelings of being successful, and a positive image of a day in the future when she no longer would be compelled to consume sugar drinks, would no longer be in danger of developing diabetes, and would be at her desired weight (approximately 80 pounds less than her weight at the time of this session). We identified, and then specifically targeted, certain situational triggers that tended to activate a high intensity of urge to drink cola. In this session, and in two subsequent sessions using the DeTUR method, she was able to reduce the intensity of her urges to some degree, from about 9–10 to 5–6, but never down to zero. Moreover, her intake of colas, during the time between sessions, continued at a high level.

The reason appeared to be that, in spite of her previous reconciliation of her adult self with the child part, "Mimi," there now was a disagreement—a renewed ego-state separation—between these parts regarding the ongoing drinking of sugar drinks. The previous therapy work remained successful—she still reported zero disturbance in thinking of the "worst-part-of-the-worst-part" sensations and images. But given the extreme nature of her soft drink intake, and the significant health-damaging effects of this behavior, it appeared likely that some additional piece of memory material still remained unprocessed. In other words, relying on the assumptions of the Adaptive Information Processing model, there had to be additional hidden posttraumatic disturbance and/or some type of psychological defense in place that was driving this continuing dysfunctional behavior.

As we discussed this problem in detail, it became clear that her adult self—her ANP—was now experiencing an unwelcome *intrusion* of an intense urge to drink excessive amounts of cola. In other words, her adult self, when looking at the situation realistically and objectively, was ready to discontinue drinking sweet drinks. However, her separate Mimi part had a very different opinion. The Mimi part not only was continuing to have a very high urge, but also seemed to have no interest in even addressing the problem.

Therefore, because this situation seemed to be much more of a conflict between previously dissociated parts (now coconscious but separate ego states) rather than an issue of unwanted urges, we shifted over to conceptualizing her problem as one of her child part having an overinvestment in an idealized action—an idealization defense with regard to ingesting colas.

In her previous course of therapy, approximately 2 years earlier, she at one point had mentioned parenthetically that her father had often given her a soft drink following the abuse. Neither she nor I made much of this at the time, but this suggested a connection—the possibility that she had learned early to use sweet drinks as a defense—as a way to somehow reduce the disturbance about the abuse, and this defense, learned early, was possibly still having a powerful and dysfunctional influence in her life.

The following transcript is verbatim from a video recording made during this session, and is an example of targeting a personality part that contains dysfunctional *positive* affect, using the level of positive affect (LOPA) method, described in Chapter 5. Figure 15.6 illustrates the structure of parts at the beginning of this session. The idealization defense is primarily held by the child EP, Mimi.

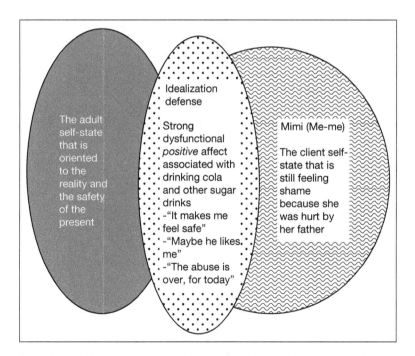

Figure 15.6 Structure of Veronica's parts at the start of the second transcripted session within this chapter. Sweet drinks were idealized because they signaled several "positive" pieces of information at the time of the trauma (e.g., that the abuse was over for that day).

Veronica: I know what's going to happen. I have to go to the doctor and do the A1C test, and I'm going to have to do insulin. And I don't want to. I need Coke. Or Pepsi. Everything's hard! *(Therapist: Does that have to do with your father?)* I don't know. I feel like . . . I'm not as afraid now about my father . . . I don't know why I'm drinking it. . . . It's because I like it, maybe. And I need it. . . . I guess I had better work on Pepsi because if I don't, my doctor is going to yell at me. It's because she cares (shrugs shoulders). That's all. She's not going to yell at me— she'll just be disappointed.

Therapist (talking to the child part): Mimi, can you remember how it was after your father did all that bad stuff, and he went to the refrigerator, and he got you a Pepsi? Do you remember when that happened? **(Veronica nods, to indicate "Yes," and says, in a childlike voice: That made it better, at least. Nothing else could make it better.)** *Could you do this right now? Could you hold in mind when you saw what he was doing? Can you get a picture of that in your mind?* **(Veronica, child voice: In the kitchen?)** *Yes. When you saw he was going to get Pepsi out of the refrigerator.* **(Veronica, child voice: Well, he likes me, at least some. Even though he did bad stuff, at least he's going to try to make up for it.)** *Okay. So now, what I'm going to ask you to do, Mimi—and just see if you can do this—I'm going to turn on the sounds, and I would like to ask you to think of how it was for you when you saw he was getting the Pepsi.* [BLS alternating tones]

Veronica (child voice): It was so disgusting before he went to get the Pepsi, and at least the Pepsi helped. *(Therapist: Think of that.)* [BLS tones]

Veronica (adult voice): It really wasn't Pepsi, it was RC Cola, or root beer. *(Therapist: Stay with that.)* [BLS tones] Everything was bad, and at least he is trying to make it better. *(Therapist: Stay with that.)* [BLS tones]

Veronica (adult voice): That made me think my father is good, not bad, because he is giving me Pepsi. It's like—not exactly rewarding me— but making it all better. It showed he did care a little bit. And I could think about that. When I drink the Pepsi, I think, "He cares." But when he is doing the other thing, I think he doesn't care. He hates me! And then he loves me! And then it gets all confusing, but I know that when I see the Pepsi or the root beer, something that he is bringing in a nice cold bottle, I know that it's going to make everything seem a little better. *(Therapist: Stay with that.)* [BLS tones]

Therapist: Maybe, what happened with your father made Pepsi into something that it isn't.

Veronica (adult voice): Like a savior! It's like, this is going to make me like my dad, and not think bad of him, and make me be able to look at him without getting sick. Because when I look at him, I think, "He is the one who gave me Pepsi." I don't think about how he's the one who hurt me. *(Therapist: Stay with that.)* [BLS tones]

Veronica (adult voice): And he knew I really liked Pepsi. He knew I really liked it, and that's why he gave it to me. . . . He must have really liked me, if he gave it to me, right?

Therapist: Well, are you asking me, if that proves he really liked you?

Veronica (child voice): I'm asking you. He must have really liked me, if he gave me Pepsi, right?

Therapist: Well, my opinion is that that doesn't prove he liked you.

Veronica (child voice): Why!? He gave me something I liked. Why do you think he gave it to me? (pause) To make me be good? So that I wouldn't tell? He already knew that I wouldn't tell. He told me that if I told, my mom wouldn't like me anymore. But then he showed me how much he liked me by giving me a Pepsi.

Therapist: Mimi, go back to the picture we started with, of when he went to the refrigerator to get you a Pepsi. See if there is a good feeling connected with that right now.

Veronica (adult voice): A good feeling? Connected with that?

Therapist: Yes. A good feeling connected with thinking of him going to the refrigerator, getting out a Pepsi.

Veronica (adult voice): Well, I was feeling pretty sick when he was doing it, but the good thing was that I was getting a treat.

Therapist: Stay with that. [BLS]

Veronica (child voice): I wanted to like him. He was my dad. Everybody I knew liked their dad. *(Therapist: Stay with that.)* [BLS] It makes me feel safe. When he gives me a soda, it means the abuse for the day is over. And . . . it makes the bad taste in my mouth go away. And it makes me like him. *(Therapist: Stay with that.)* [BLS tones]

Veronica (child voice): Am I making big Veronica drink Pepsi?

Therapist: You are asking me. What do you think?

Veronica (child voice): Maybe. Because I—when I start to get scared about something—that's when I want to make it better. *(Therapist: Stay with that.)* [BLS] **It's not happening to me anymore, and I still think I need to have the Pepsi!** *(Therapist: Stay with that.)* [BLS]

Veronica (adult voice): And I know it's bad for me now. *(Therapist: Stay with that.)* [BLS]

Therapist: Think again right now, of when he handed you the Pepsi. Is that a good feeling, right now, when you think of that?

Veronica (child voice): It means I'm a good girl. If I weren't a good girl, he wouldn't give me it. *(Therapist: Stay with that.)* [BLS] **Even though a little while before that, I wasn't being a good girl. I was fighting, and crying. But when he gives me this, I can stop crying, because it's over, and I'm a good girl. It also means that mom is coming home soon.** *(Therapist: Stay with that.)* [BLS] **He was very smart. But he was very bad.** *(Therapist: Stay with that.)* [BLS]

Therapist: You started out today saying that you want Pepsi, and that you need Pepsi. Check and see right now—see if that is still your opinion.

Veronica (child voice): I probably don't need it. But I want it.

Therapist: Do you still want it as much as you did when we started our session today?

Veronica (child voice): Maybe not as much, but I still want it! I like the way it tastes! And I like the way it makes me feel!

Therapist: Right now, 0 to 10, how much do you want a Pepsi?

Veronica (child voice): Eight. I like the way it makes me feel.

Therapist: Can you stay with that 8? Where's that 8 in your body? Where do you want a Pepsi? **(Veronica waves hand all over upper abdomen and chest.)**

Veronica (child voice): I especially like the way it tastes. I like the way it fizzes. *(Therapist: Stay with that.)* [BLS tones] **I don't like to think of it as being part of the trick.** *(Therapist: Stay with that.)* [BLS tones] **I don't like to think of my father going to the refrigerator, after everything he did, and then trying to make it all right by giving me a Pepsi.** *(Therapist: Stay with that.)* [BLS tones] **He tried to make something bad, good. You can't make something bad into something good by covering over it. That would be like putting siding over a house that is full**

of termites and then trying to sell it. They call that covering over a multitude of sins. That's what he was trying to do.

Therapist: What do you, the adult, want to say, when you look at all this?

Veronica (adult voice): Poor little Mimi! I can understand why she wants Pepsi. I need to reteach her. I need to say, "I know you want Pepsi, especially when you're feeling upset, but it's not the same kind of upset. We can work through it."

Therapist: Mimi, did you just hear the grown-up say that she understands now? She understands now why you like Pepsi so much? (Veronica nods, "Yes.") *How did you feel when you heard her say that?*

Veronica (child voice): I feel better now, knowing she understands. It's not like when she is fighting me all the time. I always have a reason for what I do.

Therapist: So, right now, Mimi, how much do you want a Pepsi? 0 to 10?

Veronica (child voice): Three.

Therapist: Okay, it still pulls a little bit, but not like before? (Veronica [child voice]: Yes.) *It was an 8 before. It was an 8, and now it is a 3—what's different?*

Veronica (child voice): When I'm thinking about it right now, maybe it's a 2. Because when I think about the Pepsi, I think about what he did.

Therapist: Okay, just think about how cold that Pepsi was, on a hot day, and how good it felt when you drank some. And when you think of that now, when you think of all that—you are still able to think of it—you may not have the same reaction to it, right now, but what do you get now when you think of that?

Veronica (child voice): I remember that it was part of the trick, and I don't like the trick. The trick was mean. Bad. [BLS tones]

Veronica (adult voice): I never thought of it before as being connected to the abuse. And that makes me wonder why I would still drink it!

Therapist: When you think of the image we started with, of your father going to the refrigerator, how much, 0 to 10, right now, do you want a Pepsi?

Veronica (adult voice): It is less than 0! Not just when I am thinking of that, but any time! It was part of the trick, and I don't want to have anything to do with it!

When Veronica returned for her next session she reported that, after the previous session, she had gone home, taken all of her soft drinks out of the refrigerator, and taken them to a local Goodwill Industries as a donation! She said, "I think the guys at the loading dock probably just drank them! That's okay." She reported that the thought of a cold soft drink, previously highly desired, was now disgusting to her, because of what she had realized with regard to the connections with her abuse.

Several weeks after this, though, she reported a brief relapse. She had purchased some soft drinks, and placed them in a warm closet, with the idea that, "The warm Pepsi's are not the same as the cold Pepsi's." As she told me this, she recognized right away that this represented a repeat of the conflict between her adult and child parts—although one that actually had much less intensity. This disagreement was resolved using very similar procedures to the previous session, with a continued compassionate conversation between her ANP and the "Mimi" part that still had a small degree (LOPA of 2–3) of positive affect connected with soft drinks. Following this work, her child part was able to entirely relinquish interest and positive investment in soft drinks. She reported that she had stopped drinking sweet drinks entirely, and in fact this report was verified, during subsequent months, as she experienced significant and positive weight loss, and a normalizing of her measured blood sugar levels. Her doctor told her that she was no longer prediabetic. Given the previous premature termination of her therapy, we cautiously continued our sessions, spreading them out to occur every 6 to 8 weeks, and then with brief phone contacts every 12 to 16 weeks. One year after the previous session, she was feeling fully integrated within herself. ("I remember how it was to have all the little separate parts inside, but Mimi and all the others are just part of me now. It isn't separate. It's all me.") Her integration and resilience were tested during the year following her therapy, when she had major surgery for cancer. The surgery appeared to be successful in removing the cancer. Throughout the stresses of this year, her personality structure remained integrated—that is, she was able to cope effectively with each stress without dissociating. In the years since ending therapy, she has sent occasional email messages, but she has not had any recurrence of her previous problems of dissociative symptoms, panic, or low self-esteem.

Veronica's course of treatment illustrates several important issues. The portion of her treatment that occurred from 2005 to 2007 (Knipe, 2007) focused on helping her overcome and resolve her fear of disclosing inner parts of the self, helping her resolve her avoidance defenses with regard to specific traumatic memories as well as avoidance of trauma-reliving child parts. During the earlier episode of therapy, she was also able to significantly reduce her phobias of certain foods that reminded her of her father's abuse. In this second, briefer episode of therapy, described in the previous transcripts, she was able to utilize the CIPOS method to fully resolve her feelings of shame, horror, and disgust regarding specific sensations and associated memories, and then, using the

LOPA method, reduce her dysfunctional and defensive emotional investment in excessive consumption of soft drinks. This last therapy work that we did seemed to remove the remaining obstacles to personality integration.

REFERENCES

Knipe, J. (2007). Loving eyes: Procedures to therapeutically reverse dissociative processes while preserving emotional safety. In C. Forgash & M. Copeley (Eds.), *Healing the heart of trauma and dissociation with EMDR and ego state therapy*. pp. 181–226. New York, NY: Springer Publishing.
Schwartz, R. (1995). *Internal family systems therapy*. New York, NY: Guilford Press.

16

Doug

- Constant Installation of Present Orientation and Safety (CIPOS) with a highly disturbing combat memory held by a dissociated part of the personality

"Doug" was a Vietnam veteran who came to therapy in 1993, 25 years after his deployment. His initial presenting problem included chronic general anxiety as well as indecision regarding whether to continue his 20-year marriage. Very early in the process, within the first three sessions, he also mentioned an additional problem—one that appeared to be linked with Vietnam. He said that he had been having severe migraine headaches, six times per week on average, for the entire time since returning from the war. He said that the only ways of finding relief from these headaches were (a) get into the shower and turn the water on his forehead, as hot as he could stand it, and/or (b) think about a particular incident from Vietnam. This suggested the possibility that he was strongly defending against the emergence of one, and possibly more, combat memories, and this was confirmed as he later told me, "I really don't want to talk about Vietnam. I don't need it. But there is this 19-year-old kid who is always wanting me to think of it." At the time, I did not know enough about dissociation, and when he started to tell me about "this 19-year-old kid," I interpreted this as just his manner of speaking about his Vietnam experience. As time went on, it became more and more clear that he was experiencing this "kid" as someone else, as a separate, unwelcome presence inside his mind. He said, "There is this 19-year-old here! It's not like I'm telling you what happened in Vietnam. It's that, he is telling me what to tell you, and he wants me to think about it, and *I don't want to!*" It became clear that these were differentiated and separate personality parts, with very different agendas. His present-oriented part was extremely avoidant of both the 19-year-old part and the actual memory images. I asked him, 0 to 10, how much he did not want to think of his combat experiences, and he said, "I could easily tell you it's a 15!" Because of the strength of his avoidance, and his wish to work on other issues, we agreed to put his combat experiences off to the side, at least temporarily.

Doug had also had some very difficult times growing up. He described his father by saying, "I never knew what he would do. Sometimes he was the meanest man in the world, when he was drunk," and "At other times he would apologize and cry." Doug was severely beaten by his father all through his childhood, and, in addition, he remembered other traumatic times—for example, one very cold Wisconsin night at age 6, when he waited alone in a car while his father was in a bar for several hours. Several representative memories were targeted with eye movement desensitization and reprocessing (EMDR) with good results, in that Doug was able to view these events much more from an adult perspective and let go of the feelings of fear and unworthiness that had previously been connected with these particular memories.

These positive results with childhood memories helped him take a second look at what could be done with the memories from Vietnam. He continued to have a strong avoidance wish with regard to thinking about his war experiences (although he also reported, paradoxically, that Vietnam was with him "all the time"), but he was also now able to view this avoidance impulse from a place of some emotional distance and perspective. He decided that he would be able to use the EMDR procedures to target the one memory that he allowed himself to think of—the memory that he would go to when he was having a headache.

At the start of this session, when I asked if he could tell about the memory, he said, with much intensity,

> **I always get this one day in 1968. My insides are racing. I get visions of the people I was with, and the faces are not happy faces. We are dirty. We smell. We have lost weight. We're tired. We are standing in a group, ready to go out. I can hear choppers in the distance. I don't know if this is going to *be it* or not. It was like going into a game. I liked it. I went out and killed people. But when I think of it right now, I'm terrified! I think there is something wrong with me.**

This description expresses many emotions that are often experienced by traumatized combat veterans—a confusing mix of terror, exhilaration, physical fatigue, personal inadequacy, and moral injury. He told me that this image was always there, if he let himself think about it. We proceeded through EMDR Phases 3 to 7, and this session had very good results, with the thought, "There is something wrong with me," shifting to a Validity of Cognition of 7 for the preferred positive cognition (PC) of "I'm okay." His Subjective Units of Disturbance Scale for this incident did not go to "0," but dropped from "10+" to "2 or 3" during the session. The next week, he said, "It's down to about a one, now." I asked if there were other memories from the war, and he said, "Yes. I don't want to think about those either. But he (the 19-year-old) is here, and he says I have to."

In spite of this reluctance, and somewhat encouraged by this first use of EMDR, he was willing to proceed cautiously in identifying a list of primary incidents ("10, and there's probably more"). In Vietnam, he had been involved in numerous firefights in which he had had intense feelings of both exhilaration and terror, with these feelings often blended within a single memory image. In the months that followed, each time we met, he would briefly restate that he did not like thinking about Vietnam, but, nevertheless, he was willing to put his avoidance wish aside, after this wish had been acknowledged, and proceed to use EMDR to work through his list. When we would target a particular incident, the negative cognition would generally be voiced by the 19-year-old part (e.g., "I could die right now! I'm in danger.") and the corresponding PC (e.g., "I'm safe now. It's over.") would be identified by his present-oriented part. Several sessions were usually required for each incident. He was highly encouraged by the fact that, during this time, his migraine headaches stopped completely, and he attributed this to the work we had been doing. But, in spite of this progress, he remained ambivalent, saying, "This is helping, but I don't enjoy coming here."

This ambivalence was also reflected in the fact that he did not want to schedule on a weekly basis, but instead would let long periods of time go by between sessions. Because of the strength of his avoidance need, I did not push him to come more often, assuming that he was trying to balance his twin goals of therapy progress and emotional self-protection as best he could. I learned to trust him to call for another appointment when he was ready. When he would call, and then come in, usually his internal debate would still be continuing between the present-oriented, avoidant part (essentially, within a later definition—his apparently normal part [ANP]) and his 19-year-old emotional part (EP; van der Hart, Nijenhuis, & Steele, 2006).

Nevertheless, in spite of the fact that his therapy was occurring in a start–stop–start pattern, he appeared over time to be benefiting from it. As we proceeded through disturbing memories, one by one, he reported that his general anxiety was significantly diminished. He still was experiencing himself (as ANP) as separate from "the 19-year-old," but he was referring now to this separate self-state as "my buddy." In January 1997, his therapy prematurely ended when he had to take a new job in a different part of the United States, and he did not continue with another provider (even though I suggested some other therapists in his new location). In 1999, he sent me a postcard saying that he was "doing fine."

I did not hear from him again until the spring of 2012, when he called me unexpectedly. He had been suffering from severe parkinsonian symptoms due to Agent Orange exposure in Vietnam. The Veterans Affairs (VA) doctor had asked him for the names of all previous healthcare providers. It was at that point that he decided to contact me directly.

On the phone, I asked him how he was doing, and he said, "Those sessions really helped." He went on to say, "I'm doing great!—except when I'm trying to go to sleep at night, or when I am just relaxing or trying to read a book." It was at these times that the other, still very separate and differentiated part of self, the "19-year-old," would come into his consciousness, always in the jungle of Vietnam, always pointing in the direction of a path. He said, "He wants me to look at something, but I don't need it. I don't want it. I left him (the "19-year-old") in Vietnam."

He had briefly been to see a counselor in the VA, who did not treat him for a dissociative disorder, but instead had advised him to try, when he was having trouble going to sleep at night, to have "happy thoughts." He said that he had tried this, but it did not help very much. As we continued talking over the phone, he said, "Maybe it would be a good idea for us to get together again. Would that be okay?" His wife had planned a business trip to Colorado, where I live, and he arranged to come with her. We had an extended therapy session for several hours on a Saturday. He agreed in advance that if following this session he still needed additional sessions, he would return again, or contact a therapist in his current location.

Fifteen years earlier, at the time of our previous session, I had not developed the Constant Installation of Present Orientation and Safety (CIPOS) procedure. If we had used CIPOS during this earlier therapy, I think the therapy process would have reached completion at that time. In our extended 2012 session, in light of his continuing dissociative personality structure, it seemed that CIPOS would be a possible option. He arrived at this session saying, "I'm ready to work," and appeared to quickly reestablish his previously comfortable relationship with me as his therapist. After catching up with each other for about 40 minutes, we proceeded to focus on the issue that was most troubling to him—the continuing intrusions from his 19-year-old EP. The verbatim transcript, taken as an excerpt from a video recording of this 3½-hour session, follows. In the transcript, wherever [**EM**] appears, I have said, "Stay with that, think of that, notice that," or something similar, followed by a set of 20 to 30 eye movement sweeps. Wherever ******* appears, that indicates the period of seconds in which Doug is going into the traumatic memory material, with *no* bilateral stimulation.

I asked him what came to mind when he thought of the work we had previously done in therapy.

> **Doug: That just took me over a lot of guilt, and to this day, as we sit here right now, that really helped me.** (*Therapist: I'm so glad. Do you remember talking about the 19-year-old?*) **Yup. I definitely do.** (*Therapist: I remember you saying before—he was someone who was perfectly adapted to what you had to do in Vietnam, so when you came back here, you left him there.*) **Yes. I did. But now, when I'm trying to go to sleep—here we go, from my subconscious!** (*Therapist: So, when you're not working at it, your mind tends to go back in that direction?*) **Doug: Yes.** (*Therapist: If you can tell me right now where it is that your mind still keeps wanting to go, we can identify that, and work with it, so that it won't pull you anymore. Does that make some sense?*)
>
> **Doug: It does. (Pause.) There were always patrols. There were always incidents that we got involved in. We covered a lot of that when I came to you before. What I keep falling back on, Jim, is that guy in**

the white T-shirt. When I see him, now he takes me somewhere else. I don't go to that firefight at Ben Het. I don't go immediately to those situations. I still see that 19-year-old, sitting on the side of that bridge with a can of C-rations and a spoon. It was almost like—"Yeah, you are getting there. You have been through a lot." But he wants to show me some more. He's just not letting me loose.

Therapist: I am going to ask you some focused questions. Okay? **(Doug nods, yes.)** *Just answer whatever is true. The things he would like to show you right now—how much, 0 to 10, is that gut urge, that feeling you have, of "I don't want to look at that?"—10 the most. What number would you say?*

Doug: I would say we're up around a 10. (Pause.) He has already told me, "We've been down this path before." Not a road—it's a "path." Because that's what we said—we walked "paths." We have been down this path before. What am I afraid of?

This distinction was important—roads and trails were more exposed than paths, and more dangerous.

(Therapist: Now, as I remember, he was always saying, "Don't be afraid. You can look at this. You don't have to be afraid.") **Doug: Pretty much, yeah.** *(Therapist: How can we go to the places he would really like to show you, so that he knows you have seen it all, and he, then, will be at peace about it, and you can be at peace too? What do you think of that idea?)* **Doug: I think it's a good *idea*. (With some hesitation.) Is it too aggressive?** *(Therapist: Let's say that there is a way to do it. Would you like that outcome?)* **Doug: Yes, definitely.**

Doug's ANP continued to be avoidant with regard to his younger soldier self, but it appeared also that he was able to experientially pull back from this avoidance impulse and continue to remain oriented and aware of present safety, separating that out from his avoidance urge. This allowed us to continue using the CIPOS procedure.

Therapist: Good, and I think there is a way. Is there a picture, a memory image, in your mind, that represents the worst part? **(Doug: Yes. Got it.)** *(Therapist: I'd like to ask your permission, and I'm asking his permission, to work on that today.* **(Doug: Yes. He's with it. He's there right now.)** *So it sounds like he is all for it.* **(Doug: He is. He is right there.)**

Therapist: So here are some more questions. Before we start, in order for me to get a sense of what you're experiencing right now, can you think of a line that goes from out here (Therapist wiggles his fingers about 24 inches in front of Doug's face) where my fingers are, all the way to the back of your head? Let this place on the line (wiggle fingers) mean that you are completely present here in my office. It is 2012, and you are here, and there is nothing else on your mind except being here—we're talking, and it's a nice sunny day out that window—and you have no other thoughts at all. That's what this place on the line means—that you are completely present here with me. **(Doug: Got it.)** *The other place on the line, at the back of your head, means that even though your eyes are open, you are in this moment, this memory of the worst part.* **(Doug nods his head.)** *So this place on the line means you're completely present; this means you are in the worst part. Doug, take your finger right now and point to where you are on this line right at this moment.* **(Doug points to a place about 8 inches in front of his face, and says, "Right here.")** *So, in order for us to work with this, I would like to do some things to help you feel more present in the room right now.* **(Doug: Okay.)** *Can you hear an airplane?* **(Doug: Yes.)** *Just listen to it. As you are listening to it, just realize you are listening to something that is real, here, right now, and follow my fingers.* **[EM]** *Now, can you catch this pillow?* **(Pillow is tossed back and forth five times.) (Doug smiles.)** *Good. Now let me ask again. Where are you on the line right now, right at this moment?*

Doug: We haven't moved too much, because my friend is anxious! He wants to get it out. *(Therapist: It sounds like he's ready to talk about it. And what is your point of view about that?)* **We'll get there.**

His response indicates that the "19-year-old" is also present in his awareness, and not willing to let his ANP take full control. I need to check to make sure that the presence of this EP does not interfere with his ability to remain oriented to my office. This is something that frequently occurs when CIPOS is used with a client who has been trying over many years to avoid and suppress the emergence of an EP. The EP may not want to relinquish full control, and thereby lose an opportunity for expression, and perhaps for healing. I check with Doug to make sure that in spite of the presence of his younger part, he still is able to maintain awareness of present safety.

Therapist: So here is a question. Are you present here in this room? **(Doug: Yes.)** *And does he want you to go to this other place, to do some time travel?* **(Doug: Yes. He's not anxious. I'm just getting this message, "Come on! Come on!")** *So, I want to talk to him for a moment. (Speaking to the 19-year-old.) We will get to you in a minute. But in order to do what you would like to happen here we have to first have a clear awareness of being here in the present, in this room. So that's what I am asking him to allow—to let you be fully aware of being here, and then, go there to where he is. What does he say back to that?* **(Doug—speaking from the 19-year-old: Pretty much, do what you have to do, but don't leave me.)** *Yes. I promise, and can you promise also, that we won't leave him today?*

Doug: We are not going to leave anybody behind. *(Therapist: Okay. Now in order for us to do what is needed here, first of all, is for you to be real clear in your mind where you really are right now. So, in all honesty, where are you on the line?)* **I'm out here. I'm not quite all the way to your fingers, but I'm knocking on the door. I'm almost all the way out.**

Therapist: Good. Now in a moment, when you are ready, I'm going to ask you to close your eyes for 8 seconds. I will keep track of the time on my watch. Don't close your eyes until you are ready, and when your eyes are closed, just let yourself go completely to where he wants you to go. For 8 seconds. And then when 8 seconds are up, I will say, "Open your eyes and come back." Now, before we do that, let me ask you, is 8 seconds something that is possible? I want to be sure that you don't go into the memory so far that you can't come back easily. What would you say?

Doug: I think we can do it. *(Therapist: Okay. Would 6 be better?)* **I think we better do the 6.** *(Therapist: Okay. How about—we do 5?)* **Okay. Yup.**

*Therapist: This is not a contest. This is not about trying to prove something. Five is fine. So when you are ready, go there for 5 seconds, and I will keep track of the time. At the end of the 5 seconds, I will say, "Open your eyes and come back." When you close your eyes, I will start. And I will talk the whole time, just so you'll know that I'm still here. (Five seconds ***) Okay, now open your eyes, and come back. That's good! So here is a really dumb question: Where are you right now, in actual fact?*

Doug: Right here with you.

Therapist: Can you take some comfort in that? **(Doug: Yes.)** *That's good. Just think of that. [EM] Would it be possible for you to go back in for 5 more seconds?* **(Doug: Yes, it would.)** *Okay. We will start again when you're ready, when you close your eyes. Don't do it until you're ready.* **(Doug closes eyes. ***)** *Okay, now open the eyes and come back. Good. How was that? It looks like you came back a little more easily that time.*

Doug: I did. Because I was told (by the 19-year-old part), the first time, "Listen up!" The second time, I heard, "You're getting help!" Those two things. *(Therapist: Good. And that was helpful for you?)* **Yes.** *(Therapist: Good. Think of that.)* **[EM]**

Therapist: Good. So, now, how about 5 more seconds? **(Doug nods yes.)** *Again, I will start when you close your eyes. (Five seconds ***) Okay, and open your eyes again.* **(Doug is laughing and nodding his head.)** *You're laughing. Say what's happening.*

(Doug leans forward, smiling, and moves his arm as if he has someone in a choke hold.) I got an arm around the neck and a jab in the stomach! That's why I'm laughing. (Pause.) This is good! (Pause.) We're at a place there, that was *not* a good place. That's where *he's* at. It's the entry to a cave. He's saying, "Follow me in, brother!" We are right at the doorstep, the entrance.

Therapist: Let's take a moment to check—where are you on the line right now?

(Doug points out with his finger, and says "I'm still with you.") *I'm just checking to be extra sure that we don't go too fast with this. So now, when you're ready, go back in again for 5 more seconds. When you're ready. (Five seconds ***) Okay, open the eyes again now, and come back here. Good. And again, my dumb question, where are you right now, in actual fact?*

Doug: I probably slipped a little.

Therapist: Do you mean you went in a little bit more than before? **(Doug nods yes.)** *That's understandable, and it's even part of this process. But, are you back here again now?* **(Doug: Yes.)** *Can you see how this may be helping?* **(Doug: Yes.)** *And maybe he can see it too. Can he see it too?* **(Doug: He hasn't said anything yet.)** *What are you seeing, so far? Is this helping?* **(Doug nods yes.)** *If it is helping, how is it helping?*

Doug: Well, there is a release. I told you earlier, sometimes when I'm reading, and I would get distracted, I would always end up with him. And he was always pointing. *(Therapist: So you would be daydreaming, and then all of a sudden. . . .)*

Right! I would end up back with him, a good 90% of the time. But he was always pointing. Always pointing . . . somewhere, someplace. (Pause.) Now, where we are in this, today, right now—he is with me! He's not pointing any more. He is with me! *(Therapist: Is that okay with you? Because there have been times when you tried to push him far away.)* **But not this time. It is okay. We're walking together now, in this place. We're together. We're going to come to grips!**

This statement by Doug indicated that he was no longer pushing the 19-year-old part away. He was now able to maintain dual attention—simultaneous awareness of both the safe present and this other part that was reexperiencing trauma material. With this dual attention, we are now able to cautiously proceed with EMDR Phase 4, the combining of bilateral stimulation with information from the trauma memory. However, because his access to present safety still appeared to be fragile, we also continue to use CIPOS procedures, alternating back and forth with Phase 4 procedures, to ensure that Doug is able to stay in the dual attention zone.

Therapist: Good. It sounds like everybody's on the same page.

Doug: Yes. Yes. *(Therapist: I would guess this is not easy.)* **That's right. It's not easy. But this is going in a good direction.** *(Therapist: So let's check again. I think I know the answer, but where are you on the line?)* **I'm away from being all the way out to your fingers, but I'm mostly out. I think if we go beyond that 5 seconds, I will be all the way back in it (points to back of head).**

Therapist: There is no reason to go beyond the 5 seconds. It's probably best that we keep it at 5. **(Doug: I can see that now.)** *So, when you're ready, go back in for 5 more seconds. (Five seconds ***) It looks to me—tell me if it's true—that it gets easier for you to come back each time. Is that true?* **(Doug: Yes. It is easier.)** *Is that a good thing?* **(Doug: Yes, because he knows we're coming back. Because the trail isn't—the path, he corrected me—is not complete.)** *Stay with that.* [EM] *Is he ready to show you something? To take you to where he has been pointing?*

Doug: (Long pause.) Yes. *(Therapist: Would you be willing to go there for 5 seconds?)* **I'm not sure we will get there in this first 5 seconds, but let's go.** *(Therapist: Okay. There's no rush. We'll just go where we go. Go there again for 5 seconds and just observe whatever there is to observe. And at the end of the 5 seconds, I will say, "Come back here." Start when you're ready.)* **Okay. (Five seconds ***) I'm not afraid, because I've been there.**

Therapist: Okay. Good. With that in mind, would you be able to go back in for another 5 seconds? **(Doug: Yes.)** *Five seconds *** It looked like it was a little harder to open your eyes that time. Is that true?* **(Doug: Yes, it was.)** *Is it like you were pulled to stay there a little longer?* **(Doug: No. It was just . . . it was the shock.)** *I see. Okay.*

Doug: I just heard, as I was trying to come back, "This is what you had to see!"

Therapist: After all that, are you able to be here, again?

Doug: Oh, yeah. *(Therapist: Is it kind of nice to be here?)* **Oh, definitely! Definitely!** *(Therapist: Notice that good feeling, that it's good to be here. Stay with that.)* **[EM] It's a relief in my chest.**

Therapist: That's a nice thing, to be here. Stay with that. [EM] *What's good about being here? That may be a very odd question.* **(Doug: I'm safe.)** *Stay with that.* [EM] *Is that a good feeling in your chest?* **(Doug: Oh, yeah. I even feel like I'm breathing better.)** *Stay with that. Just notice that.* [EM]

Doug: I'm out here (points to the out place on the Back of the Head Scale line). I hear the airplane outside! *(Therapist: Okay. How about 5 more seconds, and pick up where you left off.) Five seconds *** Okay, now open the eyes and come back. It didn't look like it was too hard to come back that time.*

Doug: It was okay that time. I knew right where I was going. And then it was easier to come back in the room here. But now I'm trying to find my buddy! Because when I went back this last time, he wasn't there! *(Therapist: He wasn't! Where is he right now?)* **I don't know! He's not there (laughs while shaking his head).**

Therapist: When you're ready, go back again. Five seconds *** Now, open the eyes again.

Doug: We are at the place that he wanted me to go. Maybe it makes sense that he's in me now (points to his own chest). *(Therapist: Maybe he's occupying the exact same space as you are, right now.)* **Yes. And now, what I have to deal with, I'm on my own.** *(Therapist: Stay with that. Just notice that.)* **[EM] I think I can do that.** *(Therapist: Stay with that. Just notice that.)* **[EM]**

Doug: It was a trap. And we walked right into it. And no way out. Minimal supplies—food, water, ammunition. It went on for days. That's what he wanted me to see.

Doug went on to describe to me, in detail, what he now was able to look at. It was visually, and morally, gruesome.

Therapist: And are you seeing it right now? **(Doug: Yes.)** *And as you see it right now, are you able to also be here, too?* **(Doug: Yes. I'm pretty much here. But I want to do 5 more seconds.)** *Five seconds *** How hard was it to come back that time?* **(Doug: Not hard at all.)** *Just think of how it wasn't hard.* **[EM]**

Doug: The last couple of times, going in—it's been harder to go back in.

This is a report that clients give sometimes during a successful CIPOS session. A similar report sometimes occurs during standard EMDR processing. A client might be initially alarmed by his or her own inability to access previously terrifying memory material. The client might think, erroneously, that he or she is doing something wrong, whereas actually, the difficulty in reaccessing the "reliving" aspect of the memory is a clear consequence of the successful processing, and is actually the goal of the therapy.

Doug: And I still haven't found him! (Laughs.) *(Therapist: I wonder if you're seeing what you're seeing through his eyes?* **(Doug nods yes.)** *and that's why you can't see him.)* **That makes sense.**

Therapist: And the fact that it is harder now to go back into it, Doug, is really the point of why we're doing this. What used to be something you tried to push away, three miles away, and you didn't want to get near it, because it would pull you in, that can become something different now that you can let yourself think about, and go right up to it, and it isn't the same anymore. It's losing the charge. Is this what you wanted?

Doug: Yes. Let's do a little longer. How about 8 seconds? *(Eight seconds ***)* **This is the very first time—in the past, when I was reading, I could be thinking about anything, and yet I would always come back to him. He would always point. He would never say, "Come on, let's go." But at night, when I would be trying to think my "happy thoughts," that's when it would occur. I've never been at this point. In all fairness, am I safe to say that I've been afraid of him? Was I worried he was going to get mad at me? And make things worse? I'm just talking through this.** *(Therapist: How is it now?)* **He's not here!!** *(Therapist, pointing at Doug: I'm wondering if he's right* here.*)* **Right. (Pause.) When I would see him, I always would see him—that cocky look at the bridge in that white shirt. Right now, I can remember that. Maybe he's here, but he's not here in the same way, in my face.**

Therapist: Can you go back again to the place, to see what you get?

Doug: Yes. [EM] Can I tell you what I saw? I saw nothing but vegetation. I saw butterflies, insects, and no scars, nothing of yesterday. It was quite nice, actually. Flowers. Vietnam, believe it or not, is a beautiful country, aside from. . . . But, there was nothing for me to see anymore. *(Therapist: Think of that.* **[EM]** *When you try to think again, right now, of the worst part, what do you get?)*

Nothing! I didn't even give it a thought until you asked me about it again! I wasn't even thinking about it until you just said that. *(Therapist: Did that make it all come back again?)* **No! No! Was like—What am I even doing here!?**

(Therapist: Okay. Stay with that.) **[EM]**

Doug: When I went back, there was nothing there that was bad. I was in the same place where those things happened, but at first I didn't recognize it. All the bad things were gone—the smell, the carnage

of bodies—that wasn't there! It was just humid, with the smell of the woods.

Therapist: Doug, when you think of this incident that happened, the cave, and where you were ambushed, and trapped for days, up against that wall, and you saw the bodies. . . . I'm saying all the words that describe the worst parts of this that you've told me. When you think of it right now, what is different from when we started, when you also were thinking of it?

Doug: What's different now—it's fuzzy. It's almost like it isn't even real. It's almost like it didn't even happen. I do know it happened, and I still can remember it now. But it's not overpowering. It feels over. Because I can see these beautiful flowers! (Laughs.) That's what I see now! I'm seeing it right now. I see it perfectly!

Usually, after an intense session like this, I would want to do a follow-up session fairly quickly, but he had to return home the next day. I did the follow-up by phone 1 week later and then again after 4 months, and again after 13 months, just to be extra sure that his outcome from this therapy session was as positive as it appeared.

He stated that he did not feel the need to return to have additional sessions with me or have a referral to a local therapist. He said that the memory that had been the focus of the session was, "different now, and just a picture, not something that bothers me." I asked him about whether he had had any additional experiences with "the 19-year-old." He said, "I still can remember him, but it's really different now, hard to describe. No problem. I still get some memories when I hear something in the waiting room at the VA, but I just let myself think about it now, and I get past it." My impression was that an integration of parts occurred during and following this therapy work. A key element in this may have been what occurred toward the end of the session, following the release of his memory disturbance, when, with the continued sets of eye movements, he reported visualizing that "the 19-year-old" was now occupying the same space as the man living in and oriented to the reality of the present.

REFERENCE

van der Hart, O., Nijenhuis, E., & Steele, K. (2006). *The haunted self: Structural dissociation and the treatment of chronic traumatization.* New York, NY: W. W. Norton.

17

Rhonda

- Targeting of a shame defense that is an obstacle to personality integration
- Use of the Internal Healing Dialogue procedure to assist the client in resolving "the problem of attachment to the perpetrator"

The case described here illustrates how an individual with complex post-traumatic stress disorder (Complex PTSD) may have issues not only of unresolved traumatic experiences, but also very strong attachment to a perpetrating caretaker, as has been described by Colin Ross (1998, Ross & Halpern, 2009). This type of attachment is often lurking behind the client's initial presentation, and can contribute in a major way to the development of dissociative personality structure.

At the time of our first session, "Rhonda's" personality structure was highly dissociative, with a strongly established apparently normal part (ANP) and three clusters of clearly differentiated first-person identities centering around age 2, ages 3 to 12, and age 14. Prior to her late 30s, Rhonda was only aware of herself as her ANP, but then, following the death of her grandmother, she began having flashbacks of previously dissociated childhood sexual abuse, and these memory images were very distressing to her. At that time, she entered therapy with a very good therapist, but one who did not use eye movement desensitization and reprocessing (EMDR), and was not trained in treating dissociative conditions. In this therapy, many traumatic childhood events were uncovered, but these remained largely unresolved and were continuing to give this client intense ongoing disturbance—not only chronic anxiety, but also deep shame—despair that she was defective, morally disgraceful, and irreparably broken. She also was experiencing auditory hallucinations (the repeated voice of a young child crying for help) and, at times of high stress, self-harming behaviors (nonlethal cutting). She continued in that therapy for 9 years before being referred to me by that therapist, to see if an EMDR therapy approach could be helpful. Her previous therapist sat in on our beginning sessions, and continued to see the client intermittently, in a supportive role, during the client's time in therapy with me.

Rhonda described her family home as one of "a constant atmosphere of rage" from her mother. Her father was described as very passive and uninvolved. The previously dissociated sexual abuse memories were each vivid and highly disturbing—the most disturbing being memories of sexual abuse by her mother, beginning in infancy. Rhonda had clear explicit memories of her confusion and fear when her mother was sexually stimulating her while nursing, or while changing her diaper, during the first 2½ years of life. Beginning at about age 3, she was taken by her mother to the maternal grandparents' house as a "gift" for sexual abuse. (We can guess, without specific evidence, that her mother, as a child, was also sexually abused by these grandparents.) When, as Rhonda got older, she would attempt to escape the abuse, she would be beaten and often drugged. In addition to the ongoing physical and sexual abuse, there was repeated mind-control manipulation by both her mother and grandparents—manipulation designed to inculcate in this child an entrenched identity of shamefulness, with the aim of making the child more compliant. For example, her mother, after a miscarriage, took the dead fetus to this client, at age 4, and said, "Look what you did! We should call the police, but we won't, if you do what we say!" Children believe what they are told, and the adult Rhonda remembered thinking, "I'm sorry! I didn't mean to do it!" It was shortly after this incident that this client tried to kill herself by biting down on an electrical cord. The scar on her lip was still evident when I met her decades later. Due to these ongoing traumatic experiences, she lived in constant fear throughout her childhood. She grew up in a very rural place, and her experiences outside the home (except for school) were very restricted. Her separate, dissociated identities were an adaptation to this environment.

The sexual abuse at the hands of these perpetrators continued until this client's late teenage years, at which time she left the house, became self-supporting, and continued her education, ultimately to the point of obtaining a graduate professional degree in her mid-20s. For the next 25 years, she lived as, and was only aware of herself as, her ANP.

When I first met her, she said, "People that think they know me don't really know me. There are children inside me, crying, and I wish they weren't there. I hate the way that I am. I don't think I can ever be any different! But I can't give up." When we began our sessions, her ANP was phobically avoidant of the internal emotional parts (EPs), the associated trauma memories, and auditory hallucinations (a child's voice crying, "No, Mommy, no!"). The ANP simply wanted to be a person free of these posttraumatic intrusions, and someone positively regarded by others. In her life outside the sessions, she would frequently do things that involved high risk. On vacations, she climbed mountains in Tibet and rafted down raging rivers in Africa. She said, "I do these things to prove I'm okay, and also to build up my courage for what I am doing in here!"

The first 3 years of her therapy with me were primarily devoted to treatment of these specific disturbing memories, sometimes using standard EMDR procedures, and very often supplementing standard procedures with the "Tools" described in the previous chapters of this book. Within her awareness, there was a separate and distinct 2-year-old identity who had learned very early to comply without opposition to her mother's sexual abuse. We used the Loving Eyes procedures to access and target a representative moment of abuse, held by the 2-year-old part. The adult part was able to observe the thoughts of the 2-year-old: "I always knew there was a bargain. I had to give her something to get something back. She was angry and disgusted all the time. I wanted to make her happy. I knew if I let her do those things, I would feel ugly and dirty, but it would make her happy." The result of this intervention was that the younger part—the EP—no longer felt terror and shame.

This chapter describes the next step in her therapy. The following session transcript illustrates the use of the Internal Healing Dialogue procedure to facilitate resolution of this client's ambivalent and very damaging "attachment to the perpetrator"—attachment to mother—that continued in spite of her successful prior work. As stated in Chapter 14, for clients with severe dissociative conditions, resolution of the posttraumatic, vivid "relivings" associated with traumatic experience is not always sufficient to bring about personality integration. This was true for Rhonda. After much hard work with specific troubling memories, she still was unable to shake a strong feeling of badness. She said, "I can forgive the 2-year-old for having sexual feelings with my mother. She had no choice. But it continued into my teenage years. I can't forgive myself for that. I don't want that 14-year-old girl to be part of me. She did bad things. I hate her, and I hate my mother for what she did." Her intense feeling of shame about herself was still a significant obstacle to her being able to achieve her larger therapy goal of personality integration—being "one person."

About 5 weeks after the session with the 2-year-old part, we shifted the focus of the therapy work to the deep sense of shame still held by the adult. This session illustrates one way of therapeutically working with the issue of ambivalent attachment to a perpetrating caretaker. In treating this issue of extreme ambivalence, with regard to her mother, a particular interweave is used. It is suggested to the client that she create separate visual representations of each side of her internal conflict, in order to clarify her ambivalence between these parts, and then facilitate an internal healing dialogue. The edited, but verbatim transcript for this session, taken from a video recording, follows, beginning from the first minutes. Whenever EM appears in the transcript, there is a statement from the therapist of "Notice that," "Think of that," or Stay with that," followed by a set of eye movements.

Therapist: Who is here today?

Client, as ANP: I think the teenage part of me is here and that is the one that I am most distrusting of, actually—the one that I want to push aside the most. I look at her with a great deal of shame. *(Therapist: You* *have shame about her?)* **Shame and disgust. I don't like her. I don't wish to have that part of me be connected.**

What am I going to do to look at her in a kind, compassionate way?

The client has been in psychotherapy long enough to know that compassionate acceptance of all of her parts is the ultimate goal of what we are doing. Nevertheless, she is honest in stating that that is not how she truly feels. She is expressing the feelings of fear and shame that have prevented integration of these personality parts.

Therapist: So, you would like to be able to do that?

Client, as ANP: I would! What is holding me back is just how sad it is. My God! What was I—12, 13, 14, 15-years-old? Maybe older?

This is a direct statement from the client describing how shame is continuing to serve as a psychological defense against full realization of the sadness connected to the ongoing losses of her childhood. But this cognitive insight does not resolve the issue.

Therapist: What if therapy here continues on, and it goes beautifully? It goes beautifully. If that happens—you talk about your sadness, if you were to fully realize that you were not really at fault when you were 14. If you really came to realize that you were not at fault, there would be such incredible sadness. . . . **(Client, as ANP: I am welling up with tears right now thinking about it.)** *What would you like to have happen with regard to that sadness? That's a hard question.*

Client, as ANP: I would like to think that I am strong enough to look at it the way it really was and be able to see the sadness, feel the pain, feel the grief and go through it.

My question is, then, who would I be? I feel like I was a bad person, that I did bad things. Who was I!? What was I doing? Why was I doing that? How do I identify myself as being any different from a street girl?

Shame is clearly connected to what occurred at 14—her difficulty as a girl in stopping the sexual abuse by her mother. I asked the following question to identify a memory of the moment—burdened by shame—when this difficulty arose.

Therapist: Can she (the 14-year-old part) bring to mind a representative image of the moment of choice? A representative moment of when she said to herself, "It is going to happen again. I have to let it happen again." What does she get?

Client, as EP: I guess I heard her on the steps coming upstairs. I heard the door quietly open, and close.

Client, as ANP, observing the age 14 part: Right now, the 14-year-old wants to say, "Don't take this away from me!" These are the words that she wants to say, "Don't take this away from me!" (Long pause, with tears.) Wow!

This realization was a shock to the client. Previously, in many, many therapy sessions, the client would express intense anger at her mother for sexually abusing her. But at this moment, the client is realizing the other side of her childhood ambivalent dilemma.

Therapist: Okay. Can we continue to talk about it? "Don't take this away from me!" Can she stay with that? **(Client, as ANP, observing the age 14 part: Yes.) EM**

And I want to ask her now, how much do you want to keep that? How much do you want to hang on to that? Use the numbers, 0 to 10. How much do you want to hang onto what you got from your mother when this occurred?

Client, as age 14 part: 10!

The client is expressing her strong attachment to her mother. We target it as an idealized image—one that is coming up as a channel of processing.

Therapist: Can she stay with that? And you help her watch my fingers. If it is too hard, for you or for her, you tell me. EM. Okay, now, just let it go.

The client, as ANP, appears to be shocked by the affection expressed by the 14-year-old toward her mother. I ask the ANP to step back, if possible, and allow the processing to continue.

Therapist: You, the adult, may have lots of comment about her feeling that way— about wanting mother to come in the night—but can you stay back a little bit, and observe, because she needs to talk about this.

Client, as ANP: The only thing going on between my mother and I—the only connection that ever was or ever will be—was the sexual connection. Without that, I feel like I would not have been able to survive. That decision did not come at age 14. It came at 2, and before that. *(Therapist: Is the 2-year-old here right now?)* **She is here. She knows. I remember when I had to make the only decision I could. And that was—"Okay, there is a bargain. There is a deal. If I want anything of my mother, this is what she's offering." Of course, I have to take that**

deal. I have to. If I don't, how am I going to be fed, how am I going to be clothed, who is going to take care of me, who is going to pick me up, who is going to whisper nice things every once in a while? I just was filled with so much guilt and ugliness, and shame, and confusion. So, I stuck to that, to a certain age, and then I threw up my hands and said, "No more!" Then all hell broke loose. But then I was in a position where I could take care of myself. I could leave. I didn't have to ask her for anything anymore. *(Therapist: So, looking at all this, are you having that flood of sadness?)* Not in the way that I thought—that I would be so uncontrollable that I would be just wailing on the floor. Is there another choice that I could have made? *(Therapist: Let's talk about that. What might it have been? You could have chosen to die.)* Yes. Tried that. And then I came up with a different solution—that I wasn't there. I wasn't there. I can still be this, this and this, and be separate too. She could have snuffed me out at any point in time. She showed that.

The client is describing how she, as a child, invented dissociation, as a desperate response to an impossible situation. Her mother had threatened her with death, and had killed animals in front of her. She could not prevent what was about to happen at age 14 when her mother entered the room. Her solution was that she simply was no longer there. Of course, when these events actually happened, another identity then took over and experienced the abuse.

Client, as ANP: I don't like how much I loved her despite who she was and what she did. I really, really struggle with that.

Therapist: Look at the 14-year-old right now. Can you look at her and see her love for her mother?

Client, as ANP: Oh, yes! . . . But then there was part of me that just hated her, just hated her for what she was doing—hated her for the control that she put over me and everybody else in the family. The terror that she reigned.

The following is a cognitive interweave that can be useful when a dissociative client is struggling with an internal EP that is highly ambivalent about an important relationship (i.e., the ambivalent EP has separate parts, each of which holds one side of the ambivalence). Note that both parts of the EP are "living in trauma time."

We start with the Loving Eyes procedure.

Therapist: Look at her. Can you see her, in your mind, right now? You know what 14-year-old girls look like. [Client, as ANP: Yes.] Can you just look at her right now? [Client, as ANP: Yes.] And see both of these things—not just one, not just the other, but see them both together.

Client, as ANP: I see them both. I just despised her (mother) with every ounce of me, and with that much hate, I cared about her that much too.

Therapist: Think of that. Just look at her, realizing that. EM.

Therapist: Let's imagine something. This will help. Imagine that the 14-year-old girl who loves her [**Client, as ANP: Yes.**] *could have a conversation . . . with the 14-year-old girl who hates her. Imagine that they can look at each other.* [**Client, as ANP: Yes.**] *Have them look at each other. What would the part that hates her say, to the other one?*

Client, as ANP: The one that hates would say, "Ahh, Are you going to let her continue to abuse you? You are not going to stop her? You are not going to say no? You're not going to tell anybody else about this? Are you going to even be complicit, to an extent? And you are going to even make it easy for her, making yourself available to our mother? Are you going to do that?"

Therapist: Think of that. EM . . .

And what does the one who loves your mother say back to that, in all honesty?

Client, as 14-year-old part who loves her mother: Yes, I am going to do that. *(Therapist: Tell the good reasons, from that side of you.)* **Well, I think she really does care about me. She's a little mixed up, a little messed up. But I think she really wants to care about me. And so that is good enough for me. I will take that.**

Therapist: Okay. And stay with that. Let both parts watch my fingers. EM . . .

What does the one who hates your mother say back to that?

Client, as 14-year-old part who hates mother: You have to stop her! You have to put a stop to this!

Therapist: And what does the one who loves your mother say back to that?

Client, as 14-year-old part who loves mother: You just have to step back, because nothing is going to change, yet, for a while. I am going to go ahead and do the same that I've always done. So just step back.

Therapist: So, is she telling the one who hates—we have to put aside that hatred? [**Client, as ANP: Yes.**] *EM.*

Client, as 14-year-old part who loves mother: I am not going to listen to that part of me that hates—who says, "You have to stop this." I am saying, "No, I am not going to deal with you. You are not going to exist here. This has to go on the way it is. I am not going to give her up, no matter what you say!"

Therapist: Stay with that. EM.

Client, as ANP: The angry part of me has validity: "Whoa—look what she's doing to you! Look what she's doing. I am pissed off and angry about that!"

The following cognitive interweave is useful in helping a dissociative client see that parts that are in some type of internal conflict are also each created to help meet the needs of the client, in a larger sense.

Therapist: Now, here is something to realize—something that might be helpful. Both the one part of you and the other part of you have something in common. **[Client, as ANP, with a tone of scepticism: Hmm.]** *They both are trying to do something good for you, in some way.* **[Client, as ANP: Hmm. Yes.]** *Isn't that kind of interesting to think of it that way? Both parts are going about it, though, with very different agendas.* **(Client, as ANP: Yes.)** *But they do have that in common.* **(Client, as ANP: The one that wants to stay sexual with my mother wants to keep that, and then the part of me that is real angry, and doesn't like what she is doing to me. . . .)** *The anger is a natural reaction too.* **(Client, as ANP: But at that time, I couldn't allow that to enter in.)** *Yes, it may be important to recognize now that these parts could not be put together. But both were ways of you trying to help yourself—they did have that in common. But they were so different. They couldn't be together—being one person. So, go back again now, and just visualize them both now—there is the one who hates your mother, and there is the other one who loves your mother. And, have it be that they are looking at each other, they are together. Is there anything different about the quality of their interaction or their relationship right now, as compared to 10 minutes ago?*

Client, as ANP: Well, they are aware of each other now. They are aware of each other. They are looking at each other, and sizing up this whole thing. It is like, "Okay, you felt this way, but I felt this way. It is going to stay the same . . . (but) it has to be different."

Client, as 14-year-old part who loves her mother: I couldn't allow that angry part to come in. I remember writing with such anger and pulling out the bottom drawer of my dresser and putting the letter in there so it wouldn't be seen. I think I eventually took it out and destroyed it. I couldn't change it.

Therapist: Stay with that. EM

Client, as ANP: But I got to a certain age where I said I was going to change it! And I walked out. I have been on my own ever since—I've been able to take care of myself, and support myself, and make all kinds of decisions on my own, and get along just fine. So, I must have done something right.

Therapist: Yes. So, go back and see them again. They never used to talk to each other. (**Client, as ANP: Yes.**) *And now they are talking to each other. And there is a little bit of contentiousness here.* (**Client, as ANP: Yes!!**) *But this is a conversation that never happened before. It didn't happen back then.* (**Client, as ANP: Yes, that's right.**) *Right now, what does the part who hates your mother have to say, based on everything we've been talking about? What does she have to say, right now?*

Client, as 14-year-old part who hates mother: So, what are you going to do now, now that you don't have her hovering over you and threatening you, at this point in your life? What are you going to do now with the information?

Her mother died about 2 years prior to this session.

Therapist: Good. What does the part who loves your mother say back to that?

Client, as 14-year-old part who loves mother: I still want to be quiet about it.

Therapist: Stay with that. EM. Just realize that. . . .

What if the part of you that loves your mother, even today, would say to the other part of you, "What am I supposed to do with this love, or this need for love? What am I supposed to do with it?"

Client, as 14-year-old part who loves mother: Yes. If I didn't have love for her, I think I would just be totally psychotic. I might be homicidal to her. If I hadn't had some sort of love for her, some compassion, my life would have gone a very different way.

Therapist: So, what does the other part that hates her say back to that?

Client, as 14-year-old part who hates mother: I agree. I agree that you should not throw out or dismiss this feeling of love you have had for her, because it was something you so, so deeply needed. And wanted.

I think you should keep that, just as much as I am going to keep my anger and hate for what she did.

Client, as ANP: Can they coexist like that? I would like to have just one or the other.

Therapist: Well, the fact is that they do coexist. **(Client, as ANP: Hmm. . . . Yes.)** *Whether they are logical together—that's another question. But just look at the two again. See the one who hates your mother. And the one who loves your mother. How are they doing, right now?*

Client, as ANP: They are there. They are together. They are listening. They are aware of one another. They are having this dialogue together. So, I can love her even though I can hate her for what she did. What she did!!

It feels like a letting-go, that this sexuality thing between my mother and I—it feels like grief.

Therapist: Let's talk to the 14-year-old who still loves your mother. Is she okay with what we are doing here? I say that because we are talking about her love. **(Client, as ANP: Yes.)** *I asked her a while ago to say, 0-10, how much she wanted to keep that feeling of love. She said, "10." What does she say right now? It might still be a 10.*

Client, as 14-year-old part who loves mother: It is not a 10. I feel a sense of relief, that it is okay for me to let go of some of that. *(Therapist: Stay with that. EM.)* **I can imagine, that when she was in a partially healthy state of mind, that she really did have some care for her kids. But there would be things that would take over for her—things she couldn't understand. She made, for each of her kids, for every birthday, a cake that she decorated. She made it herself. . . . But I feel she was a walking tragedy, and she never made her own personal decision to make any changes in her life. She was very, very much invested in continuing to live the way she wanted to live. But I want to say—it is going to end here, with this generation! It can only end with me, and what I do with my life. The understanding that what I have is really . . . a *proudness* of myself. Oh, my God, my mother couldn't ever do this. And I didn't think I could ever do this. I can! And there is a proudness for all the parts of me that made the decisions that they made, at the time, with the information that they had, about what was the right thing to move forward . . . I'm aware now.**

Therapist: Stay with that. EM.

Client, as ANP: I always thought that there were so many different parts of me, fragmented all over the place. We had to stay separate. We had to.

Therapist: This one had to, because of being afraid of that one, this one had to stay away from this one. This one idealized your mother. This one hated your mother. And they never could talk to each other, because there was just too much disagreement. Just notice how nice it is to have all of that be over.

Client: Wow!

This was a breakthrough session for Rhonda. In subsequent meetings, she was able to report that she was at peace with all parts of herself, and she was beginning to get used to the idea of having one integrated identity, one Self, with memory access to her life experience. Previously, all of her trauma history was a closely guarded secret, unknown to friends, family, and coworkers. Following the session, she made several contacts with selected members of her family, and several close friends, to let them know of these events in her history, and her recovery in therapy. There still was additional work, having to do with some remaining apprehension regarding trauma-related actions such as sexual arousal. It was helpful for her to observe (using Loving Eyes procedures) that when really was 14, her primary motive through all of these contacts with mother was not arousal but whatever scraps of connection might be available through the abuse experiences. She also was initially somewhat disoriented with the novelty of her integrated experience. However, over the course of several weeks, she was pleased to notice that she was no longer troubled by memories of her childhood and she enjoyed bringing up images of her 2-year-old and 14-year-old parts, now comfortably settled in her mind.

Over a period of 2 additional years, she faded from therapy with sessions scheduled every 3 weeks, then every 8 weeks, then occurring at longer intervals. At last contact, she reported, with a sense of satisfaction, that she no longer felt internally divided into separate first-person identities, but now was living as "one person." She was enjoying a variety of activities with other people—a yoga club, a hiking club, and volunteer work as a mentor for teenage girls who had been taken out of dysfunctional homes.

REFERENCES

Ross, C. (1998, Spring). The problem of attachment to the perpetrator. *Inner Voices*. Available at *Sanctuary for the Abused*. http://abusesanctuary.blogspot.com/2006/09/problem-of-attachment-to-perpetrator.html

Ross, C., & Halpern, N. (2009). *Trauma model therapy*. Richardson, TX: Manitou Communications.

18

Some Closing Thoughts

When a powerful method like eye movement desensitization and reprocessing (EMDR) is used with people who are highly vulnerable, the path of therapy can be quite narrow, bounded on one side by the need to keep the client within the zone of emotional safety, and on the other side by the need to help the client move forward in the healing process. The intention of this book is to help therapists help their clients widen this path, to help these individuals who have the double unfairness of a difficult childhood, and then an adult life in which they are still suffering from the residue of that childhood.

A final thought: If you think there have been interesting ideas in the chapters of this book, I would like to recommend that you take the next step. With your client's permission, and with appropriate safeguards, begin to implement these methods. Use this stuff! Make it yours! When, in the past, you purchased a computer, took it home, took it out of the box, and booted it up—at that point, it was not yet yours. It became yours when you used it. When I present some of this material in a 2-day workshop, I always try to say at the end, "This training has a shelf life of 2 weeks. If you don't use it right away, it will be harder to come back to, 4 weeks from now, or 6 months from now." I hope you will be able to actively use the ideas in this book, and do the thing that is one of life's most valuable experiences—to make a difference with people, guided by your own empathetic observations, and by your heart.

Index

AA. *See* Alcoholics Anonymous
acute stress disorder (ASD), 3
adaptive information processing (AIP)
    model, 7, 27, 29, 32, 38–39, 162, 250
    addiction memory, 126, 127, 129, 130,
    134, 140
    addictive defense, 66
    addictive disorders, 125–154
    of dissociation, 70
    dissociative table, 203
    ego state disorder, 57
    eye movement desensitization and
        reprocessing, 27, 51, 68
    internal family systems (IFS), 70–72
    personality parts, 52
    psychological defenses, 51–72
    treatment strategy, ego-state disorder, 57
addiction memory, 126, 127, 129, 130,
    134, 140
addictive disorders
    bilateral stimulations (BLS) for, 139–140
    childhood stresses, 127
    clenched fingers, 142
    CravEx model, 142
    Desensitization of Triggers and Urges
        Reprocessing (DeTUR) protocols, 125,
        134, 142–143, 154
    ego state structure, 130–131
    EMDR Humanitarian Assistance
        Program, 142
    eye movement desensitization and
        reprocessing (EMDR) phases, 133
    feeling state approach, 142

genetic vulnerability, 128
hands, illustration, 142–144
level of motivation (LOM), 134
level of positive affect (LOPA), 126, 154
level of urge (LOU), 126, 144
positive affect states, 140–141
primary triggers, 139
sequence of events, 128
substance related, 131–133
trauma related, 131
12 step program, 133
addictive ego state, 131
affect bridge
    in avoidance defense, 77
    dissociative table, 207
    in idealization defenses, 115–117
AIP model. *See* adaptive information
    processing model
alcohol dependence, 128–132, 134, 140
Alcoholics Anonymous (AA), 138
animals
    avoidance defense, 75–76
    survival mechanism, 226
ANP. *See* apparently normal part
anxiety disorder, 5, 228
apparently normal part (ANP), 60, 247
    Constant Installation of Present
        Orientation and Safety (CIPOS)
        procedure, 243–245
    dissociative personality structure, 200,
        203–204
    in idealization defenses, 82
    loving eyes procedure, 211

apparently normal part (ANP) (*cont.*)
in oval language, 188–191
stability maintenance, 192
ASD. *See* acute stress disorder
attachment style, 163
avoidance defense, 18
in animals, 75–76
conscious, 62
eye movement desensitization and
reprocessing (EMDR) with, 75–94
internal family systems (IFS) model, 90
issues, 86
method for targeting, 81–90
resource installation, 91–93
avoidance impulse, 56
avoidance response, 18
avoidance urge, 76

Back-of-the-Head Scale (BHS), 22, 238–
239, 242, 250, 262
BBQ. *See* Blocking Beliefs Questionnaire
behavior, affect, sensation, and
knowledge (BASK) model, 82
behavioral addictions, 128, 132
behaviors, addictive pattern of, 132–133
BHS. *See* Back-of-the-Head Scale
bilateral stimulations (BLS), 22, 126, 127,
140, 250, 252
addictive disorders, 140
avoidance defense, examples, 76–80
Constant Installation of Present
Orientation and Safety (CIPOS)
procedure, 236, 243
dissociative table, 203
distortion of perception, 97
ego states or dissociated parts, 54
eye movement desensitization and
reprocessing (EMDR) phases, 33–42
focused sets, 40–41
idealization defenses, 98
loving eyes procedure, 211–212, 221
personality parts, 53–59
specific effects, 38–43
targeting of the avoidance urge, 58
Blocking Beliefs Questionnaire (BBQ),
135–137
BLS. *See* bilateral stimulation

case studies
addictive disorders, 144–154
avoidance defense, 76–94
Complex posttraumatic stress disorder
(Complex PTSD), 14–16, 291–302
Constant Installation of Present
Orientation and Safety(CIPOS),
259–271, 279–290
dissociation, 159–166
dissociative personality structure,
175–182
drawings, 203–209
dual attention, 34
idealization defenses, 100–102, 104–108,
113–122
level of positive affect (LOPA), 272–277
loving eye procedure, 215–221
oval, 193–196
psychological defense, 54–59
shame, 226–229
childhood-onset posttraumatic stress
disorder, 228
children
adaptive ego states, 195
attachment experiences, 164
with bad parents, 223
caretaker abuse, 166, 232
dysfunctional environment, 188
means of connection with parents, 191
as "narcissistic object," 193–194
CIPOS. *See* Constant Installation of
Present Orientation and Safety
procedure
client, 175
dissociative, 175, 176
common defense, 62
Complex posttraumatic stress
disorder. *See also* posttraumatic
stress disorder
avoidance defense and, 76, 90, 93
caretaker abuse, 226
case study, 291–301
concept of self, 72
definition, 31
idealization defenses, 99, 104
primary characteristics of clients, 4
resource installation, 53
conference room method, 203–209

Constant Installation of Present
   Orientation and Safety procedure
   (CIPOS), 207, 209, 221, 245
   apparently normal part (ANP), 242, 245
   Back-of-the-Head Scale (BHS), 238–239
   bilateral stimulations (BLS),
      235–237, 239
   case study, 259–277, 279–290
   definition, 235
   dual attention, 235, 237, 239–242, 265,
      267, 286
   emotional part, 243
   eye movement desensitization and
      reprocessing (EMDR) therapy, 235,
      237, 243
   sequence of procedures, 240
   short-term memory (STM), 237–238
constructive avoidance, 93–94
contract for therapy, 175
CravEx model, 142

defense of denial, 62
defensive avoidance, 18
defensive shame, treating. *See* shame,
      treating
denial of anger defense, 64
depressive disorder, 187
Desensitization of Triggers and Urges
      Reprocessing (DeTUR) protocols, 125,
      134, 142–143, 154
developmental trauma disorder, 3
disorders of extreme stress, 3
dissociated memory
   disorientation, 61
   event(s), 61
dissociated parts, 52
dissociation
   bilateral simulation, 170
   childhood environment, 160, 162,
      168–170
   conceptual/cognitive, 161
   Dissociative Experiences Scale
      (DES), 167
   eye movement desensitization and
      reprocessing (EMDR)-related
      methods, 161
   hostile/self-referential pattern, 168

human personalities, 160
   internal working model (IWM), 167, 169
   parental nonengagement, 167
   phase-oriented treatment, 176, 179
   posttraumatic stress disorder (PTSD)
      and, 161
   self-concept, 159–170
   from social interaction, 162
dissociative abreaction, psychological
      defense and vulnerability, 60
dissociative client, 175
   phase-oriented treatment, 176
   therapeutic interventions, 176
dissociative disorders, 161
   affect resetting procedure, 181
   bilateral stimulations (BLS), 178–179
   dual attention, 179
   Early Trauma Protocol (ETP), 181
   phase-oriented treatment, 176–178
   resource installation, 180–182
   Theory of the Structural Dissociation of
      The personality (TSDP), 181
dissociative identity disorder (DID), 185
dissociative individuals, 66
dissociative personality structure, 163, 247
   internal healing dialogue procedure,
      250–255
dissociative table
   adaptive information processing (AIP)
      procedures, 203
   affect bridge procedure, 207
   bilateral stimulations (BLS), 206
   imagery, 208
   low-subjective units of disturbance
      scale (SUDS) target, 205
   two-part states, 209
distortion of perception, 97–99, 104
disturbing events/memories, 27, 29,
      33–36
   after time passes, 29
   avoidance defenses and, 75, 76, 78, 90,
      91, 93
   psychological defenses, 42–43, 51–53,
      60, 67, 68, 75
   without therapy, 28
drawings by clients, 197–203
   dissociative identity disorder (DID)
      client, 196

drawings by clients (*cont.*)
  example (inadequate parental
    engagement), 194
drug education program, 133–134
DSEs. *See* dysfunctionally stored elements
dual attention
  adaptive information processing (AIP)
    model, 27–43
  Back-of-the-Head Scale (BHS), 241–242
  challenges, 211–213
  Constant Installation of Present
    Orientation and Safety (CIPOS)
    procedure, 235, 237, 238, 242, 265,
    267, 286
  eye movement desensitization
    and reprocessing (EMDR), 34–36,
    179, 235
  level of urge to avoid (LOUA) score, 55
  loving eye procedure, 195
  situational barriers, 211–213
dysfunctional positive affect, 127
dysfunctionally stored elements (DSEs), 42

Early Trauma Protocol (ETP), 181
ego state structure, 127, 130
  adaptive information processing (AIP)
    model, 57
  addictive disorders, 130–131
  bilateral stimulations (BLS), 54
  example, 57, 87
  ovals, 194
  shame, 231
EMDR. *See* eye movement desensitization
    and reprocessing therapy
EMDR Humanitarian Assistance
    Program, 142
EMDR International Association, 34
emotional part (EP), 68–70, 190–191, 200,
    202, 204, 248
EP. *See* emotional part
excessively controlling defense, 64
eye movement desensitization and
    reprocessing therapy (EMDR), 211,
    227, 249
  adaptive information processing (AIP)
    model and, 27, 51, 68
  adaptive resolution, 28

bilateral stimulations (BLS), 33, 38–43, 53
dissociated disorders, 71
dissociative clients, 176, 178
dual attention and, 34–36, 179, 235, 237
dysfunctionally stored elements
    (DSEs), 42
eight phases step, 37, 178
idealization defenses, 97–100, 104–105,
    113, 125
internal family system (IFS) theory
    and, 68
negative self-appraisal, 224
phases, 35–36
resource installation during, 182
standard phase psychological defenses,
    33, 55–59
targeting of the avoidance urge, 57
therapeutic effects, 38
tools, 53, 59, 72

false self, 103
fast thinking, 18, 75
feeder memory, 116–117
feeling state therapy, 127
feelings of anxiety, 84–85
fight-or-flight response, 226
"firefighter," concept of, 70
flash technique, 244

genetic vulnerability, 128

heroin, 139
hysteria, 176

idealization defenses
  of another person, 110–122
  bilateral stimulations (BLS) and, 97
  concept of self, 102
  definition, 98
  dysfunctional level of positive
    affect, 103
  eye movement desensitization and
    reprocessing (EMDR), 97–100,
    104–105, 113, 121

idealization defenses (*cont.*)
  in marriage counseling, 109–112
  personality trait, 116
  religious beliefs, 99
  self-defeating personality trait, 116
  therapeutic barriers, 99
idealized distortion, 104
IHD procedure. *See* internal healing
    dialogue procedure
implicit memory, 56, 76
information processing system
  resource installation during
    EMDR, 182
  traumatic memories, 31, 32
internal family systems (IFS)
    theory, 250
  adaptive information processing (AIP)
    model (dissociation), 70–72
  avoidance defenses, 90–91
  concept of self, 70
  dissociated self-states, 21
  psychological defense, 68
internal healing dialogue (IHD)
    procedure, 22, 221, 250–255, 291, 293
internal personality, 111
internal phobias, 248
intimate partner violence (IPV), 109, 110
IPV. *See* intimate partner violence

language of ovals. *See* ovals, language of
"learned helplessness," 168
level of motivation (LOM), 134, 135, 138
  addictive disorders, 140
level of positive affect (LOPA), 110, 112,
    126, 127
  addictive disorders, 126, 154
  case study, 271–277
  idealization defenses, 103–105, 109,
    115–117
level of urge (LOU), addictive disorders,
    126, 144
level of urge to avoid (LOUA), 126, 245
  dual attention, 59
  targeting avoidance, 76–80
"locus of control shift" phenomenon,
    188–189
LOM. *See* level of motivation

LOPA. *See* level of positive affect
LOU. *See* level of urge
LOUA. *See* level of urge to avoid
Loving Eyes procedure
  apparently normal part (ANP), 211
  bilateral stimulations (BLS),
    212–214, 221
  Constant Installation of
    Present Orientation and Safety
    (CIPOS), 221
  definition, 212
  dual attention, 211–213
  emotional part (EP), 211
  eye movement desensitization and
    reprocessing (EMDR) standard
    phases, 213–215
  steps, 213–215
  for too little disturbance, 217–221
  for too much disturbance, 215–217

memory, 7–9. *See also* traumatic memory
  addiction, 126, 129, 133, 134, 140
  dissociated, 61
  feeder, 116–117
  positive, 102, 121
  short-term memory (STM), 237
mental actions, 248
methamphetamines, 139
mindfulness, 180
modes of thinking, 39

narcissism, 229
narcissistic defense, 65
Nathanson's concept of shame, 225, 226
NC. *See* negative cognition
negative cognition (NC), 30, 35, 114, 227
negative influence, difficult early life
    experience, 8

ovals, language of
  communication, 194
  different adaptive parts, 191
  for different situations, 192
  in dissociative identity disorder, 194
  ego states, 195

ovals, language of communication (*cont.*)
    parts development (in children),
        188, 191
    personality structure, configurations, 185

PC. *See* positive cognition
personality integration, 249
personality parts
    adaptive information processing (AIP)
        model, 52
    avoidance defense, 81–90
    bilateral simulation and, 53–59
    categories, 52, 67
    concept of self, 71–72
    dissociative structure, 67, 200, 204
    idealization defenses, 116
    neurological networks, 66
    separate, 21
    Theory of the Structural Dissociation of
        the Personality (TSDP), 68
personality structure
    avoidance defense, 78, 82
    idealization defenses, 82
    oval configuration, 185
    transcripted session's end, 85
Popky's concepts. *See* Desensitization of
    Triggers and Urges Reprocessing
    (DeTUR) protocols
positive cognition (PC), 35, 227
positive goal state resource, 138, 144
positive memory, 102, 111, 121
positive self-referencing cognitions, 111
posttraumatic "relivings," 60, 237
posttraumatic stress disorder (PTSD), 249.
    See also Complex posttraumatic stress
    disorder
    avoidance defense and, 76, 90, 93
    caretaker abuse, 226
    concept of self, 72
    definition, 31
    distortion of future perception, 34
    distortion of present perception, 33–34
    driving-related, 34
    eye movement desensitization and
        reprocessing (EMDR) for, 33–37, 51
    idealization defenses, 99

posttraumatic dysfunctional memory
    storage, 30–33
primary characteristics of clients, 4
resource installation, 53
single-incident, adult-onset problems, 71
principle of utilization, 51
psychological defense
    adaptive information processing (AIP)
        model and, 51–72
    dissociative abreaction, 60
    examples, 60–72
    internal family systems (IFS) theory, 68
    posttraumatic disturbing memory, 12
psychological defenses, 229
psychotherapy, 252
    Alcoholics Anonymous (AA) and, 138
PTSD. *See* posttraumatic stress disorder

quality of happening, 31

RDI. *See* resource development and
    installation
real self, 103
relivings, 9
    experience, 9
resource development and installation
    (RDI), 22, 53, 121, 139, 180–182
rigid defense, 60

Schwartz's Internal Family Systems
    model, 70
self-assessment, 223
self-blame, 223, 228
self, concept of, 71–72
    in children, 165
self-esteem, 228, 230
"self-states," identities, 21
sexually addictive behavior, 69
shame defense, 19–20, 291, 293–294
shame disorder, 228
shame, treating
    action system, 231–232
    bilateral stimulations (BLS), 250
    case studies, 226–229

shame, treating (*cont.*)
  childhood-onset posttraumatic stress
    disorder (PTSD), 228
  dissociative personality structure, 231
  ego state, 231
  eye movement desensitization and
    reprocessing (EMDR), 224, 230, 233
  guilt *vs.*, 230
  Nathanson's concept of, 224
  negative identity, 225
  neurological mechanisms, 224–226
  physical sensation, 225
  Polyvagal Theory on, 225
  self-definition, 227
  sympathetic activation, 226
  vs. pride, 224
shocking trauma, 228
short-term memory (STM), 237–238
shutdown disorder, 228
slow thinking, 18, 75, 76
specific events memories, 67
spontaneous integration, 249
STM. *See* short-term memory
Stockholm syndrome, 189
structural dissociation theorists, 190
structural theory of dissociation, 250
Subjective Units of Disturbance Scale
  (SUDS), 36, 38, 55–56, 204, 211
subsequent triggers, 130
substance addiction, 128–129, 132–133
substitute action, 69–70
Subjective Units of Disturbance Scale
  (SUDS)

TAU. *See* treatment as usual
Theory of the Structural Dissociation of
  the Personality (TSDP), 10, 68, 72,
  181, 247
thinking
  fast, 75
  slow, 75, 76

trauma-reliving part, 52, 67, 91, 179,
  203, 237
traumatic memory, 8, 9, 236
  avoidance defense and, 18
  bilateral stimulations (BLS) combined
    with dual attention, 37
  causes, 42
  distorted perception, 34, 43
  dysfunctionally stored elements
    (DSEs), 42
  information processing system, 29, 30
  quality of happening, 31
  storage, 30
  unresolved, 32, 42
  visual images, 33
treatment as usual (TAU), 126
triggers
  desensitization of, 141
  hidden, 135
  identification of, 138
  internal, 127
  present, 134
  primary, 139
  situational, 36, 126, 127, 129, 133, 142,
    154, 270
  subsequent, 130
TSDP. *See* Theory of the Structural
  Dissociation of the Personality
TV addiction, 132
12-step program, 131
two-handed interweave method, 101, 251

unresolved posttraumatic disturbance, 254
unresolved traumatic memory, 32, 34,
  42, 51
urges, 76, 127, 130, 133, 139–142, 154

validity of cognition (VOC), 35–36, 202
VOC. *See* validity of cognition

CPSIA information can be obtained
at www.ICGtesting.com
Printed in the USA
BVHW011752131122
651856BV00014B/294

9 780826 172556